UNITED NATIONS CONFERENCE ON TRADE AND DEVELOPMENT

E-COMMERCE AND DEVELOPMENT REPORT 2001

Prepared by the UNCTAD secretariat

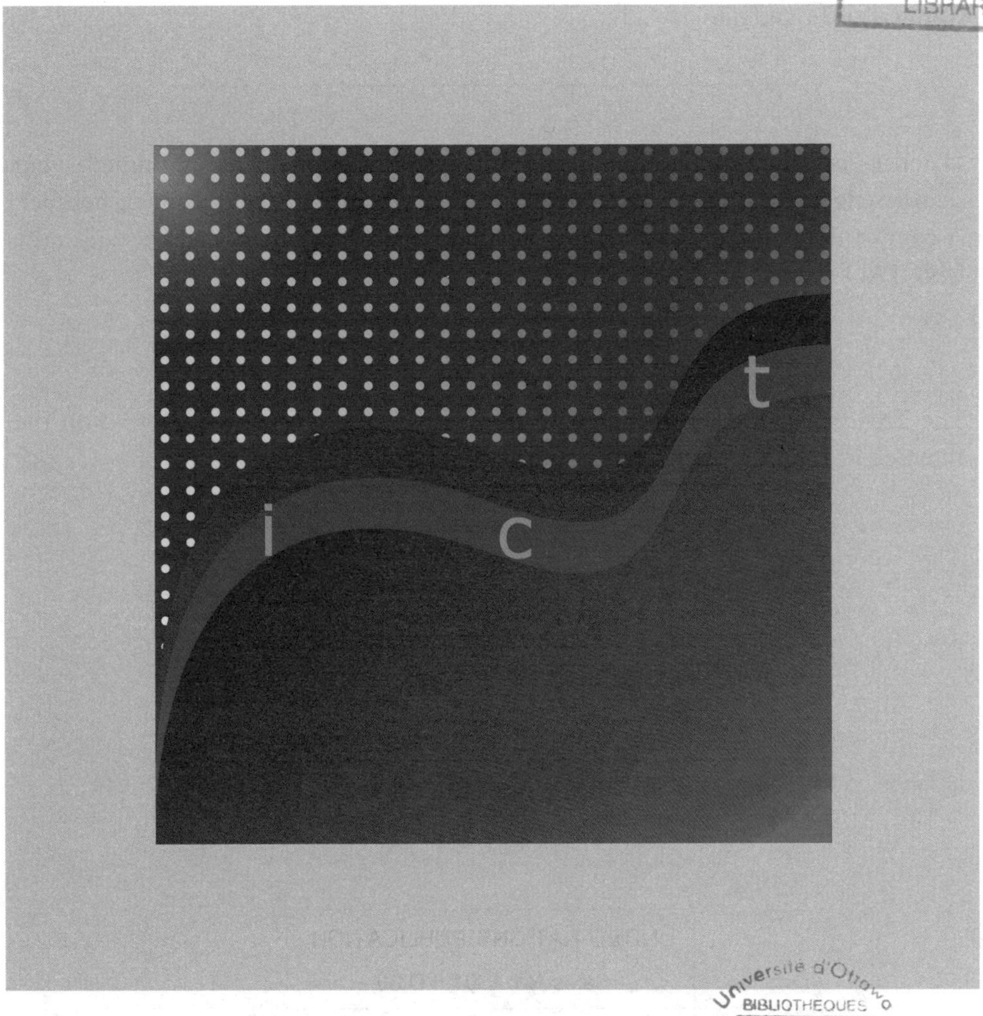

UNITED NATIONS
New York and Geneva, 2001

Note

Symbols of United Nations documents are composed of capital letters with figures. Mention of such a symbol indicates a reference to a United Nations document.

The designations employed and the presentation of the material in this publication do not imply the expression of any opinion whatsoever on the part of the Secretariat of the United Nations concerning the legal status of any country, territory, city or area, or of its authorities, or concerning the delimitation of its frontiers or boundaries.

Material in this publication may be freely quoted or reprinted, but acknowledgement is requested, together with a reference to the document number. A copy of the publication containing the quotation or reprint should be sent to the UNCTAD secretariat.

The Trends and Executive Summary from this Report can also be found on the Internet, in English, French and Spanish, at the following address:

http://www.unctad.org/ecommerce/

UNCTAD/SDTE/ECB/1

UNITED NATIONS PUBLICATION
Sales No. E.01.II.D.30
ISBN 92-1-112541-3

Foreword

The emergence of electronic commerce over the past decade has radically transformed the economic landscape. For developing countries, the digital revolution offers unprecedented opportunities for economic growth and development, as entrepreneurs from Bangalore to Guadalajara to Dakar will testify. On the other hand, countries that lag behind in technological innovations risk being bypassed by the competitive edge of those using the new technologies.

The *Electronic Commerce and Development Report 2001* reviews trends that developing countries need to be aware of as they try to position their economies to take advantage of ICT and the Internet. It provides basic facts and figures about electronic commerce and discusses the impact on sectors of particular relevance to developing countries. It also suggests, with concrete examples, ways in which developing countries can create the necessary enabling environment for e-commerce.

The ICT age has dawned, but not yet for all. This Report, which will serve as a useful reference for the United Nations Task Force on ICT, aims to help policy makers and practitioners in developing countries understand the nature of the network economy, and develop the infrastructure, capabilities, flexibility and openness with which they can reap its benefits. As a contribution to our collective efforts to unite the great promise of ICT with the needs of the poor, it merits the widest possible readership.

Kofi A. Annan
Secretary-General of the United Nations

Acknowledgements

The *Electronic Commerce and Development Report 2001* is the product of a collective effort led by Jean Gurunlian, Director of UNCTAD's Division for Services Infrastructure for Development and Trade Efficiency, and coordinated by Zhongzhou Li, Chief of the Electronic Commerce Branch. The following UNCTAD staff members participated in the preparation of this publication: Cécile Barayre, Pilar Borque Fernández, Dimo Calovski, Angel González Sanz, Rouben Indjikian, Lorenza Jachia, Yusuf Kalindaga, Carlos Moreno, Juan Pizarro, Susan Teltscher and Haijuan Yu.

The UNCTAD team wishes to express their recognition to the following consultants who provided background material for specific chapters of this Report: Bill Pattinson, Catherine Kessedjian, Donal O'Mahony, Shaun Lake and Philippe Monnier.

The cover of the Report was designed by Diego Oyarzun Reyes, and the text was edited by Graham Grayston and Chris Macfarquhar. The overall layout, graphics and desktop publishing were done by Madasamyraja Rajalingam.

Contents

Part One
Facts and Figures about Electronic Commerce

Part Two
Impact of Electronic Commerce on Selected Sectors

Part Three
Electronic Commerce Environment and Practices

Part Four
Experiences and Opportunities

List of Boxes

List of Charts

List of Tables

Explanatory Notes

The term "dollars" ($) refers to United States dollars unless otherwise stated. The term "billion" signifies 1,000 million.
Two dots (..) indicate that the data are not available, or are not separately reported.
A hyphen (-) indicates that the amount is nil or negligible.
Details and percentages do not necessarily add up to totals, because of rounding.

Abbreviations

A

ABA	American Bar Association
ABoC	Agricultural Bank of China
ABS	Australian Bureau of Statistics
ACH	automated clearing house
ACIS	Advance Cargo Information System
ADR	alternative dispute resolution
AIG	American International Group Inc.
AOL	America Online
APEC	Asian-Pacific Economic Cooperation
ASEAN	Association of South-East Asian Nations
ASYCUDA	Automated System for Custom Data
ATM	automated teller machine

B

BIAC	Economic and Industrial Consultative Committee of OECD
BIPS	bank internet payments system
BIS	Bank for International Settlements
BOC	Bank of China
BTA	British Tourist Authority
B2B	business-to-business
B2C	business-to-consumer
B2G	business-to-government

C

CA	certification authority
CBC	Construction Bank of China
CCPIT	China Council for the Promotion of International Trade
CCRTU	China Central Radio and Television University
CDMA	code division multiple access
CEPS	common electronic purse specification
CFCC	China Financial Certificate Center
CGE	computable general equilibrium
CIECC	China International Electronic Commerce Center
CIF	cost, insurance and freight
CMB	China Merchants Bank
CNNIC	China Internet Network Information Center
COD	cash-on-delivery

COFACE	Compagnie française d'assurance pour le commerce extérieur
COGSA	Carriage of Goods by Sea Act (of the United States)
CPN	controlled payment number
CRS	computer reservation system
CSRC	China Security Regulatory Commission

D

DMO	destination management/marketing organization
DP	digital products
D&B	Dun and Bradstreet

E

ECB	European Central Bank
ECN	electronic communications network
EDI	electronic data interchange
EDIFACT	electronic data interchange for administration, commerce and transport
EMPS	electronic mobile payments system
ERP	enterprise resource planning
EU	European Union

F

FAQ	frequently asked questions
FDI	foreign direct investment
FEDWIRE	US Federal Reserve electronic payments and gross settlements system
FOB	free on board
FTC	Federal Trade Commission (of the United States)
FSTC	Financial Services Technology Consortium (of the United States)
FSML	Financial Services Markup Language

G

GATS	General Agreement on Trade in Services
GATT	General Agreement on Tariffs and Trade
GBDe	global business dialogue in electronic commerce
GDP	gross domestic product
GDS	global distribution system
GNP	gross national product
GPRS	General Packet Radio Service
GSM	Global System for Mobile Communications
GSP	generalized system of preferences
GTAP	Global Trade Analysis Project
GTPNet	Global Trade Point Network
GTW	global trading web
G3	third generation mobile communications technology, ITU specification

H

HCOPIL	Hague Conference on Private International Law
HTML	hypertext mark-up language
HTTP	hypertext transfer protocol
HTTPS	HTTP using a Secure Socket Layer (SSL)

I

IBM	International Business Machines
ICANN	Internet Corporation for Assigned Names and Numbers
ICBC	Industrial and Commercial Bank of China
ICC	International Chamber of Commerce
ICP	Internet content provider
ICT	information and communications technologies
IDC	International Data Corporation
IGC	International Gateway
ILPE	Internet Law and Policy Forum
IMF	International Monetary Fund
IP	Internet protocol
IPO	initial public offer
ISP	Internet service provider
ISTAT	Italian National Statistical Institute
IT	information technology
ITF	Internet trade finance exchange
ITP	international trade prototype
ITU	International Telecommunication Union
iTV	interactive television

K

KNSO	Korean National Statistical Office

L

L/C	letter of credit
LDC	least developed country
LLP	lead logistics provider

M

MFN	most favoured nation
MII	Ministry of Information Industry
MLES	UNCITRAL Model Law on Electronic Signatures
MoE	Ministry of Education
MoFTEC	Ministry of Foreign Trade and Economic Cooperation
MOTO	mail order telephone order
MPS	Ministry of Public Security

MRO	maintenance, repair and operations
MULTIMOD	multi-region econometric model

N

NACHA	National Automated Clearing House Association
NTO	national tourism office

O

ODR	online dispute resolution
OECD	Organisation for Economic Co-operation and Development

P

PBoC	People's Bank of China
PC	personal computer
PIN	personal identification number
PKI	Public Key Infrastructure
P2P	peer-to-peer or person-to-person

R

RA	registry authority
RFP/RFQ	requests for proposals/requests for quotes
ROM	read only memory

S

SAR	special administrative region
SAT	State Administration of Taxation
SET	secure electronic transactions
SIM	subscriber identity module
SMS	short message service
SME	small- and medium size enterprise
SSL	secure socket layer
STEP	straight through Euro processing
SWIFT	Society for Worldwide Interbank Financial Telecommunications

T

TARGET	Trans-European Automated Real-Time Gross Settlement Express Transfer System
TCP/IP	transmission control protocol/Internet protocol

U

UBS	Union Bank of Switzerland
UDRP	Uniform Domain Name Dispute Resolution Policy
UN/CEFACT	Centre for the Facilitation of Procedures and Practices for Administration, Commerce and Transport of the United Nations Economic Commission for Europe

UNCITRAL	United Nations Commission on International Trade Law
UNCTAD	United Nations Conference on Trade and Development
UNECE	United Nations Economic Commission for Europe
URL	uniform resource locator
USBOC	United States Bureau of the Census

V

VAT	value-added tax
VoIP	voice-over-Internet protocol
VSAT	very small aperture terminal

W

WAP	wireless application protocol
WATCH	worldwide automated transaction clearing house
WCO	World Customs Organization
WIPO	World Intellectual Property Organisation
WTO	World Trade Organisation
WWW	World Wide Web

X

XML	eXtensible Markup Language
3PL	third-party logistics

TRENDS AND EXECUTIVE SUMMARY

Contents

A. TRENDS

It seems that the "new economic paradigm", according to which new information and communication technologies (ICT) would deliver ever higher rates of inflation-free growth, was among the first victims of the dotcom crash. The recent sluggish performance of the United States economy, the most visible exponent of the benefits of the widespread use of ICT and the Internet,[1] has not helped to keep it alive. As far as the most exaggerated versions of that paradigm are concerned (for instance, the assertion that the business cycle was dead or that the Internet had rendered competition policy irrelevant) this is a healthy development. However, it would be a dangerous mistake to discard offhand the great and lasting changes that the ICT revolution has made, and will continue to make, to the ability of enterprises to create value and to compete in increasingly globalized markets.

The ICT revolution should not be different from previous technological upheavals that have had profound consequences for the economy. The steam engine, railways, the internal combustion engine and the industrial application of electricity spelt the end of entire sectors of activity, generated new industries and services, and most importantly, allowed enterprises to work differently and more efficiently. These changes, and the ensuing improvements in living standards, were always the result of productivity gains that took a long time, even decades, to spread from the sectors first affected by technological change to the rest of the economy, first in those countries where these inventions were first applied and then gradually in the rest of the world.

The first important question is therefore what impact ICT and the Internet have had on productivity growth. With regard to the experience of the United States, where investment in ICT has been most intense, data from the Bureau of Labor Statistics show that between 1995 and 2000 output per hour in the non-farming sector grew at an annual rate of 2.5 per cent, significantly higher than the rate of the previous two decades and closer to the growth rates of the "golden age" of 1959–1973. Economists are not unanimous in their assessment of these data, and it will be necessary to wait until the end of the current cycle before the debate about how much of this acceleration of the growth of productivity is structural rather than cyclical can be closed. However, the UNCTAD secretariat agrees with those[2] that think that there are reasons to believe that much of the acceleration of productivity growth in the United States is structural and attributable to changes induced by ICT and the Internet, through improvements in all aspects of corporate organization, production, finance, marketing and logistics.

Although the speed at which companies in several advanced countries invest in ICT has decreased in the past few months, in the medium term there are several reasons to expect that ICT will continue to support rapid productivity growth. First, the cost of computing power is predicted to keep falling at a steep rate for several years.[3] Secondly, most enterprises are still learning how to reorganize themselves in order to benefit fully from the Internet. Finally, even if productivity growth does not maintain its recent phenomenal pace in the United States, the rest of the world has a lot of catching up to do in the application of ICT to business. As firms in other developed economies and, most importantly, in developing countries engage in e-business, global productivity growth should accelerate.

If the comparison with other disruptive technologies of the past is accepted, there is nothing surprising in the Internet share bubble and its implosion or in the high mortality rate prevalent among early Internet start-ups. Hype, herd instincts and unrealistic business models also accompanied past technological revolutions. A short-term phenomenon in the stock market does not give us any significant message about the implications of the Internet for the economy, in the same way as the disappearance of all but a handful of the many car makers that existed when that industry came of age hardly means that the road transport industry they brought into existence is irrelevant in today's economy.[4]

In any case, from the point of view of new entrants to e-commerce and especially for developing countries, what matters now is not who is the winner of an academic argument about how new the new economy is. What they need to know is how they can avoid the mistakes of the pioneers.

We are still at a too early stage of the process to claim that we have a complete picture of the changes that economies will go through. A comparison with electricity may be illustrative. The rate of penetration of ICT in the most advanced economies (in terms of the number of personal computers (PCs) per hundred people) is close today to the share of electricity in the total power used by industry in the United States around 1920, i.e. 50 per cent.[5] It seems, therefore, that identifying some of the trends and patterns of change, and the lessons for practitioners that can be extracted from the events of the last few months, is a more realistic ambition for now. The next pages will attempt to answer three general questions:

- What lessons for the future of the digital economy can be learned from the Internet crash?
- What assumptions of the business models of failed dotcoms were wrong?
- To what extent will ICT and the Internet change the different sectors of the economy?

Venture capital and the digital economy

For reasons mentioned above, a detailed account of the collapse of the price of the dotcom shares is not directly relevant to this publication. Suffice it to say that UNCTAD participates in the almost general consensus that the cause of the crash was an excess of investment, generated by unrealistic expectations about the disappearance of the business cycle. The result was the weeding out of many dotcoms that had been launched without a viable business model (although companies with more solid projects have also suffered). However, a few comments about the role of venture capital in this process are justified because easy access for entrepreneurs to venture capital finance is among the factors that explain the lead of the United States in the Internet economy.

Venture capitalism is mainly an American phenomenon: according to some estimates, the United States represents nearly 75 per cent of the global private equity and venture capital markets. Western Europe is a relative latecomer, with the United Kingdom having around 12 per cent and Germany and France about 3 per cent of the global market. In Asia, which has a very small share of the global venture capital market, two economies (Taiwan Province of China and Hong Kong, China) represent more that half of Asian venture funds while Japan lags far behind.[6]

A number of reasons are often given for the leadership of the United States in the venture capital industry: access to institutional financing and liquid stock markets; strong links between research centres and the private sector, and hence a clear focus on the applicability and commercialization of the outputs of research and development; flexible regulations; low capital-gain taxation; managerial ownership through widely used share option schemes; and the possibility for entrepreneurs to return to business after a bankruptcy. In the United States, as in its major competitors, there is a strong research and development capacity in the private sector, government agencies and universities, but it has also been possible to develop a vibrant venture capital sector with the initial support of the Government and close cooperation with academic centres. American venture capital funds have thus been investing in high-tech start-ups (by no means limited to the Internet sector) for years and have helped maintain the momentum of technological innovation and its rapid commercial application.

Venture capitalists operate on the assumption that although many (or most) of the companies they nurture (with funds, but often with managerial involvement too) will fail, some will be highly successful. Losses can thus be more than offset against the huge profits to be made through initial public offerings that introduce successful start-ups into the stock market. The expectations of spectacular growth rates in e-commerce businesses, where it was said that market dominance was ensured to the first to arrive, provided a rational incentive for intense venture capital infusion into the dotcom sector. But in the rush to seize a share of the market, many venture capital funds were financing Internet business projects without first undertaking realistic risk assessments and due diligence procedures. The large amounts of funds that were thus available to start-up companies allowed them to grow at an accelerated rate — often much faster than what underlying infrastructure or demand for their products and services could support.

Since mainstream investors became nervous about the lack of profitability in the Internet sector and the stock market bubble was punctured, venture capitalists have had to face the risk of holding shares of newly formed private companies which, under the conditions prevailing in the stock markets, they no longer can leave through an initial public offering.

UNCTAD has approached a sample of venture capital funds, seeking information about any new strategies they might have adopted in the aftermath of the Internet crash. Have they become more selective? Do they apply more stringent due diligence procedures? Are they using new criteria to analyse the business plans and the managerial strengths of the companies they consider for investment? If so, what are the differences?

Unsurprisingly, the majority of the answers received indicate that both before and after the crash venture capital funds were scrutinizing the business plans of dotcoms, assessing the quality of their management and undertaking all other necessary steps required by due diligence procedures. Apparently, no new investment criteria are considered necessary. It is as though the short-sightedness of mainstream investors and their herd psychology were the only culprits of the dotcom débâcle. This seems hardly credible. Perhaps the explanations are inherently systemic to the business environment. Like the last driver in a line of vehicles, who has to speed up or slow down in excess of the leading car in order to keep up, maintain a safe distance or avoid a crash, investors and entrepreneurs may drastically have to speed up or slow down investing or producing in order not to miss out on the boom or go down in the bust phases of the cycle. What appears to be mindless short-sightedness is an objective and defining characteristic of the system. The following section will look at some of the myths that have been exposed by the crisis and will try to extract some lessons from them.

Some myths, lessons and trends

"Profits can wait (almost) for ever, only market share matters now"

When the high prices of the shares of e-retailers such as Amazon.com were questioned in the light of their inconsistency with traditional stock valuation yardsticks, the usual explanation was that the key to long-term success in e-commerce was achieving a large market share fast. If this required huge investments with implausibly long payback periods, so be it. Profits would come later, as e-commerce matured.

But the time horizons of many investors are not as distant as such business plans would have required. As financial markets grew nervous about the dotcom world and virtually cost-free capital stopped flowing in, many companies found that they lacked the resources to sustain the expansion that should, eventually, generate the profits investors want. A vicious circle was closing on them.

A few players (such as Amazon.com), who have built strong brands and generate sizeable revenue streams, have been able to escape it by establishing alliances with offline players, or radically reducing their expansion plans, or both. In all cases, the objective is to achieve positive financial results at a more clearly defined (and much closer) point in time.

The danger now is a move to the opposite extreme: unrealistic short-termism. No new business, in e-commerce or in traditional sectors, can be instantaneously profitable. Long-term success cannot be built on short-term financial strategies. Business plans must be precise about when profits will be achieved, and investors will not accept that any amount of investment is justified. But at the same time, an e-commerce project that is based on a rational market analysis and has a credible medium-term time horizon before profitability can be as valid a business proposition now as it was before the crash.

"The first mover has all the advantages"

Many Internet start-ups went into business far before their projects were mature enough, on the assumption that being the first to arrive in a fast-growing market would help them capture a large customer base at a lower cost than if they had to fight competitors. They would then be in an impregnable position.

In reality, many of the Internet pioneers have either closed (eToys) or been bought (Netscape) by relative latecomers. Especially in the retailing sector, many "first movers" underestimated the cost of making consumers change their habits, of building a new brand from scratch or of mastering the complexity of distribution logistics. In all these examples, latecomers, particularly those that already had a brand and physical assets (stores, warehouses, catalogues) they could leverage, have enjoyed an important advantage. And, to some extent, they have been free riders since earlier entrants made a substantial effort to educate consumers and enterprises about e-commerce.

Speed does matter in e-commerce, because technological change makes competition a much faster game online than offline. Enterprises can hardly afford to stand still while their online competitors are learning by doing. Therefore, it may be necessary to launch an e-commerce project before everything is perfectly ready. But this does not mean that the basic rules of marketing do not apply to e-commerce.

E-commerce enterprises, like their traditional counterparts, cannot go into business without knowing clearly what their customers' needs are and what value the enterprise can offer to them. Products and distribution channels to provide that value at a profit need to be identified. Customers need to be made aware of the existence of the product or service in a cost-effective, consistent manner. And there must be clear targets so that progress can be measured and corrective action taken in time. Having a good idea for a product or service that can be sold over the Internet is just not enough.

"On the Internet it does not matter if you are big or small"

While it is true that in theory the Internet gives small and medium-sized enterprises (SMEs) new opportunities to compete, because it reduces transaction costs and barriers of entry, their e-commerce business models must be adapted to their competitive strengths and not just replicate the approaches of bigger players. If a small enterprise tries to compete with a large multinational simply by making a large investment in powerful equipment for its website, the chances are that its productive and/or distribution capacity will never allow it to recover the costs.

For SMEs and enterprises in developing countries, e-commerce may create new opportunities to participate in international trade. But although putting up a website opens a window to global markets, it is not a substitute for a full export strategy. Is the product range adapted to foreign demand? What regulations and standards apply to a firm's products in other markets? What impact will transport, insurance or tariffs have on product competitiveness? Are the staff able to deal with foreign customers? These and similar questions must be asked and answered at the same time as those related to the purely technological aspects of an e-business project. The good news is that the Internet makes it easier and cheaper to find answers to most of them.

In this context, the importance of brand management cannot be underestimated, both in international and in domestic markets. In the Internet one may be a click away from the competition, but customers are more likely to click on a web page that carries a brand they recognize. The Internet allows SMEs to implement new, cheaper strategies to build brand names and images in markets to which they had little access in the past (particularly for enterprises in niche markets). Sufficient resources – and thought – need to be given to them.

"On the Internet everything must be for free"

Even though there are well-known — and successful — examples of companies that have been charging consumers for their services from the beginning (AOL), many business-to-consumer projects were based on the concept that the culture of the Internet was inherently incompatible with charges for content or services. Advertising was seen as the only viable source of revenue. Now it is clear that business models in most business-to-consumer sectors will have to rely on alternative income streams, mostly in the form of subscriptions and fees.

Internet advertising is not yet the income earner it was supposed to become. Although the Internet allows personalized, interactive advertising campaigns that cannot be conducted through any other means, it also has distinct disadvantages. While it is not always easy to distinguish the specific influence on consumer decisions of each of the various elements of a marketing campaign (television, radio and press advertising, sponsoring, price discounts, point-of-sale events etc.), click-through rates (the number of people who click on a advertising banner) are easy to measure and they have often been disappointing. There is also much to be discovered about how to use online advertising without putting off Internet users. In the meantime, advertising budgets have been reduced as a consequence of the economic slowdown. And it was online businesses, many of which are now struggling, that made up the bulk of Internet advertising.

Providers of generic information that is convenient online but is also available offline (for instance, newspapers) will not be able to charge for it until a cost-effective means to handle micropayments takes off. Search engines or websites that help consumers to carry out product comparison will also have to keep relying on advertising and, in the case of search engines, charges for listing a website in a prominent place. Apart from these businesses, most online services will have to turn to fees as their main source of income. This includes fees for Internet access (especially for premium, broadband service) and any value-added services such as translation, financial analysis, buying guides and, in general, information that is more than raw data.

Even those e-commerce companies that do charge for their products often make the mistake of assuming that because on the Internet price comparisons are easy and cheap, price is the only factor in their customers' decision-making. As a result, prices are often fixed at too low a level and the possibilities for price segmentation and/or quick price adjustment in response to changing market conditions are not always used.

While it is true that in the business-to-business sector the enhanced transparency brought about by the Internet places buyers in a stronger position, this is not always the case in the retailing sector. In reality, most online consumers are not necessarily looking for the lowest possible prices. Issues such as the user-friendliness of a website, and the choice, security and reliability provided by the online merchant are often as important as prices. Also, more use should be made of techniques that allow companies to detect the reaction of customers to changes in prices — which is more difficult to do offline — and to charge different prices according to fluctuations in demand (as airlines, for instance, charge different prices for same-class tickets as seats in a given flight are sold).

"E-commerce needs PCs and web browsers"

Business models based on a PC-centric approach to the Internet ignore the fact that most of the potential (and the actual volume) of e-commerce does not involve a consumer sitting at home in front of a PC and surfing the World Wide Web through one of the two more widespread browsers. E-commerce today is very much a business-to-business affair. Enterprises in developing countries should not let themselves be fooled by the much higher visibility of the business-to-consumer dotcoms. Those enterprises in developing countries that make goods or deliver services that are necessary for the productive process of other enterprises are the ones that should first consider incorporating the Internet (which does not necessarily mean the web) as an instrument to enhance their opportunities to compete and grow.

There is another reason why the prevalent model of web-based e-commerce need not be the only course that enterprises in developing countries can follow. In spite of the spectacular decline in the price of computing power, PCs remain unaffordable for the vast majority of the population of the world. On the other hand, mobile telephones and other Internet-enabled devices, although expensive, are already accessible to a sizeable number of people and enterprises in developing countries. While wireless web applications have fallen short of expectations, there is a vast potential for mobile commerce (m-commerce) if the approach of transplanting the web onto a mobile phone is abandoned. It seems that in the developed countries m-commerce will focus on consumer-oriented location-dependent services, but it is possible that in the market environment of developing countries more general applications (including in business-to-business) of m-commerce can be developed.

"The Internet kills monopolies"

Except in the few industries that are affected by increasing returns to scale, the Internet tends to reduce economies of scale, for it creates new opportunities for outsourcing and lowers fixed costs. Because it makes it much easier and cheaper to exchange information across borders, it also helps the emergence of truly global markets in some industries, notably in the financial sector. It would therefore seem that the Internet is bringing the economy closer to the theoretical model of perfect competition.

Paradoxically, the industry that has made the Internet possible is itself subject to monopolistic or at least oligopolistic pressures. One single company builds nearly 80 per cent of the routers (the computers that put order into the flow of bits on the Internet). Another one sells about 90 per cent of the browsers people use to navigate the World Wide Web. Beyond this, data seem to indicate that a strong concentration is also taking place in the domain of contents and services, at least in the business-to- consumer sector. According to a study published in June 2001 by Jupiter Media Metrix (an Internet analysis and measurement firm), between March 1999 and March 2001 the number of companies that control 50 per cent of the time Internet users in the United States spend online (at home and at work) went down from 11 to just four. The number of companies controlling 60 per cent of the time Americans spend online went down from 160 to 14, an 87 per cent fall. The first in the ranking, AOL Time Warner Network, accounted for 32 per cent of online time.[7]

There is no reason to believe that this trend will not be replicated in other Internet markets as they become mature. Smaller players should be alert. The Internet, or at least the business of providing access and content, is as open to the forces of economies of scale and market concentration as the rest of the economy. Indeed, in the digital goods sector (in which some developing countries have a chance to exploit profitable niches) increasing returns to scale may make monopolistic and/or oligopolistic market structures more frequent than in the past.

"The Internet changes everything"

This assertion sums up most of the misconceptions presented above. It was on the assumption that business in the Internet would work outside the traditional laws of economics that sky-high share prices were justified and many new dotcom start-ups behaved as though they had a definitive competitive advantage over their bricks-and-mortar rivals.

In reality, the laws of economics have proved rather resilient. The business cycle is very much alive. Investors, after all, want to see profits. Sensible financial planning, marketing strategies, and such unglamorous business problems as logistics remain as important as before. Intermediaries, whom the Internet was supposed to render irrelevant, have flourished in the Internet — although in different shapes. In many sectors, customers (both retail and wholesale) are still adapting to the new business models, and enterprises need time to incorporate ICT and the Internet into their day-to-day operations.

Because of that, it will not be Internet pure-players but brick-and-mortar firms that integrate the Internet into operations who will profit most from e-commerce. Many established "old economy" companies have already succeeded in making e-commerce part of their strategies, using the Internet to cut procurement costs, to help employees work together more efficiently (which can improve quality or shorten product development cycles), to improve customer service, and, of course, to reach more customers and to enter new markets. For example, such an emblematic "old economy" company as General Electric already apparently does more business through its own market place than all public e-markets together (although the precise volumes handled by public e-markets are difficult to estimate).[8]

"The Internet changes nothing"

Of course, this was not a "new economy" myth, although it is probably a more dangerous proposition than any of the ones listed above. A natural reaction to the dismal performance of many dotcom start-ups, especially for most companies in the developing countries that have been only marginally affected by the Internet boom and crash, would be to consider that e-commerce is a risk not worth taking. They would be wrong.

First of all, the dotcoms always represented a small part of e-commerce and Internet business. Many of them have disappeared, but e-commerce (and particularly business-to-business e-commerce) continues to grow, although not at the breathtaking speed that was predicted some time ago. And many other dotcoms have indeed succeeded in establishing themselves as global companies with solid brands and business models in which new entrants in e-commerce can find inspiration.

Secondly, it is a mistake to think that e-commerce does not change an enterprise's competitive environment just because its products or services do not lend themselves easily to being traded online. A business transaction consists of many successive processes (information gathering, comparison, negotiation), most of which can be carried out more efficiently over the Internet, even if the final step of the transaction is taken offline. For instance, very few cars are bought online. Yet in Europe and the United States there is evidence that many purchase decisions are strongly influenced by information collected on the Internet.

Thirdly, marketing and sales are only a part of the value-creation chain. As mentioned above, an enterprise can become more competitive by using the Internet to get cheaper finance, reorganize its procurement, improve customer service etc. A major obstacle to the participation of SMEs from developing countries in international trade is the lack of adequate trade-supporting services — finance, insurance, transport, business information. The Internet makes it easier for them to access new, better-quality suppliers.

Finally, as many established companies in the developed countries, and in particular large multinational corporations, integrate the Internet into their operations, buyers and suppliers located in developing countries will increasingly come under pressure to adapt to the new business models. Enterprises in developing countries that are or plan to be involved in international trade need to start incorporating ICT and the Internet into their business models in order to stay competitive.

It is true, however, that the Internet will not transform all productive sectors equally. At the end of the day, Internet or no Internet, most garment makers must still make a profit by cutting, stitching, ironing and packaging clothes — or they will go out of business. For a banker, the possibility of using the Internet to cut the cost of handling an account by a few cents may be a decisive competitive edge. The following section will discuss how the impact of the Internet and ICT in general will vary across economic sectors.

The future spread of the effects of ICT and the Internet, and the prospects for developing countries

A look at the list of the fallen and the survivors of the dotcom crisis shows that the value of ICT for development lies not so much in the share of the global economy that this sector may come to represent (undoubtedly a sizeable one), but in the changes that ICT will introduce in the functioning of enterprises across the economies that assimilate them.

Technological revolutions have always affected different sectors in different ways. Railways helped create the first nation wide markets in Europe and the United States, but one cannot say that they had a dramatic effect on financial services — other than generating a huge stock market bubble. The industrial application of electricity radically changed manufacturing, but had little direct impact on farming or retailing. Information technologies and the Internet will have more widespread effects because they can be applied in most aspects of production, distribution and consumption. For instance, unlike previous technological changes, they have the potential to improve productivity in services. However, and particularly while enterprises undergo the necessary learning process, the transformations brought about by the Internet will be more important in some sectors than in others. This will, of course, have implications for the speed at which changes will be felt in the economies of developing countries, which will be directly proportional to the weight in their economies of the sectors in which the impact of the Internet and ICT will be deeper and faster.

Information-intensive activities are being — or will soon be — radically transformed by the combination of powerful, cheap computing and connectivity. This includes financial services, education, the cultural industry, professional services (consulting, design, translation, accounting etc.) and government services. In some of them (such as back-office services) certain developing countries may find new opportunities for diversification, as illustrated by the examples discussed in the chapter of this report dealing with e-commerce in the least developed countries.

Although these sectors are the ones in which more far-reaching changes are to be expected, they are also among those where technological and/or regulatory problems can be more important. For instance, privacy can be a serious concern for the potential customers of some professional service providers; the commercial exploitation of digitized goods (books, music) requires effective protection of intellectual property rights; and the availability of broadband Internet access will be crucial for the prospects of online entertainment services.

In other, less information-intensive sectors of the economy, changes will be incremental and mostly due to reductions in transaction costs: manufacturing and retailing are examples of industries where deep, although slower, changes can be expected. The benefits of e-commerce and e-business that have been mentioned before (cheaper procurement, faster knowledge accumulation, dissemination and application, more effective management of the relationship with the customer etc.) can translate into significant savings. These savings will not materialize without significant investment and organizational and cultural changes that will not happen overnight. It is therefore important that developing countries prioritize areas where results can be expected earlier, so as to minimize the financial effort and encourage people to embrace change.

Within each individual enterprise the effects of introducing ICT will be directly proportional to the organizational changes that accompany technological change. In considering investment strategies to equip themselves to participate in e-commerce, the Governments and enterprises of developing countries should keep in mind that neither computers nor the Internet, by themselves, can make a country or a company radically more productive. It is when its potential to allow more efficient business processes to operate is exploited that ICT makes a real difference.

This means that the potential of e-commerce to become an engine of development will not be realized if investment in infrastructure, equipment and human resource development does not go hand in hand with profound modifications in the organization and management of companies and (as far as they have an impact on the operation of businesses) government agencies. Fundamental changes need to be made, in particular in assigning authority and responsibility in public and private organizational structures. In the digital economy information flows more quickly and in more directions than in traditional organizations. Decision-making thus becomes a less centralized activity than in the past, and workers need to be able (and feel empowered) to perform a wider range of tasks. This represents a serious challenge for many developing countries and economies in transition, where traditional notions of authority and hierarchy may be more deeply entrenched. These notions will have to be redefined, for competitiveness in the digital economy requires a workforce that is equipped with the skills to master change rather than to undergo it.

Of course, the changes in business processes that are needed for benefit to be derived from the Internet are not limited to the internal organization of the enterprises. Among other things, enterprises in developing countries will also need to rethink the way in which they interact with their customers and suppliers, ensure compatibility of technical standards and business models or learn to share information with other enterprises. The networking effects of the Internet will also create new opportunities for innovative inter-firm cooperative arrangements and strategic alliances. Many of these aspects are examined in detail in the chapters of this report dealing with specific sectors of interest to developing countries.

At a more general level, the impact of the Internet on many key productive sectors of the developing countries will depend not only on the depth of the organizational changes that enterprises and their customers are ready to accept, but also on the linkages they establish between the information and the physical components of their activity. In concrete terms, the efforts of developing countries to adopt e-commerce and e-business will be futile if supplies spend weeks in a warehouse waiting for customs clearance, or the goods are not up to quality standards — because the workforce is poorly trained — or they cannot be brought to the market — because they lack reasonably priced transport.

Developing countries' policy-makers and entrepreneurs also need to be aware that the process of adoption of the Internet and related technologies by businesses will depend on, and at the same time change, the competitive environment in which enterprises operate. In some markets, the move to e-commerce will be a defensive reaction as enterprises see online rivals gaining market share. The most likely winners in this case will be consumers, as the process will result in increased competitive pressures on producers. In other sectors or markets, individual enterprises may use e-commerce to create a more or less durable competitive advantage (not necessarily in sales and marketing) and will reap the ensuing financial rewards. In every case the key factor will be the ability of entrepreneurs to identify the way in which the Internet can help them improve quality, reduce costs and, in the end, create value. Selling online will only be part of the process — and not necessarily the most important one.

In the end it will be as the efficiency gains derived from these and other changes in the business processes seep into the productive tissue of the developing countries that ICT and the Internet will contribute most to global economic growth and improved living standards. Indeed, it is because the Internet revolution is relevant not just to the high-tech, information-intensive sectors but also to the whole organization of economic life that its positive effects are spilling over more quickly into most sectors of the economy and that developing countries stand a better chance of sharing in its benefits earlier than in previous technological revolutions.

B. Executive Summary

1. Measuring Electronic Commerce

A crisis of e-commerce data?

Imagine gross domestic product (GDP) growth rates for the coming year (of, let us say, the United States economy) based on estimates provided by five different private companies and varying by as much as a factor of 10. These figures would then serve as a basis for taking decisions on economic policy and private sector investments in a large number of countries. While one would assume that most rational people would refrain from using the figures, such a scenario reflects the current situation of e-commerce-related data. No other economic sector has been subject to similar far-fetched growth forecasts (which had to be sharply readjusted after the Nasdaq crisis of the past year) and sweeping statements about the future of the sector and its "revolutionary" impact on the global economy. Venture capitalists and financial sector analysts alike have blindly used particularly optimistic e-commerce forecasts to take decisions on investments in start-up companies and the stock market.

E-commerce data are largely provided by private sector companies, which regularly publish reports on the latest developments in e-commerce, including short- to medium-term growth estimates. Unfortunately, the numbers differ considerably among the data providers given their use of different methodologies, definitions and indicators. Furthermore, private data providers need to be distinct from their competitors and serve their main clientele (largely e-businesses and investment analysts).

E-commerce statistics: Comparable and predictable

While there is little doubt about the ever greater role of electronic commerce and the use of ICTs in the global economy, the lack of reliable and internationally comparable data has been lamented by policy makers, researchers and business people alike. Therefore, a number of national statistical offices have started to collect data on e-commerce and, more generally, the use of ICT and the Internet. They have the advantage of guaranteeing the confidentiality of the collected data, having a more neutral position when it comes to collecting and interpreting the data and being able to use their existing methodologies and infrastructure for data collection, processing and analysis. Some countries are already benefiting from the results: they are now in a position to benchmark their economies with competitors internationally; they are able to identify the number of qualified people needed to advance their country's information economy or to calculate the amount of investments needed to provide businesses with access to the Internet. The United States is planning to include the measurement of e-commerce transactions in its entire statistical programme, which will enable it to measure the impact of e-commerce on the overall performance of the economy. In short, both policy-makers and business people are able to take well-informed decisions about the best public policy measures and private investments in e-commerce-related sectors.

Defining e-commerce before measuring it

There are a number of important steps involved in collecting e-commerce-related data. First, a country needs to decide what kind of data it wants to measure, reflecting the level of its e-commerce activity. Most developing countries would probably focus on collecting "readiness" indicators, such as the number of businesses with computers and access to the Internet, and "intensity" indicators, such as the number of businesses that receive orders over the Internet and the value of those orders.

But how does one define these indicators? The member States of the Organisation for Economic Co-operation and Development (OECD) have agreed on a working definition of e-commerce that could be used in the measuring process. The definition includes the networks over which e-commerce activities are carried out (Internet or others), the specific business processes related to e-commerce and the different actors involved (businesses, households or Governments). On the basis of this definition, a set of priority indicators for e-commerce have been established by a number of international and national bodies. Some of them, in particular those suggested by the Asia-Pacific Economic Cooperation (APEC), could be a useful starting point for developing countries wishing to compile e-commerce statistics.

New e-commerce surveys or add-ons?

At the empirical level, the two most common methodologies adopted for measuring e-commerce are (i) adding questions to existing surveys, and (ii) developing new surveys. Adding questions is more cost-effective, an important criterion for poorer countries. On the other hand, it provides limited information as it is attached to an existing survey. A good example of a new e-commerce survey is the Nordic Model survey, which has been tested across the Nordic (and other) countries and currently represents best practice in this field. It could thus be a useful input into the questionnaire design stage, in particular for developing countries.

What are the prospects for developing countries?

Most developing countries are at an early stage in collecting their own e-commerce statistics. They can thus take advantage of the experiences of some of their counterparts in the developed countries. Given their resources and statistical infrastructure, national statistical agencies in the developed countries are in a better position to contribute to the development work and are encouraged to do so. They should, however, help their counterparts in developing countries to develop the statistical infrastructure needed for the compilation of electronic commerce indicators.

2. Electronic Commerce and Developing Countries: A Computable General Equilibrium Analysis

Does e-commerce accelerate productivity growth?

The impact of e-commerce on the business sector has been widely accepted: it reduces transaction costs, allocates resources better, increases economies of scale and improves the competitiveness of businesses in general. On the other hand, doubts have been raised about the impact of e-commerce on macroeconomic growth, and in particular on productivity growth. At the root of this debate is the observation that the United States, the leading country in information technology and e-commerce, has experienced impressive GDP growth since 1995. This output expansion has been characterized by an acceleration in productivity growth, very low unemployment rates, low inflation rates and a reduction of fiscal deficits. However, productivity statistics have not provided any evidence of the impact of ICT and the Internet on this accelerated growth, also known as the "productivity paradox".

Recent studies on measuring industrial productivity in the United States show that productivity growth could in fact be widespread and not concentrated specifically in a few sectors of the new economy. It was found that productivity growth occurred in both computer and non-computer sectors. Productivity growth in the non-computer sector therefore would be a result of technological progress and production system improvements outside the computer sector, such as those related to e-commerce or computer- and web-based learning. Hence e-commerce seems to have a positive impact on the productivity and growth of countries (at least in the United States). It is expected that European countries will catch up quickly with the United States, and developing countries, with a certain degree of preparedness, could also converge in productivity with the leading e-commerce countries.

The risk of staying behind

UNCTAD's quantitative analysis focuses on the impact of e-commerce on the global economy by looking at two scenarios: first, if developing economies fall behind technologically; and, second, if they catch up with developed countries. The analysis is centred on cost savings and assumes that e-commerce can reduce the costs of services, particularly in retail and wholesale trade, transport, financial and business services. Cost savings in services are simulated through a productivity growth scenario.

The results of the first scenario reveal that while developed countries will have welfare gains of US$ 117 billion (based on 1997 data), the developing world, except for Asia, will lose welfare of US$ 726 billion. The Asian region, on the other hand, will increase welfare by US$ 802 million, largely from gains in the transport services sector. In addition to welfare and GDP losses, developing countries will experience a reduction in wages and deteriorating terms of trade. E-commerce could constitute, therefore, an additional factor increasing the gap between developed and developing countries.

Catching up quickly

The results of the second scenario, however, show that convergence in productivity in the services sectors (i.e. catching up with developed countries) allows developing countries to increase their external competitiveness and increase output, wages and welfare. A 1 per cent productivity growth in the services sector in Asia, for example, would result in welfare gains of US$ 12 billion, GDP growth of 0.4 per cent, a wage increase of 0.4 per cent and a growth in services exports of between 2 and 3 per cent. By reducing costs, increasing efficiency, reducing time and distances, e-commerce could thus become an important tool for development.

3. Electronic Commerce and Tourism

E-tourism: A chance for developing countries?

Developing countries generated US$ 131 billion in 1999 (according to the World Tourism Organization) by selling tourism services to international visitors. In many developing countries the tourism industry's role as an employer and earner of foreign currency is important and policy should be oriented to maintaining and improving its competitive advantages over developed country destinations. An important tool for doing this is e-commerce. While computer penetration and Internet penetration, as well as credit card and online payment facilities, may be lacking in many developing countries that are popular tourism destinations, this is not necessarily an overwhelming disadvantage as consumers come mostly from developed countries with modern ICT and financial infrastructures.

An information-intensive industry

The tourism industry is among those sectors most quickly adopting the Internet as a business medium. Tourism is very information-intensive and substantial resources are used in advertising, market research and consumer profiling. Purchase and delivery are often remote occurrences and during the intermediary period the tourism product exists in the form of information (reservation number, ticket, voucher), which requires consumers to have confidence that it will materialize. Confidence is best gained through the quality of information provided by the seller or producer. Value added by international tourism intermediaries, who are often no more than information handlers and who rarely own or manage physical tourism facilities, can be as high as 30 per cent or more, thus controlling general terms and conditions throughout the whole value chain. Keeping this in mind, it is easy to see that tourism and e-commerce are natural partners.

The "set-up"

The traditional international tourism market was, and to a large extent still is, a linear value chain. At the starting end we find the producers of tourism services in developing country destinations. These commit or sell their capacity to international distributors or intermediaries, who take the form of international tour operators such as Thomas Cook and JTB. Alternatively, they may commit capacity to computer reservation systems (CRSs), such as Sabre, Galileo or Amadeus, which are usually run by the largest international airlines. These distributors then retail this capacity in developed country markets through own or licensed agencies.

An often-heard complaint is that with each party taking a commission, little remains for the destination, where in fact the consumer or tourist will actually spend some pleasant or exciting time. It is the destination's socio-economic, cultural or geographical content that forms the fundamental tourism product. The common explanation for this perceived imbalance is that many developing country destinations are far away and there is not enough competition in air travel to bring down transport costs. Travel costs regularly account for more than half of the total price of a packaged product.

Another characteristic of this "set-up" is that tour operators typically provide a very comprehensive packaged product, including lodging, transport, recreation, some sight-seeing and popular cultural and historical tours with little or no flexibility for "tailoring". On the other hand, CRS operators provide full flexibility but little comprehensiveness. Besides lodging, air tickets and some car rentals from major international companies, little else is on offer.

What could change?

E-tourism may change all this and create a more dynamic and networked industry and disintermediate and deconstruct the value chain. Each and every participant in the tourism industry is trying to establish itself as the entry point for the prospective tourist surfing the web for ideas and information about where to go or what to do. Some are trying to establish themselves as an Internet generalist, while the others may become niche "portals", depending on where they see their competitive advantage. By creating a business network through freely and voluntarily associating their diverse offers in a competitive environment, tourism producers, including those in developing countries, may provide, directly to the client, a flexible and tailored product, while avoiding commission costs imposed by international distributors and high-street retailers.

Even the large distributors are transforming themselves into Internet-based operations and are transferring their proprietary/legacy computer systems to the Internet. The Open Travel Alliance, an association of leading tourism and travel industry companies, is creating a working, public and open Internet-XML data interchange protocol that will enable businesses to exchange specific tourism capacity data using the Internet as the data conduit.

Creating consumer confidence

The fundamental question is: why would an Internaut buy a tourism product from one portal and not from another? The key issue is confidence. This is why the international distributors and agents still manage to capture a large part of the buying public's orders. Their legal presence in tourists' countries of origin and their physical presence in the high street serve as a guarantee that the actual purchased product will be delivered, often weeks or months after purchase. How can distant developing country tourism producers compete with this? Only by offering quality information, and products that are better tailored, more interesting and priced more competitively compared with what international distributors and agents can manage.

Establish the dot

The ultimate goal is to improve competitiveness through the use of the Internet and e-commerce tools. To do so, a developing country tourism industry can adopt appropriate and often diverse technological solutions: the state of the art is not necessarily feasible for each and every business. It should consider very carefully the way e-tourism will interface with the traditional physical industry that needs to become the content provider. If it is disowned or technologically alienated from the content of its web, any advantages will be short-lived. It is necessary to build a business web to provide comprehensive and flexible tourism products: local businesses must co-operate and see their joint interests.

Knowing the customer and speaking his or her language is vital. This often entails establishing co-operative and reciprocal relationships with similar businesses or organizations in other countries. Online payment possibilities are fundamental to closing sales and a lack of local financial infrastructure regularly forces e-businesses to establish offshore subsidiaries and accounts. Finally, all this is impossible without trained and educated IT and tourism professionals.

More room for the destination marketing organizations

The activities of national tourism offices, or destination management organizations, could be crucial for the success of e-tourism endeavours in many developing countries. Often, they may best understand the need for quality information and typically have a broad overview of the national tourism industry. They may be the industry's best representative in securing technical support and training, as well as negotiating terms and conditions with local financial institutions for securing online payment facilities. In many countries they may develop themselves into the national portal for prospective tourists, provided that they are able to respond to the information and online transaction needs of consumers in developed countries.

4. Business-to-Business Electronic Marketplaces: Their Nature, Impact and Prospects in Developing Countries

Are e-marketplaces the future of e-commerce?

B2B e-markets, also referred to as "net markets" or "exchanges", are expected to play a pivotal role in the future of e-commerce. The sheer total value of their transactions and the fact that they are created and supported by established bricks-and-mortar companies should ensure their long-term viability and growth. These market-places are forums that bring together many buyers and many sellers not only to exchange goods and services, but also to share a variety of value-added services. Furthermore, they involve contractual relationships that are more long-term than other e-commerce models such as B2C trading. Their future growth is expected to involve a variety of changes, the main ones being consolidation and the formation of strategic alliances, greater focus on the provision of differentiated and specialized products and services, and a shift towards the creation of industry-based or consortium-type and private e-markets as opposed to independent third-party markets. The lessons learned from the experiences of early dot. com companies may provide B2B e-markets with a vision for adopting sustainable business strategies.

The benefits of B2B e-markets to enterprises

B2B e-markets considerably enhance the various benefits that are generally attributed to e-commerce. They reduce transaction costs by minimizing search costs, as they bring a large number of buyers and sellers into one trading community. They also facilitate a more efficient processing of transactions by facilitating online auctions and online processing of invoices, purchase orders and payments. In addition, B2B e-markets provide a framework by means of which traders can optimize online transactions in other ways across the entire supplier chain, for example by linking the processing of goods transactions directly to logistics functions.

B2B e-markets both eliminate intermediaries and create new ones. Independent, third-party e-market-places themselves are intermediaries by definition, as they are placed in between suppliers and customers in the supply chain. On the other hand, market-places established by bricks-and-mortar companies and private e-markets enable companies to link with established trading partners, thus eliminating the role of intermediaries.

B2B e-markets also have the benefit of increasing price transparency. By bringing together large numbers of sellers and buyers they reveal market prices and transaction processing to participants. As a result, price differences are reduced in the market-place and also buyers are allowed greater opportunities to compare prices and make better purchasing decisions. Finally, e-markets provide scope for economies of scale, largely because of substantial upfront expenses involved in setting up an e-market, such as programming costs. Also, by linking large numbers of buyers and sellers, e-markets provide demand-side economies of scale or network effects in that the addition of each incremental participant in a market creates value for all existing participants on the demand side.

The success and failure of an e-market

There is a wide range of capabilities or functionality that e-markets can offer to traders. These relate to the content or information they provide, support for collaboration between trading partners and the handling of online transactions, including payments, online exchange of documents and providing linkages to logistic services. The e-marketplace that offers the most functionality that traders require will have an advantage. Coupled with functionality is the attainment of a critical mass or liquidity that makes the e-marketplace viable and sustainable. In addition, technology is a critical input that enhances the functionality of an e-marketplace. This explains why many B2B e-markets have created strategic alliances with technology companies or have outsourced the hosting of e-marketplaces to them.

Do B2B e-markets lead to competition or oligopolies?

A large number of B2B e-markets have been established in different industries, thus giving rise to intense competition. E-markets tend to have low barriers to entry, but the attainment of liquidity and critical mass determines which e-markets will survive the competition. Generally, first movers, but in certain cases newcomers, may have the advantage in attaining critical mass and thereby creating barriers to entry to other entrants. Also, because of the ability of B2B e-markets to engage in exclusionary behaviour and share information about prices and other commercial data, they have the potential for creating market dominance and anti-competitive behaviour. Competition authorities, however, have not so far established specific rules to address B2B e-markets.

It is an uphill task for developing countries to play a role in B2B e-markets

There are challenges and opportunities for developing countries to participate in B2B e-markets. So far they have accounted for a negligible share of transactions in such markets. For an enterprise to decide to participate in e-markets as a buyer or seller, it is essential to consider a number of strategic factors and to assess the expected return on investment.

Developing countries may find opportunities to participate in or create B2B e-markets in sectors where they have a significant presence, such as travel/tourism and primary commodity marketing. In tourism the Internet opens new channels through which developing country enterprises can participate in the supply and distribution of tourism products. To this end, a number of schemes, such as regional cooperation and affiliation with major players, are available to enterprises, including SMEs.

Primary commodities play a key role in the economies of many developing countries. Traditional marketing and export channels tend to be inefficient and dominated by multiple intermediaries. This situation can be improved by using the Internet for electronic trading. Online B2B exchanges have already been created in trades such as coffee, tea and cotton. Most of these have been created by developed country companies, but a few have been established by developing country enterprises. Developing countries, using existing local commodity exchanges and commodity export associations as a foundation, can use B2B online trading as a means of transforming existing commodity marketing systems to great advantage.

5. Towards Digital Government

Why should Governments go online?

The Internet, with its capacity to allow the sharing of information across organizations and to help people work together, creates new possibilities to reorganize and network government services so that they can become more user-centred, transparent and efficient. In UNCTAD's experience of the application of ICT to government services, the first prerequisite for success in this process is political will and motivation. Government agencies will also have to overcome obstacles derived from their size and complexity, address concerns about inequality of access to the Internet and revise the way they are organized and operate. In developing countries they will also have to deal with the same problems of telecommunications infrastructure, poor computer and general literacy, lack of awareness of the potential of the Internet and regulatory inadequacy that also hinder other applications of the Internet there.

At the same time, there are many reasons to expect that the changes brought about by the Internet regarding the delivery and management of public services will be significant. As in the private sector, adopting e-government practices will allow Governments to achieve significant savings in areas ranging from procurement to personnel management. Not only can resources be saved, but also the quality of services provided to citizens can be dramatically improved. Furthermore, e-government will provide an example and an incentive for firms (especially SMEs) to adopt e-business practices, thus spreading the efficiency gains to the economy as a whole.

E-government is not about setting up a website

Even though the expectations about e-government are high, its reality today is uneven. Many government agencies around the world have set up websites that provide information about their services, include downloadable forms that can be submitted offline and let users interact with the staff of the agency through e-mail. These applications of the Internet, although useful, cannot be said to be true e-government tools, because they cannot support formal transactions.

The majority of government agencies that have started to provide some e-government services are concentrated in developed countries and a few advanced developing countries. Their sites support some formal online transactions that involve either payments or the creation or transfer of legal rights (for instance, filing a tax return, renewing a driving licence or claiming social security benefits); they may include tools to help users complete online transactions, but they normally need to be combined with more traditional support systems, such as a telephone "hot-line". These sites tend to replicate the procedures of the offline service, they rarely include the whole range of services and do not support transactions that involve more than one agency.

Finally, only very few operative government sites aim at providing services not on the basis of the organization of the agency entrusted with their delivery but according to the needs of the user. This means that they integrate a wide range of governmental services, normally under the same overall political responsibility. The objective is to build comprehensive government portals that people can use to find information or to carry out transactions without having to deal directly with the various agencies that can be involved in a single "life event", such as setting up a small business or changing residence.

How to go about building e-government

To succeed in e-government, agencies will need to learn to see the citizen as their customer, which represents a radical cultural change for many organizations. Becoming a user-centred organization will require a change in resource allocation priorities and a thorough review of business processes. A user-centred agency will also need to give credible answers to concerns about the integrity and confidentiality of the sensitive data that government agencies often collect.

The move towards e-government will be incremental. The current phase can be considered an experimental one, with Governments concentrating on limited, relatively simple applications of the Internet. As demand for e-government grows, and agencies progress in their understanding of its benefits and the changes it requires, e-government will enter a second phase in which portals integrating a wider range of online transactions in a secure environment will be more widespread. The areas in which progress is likely to be faster coincide in part with those in which the private sector is getting more benefits from the Internet. They include procurement, applications to help agencies share information more efficiently and websites that provide convenience for citizens (renewing licences online, for instance) and reduce transaction costs for the agency.

The following are some other basic points that should be kept in mind by agencies considering how to use the Internet to enhance their operations:

- Technology for e-government does not need to be complicated, but it must be reliable and fast;
- As long as a large part of the population remains without easy access to the Internet, traditional channels such as counter service or the telephone will retain an important role. The requirements of people with special difficulties to use technology need to be taken into account too;
- Citizens and businesses need to be made aware of the availability and advantages of e-government services;
- E-government projects are an excellent opportunity for new partnerships with the private sector, which can contribute financial resources and its experience of e-business;
- E-government poses a complex challenge that calls for political commitment and a clear strategic vision at the highest possible level.

6. Overview of Selected Legal and Regulatory Issues in Electronic Commerce

Finding global solutions to address global transactions

Ensuring users and consumers effective redress for disputes arising from transactions in the online environment is a key element in building trust. There is a widespread awareness of the potential legal barriers arising from recourse to courts in disputes resulting from cross-border online interactions. Which law applies? Which authority has jurisdiction in the dispute? Which forum is competent to hear the dispute? Is the decision enforceable? These are some of the questions that all too often arise and for which there is not yet a clear answer. Electronic commerce has increased the need to rely on party autonomy, the choice-of-court clauses becoming central to any discussion of court jurisdiction. Thus, it is essential that national legal systems clearly provide for rules on which parties can rely in order to ensure that their choice-of-court clauses will be deemed valid. Uncertainty in this respect is detrimental to the trust which private operators will have in the judicial and legal systems of a particular country. To assist States in their efforts to accommodate e-commerce, this chapter analyses a number of options for countries wishing to develop a set of choice-of-court rules. A difference is made in this regard within business-to-business (B2B) and business-to-consumer (B2C) contracts, as well as between (i) contracts concluded online and performed offline, and (ii) contracts concluded and performed online.

Disputes in cyberspace: Online solutions needed for online problems

It is well known that public law-making is too rigid, too slow in responding to the need for immediate adjudication, and too slow adapting to changes to the social, technological and commercial customs of cyberspace. In contrast, private law-making and private adjudication are more flexible and readily adapt to the diverse evolving technological and social nature of cyberspace and its changing commercial practices. Given that traditional dispute settlement mechanisms may not provide effective redress in electronic commerce transactions for a large number of the small claims and low-value transactions arising from B2C online interactions, this chapter analyses the various alternative dispute resolution (ADR) mechanisms that would provide speedy, low-cost redress. When ADR takes place using computer-mediated communications in the online environment, it is often referred to as online dispute resolution (ODR). Both e-disputes and bricks-and-mortar disputes can be resolved using ODR. The system could be used in a variety of contexts, including within a particular online market place (e.g. mediation in online auction sites, arbitration in the domain name system and in the automated negotiation process for insurance disputes), as part of a trustmark or seal programme, or on an independent basis. These ODR mechanisms range from those which are fully automated — in that a computer program without human intervention generates outcomes — to most other ODR providers that offer dispute settlement with human intervention. Parties may contract for a range of ODR services from mediation, which aims at encouraging the parties to reach an amicable settlement of their disagreement, to binding arbitration, which imposes on the parties a legally enforceable arbitral award. As of December 2000, more than 40 ODR providers had been identified.

Jurisdiction: Is your enterprise website regarded as a branch?

Concerning jurisdiction, two main questions are addressed: (i) can an Internet site be regarded as a branch or establishment for any legal purpose? and (ii) is the level of interactivity relevant? As regards the first question, it seems that the tendency is to consider that a website does not qualify as a branch or permanent establishment. Thus, the place of establishment of a company providing services via an Internet website is not the place at which the technology supporting its website is located or the place at which its website is accessible, but the place where it pursues its economic activity. The answer to the second question for a large number of countries is also clear: whatever the level of interactivity of the website, it will not change the answer to the first question. However, if a site is an interactive one, it may lead some countries, which apply a doing-business concept for court jurisdiction to assert jurisdiction as long as the interactivity can be seen as a clear link with the State whose courts assert jurisdiction.

Applicable law: A new concept of consumer protection

As regards applicable law, an important difference has to be made between B2B and B2C contracts. Concerning B2B contracts, there is a renewed interest in codes of conduct. Thus, States are confronted with an ever-increasing duty to define carefully the limits of their public policy rules, since operators over the Internet often develop their own codes of conduct. Whether or not operators can include a choice-of-law clause in their contracts will be determined by the public policy of each State. In the case of B2C contracts, and for a large majority of countries where consumers are protected, the law applicable would be the one which is more favourable to the consumer. Therefore, if the law of the location of the consumer is more favourable, it will apply; but if, on the contrary, it is not, the law of the professional who supplied the service or the goods will apply. This is the main reason why Internet operators have been so keen to block all adoption of rules of the same nature for the Internet. This is one of the areas that would greatly benefit from an international agreement on common rules of protection for consumers. Concerning torts, most decisions which have been taken by national courts around the world apply the law of the place where the effect is felt, and not that of the country where the tort was committed. This rule needs to be reassessed against Internet specificity.

Data protection: Convenience at the cost of privacy?

The question of privacy and data protection over the net is another important issue. It is well known that the value of many Internet corporations depends on the amount of data they are able to gather. Thus, personal data about consumer habits, tastes and the like are of great value to any corporation wishing to operate over the net. A consumer may want to limit the availability and use of each of these types of information and may make decisions about entering into a transaction based on the extent to which the information will be protected. The problem is not new, what is new is its scale. It is this dilemma — keeping our personal information private, while allowing use of that information to make our lives easier — that is the crux of the current data protection debate. The more legal protection and control individuals are provided with as regards their personal information, the more costly it becomes for companies to comply with those protections, and for Governments to investigate and prosecute violations of those rights. Removing legal barriers to the free flow of information, while allowing for more innovation, development, and more personalized service, will lessen legal protection of personal information. Although the unification of substantive law remains the best solution for international protection of privacy and personal data, in practice it is not always possible to unify all aspects of the law. Therefore, the question of applicable law (e.g. the law of the location of the person whose data are collected) is still pertinent in this context. However, when the conflict rule clashes with the economic needs of Internet operators, it must remain a default rule to be applied only if substantive unification is not possible.

Legal recognition of electronic signatures: The options

As regards encryption and electronic signatures, there seems to be a consensus that a mechanism for secure authentication of electronic communication is critical to the development of electronic commerce. Such a mechanism must provide for confidentiality, authentication (enabling each party in a transaction to ascertain with certainty the identity of the other party) and non-repudiation (ensuring that the parties to a transaction cannot subsequently deny their participation). This chapter provides a review of the basic approaches to electronic signature legislation together with some recent samples of regional legislation that might guide States wishing to prepare legislation on electronic signatures.

Cybertaxation: No escape

So far, businesses have enjoyed a largely tax-free e-commerce environment. In other words, goods and services transmitted electronically have not been subject to taxation. However, fears of revenue losses from uncollected taxes and duties on Internet transactions have prompted many Governments to work towards internationally agreeable solutions with regard to changing existing tax legislation to take account of e-commerce.

Who pays the VAT: Buyer or seller?

At the centre of the e-commerce taxation debate are two issues: consumption and income taxation. As far as consumption taxes are concerned, the question arises whether the tax should be collected in the jurisdiction of the supplier or the consumer. Under current legislation foreign suppliers are often exempted from VAT. This provides incentives for suppliers to locate abroad and gives an unfair competitive advantage to foreign suppliers. Therefore, there seems to be a growing tendency towards applying taxation in the place of consumption. Given the disappearance of intermediaries who previously collected the VAT, it is not clear yet who should collect the taxes now. The EU has proposed that the foreign supplier should register in a EU country for VAT purposes. The United States, being the largest exporter and a net exporter of e-commerce, tends towards an origin-based consumption tax. Furthermore, it has little interest in collecting VAT for European tax authorities on their e-commerce goods and services exports to the EU. Developing countries, which will be largely e-commerce importers in the short to medium run, would have an interest in not eroding their tax base by switching to an origin-based tax system.

Is my website a taxable business?

As far as income taxation is concerned, much of the debate has focused on the issue of the "permanent establishment" (PE) of a business. This will determine to what extent an Internet-based business will be subject to taxation. The definition of PE is important for countries that apply source-based income taxation (the majority of countries). Agreement has been reached at the OECD on the following issues: (i) a website by itself cannot constitute a PE; (ii) a web server hosted by an Internet service provider (ISP) cannot constitute a fixed place of business if the ISP does not carry on business through the server; (iii) a web server can constitute a fixed place of business and thus a PE if it is owned by a business that carries on business through the server; and (iv) ISPs cannot be PEs of the businesses whose websites they host. Developing countries, even if they are not part of an OECD agreement on Internet taxation, should use the agreed-upon rules as a basis for adjusting their own legislation. Since they are net importers of e-commerce, they will run a greater risk of losing revenues if traditional imports are replaced by online delivery, and should thus start to develop efficient tax collection systems for e-commerce.

No customs duties on digital goods: A fiscal concern?

In accordance with a WTO moratorium, no customs duties should be imposed on electronic transmissions. While a large number of (mainly developed) countries prefer to extend the moratorium, some developing countries have expressed concern about potential revenue losses resulting from uncollected border tariffs. The question of how to define digitital goods (books, CDs, software, music etc.) — as goods or as services — has held up progress on e-commerce in the WTO. While border tariffs are normally collected on goods, they are not collected on services. Developing countries have therefore raised the question of potential fiscal implications if digital products are imported duty-free. UNCTAD calculations show a potential fiscal loss of approximately US$ 1 billion on border tariffs and US$ 8 billion if other import duties (including VAT) are taken into consideration. While these amounts are small relative to total government revenue, absolute losses from forgone tariff revenues are much higher in the developing countries, owing to their higher tariffs applied to digital products.

7. Managing Payments and Credit Risks Online

Online payments: A pre-requisite for e-commerce?

The issue of online payments has been identified at several UNCTAD meetings as one of the main obstacles to the growth of e-commerce in the developing countries. In particular, the lack of know-how, the high initial costs of introducing online payments mechanisms and difficulties in ensuring secure digital transfers via the Internet are often listed among the major impediments. Although e-commerce transactions in developing countries still rely mainly on "online conclusion and offline payment", as the volume of e-commerce expands the development of online payments will become a pressing issue.

Moving from traditional to online payment

The dramatic difference in cost and speed between traditional and Internet-mediated financial services and related information delivery has led to rapid growth of online payments, e-financing and online credit risk management, thus bringing about profound changes in the whole system of financial services and intermediation. Online versions of nearly all existing payment methods are appearing rapidly. Moreover, new instruments and modes of financial intermediation such as smart cards and Internet banking are becoming the dominant features of the emerging, Internet-based international financial system.

Conventional financial instruments with online analogues include cash, money orders, giro transfers, cheques, drafts, notes and bills of exchange. The existing modes of third-party protection against the risks of non-payment and non-performance, including documentary credit, credit insurance, bonding, factoring and forfeiting, are also rapidly developing their online equivalents. The same applies to wholesale payment systems, including so-called automated clearing house (ACH) networks, "wire transfers" for large-volume payments and interbank payments networks.

Credit and debit cards, which were already the most widely accepted mode of electronic payments, especially in B2B relations, have become the principal payments instrument in B2C e-commerce. The move from cards with magnetic strips to "smart cards" with multifunctional chips that include security features is the next Internet-centred stage in the development of the payments cards industry.

In parallel, Internet technologies to provide security in online payments have been evolving. The first, and still the most widely accepted standard, is the Secure Socket Layer (SSL), a set of built-in browser protocols designed initially by Netscape to protect card-based financial transactions on the Internet. A more secure and complex bank-centred Secure Electronic Transactions (SET) software is currently being used more and more by online payments providers.

Another increasingly popular method for carrying out large B2B payments is Internet banking. Moving online transfers such as ACH debits or credits, as well as domestic and international wire transfers, became possible with systems such as the Bank Internet Payment System (BIPS), which work as an Internet 'front-end' to the existing ACH. The latter can now be initiated directly by companies. The Society for Worldwide Inter-Bank Financial Telecommunications (SWIFT) — the largest international interbank payment network — also started this year its move to the open Internet platform. Initiatives to introduce new regional and global systems for online real-time gross settlements and clearing operations all reflect the expectation of exponential growth in online payments.

New ways to secure financial transactions and financial stability?

For a successful online transaction to take place, the contracting parties should be able to find at low cost information on the corporate and financial health and performance of each other or be adequately protected by third parties. As in the case of conventional transaction protection by third parties, the Internet needs modern risk management tools. The leaders of the industry, including credit insurance, credit information, factoring and other companies or their alliances, are moving online to follow their clients and to protect them from political and commercial risks inherent in trade and investment.

The emergence of e-finance may pose new regulatory challenges related to the emergence of non-bank organizations operating electronic cash or online accounts holding substantial amounts of deposits. Monetary authorities may in the future have to take into account the effects of e-cash and other money substitutes on monetary aggregates and monetary policy instruments, although for the time being the volumes involved are too small for this issue to be more than a theoretical matter. At the same time, the blurring borders between instruments and service providers, the emergence of new entrants and the global character of e-finance make financial regulation an even more complex task and increase the importance of effective international coordination among the financial regulators.

E- finance for developing countries

Banks and financial services companies in the developing countries will need to adopt online payment systems and practices that will meet their clients' new needs arising from a shift to e-commerce. They will need to adopt systems that address the key issues of concern to users, namely security, confidentiality, identification of sellers and buyers, verification of buyers' solvency and guarantee of delivery. Similarly, regulatory authorities will need to provide the necessary supportive measures to ensure that acceptable system standards are established and maintained.

To obtain e-trade finance and equity investment, companies from developing countries need to be registered in local, regional and global Internet-based commercial risk databases. For that, company registries, public courts, accountancy and audit, and other business-related services should undergo substantial enhancements. Non-bank financial services such as credit information, credit insurance, factoring and leasing should develop. Local banks should adapt to e-banking and move online their customer credit risk databases, and their individual and corporate customer payment services and financing, including trade finance instruments. Overcoming the digital divide in finance also implies closer cooperation between local and international financial service providers, including active co-financing by development banks, as well as concerted technical assistance, including training, from specialized international organizations.

8. E-Logistics: Delivering the Goods in E-Commerce

Why logistics services are critical to the success of e-commerce

Logistics services for e-commerce (e-logistics) have proved to be an area that requires major improvements if e-commerce is to achieve its full potential. The failure of many e-tailers, for example in the United States, to fulfil orders during peak demand periods and the reluctance of some sellers to engage in international e-commerce because of the complex logistics requirements clearly demonstrate the critical role of e-logistics. The existing e-logistics problems arise largely from the fact that e-commerce and the demand for related logistics services have grown at a much faster rate than that at which suitable logistics services and solutions have been developed.

Solutions being used to improve logistics for e-commerce

Traders have responded to the increased demand for logistics services that arises from e-commerce by adopting a variety of methods. These include handling of order fulfilment by companies themselves using in-house logistics services, outsourcing fulfilment to third-party logistics service providers (3PLs), drop-shipping and various combinations of these methods. Concurrently, considerable efforts have been made to develop software applications in order to automate logistics functions such as order management, cargo and equipment tracking, transportation management and planning, customer service management and returns management. It is estimated for that by 2000 worldwide sales of software, hardware and services used in electronic logistics had reached US$ 277 billion, and they are expected to reach US$ 1 trillion by 2005.[9] While these figures appear to be on the high side, they nevertheless provide a useful indication of the importance being given to the issue of logistics in e-commerce.

Difficulties faced

Technology plays a critical role in providing systems that can enhance the ability of logistics service providers to satisfy customer demands. The main weakness of the efforts to develop applications for improving logistics is the general lack of integration between the various applications used for different logistics functions. Many of the applications are designed to handle different types of logistics functions, and this tends to lead to the existence of incompatible systems being applied to related logistics functions.

Another factor that impedes the effectiveness of e-logistics services is the existence of a multitude of constraints brought about by inefficient trade facilitation. The major problems in this area include:

- The existence of a considerable number of disparate documentation requirements, which include government documents, commercial documents and those relating to transportation;
- The lack of harmonization of customs procedures and tariff classification systems;
- The existence of custom valuation of exports and imports in many countries that is characterized by such problems as double invoicing and undervaluation, thus making assessment of the true value difficult;
- The existence of outdated trade procedures such as exchange controls, long retention of goods in customs custody and regulations that require paper documents;
- Lack of transparency in many regulations, leading to the inability to predict costs and delivery times;
- Customs administrations that are poorly equipped, as regards physical infrastructure and human resources and also lack of cooperation between customs administration of different countries. Many customs administrations are also prone to corruption, which leads to delays, high costs and a distortion in trade information;
- Limited use of automation and information technology in trade facilitation functions, leading to delays, high costs and inefficiencies.

The way forward

To achieve more efficient e-logistics and e-fulfilment, it is desirable to have a trading environment in which there is sufficient information about goods as regards their description and origins, and destinations. Sellers and buyers should be able to monitor and track goods at every point along the way from the supplier to consumer. All stakeholders should be able to check on the Internet the availability and status of orders. All this can be achieved if trade information is simplified, automated and fully harmonized in all countries and when all restrictive government export/import regulations and practices have been eliminated. It also requires sophisticated supply chain management systems for compiling and enabling global end-to-end monitoring of trade information.

To accomplish these broad objectives and also to take into account the special problems of developing countries, it is recommended that Governments, the international community and the private sector cooperate in promoting the following specific measures:

- To take advantage of the great potential provided by the Internet technology in order to capture, transfer and monitor trade information over global networks of supply chains in an open fashion;
- To enhance and improve the harmonization of the classification of commodity tariffs and facilitate the identification of individual consignments;
- To automate trade processing and particularly customs declaration systems in order to develop customs-to-customs information exchange and thereby provide a basis for the elimination of unnecessary export/import requirements, which can instead be replaced by fully integrated international transactions. In this context, the International Trade Prototype (ITP) project created by the United Kingdom and the United States

customs administrations to develop a system that could enable information provided for export declaration to be used to fulfil the data requirements for import entry in the country of destination could provide a model to be developed at the international level. This system, however, could only be implemented if all government customs requirements could be simplified and harmonized and the transmission of trade information based on internationally agreed standards. A preliminary evaluation has shown widespread support for further development of the project, and the international community should lend its support to the project as well;

- To harmonize and simplify trade facilitation regulations and procedures, and in particular to encourage greater harmonization of customs procedures through wide adoption and implementation of the revised Kyoto Convention on the Simplification and Harmonization of Customs Procedures;
- To encourage greater transparency in trade processing activities and take measures to reduce corruption and other forms of malpractice in customs administration;
- To promote greater integration of software applications for logistics functions, including the use of such systems as XML (eXtensible Markup Language);
- To promote partnerships between logistics service providers of developing countries and those of developed countries that are applying e-logistics systems;
- To provide technical cooperation programmes to developing countries in promoting services that support e-logistics, for example in customs, transportation services, cargo terminals and related services and also in the automation of trade information.

9. Electronic Commerce in the Least Developed Countries

A survey of the status of electronic commerce in 10 of the least developed countries (LDCs) was conducted by UNCTAD in 2001. The countries visited were Bangladesh, Cambodia, Ethiopia, Madagascar, Mozambique, Myanmar, Nepal, Togo, Uganda and the United Republic of Tanzania. The objective of the survey was to identify enterprises engaged in e-commerce in the LDCs, and sectors in which e-commerce may create new opportunities for these countries. The cases of 16 enterprises were selected for presentation in the *Electronic Commerce and Development Report 2001* among those identified through the survey. The criteria used to select them were potential market size, the sustainability of their competitive advantage, the qualifications of the management and the replicability of their business models.

Is e-commerce part of an LDC development strategy?

A prerequisite for international trade to make a positive contribution to the development of the LDCs is the generation of productive capacities there. The various policies implemented by the international community and national Governments over the past two decades have had little success. Adopting e-commerce may now place the LDCs in a better position to use international trade as a tool for development for two reasons. First, an important factor explaining the failure of export promotion policies in the LDCs is the impact of transport costs and inefficient trade procedures in the competitiveness of LDC enterprises (transport can amount to up to 40 of the total cost of the exportation of a product). LDCs enterprises in a number of sectors may find that e-commerce enables them to overcome some of these obstacles and thus become more competitive in international markets. Second, e-commerce may give some LDCs an opportunity for economic diversification by entering into new sectors, particularly in the field of teleservicing, where they can enjoy advantages derived mainly, but not exclusively, from their low labour costs.

It is well known that entrepreneurs in the developing world who wish to engage in e-commerce face serious difficulties, including a lack of infrastructure, IT skills, legislation, payment methods and financial resources. The participation of LDC enterprises in the digital economy is also limited by the relative lack of government interest in e-commerce issues. Very few LDCs have an e-commerce policy in place. Of those surveyed by UNCTAD, only Bangladesh is at an advanced stage in developing an information technology policy. Others are in the early phases of their e-commerce strategies and IT policy development.

However, all these problems should not obscure the fact that ICT and the Internet have a significant potential to generate new business opportunities for LDC enterprises seeking to participate in international trade. In particular, the LDC physical infrastructure for e-commerce is limiting but not prohibitive and new technologies (web enabling, cellular applications) offer exciting new opportunities to leapfrog development of a local e-commerce infrastructure. The availability and the quality of telecommunications have indeed improved dramatically in LDCs, although most of the countries surveyed still reported relatively high local telecommunications costs.

Electronic commerce niches

The survey revealed the existence of potential niches for e-commerce projects in the LDCs and identified examples of successful business-to-business, business-to-consumer and other concrete actions taking place mainly at the initiative of enterprises, and to a lesser extent, of Governments.

An important point illustrated by these examples is that the most serious problem for LDC enterprises as they embark on e-commerce is not technology but the need to change their business culture and practices. The success stories identified in the survey are the achievements of dynamic entrepreneurs that found ingenious solutions to bypass traditional obstacles to international trade. That is the case, for instance, of SMEs using the capacities of developed country-based banks or Internet service providers (ISPs) to develop their web platforms and payment facilities, or using network agents such as restaurants as their distributors around the world. Success has come to those LDC enterprises that have been able to progressively generate consumer trust by creating a loyal subscriber base, by offering information about home or by developing an agent network in the target market.

"Offline teleservicing" (B2B) is recognized as a very viable opportunity for the LDCs. This includes transcription services, data input, software development, remote access server maintenance, web development, creation of databases, digitization of old documents (i.e. architectural drawings), translations and editing. There are indeed a few case studies indicating that opportunities abound in this industry, even if the LDCs already face stiff competition from other developing countries (India, Philippines, etc.) that are also able to offer a lower labour cost environment. In addition to attractive low labour costs, e-commerce creates opportunities to exploit advantages derived from the loss of economic significance of distances and the geographical location of LDCs in various time zones.

There are also business-to-consumer opportunities, though limited, that involve servicing the diaspora market, and developments in international business-to-business exchanges will eventually provide opportunities to commodity suppliers and manufacturers.

Perspectives for the development of an e-commerce strategy

E-commerce policy and laws are important, but the lack thereof should not deter enterprises from implementing e-commerce strategies. E-commerce has flourished in the United States for many years without the existence of specific e-commerce legislation. This having been said, for the LDCs to make headway in the digital economy Governments should take a more active role, in particular in addressing the lack of an e-commerce business culture and the human resource needs of their countries.

Most of the countries surveyed had a sufficient infrastructure from which enterprises could implement some form of e-commerce strategy. This is partly due to the fact that ISPs are available in most cities, and partly due to the nature of the Internet itself, which enables companies to be serviced by ISPs based in developed countries (i.e. hosting, payments, web design etc.). Some of the cities visited have excellent connectivity for businesses, some of the ISPs offering wireless options on fixed monthly subscriptions albeit expensive, and a greatly improved telecommunications infrastructure in certain cities (i.e. fibre-optic cabling in Kampala). However, restrictive regulations such as exchange controls, protection of telecommunication monopolies, restrictive trade practices and prohibitions (i.e. encryption, Internet telephony, own gateway access etc.) are highest on the list of concerns indicated by LDC enterprises wanting to engage in e-commerce.

10. China's ICT Strategy and E-Commerce

A government-driven strategy

China adopted its ICT development strategy in the early 1980s in the context of constructing the information highway as a path to modernization and economic development. It eventually led to the launching of the Golden Projects, which include the Golden Bridge, an electronic information network linking provincial regional nodes with a central hub in Beijing; the Golden Card, an electronic money project designed to accelerate the development of electronic banking and a credit card system; and the Golden Gate, a foreign trade information network designed to promote information exchange concerning foreign trade and foreign investment, paving the way for eventual transition toward paperless trade. It is a top-down strategy with government backing and under government control. Some outside observers have criticized the Golden Projects as an attempt to strengthen government control which may prevent businesses and individuals from fully exploiting the potential of the Internet.

The substantial public investment in the telecommunication infrastructure has brought about considerable growth in the ICT industry. According to official statistics for 2000, the national telephone penetration rate by home rose to 20.1 per cent with a higher urban area rate of 39 per cent. Telephone network capacity in absolute terms has advanced its global ranking to second from 17th in the 1980s. The total length of fibre-optic cables was 1.25 million kilometres. The personal computer penetration rate is less than 3 per cent with only 30 million computers in the country. But the ICT industry has a PC production capacity of 8.6 million. A high growth of computer penetration rate can reasonably be expected in the next few years.

Internet users double every six months

Despite this impressive growth in the basic telecommunications infrastructure, e-commerce is still in its infancy. However, there are signs of increasing interest in e-commerce. The number of Internet users doubles every six months, faster than in India, Malaysia or Thailand. As of January 2001, the number of users stood at 22.5 million, with 8.92 million PCs connected to the Internet. According to the Ministry of Information Industry, by March 2000 China had 800 online shopping sites, 100 auction sites, 180 remote education sites and 20 remote medical sites. It also had 300 Internet service providers and 1,000 portals. However, a substantial increase in the number of actual business transactions conducted online has yet to materialize. In 2000, B2B transactions amounted to US$ 9.29 billion. B2C transactions have been insignificant - only US$ 47.17 million. E-commerce transactions represent only 0.87 per cent of GDP. Chinese enterprises and consumers are not e-ready for a number of reasons, including high Internet access cost, restrictions on Internet services, lack of a nationwide credit card system, slow and uncertain delivery, network insecurity, lack of awareness of the benefits of electronic commerce and lack of knowledge of e-commerce technology. Major efforts have to be made to remove these impediments in order to allow significant growth of e-commerce.

China's commitments in the WTO will spur e-commerce

The initial commitments which China made to progressively liberalize its telecommunication services upon accession to the WTO may create a competitive environment that will substantially reduce access cost and spur the growth of electronic commerce. In value-added and paging services, foreign service suppliers may hold 30 per cent of equity shares upon China's accession to the WTO. This may increase to 49 per cent one year later and 50 per cent after two years. In mobile voice and data services, foreign service suppliers will be permitted to provide analogue and digital cellular services and personal communication services. The committed liberalization of financial services will also have a major impact on electronic commerce.

A promising future

The major foreign ICT companies, and banking and financial corporations (including insurance companies), are queuing up for the green light to invest in the huge potential market. Telecommunication and financial services are the key sectors in the development of e-commerce. However, a significant growth of e-commerce would require major efforts in liberalizing telecommunication services, enhancing the Internet and PC penetration rate, establishing a comprehensive, uniform legal framework providing adequate protection of security, privacy and intellectual property rights, creating an efficient electronic payment system, creating a competitive environment to improve services and reduce access cost, and accelerating human resource capacity-building including language skills.

Despite the technological and economic obstacles, the number of the Internet users is expected to keep on increasing. As Chinese businesses increasingly incorporate the Internet into their operations, and users become more sophisticated, demand for higher-quality Internet access services will grow. In order to respond to this demand, the role of the private sector in the development of e-commerce in China will have to become more important than in the past. This, coupled with government initiatives and anticipated foreign investment in the ICT sector, will allow China to become a key player in e-commerce, matching its success in international trade.

Notes

1 Although ICT includes the Internet, a distinction is made between them because while ICT has been widely in use in businesses at least for the last two decades, it was with the development of the Internet, which enables people and enterprises to share information and to work together faster and at a lower cost, that the full potential of ICT to enhance productivity was unleashed.

2 See, for example, Jorgenson (2001), Oliner and Sichel (2000), Brynjolfsson and Hitt (2000) or Haynes and Thompson (2000). For a dissenting view, according to which most of the surge in productivity growth outside the ICT goods sector is cyclical rather than structural, see Gordon (2000).

3 Recent advancements in chip design and manufacturing should ensure that Moore's law (which states that the processing power of a silicon chip doubles approximately every 18 months) holds for another decade.

4 Indeed, there are signs that the Nasdaq crash has not made companies in the United States stop equipping themselves for e-commerce. For instance, recent data from Netcraft, a company that surveys the usage of web server software, indicate that the number of Secure Socket Layer servers (mostly used in e-commerce websites to perform encrypted transactions) in the United States increased by 50 per cent between July 2000 and July 2001. See www.netcraft.com/survey.

5 See David and Wright (1999).

6 PricewaterhouseCoopers and 3i Group (2000).

7 Press release available at http://www.jmm.com/xp/jmm/press/2001/pr_060401.xml.

8 The Economist (2001).

9 See Coleman, M. "Software gets its hands dirty" Investors' Business Daily, 5 January 2000.

References

Brynjolfsson, E. and Hitt, L.M. (2000). "Beyond computation: Information technology, organisational transformation and business performance", *Journal of Economic Perspectives*, vol. 14, no. 4, pp. 23–48.

David, P. and Wright, G. (1999). "Early twentieth century productivity growth dynamics: An inquiry into the economic history of 'Our Ignorance'", University of Oxford Discussion Papers in Economic and Social History, No. 33, October, p. 23.

Gordon, R.J. (2000). "Does the new economy measure up to the great inventions of the past?", *Journal of Economic Perspectives*, vol. 14, no. 4, pp. 49–74.

Haynes, M. and Thompson, S. (2000). "The productivity impact of IT deployment: An empirical evaluation of ATM introduction, *Oxford Bulletin of Economics and Statistics*, vol. 62, no. 5, December, pp. 607–619.

Jorgenson, D.W. (2001). "Information technology and the US economy", *American Economic Review,* vol. 91, March, pp. 1–31.

Oliner, S. and Sichel, D. (2000). "The resurgence of growth in the late 1990s: Is information technology the story?", *Journal of Economic Perspectives,* vol. 14, no. 4, pp. 3–22 .

PricewaterhouseCoopers and 3i Group (2000). Global Private Equity 2000. A Survey of the Global Private Equity and Venture Capital Markets. Report available at http://wwwpwcmoneytree.com and http://www.3i.com.

The Economist (2001). E-strategy brief: General Electric, 17 May.

Part One

Facts and Figures about Electronic Commerce

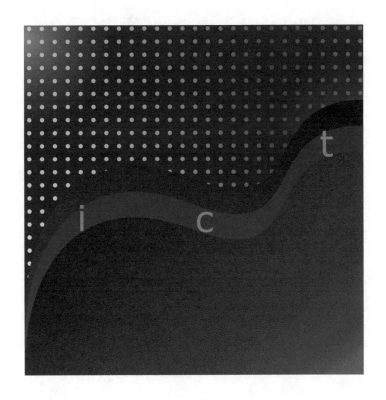

Chapter 1
MEASURING ELECTRONIC COMMERCE

A. Estimating or measuring electronic commerce?

There is little doubt that electronic commerce has penetrated many people's — and particularly businesses' — lives in one way or another during the past few years. But how many businesses really use the Internet? How do they use it? And how are they planning to use it? When it comes to a precise evaluation of the importance of electronic commerce, including its dimensions, growth rate and role in economic growth and development, uncertainty prevails. This is largely because data on e-commerce are not readily available or differ widely, depending on the definition and methodology used by the entity collecting them.

So far, figures are mainly provided by a large number of private sector companies, dedicated to continuously monitoring e-commerce around the world. They regularly publish reports on the latest developments in e-commerce, including short- to medium-term growth estimates. However, some of them have a great interest in providing data that serve their main clientele — e-businesses or financial sector analysts. Furthermore, most of the collecting agencies use different definitions and indicators for electronic commerce and have different methodologies for estimating it.[1] Hence, their data vary widely and are not always representative of a whole community or country. Table 1 shows that even estimates of Internet users vary up to 100 per cent between the different sources. Forecasts could even differ by a factor of ten.

While some of these estimates may be useful for analysing specific e-commerce markets, more precise and comparable data on electronic commerce and its role in the overall economy are crucial for a number of reasons. Without reliable data, policy makers and business people are unable to take decisions that reflect the changes brought about by e-commerce. For example, electronic commerce is said to affect the productivity, profits, procurement and distribution systems of businesses. The use of electronic websites presumably expands the potential market for, and the sales income generated by, businesses' goods and services by increasing the range of potential new customers and business hours. Electronic commerce is also expected to significantly reduce transaction costs associated with the purchase and sale of goods and services, and operating costs of firms by *inter alia* reducing the costs involved in holding stock through the use of better stock control/inventory systems. Furthermore, there could be indirect effects: for example, a business may improve the timeliness and quality of a service and so attract new customers or retain existing ones for a longer period of time. More accurate data on e-commerce would allow policy makers and researchers to analyse the impact of

Table 1
Estimates of e-commerce, 2000

Source	Global B2B e-commerce (*$ billions*)	US consumers on-line shopping revenue (*$ billions*)	Internet users in Asia (*millions*)	Internet users in Brazil (*millions*)
eMarketer	226	37.0	48.7	3.9
Forrester Research	604	38.8	..	..
IDC Research	213	..	40.0	4.2
Gartner Group	403	29.3	..	..
Morgan Stanley	200	..	82.0	5.6
Jupiter Research	..	23.1	65.1	8.4

Source: eMarketer, 2001, www.eMarketer.com

e-commerce on labour markets and income distribution, and market structures and functioning, including changes in the distribution of goods and services and changes in international and domestic competition. Both policy makers and business people would be able to take well-informed decisions about the best public policy measures and private investments in e-commerce-related sectors.

Current statistics on electronic commerce, however, do not capture these changes. Therefore, the national statistical offices in a number of countries (including some developing countries) have recently turned their attention to measuring electronic commerce. Official statistical offices have the advantage of guaranteeing the confidentiality of data collected, having a more neutral position when it comes to collecting and interpreting that data and being able to use their existing methodologies and infrastructure for data collection, processing and analysis.

Experience so far has been limited. One of the major difficulties facing government policy makers and others who have addressed the issue of measurement has been the lack of comprehensive indicators about electronic commerce. This has been exacerbated by the lack of clear guidelines and consensus on what is meant by electronic commerce. Thus, there has been a considerable effort at the international level, including by the Organisation for Economic Co-operation and Development (OECD), the Asia-Pacific Economic Co-operation (APEC) and the European Union (EU), and their respective member States, to work towards an international agreement on the definitions to be adopted. There seems to be a growing convergence towards internationally accepted guidelines and methodologies for measuring electronic commerce. Hence, the time has come for Governments to consider starting their own statistical compilation programmes.

Although the development of electronic commerce and electronic commerce indicators has been up to now concentrated in the more developed economies, some developing countries have started to become actively involved. They have realized the potential social and economic benefits that could result from e-commerce, as well as the importance of having readily available data which would highlight the role of e-commerce in their economies. Other countries have shown great interest in the subject but need further information and guidelines on how to embark on such a task. This chapter will therefore address the need for data and statistical indicators on electronic commerce and present concrete examples, including a model survey, of how to go about measuring electronic commerce, which could be of particular interest to the developing countries.

The remainder of this chapter is organized as follows. Since the first step towards measuring e-commerce is to agree on a common terminology, the second section briefly introduces some of the concepts and definitions that have been used in the work done so far on measuring e-commerce. The third section presents a number of initiatives that have been taken at the national and international levels for defining e-commerce indicators. The fourth section presents various methodologies that have been chosen by statistical offices in their e-commerce surveys, and discusses the advantages and disadvantages from the perspective of a developing country. On that basis, a model business survey is presented in the fifth section, which could be used by developing countries for surveying e-commerce. The sixth section discusses some of the key requirements for starting a statistical compilation programme on e-commerce. The last section provides concrete examples of how countries that have completed e-commerce surveys have made use of the results and proposes a number of activities which national statistical agencies could take up to further develop their work on measuring electronic commerce.

B. What do we want to measure? Towards a working definition of e-commerce

One reason for the considerable discrepancies among e-commerce estimates is the number of different terms used interchangeably and with no common understanding of their scope or relationship. For example, do we want to measure the number of Internet users, online purchasing, advertising, ordering and procurement, or total e-commerce activities? Are we interested in e-commerce-related infrastructure, electronic business processes or transactions? In order to obtain internationally comparable statistics, we need to establish a clear and consistent terminology. Hence, before embarking on the task of measuring e-commerce, it is useful to look at a few concepts and definitions that have been suggested by various entities involved in defining and measuring electronic commerce.

1. Identifying user needs

Each country or economy will first want to reflect on what kind of e-commerce data it wants to measure, depending on the stage of development it has reached in the area of e-commerce. Some countries, particularly developing countries, may be at an early stage, while others may already be very active users of e-commerce and the Internet.

A good model for identifying these needs of e-commerce data users has been proposed by Canada and is generally considered a good starting point for statistical work on e-commerce (chart 1).

The model recognizes that a distinction needs to be drawn between various situations, such as where a country might wish to know about:

- the *readiness* of its people, businesses, infrastructure and its economy generally to undertake electronic commerce activities — this is likely to be of interest to countries in the early stages of electronic commerce maturity or activity;
- the *intensity* with which information and communication technologies are utilized within a country and the extent to which electronic commerce activities are undertaken — this is likely to be of interest to countries where electronic commerce is becoming much more prevalent; and
- the *impact* of electronic commerce on national economies and business activities being carried out in the country — this is likely to be of interest to countries where electronic commerce activities are very well developed.

As depicted in the diagrammatic representation in chart 1, there is considerable overlapping of the various stages of maturity of e-commerce, and hence a unique classification of the issues and indicators into the three stages is not possible. Some issues, and the corresponding indicators, could be relevant to more than one of the stages of development. The model itself is a simplification of the situation that exists in a country. In reality, of course, different parts of a country may be at different stages of maturity. For example, the business community may have passed from the "readiness" stage of maturity to the "intensity" stage, while the Government or household sectors may have a much lower rate of Internet access and thus be at an early stage within the overall process. Even within the business sector, it is possible to have regional or industrial differences in the stage of maturity. Thus the model adopted should merely be regarded to be illustrative — suitable for helping in the derivation of relevant indicators.

2. The ICT sector, e-commerce and the use of ICT goods and services

There has been confusion among many people about the different uses of the terms "information and communications technology (ICT) sector", "electronic commerce", and about the use of ICT goods and services more generally. It is therefore useful to distinguish these terms first.

Chart 1
Maturity of e-commerce markets and need for indicators: the S-curve

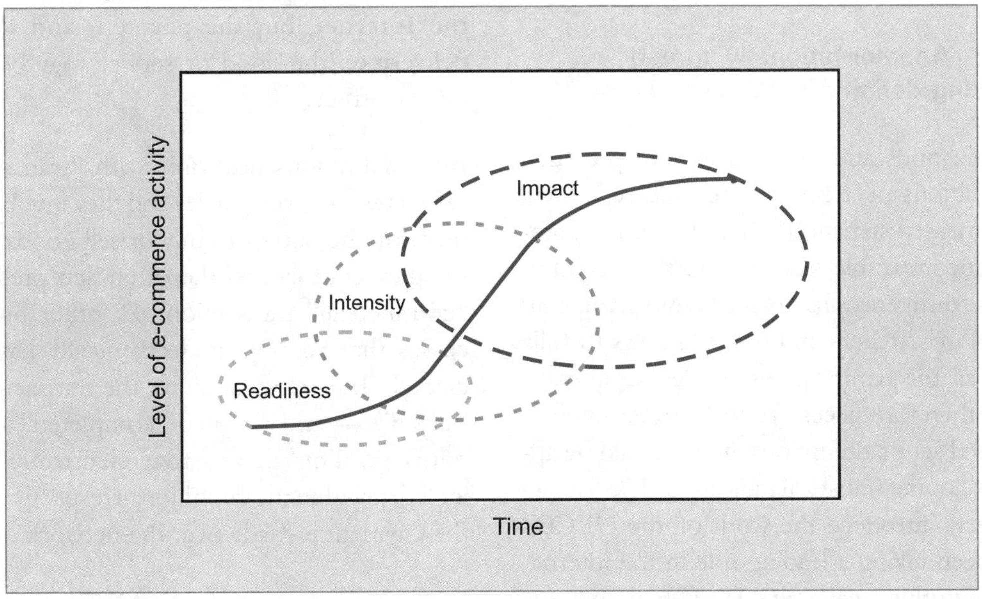

Source: Industry Canada, presented at the OECD Workshop on Defining and Measuring E-commerce (April 1999).

The ICT sector has been one area that has attracted considerable attention in recent years, particularly among the national statistical agencies. Many countries have now started compiling statistics about the ICT sector as part of their standard industrial statistics survey programmes.

In brief, the ICT sector provides a supply perspective with respect to producers of ICT goods and services. It provides standard details about the size and structure of the industry, employment, number of businesses, value added, etc. As the ICT sector contains businesses that provide both goods and services, it is not separately identified in most industrial classifications that draw boundaries between the goods and services sectors. One useful standard definition of the ICT sector has been developed by the OECD (OECD, 2000d), which brings together a number of industries identified within the International Standard Industrial Classification. Accordingly, the sector comprises the manufacturers of information technology and telecommunications goods, the providers of information technology and telecommunications services, and the wholesalers of these goods and services.

On the other hand, the use of ICT goods and services and electronic commerce is a demand perspective for ICT goods and services, i.e. how are ICT technologies used throughout the economy and, in the case of electronic commerce, what impact do they have on the sale or purchase of goods or services. In this respect, electronic commerce can be seen merely as a subset of all aspects of the use of ICT goods and services, across all sectors of the economy.

3. An internationally agreed working definition of e-commerce

Many organizations and individuals have provided various definitions of electronic commerce, which, when implemented statistically, have led to the compilation of incompatible statistics on the phenomenon.[2] These differences have significantly hampered the ability of researchers and policy makers to fully understand all the ramifications of electronic commerce. It is therefore necessary to form an internationally agreed set of definitions, which could be applied for developing statistical indicators. The following will briefly introduce the work of the OECD,[3] which has been taking a leading role in the international debate in this area (OECD, 2000b, d, e).

The efforts by the OECD to work out a definition of e-commerce have resulted in the acceptance of a need for three dimensions to be spelt out as part of the definition process. These dimensions relate to the:

(i) *Networks* over which the relevant activities are carried out;

(ii) *Processes* that ought to be included within the general domain of electronic commerce; and

(iii) *Actors* involved in the transactions.

Networks

With respect to the networks over which e-commerce activities are carried out, OECD member countries have agreed on the following two definitions to be used:[4]

Broad definition

An *electronic transaction* is the sale or purchase of goods or services, whether between businesses, households, individuals, Governments, and other public or private organizations, conducted over computer-mediated networks. The goods and services are ordered over those networks, but the payment and the ultimate delivery of the good or service may be conducted on- or offline.

Narrow definition

An *Internet transaction* is the sale or purchase of goods or services, whether between businesses, households, individuals, Governments, and other public or private organizations, conducted over the Internet. The goods and services are ordered over the Internet, but the payment and the ultimate delivery of the good or service may be conducted on- or offline.

Both definitions deal only with "transactions" between two or more parties and they involve the agreement of the parties to buy or sell goods or services, i.e. they conform to the often accepted view of a "commercial" transaction. All other business processes that take place electronically have been excluded. In both definitions, the transaction is "conducted" — and not just "completed" — over the network. This means that electronic orders are included within the definition, irrespective of whether the payment is made over the network or not.[5]

The broader definition includes proprietary networks used, for example, for electronic data interchange (EDI). This more inclusive definition is important for capturing electronic transactions in those countries where electronic commerce has been a regular feature of business activities for many years, for example in the United States, where there are well-established proprietary networks. It is less relevant to smaller and less developed economies where the major network involved is the Internet. For these cases, the narrower (Internet) definition, which is deliberately a subset of the broad definition, is more relevant. The majority of OECD member countries have expressed a preference for measuring Internet commerce. As developing countries are unlikely to have significant business activity occurring over proprietary networks, it could reasonably be expected that those countries would also favour the narrow definition.

Business processes

The second aspect of the definition relates to the activities or business processes being included, or excluded, from the electronic commerce domain. While many countries want to restrict the definition to the purchasing and selling aspect incorporated in the above definitions, many others want to include other types of business processes, such as marketing and advertising. Undoubtedly, the latter ones are going to be very important in the future, as businesses come up with more and more integrated electronic processing systems for a greater range of business functions and the productivity benefits of electronic commerce thus become much clearer. This has led to the conclusion that there ought to be one specific definition relating to purchasing and selling activities as shown above in the broad and narrow definitions, as well as another definition which lists a greater number of business processes.[6] Developing countries will also favour a definition that includes business activities that go beyond purchasing and selling, given the restrictions that some of those countries face in conducting online payments.

E-commerce actors

The third aspect of the definition relates to the actors involved in the electronic commerce process. Electronic commerce is often described as being one of three varieties — business-to-business (B2B), business-to-consumer (B2C) or business-to-government (B2G). Each of these has a set of statistical indicators about e-commerce that might be useful and hence be included. Much of the interest and the literature has focused on B2B and B2C electronic commerce and most of the statistical indicators have also been in respect of these two forms. It is generally agreed that about 80 per cent of the total value of electronic commerce in the world today is accounted for by B2B e-commerce. B2B electronic commerce also provides the greatest potential benefits in terms of productivity gains. On the other hand, B2C e-commerce has the potential to substantially affect the way in which people live and interact with each other and is therefore a key aspect for statistical measurement. Only a small number of countries have so far undertaken much work with respect to the measurement of B2G e-commerce.

C. What are the priority indicators for e-commerce?

Now that a set of definitions for measuring e-commerce has been provided, the next step is to develop a list of e-commerce indicators. Thus, it is worthwhile to look at what Governments have done so far in their respective programmes. How do their indicators differ from each other and can they be used by other countries? This section briefly presents three different initiatives on defining indicators, prompted by work programmes at the regional or multilateral levels. First, the OECD work mentioned earlier will be discussed. Secondly, the Asia-Pacific Economic Cooperation (APEC) has established an e-commerce readiness initiative which has been tested in a number of countries. And thirdly, Eurostat has just finalized the development of an electronic commerce pilot survey aimed at collecting statistics on electronic commerce and the use of ICTs in Europe.

1. OECD work on e-commerce indicators

The OECD (2000e) has established a set of priority electronic commerce indicators for both the business and the household sectors. They are shown in boxes 1 and 2.

The (initial) list includes both readiness and intensity indicators. It was decided to omit indicators designed to measure the impact of electronic commerce, as there were none available for most countries. There is statistical work going on in some countries to try

Box 1
A priority set of indicators for the business sector

1. Number and proportion of businesses with computers.
2. Employment (level and share) of businesses with computers.
3. Number and proportion of businesses with access to the Internet.
4. Employment (level and share) of businesses with the Internet.
5. Number and proportion of businesses undertaking specific processes on the Internet.
6. Number and proportion of businesses with websites.
7. Number and proportion of businesses which recognize specific barriers to e-commerce.
8. Number and proportion of businesses which plan to use the Internet.
9. Number and proportion of businesses which receive orders over the Internet.
10. Number and proportion of businesses which receive orders over computer-mediated networks.
11. Value of orders of goods and services received over the Internet.
12. Value of orders of goods and services received over computer-mediated networks.
13. Proportion of orders of goods and services received over the Internet.
14. Proportion of orders of goods and services received over computer-mediated networks.

Box 2
A priority set of indicators for the household sector

1. Number and proportion of households with computers.
2. Number and proportion of households with access to the Internet.
3. Number and proportion of householders undertaking specific activities.
4. Number and proportion of households which recognize specific barriers.
5. Number and proportion of individuals placing orders (for own use) over the Internet (irrespective of location where purchase was made).
6. Value of orders (for own use) placed by individuals over the Internet.

to develop these, but at this stage no agreed methodologies or indicators are available. In the short term, at least, impact indicators are most likely to be developed using case study methodologies. It was also decided to exclude indicators of government electronic commerce as there has been very little collection activity in member countries. Only in the Nordic group of countries, Canada and Australia are specific statistical collections conducted which provide such indicators.

2. The APEC E-Commerce Readiness Assessment Guide

APEC was one of the first regional forums to put e-commerce high on the agenda, including the task of measuring e-commerce. In their Blueprint for Action for electronic commerce, confirmed by the APEC Ministerial Meeting in 1998, APEC ministers recognized:

> "the enormous potential of electronic commerce to expand business opportunities, reduce costs, increase efficiency, improve the quality of life and facilitate the greater participation of small business in commerce." (APEC, 2000)

The ministers also recognized that the different stages of development of their member countries would lead to different challenges for each country in the development of e-commerce. Thus it was important for each Government to tailor its policies to the conditions in its country. This has led to the development of an APEC E-Commerce Readiness Assessment Guide designed to help Governments develop their own focused plans for development by measuring their level of e-commerce "readiness".[7] The guide is also aimed at helping APEC economies identify and overcome impediments to the deployment of electronic commerce.

The guide is composed of six broad categories of indicators of readiness (see box 3). Each of the categories is based on a detailed set of questions about those categories.

Box 3
The six categories of the APEC E-Commerce Readiness Assessment Guide

1. Basic infrastructure and technology
2. Access to necessary services
3. Current level and type of use of the Internet
4. Promotion and facilitation activities
5. Skills and human resources
6. Positioning for the digital economy.

Box 4
Data items included in Eurostat pilot survey

- Use of computers
- Use and planned use of the Internet
- Presence on a website
- Type of Internet connection
- Barriers to using the Internet
- Use of e-commerce for purchases
- Barriers to using e-commerce for purchases
- Plans to use e-commerce for purchases in 2001
- Length of time using e-commerce for purchases
- Processes undertaken with e-commerce purchases
- Benefits in using e-commerce purchases
- Use of specialized B2B Internet market places for purchases
- Value of purchases (percentage of purchases) made using Internet and all networks
- Use of e-commerce for sales
- Barriers to using e-commerce for sales
- Plans to use e-commerce for sales in 2001
- Length of time using e-commerce for sales
- Processes undertaken with e-commerce for sales
- Benefits in using e-commerce for sales
- Use of specialized B2B Internet market places for sales
- Value of sales (percentage of sales) made using Internet and all networks
- Proportion of e-commerce sales to households

The project is still in its early stages. Members that have so far completed the Guide include Taiwan Province of China, Hong Kong (China), Japan, Malaysia, Mexico, Peru, Thailand and the United States.

3. Eurostat pilot survey on e-commerce

In June 2000, Eurostat presented to its member States a proposal to establish a pilot survey of e-commerce by the business sector. The proposal called for the compilation of a range of ICT use data in the second quarter of 2001, with final results to be compiled and published at the end of 2001. Most of the member States have agreed to participate in the survey.

In general, the pilot survey is designed to produce statistics by industry and by size of business. Businesses with fewer than 10 employees do not have to be included in the survey.

Eurostat is trying its best to keep the pilot survey within the definitional framework laid down by OECD and to ensure that it remains consistent with the draft model survey being prepared by the Nordic group (see below). Most of the data items being collected in the pilot survey refer to intensity indicators, and are shown in box 4 (Eurostat, 2000).

D. How do we measure e-commerce?

So far, we have looked at the user framework, the e-commerce definitions and the priority indicators that have been identified for collecting e-commerce data. All of these provide the basis for an internationally comparable statistical measurement. This section moves to the empirical part of measuring e-commerce, i.e. the actual data collection. The methodologies most commonly adopted by the national statistical agencies are outlined below, together with an assessment of their suitability for the measurement of these indicators. These will be useful for developing countries that are about to embark on the task of compiling statistical indicators on e-commerce.

1. Businesses, households or Governments?

As noted earlier, there is interest in having indicators on the business sector, the household sector and the government sector. The obvious way of obtaining information about the business sector is to survey that sector; such surveys generally provide information on B2B e-commerce transactions and the actors involved in those transactions. B2C e-commerce can, however, be measured from both business sector and household sector surveys as both sectors are participants in the transactions. Similarly, government sector transactions can be measured by government surveys and business or household surveys, depending on which other sector is involved in the transaction. This chapter will limit itself to business surveys, given the fact that this is the sector where traditional surveys are well established and most e-commerce activity takes place. The following considers, first of all, the development of new surveys on e-commerce, and then the addition of e-commerce questions to existing surveys. Next it presents some alternative ways of measuring e-commerce for countries where business surveys are difficult to implement.[8]

2. New surveys on e-commerce

Many countries have adopted the approach of developing new surveys to compile indicators of electronic commerce. These have generally been broad-based, aimed at measuring the use of ICT by businesses across a broad range of industries. The surveys are usually undertaken at the level of enterprises or firms, because a number of the issues relevant to the measurement of ICT and electronic commerce are more appropriately answered by such units, rather than by establishments or statistical units at some other level. This could create difficulties as far as comparability with other statistics is concerned, given that much of the other economic information collected by national statistical agencies relates to establishments.

Since ICTs are used in a wide range of industries, the surveys are generally undertaken across as wide a range of industries as the business register available in that country can sustain. In most countries the agriculture sector has been excluded and in other countries industries such as construction, transport, education and health are also excluded because of difficulties with coverage within them, or because the industries are largely government-operated. Often there is also a cut-off based on the size of the firm because of problems either with the availability of a suitable business register covering all businesses or with government restrictions associated with the collection of data from very small businesses.

Good examples of these types of survey are found in Australia, Canada, the Netherlands, Portugal, Singapore and the Nordic group of countries.[9] The Nordic group survey provides an interesting contrast to the other surveys as part of it has been consciously designed as a "model survey".

The questions in the Nordic model survey are very similar to those contained in the other country surveys mentioned above. All are essentially surveys on the use of ICTs and incorporate questions based on the narrow definition of electronic commerce described earlier. The questionnaires are structured to ascertain the current and planned use of computers, websites and the Internet within a firm, assess the extent to which purchases and sales are conducted over the Internet, and then consider the barriers to the use of ICT and electronic commerce.

The Nordic survey has been used as the basis for the development of a model survey suitable for application more widely than just in the Nordic countries. The proposed survey has been prepared by Statistics Denmark in conjunction with the statistical agencies in many other countries and was endorsed by the OECD Working Party on Indicators for the Information Society in April 2001. So far, the model survey represents the best practice in this field and hence is described below in a separate section (see annex for the complete questionnaire). This may help countries, especially in the developing world, which are about to launch such a survey, to prepare their own e-commerce surveys.

3. The addition of questions to existing surveys

The practice of adding electronic commerce questions to existing surveys has been adopted in many countries and is an extremely cost-effective way of obtaining extra information. Hence, it may be a useful alternative for countries whose statistical offices have limited resources and statistical infrastructure. A few examples of questions being added to existing questionnaires, as well as alternatives used by countries to survey e-commerce, are given below. The data items collected in each of the examples are summarized in table 2.

Annual surveys

The most common examples of adding questions to existing collection vehicles are in respect of regular economic surveys of businesses in specific industries. An example of the use of this survey approach is in the 2000 Manufacturing, Wholesale, Retail and Service Industries surveys conducted by the United States Bureau of the Census (USBOC) (Mesenbourg, 2000). Here, a few additional questions were added to the Wholesale, Retail and Service Industries surveys and a supplementary computer use survey was added to the Manufacturing survey. The supple-

Table 2
E-commerce survey indicators

Type of survey	Data items collected
USBOC Manufacturing Survey	Type of networks used Proportion of employees with access to the Internet Use of ERP software Placing orders on-line Accepting orders on-line Type of information provided on-line Use of specific business processes
ABS Agricultural Survey	Use of computers on the farm Access to the Internet Type of use of the Internet Barriers to the use of Internet
ISTAT SME Survey	Type of use of the Internet Purchases and sales over the Internet
ABS ISP Survey	Numbers and type of Internet subscribers Volume of data sent to subscribers Time spent on-line by subscribers Number of websites hosted (total and with secure transaction capabilities) Number of subscribers, by amount billed Technical support and related services provided Point of presence
KNSO Cyber Shopping Mall Survey	Sales by type Sales by product category Operating costs by type Price competition Type of purchaser Support systems for e-commerce Plans to facilitate e-commerce
KNSO Corporations Survey	Ratio of e-commerce sales to total sales E-commerce sales by product Ratio of e-commerce purchases to total purchases E-commerce purchases by product Stumbling blocks to e-commerce Future plans to promote e-commerce

Sources: Ambler, 2000; Atrostic, Gates and Jarmin, 2000; Haltiwanger and Jarmin, 1999; Koo, 2000; OECD, 2000a.

mentary questions added to the USBOC annual Manufacturing survey sought details on the questions shown in table 2.

Another example of the approach is in the annual agricultural survey conducted by the Australian Bureau of Statistics (ABS), where questions on computer and Internet use by farming establishments have been asked in recent years. The Italian National Statistical Institute (ISTAT) has inserted a module on ICT use in its annual survey of small and medium-sized enterprises (i.e. enterprises with fewer than 100 employees).

The benefits and drawbacks of adding questions to existing surveys *vis-à-vis* conducting new surveys are set out in boxes 5 and 6.

Monthly surveys

The above surveys are examples of annual collections that generally provide information only about a year after the reference period for the survey. For some purposes, however, there is a need to have more timely information. In the United States, the Bureau of the Census has added to its monthly Retail Sales Survey an additional question about online sales. The monthly survey generally produces results within a few weeks of the end of the period and thus has the advantage of producing statistics that are available on a more timely basis. The survey provides an approximation to B2C electronic commerce and enables the results to be easily compared with the total retail sales in the United States. As this is the only example of this particular approach, it is worth considering the question in more detail. The question asked refers to:

> "the sales of goods and services over the Internet, an extranet, Electronic Data Interchange (EDI) or other online system where payment may or may not be made online" (Ambler, 2000)

Clearly such an approach is very cost-effective and provides a very timely indicator of B2C electronic commerce. The instructions and definitions are consistent with those that are being used for their measure of total retail sales, and hence the resulting statistics are comparable. It should be remembered, however, that only a small share of total retail sales is conducted online (approximately 0.8 per cent in the United States). The sampling errors associated with the measurement of such a small proportion are likely to be greater than desired.

The Korea National Statistical Office (KNSO) has also undertaken an extensive programme of adding questions to existing surveys with a view to increasing the amount of indicators of both B2B and B2C electronic commerce. It has added questions to its monthly and annual establishment surveys in the mining, manufacturing, wholesale, retail and services industry surveys. Each survey identifies whether an establishment has made any e-commerce sales and, if so, the value of such transactions.

Box 5
Benefits of adding questions to existing forms

- Costs are reduced since the only additional cost is the marginal cost of collecting and compiling the additional data items.
- The timeliness of implementation is generally enhanced as collection and computer processing systems are generally already in place.
- It is often possible to obtain additional information from the original survey to help in the analysis of results.

Box 6
Drawbacks of adding questions to existing forms

- The amount of additional information that can be added to a survey is often limited. Too many additional questions may lead to form overload.
- This increases the respondent burden on specific businesses. Respondent burden is an extremely important issue in most countries, particularly for small businesses.
- The design of the original survey vehicle may be inappropriate for the measurement of electronic commerce.
- The industrial scope of the original survey may not include all the industries appropriate for the measurement of electronic commerce.

4. Surveys of Internet service providers (ISP)

An alternative way of providing some measures of electronic commerce readiness is to survey Internet Service Providers (ISPs). While this approach will not provide the priority indicators for international comparability referred to earlier, it will provide some indicators that are useful within a national context. The ABS started such a survey in 2000 and released its first results in March 2001.

Some of the drawbacks of this approach are that it does not provide statistics on the value of sales undertaken within a period, or any of the other priority indicators listed above. However, it does provide an alternative survey type for those countries unable to conduct surveys that might meet those priority requirements. In particular, it could be a useful approach for countries without adequate national statistical business registers (see below). The survey itself is relatively cheap to conduct, as there are few ISPs operating in most countries. It also provides regional statistics, an aspect of electronic commerce and the use of ICT that has a high priority in many countries. In short, for some developing countries it might be a useful starting point for collecting e-commerce indicators.

5. Cyber shopping mall survey

The KNSO has developed a new collection of statistics from cyber shopping malls in order to measure B2C electronic commerce. As from April 2000, the Cyber Shopping Mall survey has been collecting the data items shown in table 2 as well as classificatory data on the shopping mall, including details of whether it is solely an online mall or whether it provides both online and offline services.

The advantage of this kind of survey is that it is relatively easy to implement and that it captures all businesses that have opened Internet-based cyber shopping malls for either B2B or B2C e-commerce. On the other hand, it may be difficult to identify the malls, and the survey can capture only the e-commerce conducted through the malls, thus omitting any other e-commerce.

6. Korea Corporations survey

The KNSO has also initiated a new collection of statistics aimed at measuring trends in B2B e-commerce — the quarterly Corporations survey. This is primarily a survey of private and publicly owned large businesses, based on available lists such as the Korea Stock Exchange. In addition to the general information collected regarding the firm, the survey collects the e-commerce-specific data items shown in table 2.

KNSO has acknowledged that there is considerable work to be done to improve the coverage of e-commerce measured through both the Cyber Shopping Mall survey and the Corporations survey. Nevertheless, it feels that they offer substantial promise in achieving better measures of electronic commerce transactions.

E. A model survey for measuring e-commerce

Governments and statistical offices wishing to start collecting indicators on electronic commerce may consider using a model survey rather than starting to develop new questionnaires. Model surveys that have been previously tested and improved are very useful since they help countries to learn from mistakes made by other countries. The Nordic business survey mentioned above is a good example that could be adopted by other countries, including those from the developing world. The survey has been tested across the countries of the Nordic region. On the basis of their experiences, and with inputs from statistical offices in other countries, Statistics Denmark prepared the model survey, which was endorsed by the OECD in April 2001. It can be implemented across a wider range of countries.[10] The use of this model survey questionnaire will facilitate the comparison of the results internationally and may be a very useful starting point for developing countries as they begin their own statistical programmes to measure electronic commerce.

The following outlines the main features of the survey (Boegh Nielsen et al., 2000). A complete set of the questions being proposed to the OECD is provided in the annex.

The model questionnaire is based on the following principles:

- It is designed to be flexible and modular, facilitating the development of country-specific features;
- It is designed to measure Internet activity at present, but it can be updated quickly as required by changes in technology;

- It is a general survey tool for measuring economic activity; and
- It largely takes a qualitative approach to measuring ICT use and the Internet.

The questionnaire has five main components, or modules: (i) general information about ICT systems; (ii) use of the Internet; (iii) e-commerce via the Internet; (iv) e-commerce via EDI or other computer-mediated networks (other than the Internet); and (v) barriers to the use of the Internet and ICT in general.[11] Table 3 outlines the main topics included under each module. They mainly cover readiness and intensity indicators.

Developing countries interested in using this model survey for developing their own e-commerce surveys should keep in mind that it is based on the experiences of some of the most advanced countries in relation to ICT and e-commerce use. Developing countries may therefore want to use the model as a basis and add or modify questions, which would correspond to the specific situation in their economies. For example, useful additions of indicators in a technologically less advanced country might be:[12]

- Under Module A (use of the Internet): questions on the management of the website (hosted by third parties or not);
- Under Module C (e-commerce via the Internet): questions on online sales through portals; and
- Under Module E (barriers): questions on the use of intermediaries specializing in e-commerce.

F. How do we prepare for e-commerce surveys?

Before starting a programme on collecting statistical indicators for electronic commerce, it is worth considering a few conditions that should be put in place by countries or agencies planning to carry out surveys on e-commerce. Irrespective of whether the strategy adopted relates to conducting new surveys, or merely adding questions to the existing surveys, there are a number of factors to be considered for compiling reliable statistics. This section looks at these conditions and discusses alternatives in case a country cannot meet them, taking into account the situation in developing countries.

Table 3
Modules included in Nordic Survey

Module	Topics included
A. General information about ICT systems	1. Use of PCs, workstations and terminals 2. Use or planned use of specific ICT activities 3. Percentage of employees who have access to PCs, etc. and the Internet (WWW)
B. Use of the Internet	1. Use or planned use of the Internet 2. Type of external connection to the Internet 3. Purpose of use of the Internet 4. Use or planned use of own website
C. E-commerce via Internet	1. Purchases via the Internet 2. Purchases via specialized market places 3. Expected benefits from Internet purchases 4. Sales via the Internet 5. Internet sales by customer group and destination of sales 6. Sales via specialized market places 7. Motivations for Internet sales
D. E-commerce via EDI or other computer-mediated networks (non-Internet)	1. Use or planned use of EDI or other computer-mediated networks 2. Type of use 3. Purchases via EDI or other computer-mediated networks 4. Sales via EDI or other computer-mediated networks
E. Barriers to the use of the Internet and ICT in general	1. Barriers to ICT in general 2. Barriers to the use of the Internet 3. Barriers to Internet sales

1. Check your business register

The first consideration relates to the business register available in a country. Electronic commerce can be undertaken by, and can affect, all types of businesses, small or large, irrespective of the industry to which they belong. Hence, in order to measure the type of business indicators referred to earlier, the first requirement is to have a reliable business register. It should cover all types of businesses, and for the sake of efficiency, it has to be kept up to date with the introduction of new businesses and the deletion of businesses that cease to operate, while allowing for changes in the structure of other businesses.

For efficiency in sampling, it is also important for a business register to contain as many classification variables as possible for the surveys to be undertaken. Generally this means that it is imperative to have an indicator for the size of a business and an indicator for its main activity.

Many developed countries have a reasonably good quality business register, with mechanisms in place for covering all sectors of the economy and all sizes of business (except perhaps for very small businesses). In the case of developing countries, the chances of having good-quality business registers are much smaller, a fact which affects their ability to mount statistical collections quickly and efficiently. For example, business registers that are not updated regularly miss a significant number of smaller firms, where the annual turnover is much higher compared with larger firms. In 1999, Singapore conducted a survey of electronic commerce of only the top 1,000 businesses in Singapore, and the top 1,000 firms providing information technology services (Wong and Lam, 1999). Such an approximation is likely to have to be made if no complete business register is available. If no register is available at all, countries will have to resort to other sources, such as Chambers of Commerce or Manufacturers, or telephone book listings.

2. Identify your user needs

Another prerequisite for conducting an electronic commerce survey is to develop a questionnaire based on a detailed model of the user needs from such a survey, i.e. the kind of data desired (see section B). This questionnaire-designing stage is extremely important as mistakes made in the design of a questionnaire will significantly affect the quality of the data collected. Hence, after an initial design has been made, it is important to undertake sufficient field tests to ensure that the survey works effectively. The development of model surveys is a crucial step in overcoming problems in this respect as it helps to transfer lessons learned in one country to another. By the same token, it is important to note that a question that might work very effectively in one language or country may not work quite so well in another because of language or cultural differences. In addition, the terminology used in the field of electronic commerce needs to be checked. There are significant differences in the understanding of the term, not only between countries, but also between different groups of people within the same country.[13] Thus the importance of field-testing the questionnaire must be recognized at the outset.

As noted earlier, it is likely that developing countries will have different requirements, or user needs, for indicators of electronic commerce. As shown by the S-curve discussed earlier (chart 1), developing countries, in the short term, are likely to be more interested in compiling indicators of e-commerce readiness, while developed countries appear to be more interested in indicators which measure the intensity of use. Therefore, the indicators contained in the APEC E-Commerce Readiness Assessment Guide might be more suitable for some developing countries at present than some of the indicators relating to intensity and impact of e-commerce.

3. Design your collection strategy

An important step in the development of an overall statistical process is to work out a collection strategy. National statistical agencies often have compulsory powers of collection — at least for some types of collection; policy departments in the same countries mostly do not have the same powers. General experience from around the world has been that voluntary surveys do not work very effectively, since in many cases the response rates were only 20–30 per cent. Voluntary surveys conducted by national statistical agencies often perform a little better than that, but still struggle to reach a 50 per cent response rate.[14]

It is difficult to quantify the impact of low response rates on the quality of the statistics compiled from the survey. If the non-response is purely a random happening, the low response rates will merely imply a greater degree of sampling error than desired. However, it is more likely that non-respondents will be different from respondents (as they did not answer in the first place), which means that the omission of such businesses from the survey results will bias the answers, often by an extent and in a direction that cannot be easily estimated. Thus it is important to recognize the importance of achieving a good response rate.

Developing countries are less likely to have appropriate collection systems in place to facilitate the compilation of electronic commerce indicators and their national statistical agencies are less likely to have compulsory powers of collection. For them, one option to enhance a good response rate would be to have an appropriate cover letter attached to the survey form, signed by someone who may be important to the receiver of the form, stating why it is important to participate.

4. Prepare an attractive survey form

A key consideration in achieving a good response rate is the quality of the questionnaire design and the subject matter of the survey. If the subject matter appears to be important to the reader, and the reader can answer the question without reference to a great deal of bookwork, the survey questionnaire has a much greater chance of being completed. If, on the other hand, the survey form appears to be irrelevant to the business in question, or if it was sent to a person in the organization who is unable to answer the questions, it is unlikely that it will be completed. The survey taker needs to understand these issues, otherwise the questionnaires are unlikely to be completed. Even in the case of compulsory surveys (where response rates of 90 per cent or higher are often achieved), form fillers may well take an easy option in the completion of the form and omit answering questions they do not understand or think are not relevant for their business. In the case of electronic commerce surveys, many countries have adopted questionnaire designs which feature a greater use of tick-box answers than is normally the case. This is undoubtedly one of the reasons for the good response rates (for a voluntary survey) achieved by Statistics Denmark in its most recent survey.

Another aspect affecting form completion that needs to be recognized is the overall respondent burden on an individual businessperson. Generally this is related to the overall length of the questionnaire. Respondent burden on individual businesses, particularly large businesses, is less likely to be a problem in developing countries as those countries have less developed statistical systems and hence the number of questionnaire forms being sent to these large businesses will be smaller. Thus there may be less reluctance in developing countries to complete forms about electronic commerce.

G. Conclusion and outlook for the future

1. How useful are e-commerce indicators?

While it is still early in the development of electronic commerce indicators, the experience to date has been very positive. In many countries, the collected indicators have highlighted a number of barriers to the wide implementation of electronic commerce, providing Governments with keys to future policy development. Some indicators have demonstrated digital divide issues, highlighting areas of the population and business community that have been disadvantaged. They have also pointed to areas of concern such as age and training, and to security, a key aspect when related to the actual conduct of commercial transactions, especially for small and medium-sized enterprises and private householders. So far, indicators have mainly been used in the areas of readiness and intensity. The third general area of use — measuring the impacts of electronic commerce — has not yet been subject to statistical measurement to any substantial degree.

With respect to readiness and intensity indicators, a prime example comes from Canada, where the Government made a commitment in 1997 to make Canada the most "connected" nation in the world by the year 2000.[15] To be able to test progress in this regard, it has been necessary to form an overall indicator for Canada and compare and contrast it with similar ones from other countries. The Conference Board of Canada and Industry Canada have now established such an indicator and it provides a very useful tool to measure the effectiveness of government action in attaining the overall policy objective.

The Nordic countries have for some years been concerned about the impact of ICT use on their countries. The Government of Denmark has recently set itself an objective similar to that of the Canadian Government and will undoubtedly want to undertake a similar indicator exercise. The Danish Government is using e-commerce indicators (such as the number of enterprises with PCs, the share of the workforce with access to PCs, the number of enterprises with access to the Internet, the number of enterprises with web pages, the number of enterprises with e-commerce transactions and total e-commerce) as indicators for benchmarking the Danish information society with competitors internationally. Also, information on e-commerce barriers, such as the lack of qualified people, has been used for more specific policy purposes. Information about the share of the workforce with PCs has been used to estimate the amount of investment needed for providing everyone with a PC at work.

The European Commission, in its eEurope action plan, has used data on ICT penetration in enterprises as a main indicator on the development towards the information society with regard to enterprises.

The United Kingdom is implementing a strategy that will bring together a wide range of indicators through an international benchmarking study as well as through implementation of a range of statistical initiatives as part of its overall official statistical programme. The United States has formulated a plan to introduce the measurement of electronic commerce transactions throughout its entire statistical measurement programme and is in the process of implementing this plan. In this way the United States is aiming to be eventually able to tackle the more complex task of measuring the impact of electronic commerce on the overall performance of the economy.

Finally, the APEC leaders, at their last meeting in Brunei (November 2000), agreed in their final declaration to:

> "Use the results of the APEC E-Commerce Readiness Assessments for APEC Economies to further explore collective and individual actions, including by implementing the follow-on 'Readiness Evaluation Action Partnerships' showcasing practical actions to remove roadblocks to participation in electronic trade" (WTO, 2000).

2. Suggestions for policy action

The rapid growth in electronic commerce around the world has prompted many to look for better ways of measuring the phenomenon. As more and more countries and international agencies become involved, it is important to develop plans to ensure that there is no unnecessary duplication of effort and that users have the data necessary for informed decision-making at the earliest possible opportunity. From the above discussion, it appears that there are a number of actions that could be taken by national statistical agencies in both developed and developing countries:

- Assuming leadership for the development of international standards, concepts, definitions and model surveys by associating with the relevant international agencies;
- Collaborating with other national statistical agencies (particularly national statistical agencies in developed countries collaborating with those in developing countries), to improve the quality of statistical indicators that can be made available;
- Participating in seminars and workshops organized by international agencies aimed at improving statistical standards in the measurement of electronic commerce.

Those statistical offices that are about to start their compilation programmes on e-commerce are advised to consider the checklist discussed above, which includes:

- Checking the national business register;
- Identifying user needs for e-commerce data;
- Designing a collection strategy; and
- Preparing an attractive survey form.

Bearing in mind that the priority statistical indicators of electronic commerce in some developing countries are likely to focus on the readiness of those economies for electronic commerce, national statistical agencies in those countries are encouraged to develop, as a first step, readiness indicators of the type already discussed (such as those included in the APEC E-Commerce Readiness Assessment Guide, the OECD proposed set of indicators or the Nordic model survey). Those countries that see themselves at a more mature stage in their e-commerce development are encouraged to include intensity indicators in their e-commerce statistical compilation programmes (see those proposed by the OECD and Eurostat and included in the model survey).

Given their resources and statistical infrastructure, national statistical agencies in the developed countries are in a better position to contribute to the development work and are encouraged to do so. They are, however, strongly encouraged to work with their counterparts in developing countries to assist them in the development of the statistical infrastructure needed for the compilation of electronic commerce indicators and subsequently with the derivation of electronic commerce indicators themselves.

Notes

1 For example, some studies include all business activities carried out over the Internet, while others include only those that result in the purchase of a good or service. Some use personal interviews, and others use e-mail surveys or website surveys. Moreover, the methodologies used for calculating estimates vary widely among the studies. For a discussion on methodologies used by private data collectors, see OECD (2000c).

2 Definitions have been provided by, inter alia, UNCTAD (2000) and WTO (1998). While useful for describing the current status and possible trends of e-commerce, they have not been designed as a basis for compiling internationally comparable data on e-commerce. This is partly because most existing definitions are the product of individual researchers rather than, for example, a working group representing the member States of an international organization.

3 Carried out through its Working Party on Indicators for the Information Society.

4 All OECD member countries have agreed to use these definitions in their statistical work in measuring e-commerce (including Eurostat members, the Nordic countries, the United States, and Canada). However, some will use the narrow definition, and others the broad definition, as explained in the text.

5 One aspect that has not yet been fully resolved relates to electronic commerce conducted using e-mail. Some experts view e-mail transactions as being little different from transactions taking place using fax machines or ordinary (postal) mail and would therefore like these to be excluded from electronic commerce. However, experts from other countries consider it necessary to include e-mail orders within electronic commerce, particularly in the household sector, where the majority of such transactions occur.

6 This definition is more in line with the concept of electronic business, as identified by Statistics Canada (1999).

7 The APEC Guide defines "readiness" as the degree to which the economy of a community is prepared to participate in the digital economy. This is the same concept as the one adopted by OECD.

8 Some statistical indicators on the readiness aspect can also be derived from information supplied by telecommunications carriers, rather than by the businesses themselves.

9 Denmark, Finland, Iceland, Norway and Sweden.

10 The Nordic group will also present its survey to the United Nations Voorburg Group, a group of statisticians, mainly from national statistical agencies, which was formed to facilitate the availability of services sector statistics. The Voorburg Group has had some experience in developing model surveys, having developed a model computer services industry survey in the early 1990s.

11 An additional (non-core) module X on background information about the enterprise is included where the information requested is not available from national business registers.

12 These indicators are taken from ISTAT (2000).

13 In Slovenia, surveys on the information society have been carried out since 1996. Vehovar (1999) points out that the translation of the English term "electronic commerce" into Slovene comes closer to "electronic business" rather than "electronic trade". Hence, a definition clearly specifying the activities involved is critical.

14 In this regard, it is interesting to note that Statistics Denmark (2001) achieved a response rate of 67 per cent in its most recent ICT Use in Business survey.

15 In this regard, "connectedness" can be considered to relate to both readiness and intensity.

References

Ambler, C. (2000). "Measuring the electronic economy at the United States Bureau of the Census". Paper presented to the Voorburg Group Conference, Madrid, September.

APEC (2000). *APEC Readiness Initiative: E-Commerce Readiness Assessment Guide,* http://www.ecommerce.gov/apec.

Atrostic, B. K., Gates, J. and Jarmin, R. (2000). *Measuring the Electronic Economy: Current Status and Next Steps,* http://www.census.gov/econ/www/ebusiness614.htm.

Boegh Nielsen P., et al. (2000). "Measurement of ICT usage in enterprises and electronic commerce: A proposal for a model questionnaire". Paper presented to the Voorburg Group Conference, Madrid, September.

Eurostat (2000). *List of questions for Eurostat pilot surveys on e-commerce.* Luxembourg, November.

Haltiwanger, J. and Jarmin, R. (1999). "Measuring the digital economy". Centre for Economic Studies, United States Bureau of the Census. Paper presented at the conference on "Understanding the Digital Economy: Data, Tools and Research", 25-26 May.

ISTAT (2000). *Survey on Information and Communication Technology and on Competitiveness in Enterprises – Year 2000/2001.* Rome.

Koo, J. (2000). "Measuring e-commerce in Korea". Paper presented to the Voorburg Group Conference, Madrid, September.

Mesenbourg, T. (2000). *Measuring electronic business,* http://www.census.gov/econ/www/ebusiness614.htm.

OECD (2000a). *Challenges and Lessons Learnt in Measuring Internet Commerce: Australia's Experience,* Paris, April.

OECD (2000b). *Defining and Measuring Electronic Commerce: A Provisional Framework and a Follow-up Strategy,* Paris, April.

OECD (2000c). *Defining and Measuring Electronic Commerce: A Background Paper.* DSTI/ICCP/IIS(2000)5, Paris, April.

OECD (2000d). *Measuring the ICT sector,* Paris.

OECD (2000e). "Report on the OECD Expert Group Meeting on Defining and Measuring E-Commerce", Paris, 17 November.

Statistics Canada (1999). *A reality check to defining eCommerce. A report prepared by CGI for Statistics Canada,* http://www.statcan.ca/english/IPS/Data/88F0006XIB99006.htm

Statistics Denmark, Statistics Finland, Statistics Norway, Statistics Sweden (2001). *Use of ICT in Nordic Enterprises – 1999/2000,* http://www.ssb.no.

UNCTAD (2000). *Building Confidence. Electronic Commerce and Development.* United Nations publication, sales no. E.00.II.D.16, New York and Geneva.

Vehovar, V. (1999). "Measuring electronic commerce with sample surveys: The methodological problems". Paper presented to Statistics Singapore Conference on E-Commerce, December.

Wong J and Lam E, (1999). "Measuring electronic commerce in Singapore: methodological issues and survey findings". Paper presented to Statistics Singapore Conference on E-Commerce, December.

WTO (1998). *Electronic Commerce and the Role of the WTO.* Geneva.

WTO (2000). *APEC 2000 Leaders' Declaration.* WT/L/375, Geneva, 29 November.

Annex

Nordic Model Questionnaire[1]

Indicators

Module A: General information about ICT systems

A1. Does the enterprise use personal computers, workstations or terminals? (Filter question) Yes ☐ No ☐ → Go to question E3

A2. Does the enterprise use or plan to use ICT in the following areas?[2] (Multiple choise)

	Year t-1 or earlier	Year t	Year t+1	Do not know/ not relevant now
E-mail (including e-mails reached by any means)	☐	☐	☐	☐
Internet (access to www)	☐	☐	☐	☐
Intranet[3]	☐	☐	☐	☐
Extranet[4]	☐	☐	☐	☐
Computer-mediated networks other than Internet (e.g. EDI, Minitel, Interactive telephone systems)	☐	☐	☐	☐
WAP (The enterprise as supplier of WAP services)	☐	☐	☐	☐

A3. The share of the total no. of employees using in normal work routine:

Personal computer, workstation or terminal ___%

Personal computer connected to the Internet/www ___%

Module B: Use of Internet

(asking enterprises with ICT)

B1. Does the enterprise use or plan to use Internet? (Filter question)

Year t-1	Year t or earlier	Year t+1	Do not know/ not relevant now
☐	☐	☐→Go to B3	☐ →Go to D1

B2. Type of external connection to the Internet in year t? (Multiple choise)

Modem (analog)	☐
ISDN	☐
xDSL (ADSL, SDSL etc.)	☐
Other fixed connection < 2Mbps (Frame relay or other broadband network service)	☐
Other fixed connection >= 2Mbps (Frame relay or other broadband network service)	☐
Do not know	☐

B3. For what purposes does the enterprise use or plan to use Internet?

B3-1. General activities (Multiple choise)

	Year t-1 or earlier	Year t	Year t+1	Do not know/ not relevant now
Information search	☐	☐	☐	☐
Monitoring the market (e.g. prices)	☐	☐	☐	☐
Communication with public authorities	☐	☐	☐	☐
Banking and financial services	☐	☐	☐	☐
Information about employment opportunities (recruitment and search)	☐	☐	☐	☐

B3-2. Activities related to purchasing goods and services (Multiple choise)

	Year t-1 or earlier	Year t	Year t+1	Do not know/ not relevant now
Information search on homepages	☐	☐	☐	☐
Receiving purchased digital products	☐	☐	☐	☐
Receiving free digital products	☐	☐	☐	☐
Obtaining after sales services	☐	☐	☐	☐

1 As proposed to the OECD in April 2001.
2 The ICT-indicators such as Internet and EDI should not be asked if they are used as filter-questions in other modules.
3 An internal company communications network using the same protocol as the Internet allowing communications within an organization.
4 A secure extension of an intranet that allows external users to access some parts of an organization's Intranet.

Annex (contd.)

Indicators

	Year t-1	Year t	Year t+1	Do not know/ not relevant now
B4. Does the enterprise have or plan to have a Web site? (Filter question)	□	□	□	□ →Go to C1

B4-1. Activities related to selling goods and services (Multiple choise)

	Year t-1 or earlier	Year t	Year t+1	Do not know/ not relevant now
Marketing the enterprise's products	□	□	□	□
Inquiry/contact facility	□	□	□	□
Customized page for repeat clients (e.g. customized presentation of product preferences)	□	□	□	□
Facilitating access to product catalogs, price lists etc.	□	□	□	□
Delivering sold digital products	□	□	□	□
Capability to provide secure transactions (e.g. firewalls or secure servers)	□	□	□	□
Integration with back end systems	□	□	□	□
Providing after sales support	□	□	□	□

Module C: E-commerce via Internet[5]

(asking enterprises with Internet access)

C1. Purchases via Internet

Has the enterprise purchased products via the Internet in year t? (Filter question)	Yes □	No □ →	Do not know □ →	Go to C4
What percentage of the total purchases (in monetary terms) do the Internet purchases represent?[6]	__%	Do not know □		
Has the enterprise paid on-line[7] for products purchased on the Internet?	Yes □	No □	Do not know/ not relevant now □	

C2. Has the enterprise purchased products via specialized Internet market places[8] in year t?	Yes □	No □	Do not know/ not relevant now □

C3. Expected benefits from Internet purchases (Multiple choice)

	No importance	Some importance	Much importance	Do not know/ not relevant now
To reduce costs	□	□	□	□
Increased access to, and awareness of, suppliers	□	□	□	□
To speed up business processes	□	□	□	□

C4. Sales via Internet

Has the enterprise received orders via the Internet in year t? (Filter question)	Yes □	No □ →	Do not know □ →	Go to D1
What percentage of the total turnover (in monetary terms) do the Internet sales represent?[9]	__%	Do not know □		
Has the enterprise received on-line[10] payments for Internet sales in year t?	Yes □	No □	Do not know/ not relevant now □	

C5. Breakdown of Internet sales

Please break down the Internet sales in year t into the following customer groups/destination of sales (estimate in percentage):

1) Other enterprises 2) Households 3) Others (1+2+3= 100 %)	__%	__%	__%	Do not know □
1) Homemarket (domestic sales) 2) Exports (non domestic sales) (1+2=100 %)	__%	__/%	Do not know □	

5 Depending on decision concerning definition of e-commerce. This module includes EDI over the Internet.

6 The proposal is to ask about percentage of total purchases and sales instead of accurate money values. The reason is the experiences from the Nordic surveys where respondents have preferred this option. In case, a country wants to ask directly for money values this can be done as well. As total amounts of purchases and sales are asked in module X, the percentages can be converted into money values or vice versa.

7 On-line is defined as an integrated ordering-payment transaction.

8 More than one enterprise is represented at the website. The market sells either certain goods/services or is adressed towards limited costumer groups.

9 See note 6.

10 See note 7.

Annex (contd.)

Indicators

C6.	**Has the enterprise sold products to other enterprises via a presence on specialized Internet market places[11] in year t?**	Yes ☐	No ☐	Do not know/ not relevant now ☐

C7. Motivations for Internet sales (Multiple choise)	No importance	Some importance	Much importance	Do not know/ not relevant now
Company image considerations	☐	☐	☐	☐
To reduce business costs	☐	☐	☐	☐
To speed up business processes	☐	☐	☐	☐
To improve quality of services	☐	☐	☐	☐
To reach new customers	☐	☐	☐	☐
To expand the market geographically	☐	☐	☐	☐
To launch new products	☐	☐	☐	☐
To keep pace with competitors	☐	☐	☐	☐

Module D: E-commerce via EDI or other computer-mediated network (other than Internet)[12]

(asking enterprises with ICT)

D1. Does the enterprise use or plan to use EDI or other computer-mediated networks? (Filter question)	Year t-1 or earlier	Year t	Year t+1	Do not know/ not relevant now
	☐	☐	☐	☐ → Go to E1

D2. Is EDI or other computer-mediated networks used in relation to:	Year t-1 or earlier	Year t	Year t+1	Do not know/ not relevant now
Customers	☐	☐	☐	☐
Suppliers	☐	☐	☐	☐
Other cooperating partners	☐	☐	☐	☐
Banks/Financial institutions	☐	☐	☐	☐
Public organisations/institutions	☐	☐	☐	☐

D3. Purchases via EDI or other computer-mediated networks

If the enterprise orders products via EDI, what percentage of the total purchases (in monetary terms) does this represent in year t?[13] __% Do not know ☐

D4. Sales via EDI or other computer-mediated networks

If the enterprise receives orders via EDI, what percentage of the total turnover (in monetary terms) does this represent in year t?[14] __% Do not know ☐

Module E: Barriers on the use of Internet and ICT in general

(Asking enterprises with ICT, general barriers also asking enterprises without ICT)

What significance does the following barriers have for the present and future use of ICT?

E1. Barriers on Internet sales	No importance	Some importance	Much importance	Do not know/ not relevant now
The products of the enterprise not applicable for Internet sales	☐	☐	☐	☐
Customers not ready to use Internet commerce	☐	☐	☐	☐
Security problems concerning payments	☐	☐	☐	☐
Uncertainty concerning contracts, terms of delivery and guarantees	☐	☐	☐	☐
Cost of developing and maintaining an e-commerce system	☐	☐	☐	☐
Logistical problems	☐	☐	☐	☐
Considerations for existing channels of sales	☐	☐	☐	☐

11 See note 8.
12 Depending on decision concerning definition of e-commerce. EDI over the Internet is included in module C.
13 See note 6.
14 See note 6.

Annex (concluded)

Indicators

E2. Barriers on use of Internet	No importance	Some importance	Much importance	Do not know/ not relevant now
Security concerns (e.g. hacking, viruses)	☐	☐	☐	☐
Technology too complicated	☐	☐	☐	☐
Expenses of development and maintenance of websites too high	☐	☐	☐	☐
Lost working time because of irrelevant surfing	☐	☐	☐	☐
Data communication expenses too high	☐	☐	☐	☐
Data communication is too slow or unstable	☐	☐	☐	☐
Lack of perceived benefits	☐	☐	☐	☐

E3. Barriers on the use of ICT in general	No importance	Some importance	Much importance	Do not know/ not relevant now
ICT expenditure too high	☐	☐	☐	☐
New versions of existing software introduced too often	☐	☐	☐	☐
Supply of ICT-technology not matching the ICT needs of the enterprise	☐	☐	☐	☐
The level of ICT skills is too low among the employed personnel	☐	☐	☐	☐
Difficult to recruit qualified ICT personnel	☐	☐	☐	☐
Existing personnel reluctant to use ICT	☐	☐	☐	☐
Lack of an updated ICT strategy	☐	☐	☐	☐
Lack of perceived benefits	☐	☐	☐	☐

Module X: Background information[15]

X1. Name and address of the enterprise

X2. Activity of the enterprise

X3. No. of employees end of year t

X4. Total purchases of goods and services in year t (national currency)

X5. Total sales in year t (national currency)

15 The information asked in this module might be available – or a number of them – from the Statistical Business Register and/or statistical registers and thus not included in the questionnaire.

Chapter 2

ELECTRONIC COMMERCE AND DEVELOPING COUNTRIES: A COMPUTABLE GENERAL EQUILIBRIUM ANALYSIS

A. Introduction

The United States, currently the leading country in electronic commerce (e-commerce), showed impressive GDP and productivity growth rates during the 1990s. In particular between 1995 and 2000, productivity growth accelerated significantly, reaching an annual rate of 2.5 per cent, significantly higher than the rate of the previous two decades.[1] Much of this growth is explained by the increased use of information technology, and in particular e-commerce. It is expected that European countries will catch up quickly with the United States in their use of e-commerce, and that developing countries, with a certain degree of preparation, could follow suit and converge in productivity with the developed countries. This could significantly boost their economic growth rates. On the other hand, if countries lag behind in their technological development, what will be the impact on macroeconomic growth and development?

This chapter addresses this question and analyses the overall impact of e-commerce on the global economy by simulating two scenarios: one in which developing countries fall behind technologically (characterized by less productivity growth than developed countries), and a second in which they catch up with the developed countries. It is assumed that e-commerce has a direct impact on cost savings in service sectors, particularly in wholesale and retail trade, financial and business services, and transport services. These cost savings are simulated through a productivity growth scenario, using a computable general equilibrium model. This allows for analysis of the impact of e-commerce on macroeconomic variables such as GDP, welfare, wages and terms of trade.

The chapter is organized in six sections. The second section provides a short discussion of how cost savings may result from business-to-consumer (B2C) and business-to-business (B2B) e-commerce. The third section presents briefly some recent studies on the overall impact of e-commerce on developed countries' economies. The fourth section turns to the modeling exercise. It first describes the methodology used, and then shows the results of two experiments: (a) one in which developed countries experience a 1 per cent productivity growth (developing countries fall behind); and, (b) one in which developing countries converge in productivity in services sectors and experience a 1 per cent productivity growth (developing countries catch up). Finally, the last section presents some conclusions.

B. E-commerce and cost savings

It is widely recognized that e-commerce reduces transaction costs, increases efficiency, and generates important changes in the management and production processes of businesses. For example, by linking industries and consumers through the Internet, B2C e-commerce has the potential to significantly reduce transaction costs. It also increases access to information for consumers, thus reducing search costs and allowing consumers to find the lowest price for a product or service. B2C e-commerce also reduces market entry barriers for producers, given that the cost of setting up and maintaining a web site is much lower than the installation of a "brick-and-mortar" firm. A larger number of suppliers will increase competition and reduce monopolistic profits of firms.

In the B2B sector, e-commerce contributes most to reducing costs by linking industries and suppliers electronically along the supply chain. It reduces procurement costs because it makes it possible to find the lowest supplier prices. It increases efficiency because greater competition among suppliers will reduce monopolistic profits and the number of intermediaries. It also reduces the cost of providing financial services or other services that can be made available electronically through the Internet. Moreover, a better flow of information reduces inventory stocks.

Garicano and Kaplan (2000) classify transaction costs as coordination and motivation costs, and argue that B2B e-commerce has the potential to affect both types of transaction costs. Coordination costs are related to the determination of prices and the details of a transaction, to the mutual knowledge of potential buyers and suppliers, and to bringing them together to conduct a transaction. B2B e-commerce reduces this type of costs by improving the efficiency of business processes, for example when a transaction that is normally conducted by phone or fax is made by Internet, or when business processes are redesigned. Coordination costs are also reduced when B2B e-commerce improves access to direct information, for example by reducing search costs in finding suppliers and allowing them to reach more potential buyers at lower cost. B2B e-commerce also reduces coordination costs by providing better information on the availability, characteristics and prices of products, buyers and sellers.

Motivation costs are related to the costs of informational incompleteness and imperfect commitment. Costs of informational incompleteness occur when buyers and suppliers do not have all relevant information to find out whether the terms of an agreement are fulfilled, for example whether the product provided by the supplier satisfies all the technical requirements of a productive process. B2B e-commerce reduces these costs through the standardization of products. Costs of imperfect commitments are produced when buyers and suppliers do not have the ability to bind themselves. E-commerce contributes to reducing these costs by standardizing processes and allowing for electronic tracing of products.

It is expected that most cost reductions related to B2B e-commerce will be in procurement costs. According to Goldman Sachs analysts[2], it is estimated that in the United States the percentage saving in the cost of inputs that results from migrating from traditional procurement systems[3] to B2B e-commerce varies from 2 per cent for coal to 39 per cent for electronic components. These cost savings are the result of the combined effect of reductions in transaction costs and greater competition among suppliers. Table 4 shows the savings in cost of inputs by industry.

Table 4
Estimated B2B cost savings by industry

Industry	Cost savings (%)
Aerospace machinery	11
Chemicals	10
Coal	2
Communications/bandwidth	5-15
Computing	11-20
Electronic components	29-39
Food ingredients	3-5
Forest products	15-25
Freight transport	15-20
Healthcare	5
Life science	12-19
Machinery (metals)	22
Media & advertising	10-15
Maintenance repair and operating supplies	10
Oil & gas	5-15
Paper	6
Steel	17

Source: Goldman Sachs Investment Research (1999), p.8.

C. E-commerce and productivity growth

Despite the growing evidence of the importance of e-commerce at the microeconomic level, doubts have been raised about its impact on macroeconomic growth. During the past few years, a debate has evolved as to whether information technology can explain the acceleration in productivity growth. At the root of this debate was the fact that the United States, the leading country in information technology and e-commerce, has experienced impressive GDP growth since 1995. This output expansion has been characterized by an acceleration in productivity growth, very low unemployment rates, low inflation rates, and a reduction of fiscal deficits. This debate was linked to the "productivity paradox"[4], which states that productivity statistics do not seem to provide any evidence of the impact of computer and information technologies. There are three main positions among economists to explain the productivity paradox: (i) there is a mismeasurement problem; (ii) there is nothing paradoxical[5]; and (iii) the observation of positive macroeconomic effects requires decades rather than years, as the economy is in a process of transition.

Robert Gordon believes that all of the United States productivity growth originated from the computer-manufacturing industry and that technological progress acceleration in all other industries is zero, arguing that: "For the economy as a whole, extra capital plus growth in computing technical progress constitute the whole of the increase in labor productivity: the contribution from technological progress outside computing is zero".[6]

Nordhaus (2001) evaluated Gordon's hypothesis and rejected it. Using a new approach to measuring industrial productivity, he showed that during the period 1996-1998, productivity growth in both the new economy[7] and non-new economy sectors grew faster than in the 1977-1995 period. He concluded that productivity growth is widespread and not concentrated in a few sectors of the new economy.

Similarly, the *Annual Report* of the United States Council of Economic Advisers[8] shows evidence of productivity growth in both computer and non-computer sectors. The report considers that changes in productivity have cyclical and structural components. A structural acceleration in productivity may originate from four sources: (i) capital deepening; (ii) improvements in labor quality; (iii) technological progress in computer-producing industries; and (iv) technological progress in other industries.

Table 5 shows statistical estimates of labour productivity and its components, where labour productivity is calculated as the average of income-and-product side measures of output per hour worked. These figures indicate that in the private non-farm business sector, there was a structural acceleration in productivity for the 1995-2000 period, compared to the 1973-1995 period, due to the productivity growth in both computer and non-computer sectors. The contribution coming from the productivity growth of the non-computer sector is calculated as a residual and accounts for 1 per cent of the acceleration in productivity. This last figure represents, therefore, the impact on productivity growth of technological progress and management and production system improvements outside the computer sector, such as those related to e-commerce, computer and web-based learning.

These results are consistent with the idea that the use of information technology contributes most to the expansion of productivity, but not the production of information technology products. Atkinson and Court (1998) argue that "... the animating force for productivity and wage growth in the New Economy will be the pervasive use of digital electronic technologies to increase efficiency and productivity".

Table 6 shows the productivity growth in various services industries, as measured by the value added per full-time equivalent employee. These figures show that there has been an acceleration in productivity growth since 1995 in sectors such as wholesale and retail trade, financial and business services. Although there are some data problems in certain sectors, these figures seem to give some support to the hypothesis that the use of information technology, coupled with

Table 5
Accounting for the productivity acceleration in the 1990s
(Private non-farm business sector; average annual rates)

Item	1973 to 1995	1995 to 2000	Change (percentage points)
Labour productivity growth rate (per cent)	1.39	3.01	1.63
Percentage point contributions			
Business cycle effect	0.00	0.04	0.04
Structural labour productivity	1.39	2.97	1.58
Capital services	0.70	1.09	0.38
Labour quality	0.27	0.27	0.00
Computer sector TFP	0.18	0.36	0.18
TFP excluding computer sector	0.22	1.22	1.00

Source: United States (2001), p. 28.
Note: TFP denotes total factor productivity.

improvements in business practices, has, in fact, increased productivity growth.

Some studies have tried to evaluate the impact of e-commerce on developed countries using macro-econometric or computable general equilibrium (CGE) models. Their results indicate that e-commerce could have a significant positive impact on GDP growth and other macroeconomic variables.

Brooks and Wahjai (2000) used the MULTIMOD[9] model to estimate the macroeconomic impact of B2B e-commerce on some developed countries (United States, Japan, Germany, United Kingdom and France). They first calculated savings from procurement in selected industrial sectors, and used input-output accounts to calculate price reductions of inputs for other industries. They then used the MULTIMOD model to estimate the total effect on the economy. The results indicate that in the five economies, B2B e-commerce will raise GDP by about 5 per cent, with over half of this increase expected within the next 10 years.

A study by the Australian Government[10] used a mixed methodology to estimate the impact of e-commerce on the Australian economy. It combines qualitative information provided by business leaders from selected industry sectors with quantitative analysis provided by the Monash model.[11] The study estimated that e-commerce would increase GDP by about 2.7 per cent (direct and indirect effects) by the year 2007. It would also increase imports and exports, improve terms of trade, and increase real wages. The increase in trade would result in a trade deficit.

In short, there is now a growing trend among economists to agree that B2C and B2B e-commerce can have a positive impact on productivity and growth in developed countries.

D. The impact of e-commerce on the global economy: a CGE analysis

As a contribution to this debate, this section presents the results of a quantitative analysis of the impact of e-commerce on the global economy. It discusses two scenarios: one in which developing regions fall behind technologically, and a second in which they catch up with developed regions.

The analysis is centered on cost savings, assuming that e-commerce can reduce the costs of services. As services are important inputs to other production sectors, their cost reduction will spread across the economy. In a partial equilibrium framework, a cost reduction will push the supply curve out to the right, thereby achieving a new equilibrium where output will increase and prices will decline. In this analysis, special attention is given to the effects of cost reductions in transport services, wholesale and retail trade,

Table 6
Labour productivity growth by private industry - services
(Average annual percent change)

Item	1973 to 1995	1995 to 2000	Change (percentage points)
Transportation	2.48	1.72	-0.76
Trucking and warehousing	2.09	-0.73	-2.82
Transportation by air	4.52	4.52	0.00
Other transportation	1.51	2.14	0.63
Communications	5.07	2.66	-2.41
Electric, gas, and sanitary services	2.51	2.42	-0.09
Wholesale trade	2.84	7.84	4.99
Retail trade	0.68	4.93	4.25
Finance	3.18	6.76	3.58
Insurance	-0.28	0.44	0.72
Real estate	1.38	2.87	1.49
Personal services	-1.47	1.09	2.55
Business services	-.16	1.69	1.85
Health services	-2.31	-1.06	1.26
Other services	-0.72	-0.71	0.01

Source: United States (2001), p. 32.

as well as business and financial services. Except for transport services, these are sectors where the use of information technology and improvements in business practices through e-commerce have contributed most to the productivity increase in the United States. Although, at present, there is no evidence of productivity growth in transport services (see table 6), this sector is included because it is expected that the transformation of the traditional transport chain and other features of e-commerce will produce significant gains in productivity.[12]

For the purposes of the analysis, countries were aggregated into six regions: developed countries, Eastern Europe, Asia, Latin America, Africa and the rest of the world. Commodities were aggregated into 13 sectors: primary/food, manufacturing, trade, air transport, maritime transport, other transport, communications, financial services, insurance, business services, recreational services, government and other services. Factors of production were divided into five factors: capital, land, unskilled labour, skilled labour and natural resources.

To analyse the impact of cost savings in services on the global economy, due to e-commerce, a general equilibrium framework is used.[13] Specifically the GTAP[14] model is used to run the simulations. The multisector specification provided by the GTAP model makes it possible to consider the transmission of technological change effects across sectors of a region, while the multiregion specification enables us to analyse the transmission across regions.[15]

It must be pointed out that the simulations below should be considered as an exploratory exercise that is used to understand the nature and direction of the impact of e-commerce, but not for forecasting purposes.[16]

1. Falling behind technologically: productivity growth in developed countries only

The first experiment simulates a cost reduction in services, due to e-commerce, in developed countries only. The aim of this experiment is to examine the impact of e-commerce on developing regions when they do not keep up with developed regions technologically. This cost reduction is simulated through an increase in productivity of 1 per cent in the services sectors of the developed countries.[17] It should be mentioned that an increase in productivity[18] of 1 per cent is equivalent to a downward shift of the unit cost function by 1 per cent, *ceteris paribus*. The experiment consists of seven separate simulations: a 1 per cent increase in productivity in (1) trade services, (2) air transport, (3) maritime transport, (4) other transport, (5) financial services, (6) business services, and (7) all precedent services.

It is important to point out that the 1 per cent technological shock does not correspond to the rate of technological progress of the services sector of developed countries. It is merely a working hypothesis. It can be considered as the rate at which services sector productivity grows in the developed countries relative to other regions.

Given the structure of the GTAP model, a productivity growth in services of developed countries will expand the output of services and increase the price of production factors[19] (income effect) in a first step; then it will reduce the price of services[20] in a second step (price effect). In an open economy and in a partial equilibrium framework, terms of trade will deteriorate or not depending on whether the services are exportable or not.[21] In a general equilibrium framework the impact on other markets is taken into consideration. If the income effect is larger than the price effect, it is possible that the price of other sectors increases in relative terms, bringing about an increase of the terms of trade of developed countries.[22] In this case, depending on the composition of exports and imports of developing countries, it is possible that developing countries lose welfare[23] through a deterioration of their terms of trade. This explains part of the results of the experiment, which are presented below.

Table 7 shows the results of the first experiment by different services sectors. Output of trade services mainly includes retail and wholesale trade.[24] Output of retail and wholesale trade is measured by the total value of commercial margins. As these margins are important elements of transaction costs, a reduction in the cost of trade services could capture a portion of the effect of B2C and B2B e-commerce. Column 1 of table 7 shows the results of the productivity growth in trade services. For developed countries, it can be observed that the effect of this shock in terms of GDP, wages and welfare is significant. A 1 per cent increase in productivity in this sector results in a GDP increase of 0.22 per cent, a wage increase of 0.03 per cent and 0.05 per cent for unskilled and skilled labour respectively, welfare gains of $47.9 billions (in 1997 dollars) and an increase in the terms of trade of 0.01 per cent. On the other hand, the impact on the developing countries' economies is largely negative, with a fall in welfare ($614 million), wages (0.12 per cent), and terms of trade (0.02 per cent).

If we consider transport services for goods, output is measured by the total value of transport margins. E-commerce generates improvements in the supply chain that produce productivity gains and cost reductions in the transport sector. Table 7, columns 2–4, shows the results of the simulation where productivity increases in transport services of developed countries only. For example, an increase of productivity of 1 per cent in maritime transport services will result in a GDP rise of 0.02 per cent, welfare gains of $2.9 billion and a deterioration of 0.01 per cent in the terms of trade in developed countries. For developing countries, cost reductions in maritime transport services in developed countries will improve their terms of trade, thus improving the competitiveness of exports from developing regions. The analysis indicates that developing countries will increase imports of maritime transport services from

Table 7
A 1% increase in productivity in developed countries only (experiment 1)

	Trade services *(1)*	Air transport *(2)*	Maritime transport *(3)*	Other transport *(4)*	Financial services *(5)*	Business services *(6)*	Services *(1) to (6)*
			Welfare (millions of US$ of 1997)				
Developed	47 942	3 365	2 896	17 238	12 071	35 081	117 869
Eastern Europe	-55	-13	21	11	-8	-53	-93
Asia	-121	130	528	261	-8	1	802
Latin America	-197	-5	83	-19	-52	-123	-301
Africa	-45	-4	69	-40	-12	5	-23
Rest of the world	-196	-38	96	-8	-56	-124	-309
			GDP – Quantity Index (% change)				
Developed	0.22	0.02	0.02	0.08	0.06	0.16	0.54
			Wages – Unskilled labour (% change)				
Developed	0.03	0.01	0.00	0.01	0.02	0.08	0.15
Eastern Europe	-0.12	-0.03	-0.01	-0.08	-0.05	-0.14	-0.42
Asia	-0.13	-0.02	0.01	-0.07	-0.04	-0.13	-0.36
Latin America	-0.13	-0.03	-0.02	-0.08	-0.05	-0.14	-0.44
Africa	-0.11	-0.02	0.00	-0.09	-0.04	-0.13	-0.39
Rest of the World	-0.14	-0.04	-0.02	-0.10	-0.06	-0.16	-0.50
			Wages – Skilled labour (% change)				
Developed	0.05	0.01	0.00	0.03	0.00	0.06	0.14
Eastern Europe	-0.12	-0.03	-0.01	- 0.07	-0.06	-0.18	-0.45
Asia	-0.12	-0.02	0.01	-0.06	-0.04	-0.15	-0.37
Latin America	-0.13	-0.03	-0.02	-0.08	-0.05	-0.15	-0.46
Africa	-0.11	-0.03	0.00	-0.10	-0.05	-0.16	-0.44
Rest of the world	-0.13	-0.04	-0.01	-0.09	-0.06	-0.19	-0.52
			Terms of trade				
Developed	0.01	0.00	-0.01	0.00	0.00	0.00	-0.01
Eastern Europe	-0.02	0.00	0.01	0.00	0.00	-0.02	-0.03
Asia	-0.01	0.01	0.03	0.01	0.00	0.00	0.04
Latin America	-0.03	0.00	0.02	0.00	-0.01	-0.01	-0.02
Africa	-0.02	0.01	0.04	-0.01	0.00	0.01	0.03
Rest of the world	-0.03	0.00	0.02	0.00	0.00	-0.01	-0.03

developed countries and reduce their output and that the freed resources will be allocated to more productive activities. In short, improvements in terms of trade and a better allocation of resources in developing countries will increase their welfare by $797 million.

The financial services sector includes financial services and auxiliary activities. Output of this sector is measured by the sum of implicit and explicit charges. E-commerce can have an important impact on the productivity of this sector, by reducing costs of "brick-and-mortar" establishments. Table 7, column 5, shows the results of the productivity growth in financial services in developed countries only. For developed countries, a 1 per cent increase in productivity entails a GDP rise of 0.06 per cent and welfare gains of $12.1 billions. Developing countries, on the other hand, will experience welfare losses ($136 million) and wage reductions (0.05 per cent), but no changes in their terms of trade.

The business services sector includes business activities, real estate, and renting. As business activities include professional "knowledge" services, e-commerce can reduce margins through, for example, electronic service delivery. Table 7, column 6, shows the results of the simulation on the business services sector. For developed countries, a 1 per cent increase in productivity results in a GDP rise of 0.16 per cent and welfare gains of $35 billions. In the developing world, a fall in wages and welfare will be experienced in Eastern Europe, Latin America and the rest of the world. Asia and Africa will reduce wages but their welfare and terms of trade will not be affected.[25]

To summarize, results from the analysis suggest that when developing regions fall behind technologically (i.e when they experience less productivity growth compared to the developed countries), in general the macroeconomic gap between developed and developing countries could increase. Only the Asian region experienced a positive impact, and largely in the transport (in particular maritime transport) sector. Hence, e-commerce could constitute an additional factor increasing the gap between the developed and many developing countries.

It is to be recalled that the numerical results of this analysis have to be considered with caution and interpreted not in quantitative and absolute terms, but in qualitative and relative terms. This analysis is intended not to forecast but to identify tendencies of the overall impact of e-commerce on developing countries, simulated through productivity growth in a number of services sectors. It should also be noted that the analysis refers only to increases in productivity in the services sectors, and does not take into account the impact of a reduction of inventory stocks and the increase of competitiveness in intermediate services.[26]

2. Catching up: productivity growth in selected developing regions only

It is expected that in the next few years the productivity gap between the European countries and the United States will close rapidly as European productivity growth increases faster than that of the United States. This process is known as convergence in productivity. Convergence in productivity takes place when the countries that lag behind the technological frontier grow more rapidly in productivity than the leading countries.

The same could be true for developing countries, with a reasonable degree of readiness. The impact of e-commerce on developing countries could be even stronger than that on developed countries because the scope for reducing inefficiencies and increasing productivity is much larger in the developing countries.

The second experiment therefore simulates a cost reduction in services, due to e-commerce, in a single developing region only. In other words, it simulates, for example, a 1 per cent growth in Asia (Africa, Latin America, etc.), while productivity in all other regions remains unchanged. The aim of this experiment is to examine the impact of a cost reduction on a single developing region when it converges in productivity for the services sectors, that is when the rate of productivity of these sectors grows faster relative to other regions. The experiment consists of 28 separate simulations. For each developing region and region in transition[27], a 1 per cent increase in productivity is simulated in (1) trade services, (2) air transport, (3) maritime transport, (4) other transport, (5) financial services, (6) business services, and (7) total of (1) to (6). The results should then be interpreted as the overall effect, on a developing region, of one additional percentage point of productivity growth in services sectors relative to other regions. The rate at which these services grow in productivity determines the time needed to close the gap between the leading countries and developing countries.

The results of technological progress in services in a single developing region are presented in tables 8–11. They indicate that an increase of productivity of 1 per cent in services will reduce prices, increase economic activity, wages and welfare. For example, in the case of the Asian region (table 8), productivity growth in all services combined (column 7) is expected to increase GDP by 0.43 per cent, wages by 0.42 per cent and welfare by $12 billions (1997 dollars). The results also indicate that output and exports of trade services would rise, while value added and imports would decrease. The simulations for individual services sectors (columns 1 to 6) indicate that productivity growth in trade services (which include retail and wholesale trade), followed by other transport and business services, results in the highest welfare gain for Asian countries. Similar positive results were obtained for the other regions (tables 9–11), with somewhat lower welfare gains compared to Asia.

To summarize, by cutting costs, increasing efficiency and reducing time and distance, e-commerce could become an important tool for development. A reasonable degree of e-commerce preparedness[28] of developing countries could give rise to the potential to catch up with leading countries. Thus, the discussion on the convergence of sectoral productivity could be treated as forming part of the discussion on economic convergence of the economic development literature, that is the tendency for poorer countries to grow faster than rich countries, and, consequently, to converge in living standards. Although there are many explanations for the absence of economic convergence, results of a recent study by Sachs and Warner[29] support the idea that appropriate economic and legal frameworks give developing countries the potential to catch up with leading countries.

E. Conclusions

The results of the experiments presented in this chapter indicate that the overall effect of productivity growth in the services sectors (which is assumed to simulate the direct effect of e-commerce) will be positive for a number of macroeconomic variables for regions adopting e-commerce.

They indicate, however, that when developing regions fall behind technologically, the gap between developing and developed countries could increase. Except for transport services, and in particular maritime transport services, the results show that productivity growth in developed countries' services sectors could result in a deterioration of the terms of trade, welfare and wages of many developing countries.

Convergence in productivity in services contributes to raising the external competitiveness of developing countries' exports and reducing international trade and transport margins. The results suggest that, by increasing the productivity of services, e-commerce could offer the possibility for increasing welfare in developing countries.

It has to be noted, once more, that the findings of this chapter should be interpreted carefully. The chapter has tried to identify the nature and direction of the impact of e-commerce on developing countries. Consequently, the results depend on the approach used to simulate the impact of e-commerce (cost savings in services) and on the structure and basic assumptions of the GTAP model framework.

Table 8
A 1% increase in productivity in Asia only

	Trade services (1)	Air transport (2)	Maritime transport (3)	Other transport (4)	Financial services (5)	Business services (6)	Services (1) to (6)
Welfare, $ millions							
Asia	3 601	1 914	1 530	2 389	863	1 706	12 012
World	3 766	1 970	1 626	2 536	866	1 781	12 555
GDP, % change							
Volume	0.13	0.07	0.06	0.09	0.03	0.06	0.43
Prices	-0.05	0.00	0.00	-0.02	0.00	0.02	-0.05
Terms of trade	-0.02	-0.01	-0.01	-0.01	0.00	-0.01	-0.06
Wages, % change							
Unskilled labour	0.09	0.08	0.06	0.07	0.03	0.09	0.42
Skilled labour	0.10	0.09	0.06	0.07	0.02	0.11	0.46
Output, % change							
Primary	0.01	0.00	0.01	0.01	0.01	-0.02	0.02
Manufacturing	0.01	0.01	0.02	0.00	0.03	-0.08	-0.02
Trade services	0.69	0.04	0.02	0.03	0.02	0.02	0.83
Air transport	-0.01	0.59	0.02	0.07	0.00	-0.02	0.64
Maritime transport	0.03	0.00	0.43	0.04	0.03	-0.01	0.51
Other transport	0.03	-0.03	-0.01	0.71	0.01	-0.02	0.69
Financial services	0.00	0.01	-0.01	0.01	0.14	-0.01	0.15
Business services	-0.08	-0.05	-0.05	-0.05	-0.02	1.27	1.02
Value added, % change							
Primary	0.01	0.00	0.01	0.01	0.01	-0.02	0.02
Manufacturing	0.01	0.01	0.02	0.00	0.03	-0.08	-0.02
Trade services	-0.31	0.04	0.02	0.03	0.02	0.02	-0.17
Air transport	-0.01	-0.41	0.02	0.07	0.00	-0.02	-0.35
Maritime transport	0.03	0.00	-0.57	0.04	0.03	-0.01	-0.48
Financial services	0.00	0.01	-0.01	0.01	-0.85	-0.01	-0.84
Business services	-0.08	-0.05	-0.05	-0.05	-0.02	0.27	0.02
Exports, % change							
Primary	-0.17	-0.18	-0.09	-0.12	-0.05	-0.21	-0.82
Manufacturing	-0.05	-0.02	0.01	-0.04	0.02	-0.18	-0.26
Trade services	2.68	-0.02	-0.09	-0.06	-0.01	-0.08	2.40
Air transport	-0.12	2.57	-0.01	0.16	-0.02	-0.14	2.44
Maritime transport	-0.08	-0.05	1.85	0.10	0.02	-0.09	1.74
Other transport	-0.09	-0.17	-0.06	2.70	-0.03	-0.19	2.14
Financial services	-0.25	-0.11	-0.17	-0.17	3.69	-0.10	2.87
Business services	-0.20	-0.16	-0.17	-0.16	-0.04	3.44	2.70
Imports, % change							
Primary	0.10	0.10	0.08	0.09	0.05	0.07	0.49
Manufacturing	0.07	0.04	0.04	0.05	0.02	0.05	0.28
Trade services	-0.78	0.07	0.08	0.08	0.02	0.08	-0.45
Air transport	0.14	-0.95	0.06	0.02	0.04	0.12	-0.56
Maritime transport	0.15	0.08	-1.07	0.00	0.01	0.10	-0.75
Other transport	0.09	-0.02	-0.10	-1.20	0.04	0.1	-1.11
Financial services	0.15	0.07	0.08	0.11	-1.77	0.06	-1.30
Business services	0.08	0.01	-0.15	0.08	0.03	-0.61	-0.57

Table 9
A 1% increase in productivity in Latin America only

	Trade services (1)	Air transport (2)	Maritime transport (3)	Other transport (4)	Financial services (5)	Business services (6)	Services (1) to (6)
Welfare, $ millions							
Latin America	1 920	1 199	860	1 439	949	1 236	7 614
World	1 885	1 174	879	1 454	910	1 195	7 507
GDP, % change							
Volume	0.10	0.06	0.05	0.07	0.05	0.06	0.38
Prices	-0.04	0.00	0.00	-0.02	0.00	0.01	-0.05
Terms of trade	0.01	0.00	-0.01	-0.01	0.01	0.00	0.00
Wages, % change							
Unskilled labour	0.06	0.07	0.05	0.06	0.06	0.10	0.39
Skilled labour	0.07	0.08	0.05	0.07	0.04	0.10	0.42
Output, % change							
Primary	0.00	-0.02	-0.01	-0.01	0.01	-0.01	-0.03
Manufacturing	0.02	-0.01	0.00	-0.01	0.04	0.00	0.04
Trade services	0.59	0.05	0.02	0.04	0.05	0.08	0.84
Air transport	0.00	0.76	0.02	0.06	0.02	0.03	0.89
Maritime transport	0.03	0.01	0.68	0.05	0.06	0.03	0.86
Other transport	0.03	0.00	0.01	0.75	0.03	0.03	0.86
Financial services	0.01	0.01	-0.01	0.01	0.19	0.03	0.25
Business services	-0.03	-0.01	-0.01	-0.01	0.00	0.49	0.44
Value added, % change							
Primary	0.00	-0.02	-0.01	-0.01	0.01	-0.01	-0.03
Manufacturing	0.02	-0.01	0.00	-0.01	0.04	0.00	0.04
Trade services	-0.40	0.05	0.02	0.04	0.05	0.08	-0.16
Air transport	0.00	-0.24	0.02	0.06	0.02	0.03	-0.10
Maritime transport	0.03	0.01	-0.32	0.05	0.06	0.03	-0.14
Other transport	0.03	0.00	0.01	-0.25	0.03	0.03	-0.14
Financial services	0.01	0.01	-0.01	0.01	-0.80	0.03	-0.74
Business services	-0.03	-0.01	-0.01	-0.01	0.00	-0.51	-0.56
Exports, % change							
Primary	-0.08	-0.14	-0.07	-0.11	-0.07	-0.13	-0.61
Manufacturing	-0.08	-0.11	-0.07	-0.11	0.00	-0.13	-0.50
Trade services	3.59	-0.06	-0.13	-0.15	-0.05	0.02	3.20
Air transport	-0.12	3.42	-0.05	0.10	-0.06	-0.07	3.21
Maritime transport	-0.10	-0.10	2.71	0.05	0.07	-0.06	2.56
Other transport	-0.12	-0.17	-0.08	3.21	-0.08	-0.13	2.60
Financial services	-0.19	-0.16	-0.17	-0.20	3.78	-0.13	2.90
Business services	-0.17	-0.18	-0.16	-0.20	-0.14	3.73	2.86
Imports, % change							
Primary	-0.03	0.05	0.04	0.05	0.05	0.06	0.30
Manufacturing	-0.10	0.06	0.05	0.08	0.06	0.09	0.43
Trade services	1.03	0.06	0.08	0.10	0.07	0.05	-0.96
Air transport	-0.12	-1.15	0.06	0.02	0.08	0.10	-0.84
Maritime transport	-0.08	0.05	-1.19	0.01	0.02	0.07	-0.97
Other transport	-0.09	0.03	-0.03	-1.16	0.08	0.10	-0.89
Financial services	-0.23	0.09	0.09	0.12	-1.71	0.10	-1.19
Business services	-0.16	0.09	0.03	0.12	0.10	-1.27	-0.83

Table 10
A 1% increase in productivity in Eastern Europe only

	Trade services (1)	Air transport (2)	Maritime transport (3)	Other transport (4)	Financial services (5)	Business services (6)	Services (1) to (6)
Welfare, $ millions							
Eastern Europe	664	89	56	345	122	492	1 770
World	642	79	80	350	101	416	1 671
GDP, % change							
Volume	0.22	0.03	0.03	0.12	0.04	0.15	0.58
Prices	-0.08	0.02	0.00	0.02	0.02	0.06	0.04
Terms of trade	0.01	0.00	-0.02	-0.01	0.01	0.03	0.02
Wages, % change							
Unskilled labour	0.14	0.05	0.03	0.14	0.06	0.21	0.63
Skilled labour	0.19	0.05	0.03	0.16	0.06	0.24	0.72
Output, % change							
Primary	0.04	-0.01	0.00	-0.01	0.00	-0.03	-0.02
Manufacturing	0.01	-0.04	-0.02	-0.11	-0.01	-0.14	-0.30
Trade services	0.62	0.02	0.01	0.07	0.03	0.11	0.85
Air transport	-0.04	1.49	0.00	0.06	-0.02	-0.08	1.41
Maritime transport	0.01	-0.01	1.13	0.14	0.01	-0.04	1.22
Other transport	0.03	-0.01	0.00	1.03	-0.01	-0.03	1.01
Financial services	0.00	-0.02	-0.01	-0.05	0.62	-0.05	0.48
Business services	0.02	-0.01	-0.01	-0.03	-0.01	0.88	0.85
Value added, % change							
Primary	0.04	-0.01	0.00	-0.01	0.00	-0.03	-0.02
Manufacturing	0.01	-0.04	-0.02	-0.11	-0.01	-0.14	-0.30
Trade services	-0.38	0.02	0.01	0.07	0.03	0.11	-0.15
Air transport	-0.04	0.49	0.00	0.06	-0.02	-0.08	0.41
Maritime transport	0.01	-0.01	0.12	0.14	0.01	-0.04	0.22
Other transport	0.03	-0.01	0.00	0.03	-0.01	-0.03	0.01
Financial services	0.00	-0.02	-0.01	-0.05	-0.38	-0.05	-0.51
Business services	0.02	-0.01	-0.01	-0.03	-0.01	-0.12	-0.15
Exports, % change							
Primary	-0.19	-0.11	-0.05	-0.26	-0.10	-0.43	-1.13
Manufacturing	-0.12	-0.09	-0.05	-0.26	-0.06	-0.38	-0.96
Trade services	3.76	-0.08	-0.08	-0.28	-0.12	-0.34	2.84
Air transport	-0.15	3.49	-0.02	0.07	-0.08	-0.28	3.02
Maritime transport	-0.07	-0.03	1.75	0.18	-0.01	-0.11	1.71
Other transport	-0.10	-0.09	-0.04	2.68	-0.09	-0.30	2.04
Financial services	-0.26	-0.11	-0.09	-0.39	4.08	-0.43	2.77
Business services	-0.20	-0.13	-0.09	-0.40	-0.15	3.75	2.75
Imports, % change							
Primary	0.12	0.03	0.02	0.08	0.04	0.14	0.43
Manufacturing	0.14	0.04	0.02	0.11	0.05	0.18	0.54
Trade services	-1.65	0.05	0.04	0.17	0.07	0.24	-1.08
Air transport	0.21	-1.00	0.03	0.08	0.06	0.23	-0.40
Maritime transport	0.13	0.04	-0.96	-0.02	0.03	0.13	-0.65
Other transport	0.12	0.10	0.04	-1.36	0.06	0.18	-0.85
Financial services	0.12	0.03	0.03	0.12	-1.57	0.14	-1.13
Business services	0.11	0.07	0.05	0.16	0.06	-1.11	-0.66

Table 11
A 1% increase in productivity in Africa only

	Trade services (1)	Air transport (2)	Maritime transport (3)	Other transport (4)	Financial services (5)	Business services (6)	Services (1) to (6)
Welfare, $ millions							
Africa	1 214	144	139	1 214	233	383	2 663
World	1 139	141	160	1 139	218	351	2 568
GDP, % change							
Volume	0.21	0.03	0.03	0.21	0.04	0.07	0.48
Prices	-0.02	0.01	0.00	-0.02	0.00	0.04	0.05
Terms of trade	0.04	0.00	-0.01	0.04	0.01	0.01	0.03
Wages, % change							
Unskilled labour	0.19	0.04	0.03	0.19	0.05	0.11	0.53
Skilled labour	0.24	0.06	0.04	0.24	0.04	0.14	0.65
Output, % change							
Primary	0.02	-0.02	0.00	0.02	0.00	-0.06	-0.09
Manufacturing	0.02	-0.03	-0.01	0.02	0.01	-0.06	-0.12
Trade services	0.55	0.01	0.01	0.55	0.03	0.02	0.66
Air transport	-0.08	1.35	-0.01	-0.08	-0.01	-0.05	1.25
Maritime transport	0.05	-0.01	0.76	0.05	0.02	-0.02	0.83
Other transport	0.05	0.00	0.00	0.05	0.02	-0.01	0.82
Financial services	0.02	0.00	0.00	0.02	0.21	0.02	0.26
Business services	-0.02	-0.01	-0.01	-0.02	0.03	1.13	1.09
Value added, % change							
Primary	0.02	-0.02	0.00	0.02	0.00	-0.06	-0.09
Manufacturing	0.02	-0.03	-0.01	0.02	0.01	-0.06	-0.12
Trade services	-0.45	0.01	0.01	-0.45	0.03	0.02	-0.34
Air transport	-0.08	0.34	-0.01	-0.08	-0.01	-0.05	0.25
Maritime transport	0.05	-0.01	-0.23	0.05	0.02	-0.02	-0.17
Other transport	0.05	0.00	0.00	0.05	0.02	-0.01	-0.18
Financial services	0.02	0.00	0.00	0.02	-0.79	0.02	-0.73
Business services	-0.02	-0.01	-0.01	-0.02	0.03	0.13	0.09
Exports, % change							
Primary	-0.22	-0.10	-0.04	-0.22	-0.06	-0.24	-0.85
Manufacturing	-0.26	-0.11	-0.06	-0.26	-0.04	-0.26	-0.96
Trade services	3.33	-0.10	-0.08	3.33	-0.03	-0.26	2.60
Air transport	-0.33	3.46	-0.04	-0.33	-0.04	-0.18	2.90
Maritime transport	-0.19	-0.06	2.18	-0.19	-0.02	-0.15	1.70
Other transport	-0.31	-0.10	-0.06	-0.31	-0.05	-0.21	2.52
Financial services	-0.47	-0.10	-0.09	-0.47	4.06	-0.23	2.83
Business services	-0.35	-0.08	-0.07	-0.35	0.05	3.70	3.00
Imports, % change							
Primary	0.19	0.05	0.03	0.19	0.05	0.12	0.56
Manufacturing	0.27	0.05	0.04	0.27	0.06	0.15	0.71
Trade services	-1.18	0.05	0.04	-1.18	0.00	0.13	-0.85
Air transport	0.23	-1.16	0.03	0.23	0.05	0.12	-0.69
Maritime transport	0.19	0.05	-1.37	0.19	0.04	0.12	-0.91
Other transport	0.20	0.09	0.00	0.20	0.05	0.11	-0.95
Financial services	0.29	0.05	0.05	0.29	-2.00	0.13	-1.32
Business services	0.32	0.06	0.04	0.32	0.02	-0.97	-0.37

Notes

1 Oliner, S. and Sichel, D. (2000).

2 Goldman Sachs Investment Research (1999).

3 Traditional systems are based on paper, telephone, fax, electronic data interchange (EDI) or value added networks (proprietary networks).

4 In 1987, Robert Solow, professor at the Massachusetts Institute of Technology (MIT) and Nobel prize-winner economist, said that "we see the computer age everywhere except in productivity statistics".

5 Economists adopting this position are called "computer revolution sceptics".

6 *The Economist*, 8 June 2000.

7 Nordhaus defines new economy as machinery, electric equipment, telephone and telegraph, and software. These sectors represented 9 per cent of GDP in 1998.

8 United States (2001).

9 MULTIMOD (MULTI-region econometric MOdel) is a dynamic multicountry macro model of the world economy, which has been designed to analyze the impact of shocks across countries as well as the effect of fiscal and monetary policies of developed countries on the global economy. It has been developed since 1988 by the International Monetary Fund.

10 Commonwealth of Australia (2000).

11 The Monash model is a dynamic computable general equilibrium model of the Australian economy, which has been designed for policy analysis and forecasting. It has been developed since 1993 by the Centre of Policy Studies of the Monash University, Australia.

12 UNCTAD (2000).

13 A computable general equilibrium model or CGE model is general because it specifies the behaviour of several economic agents; it is in equilibrium because prices of goods and factors adjust according to the market; and finally, it is computable because it produces numerical results.

14 The standard GTAP model is a multiregion, computable general equilibrium model, with perfect competition and constant returns to scale. The full GTAP version 5 database covers 65 regions, with five production factors and 57 commodities, and is constructed with data for 1997. It has been developed by the Center for Global Trade Analysis, Purdue University, West Lafayette, United States.

15 Although e-commerce in information goods could have an important impact on the overall economy, characteristics of these goods (increasing returns) and data restrictions (aggregation) do not allow taking into account the behaviour of information goods firms by using the current framework.

16 In fact, the analysis is a comparative static one, in which the changes between equilibria given a change in productivity in services sectors are analysed.

17 A better approach could be to simulate a reduction in margins (the difference between producer and consumer prices), but the GTAP model does not have the option to work with these margins. It gives only special treatment to international trade and transport margins (the difference between fob and cif prices).

18 In terms of the CGE notation, a shock of 1 per cent in total factor productivity is programmed by augmenting the technological augmentation parameter, ao, by 1 per cent. This corresponds to a Hicks-neutral technological change, which means that 1 per cent more output will be produced by using the same quantity of factors and intermediate inputs.

19 Wages and remuneration of other production factors are assumed to be a function of productivity.

20 The GTAP model does not have a monetary sector, that is, all results are expressed in real terms. In this case, the reduction of prices refers to relative prices.

21 For example, when the productivity growth is in the import-competing sector, terms of trade will improve.

22 That is, when "other sectors" are mainly export sectors, so that the price of exports of developed countries rises relative to the price of their imports.

23 Changes in economic welfare represent a change in income that can be allocated to aggregate private consumption, aggregate government consumption and savings.

24 It also includes commission trade, hotels and restaurants, repairs of motor vehicles and personal and household goods.

25 Results show that all developing countries will reduce output of business services but Asia and Africa will reduce the most (-1.01 per cent and -0.75 per cent respectively).

26 The impact of a reduction of inventories could be incorporated by simulating a technological change in the production sectors. The impact of the increase in competitiveness could be incorporated by simulating a reduction of the monopolistic profits of enterprises (mark-up).

27 Asia, Latin America and Caribbean, Eastern Europe, and Africa.

28 E-commerce preparedness implies *inter alia* the existence of e-commerce-related infrastructure, human capital, and economic and legal frameworks.

29 Sachs, J. and Warner, A.M. (1995). For the 1970-89 period, the authors examined economic convergence for a set of countries and found that a sufficient condition for it is that countries adopt appropriate market-based economic policies.

References

Atkinson, Robert D. and Court, Randolph H. (1998). *The New Economy Index: Understanding America's Economic Transformation.* Progressive Policy Institute, November, p. 22.

Brookes, Martin and Wahhaj, Zaki (2000). "The Shocking Economic Effect of B2B". Goldman Sachs Global Economics Paper No 37.

Commonwealth of Australia (2000). *E-commerce beyond 2000.* Department of Communications, Information Technology and the Arts, Canberra.

Garicano, Luis and Kaplan, Steven N. (2000). "The Effects of Business-to-Business E-commerce on Transaction Costs". National Bureau of Economic Research (NBER) Working Paper 8017, November.

Goldman Sachs Investment Research (1999). "B2B: 2B or Not 2B?" Version 1.1. November.

Nordhaus, William D. (2001). "Productivity Growth and the New Economy". NBER Working Paper 8096, January.

Oliner, S. and Sichel, D. (2000). The resurgence of growth in the late 1990s: Is information technology the story? *Journal of Economic Perspectives*, Vol. 14, (4) fall 2000: 3-22.

Sachs, Jeffrey D. and Warner, Andrew M. (1995). "Economic Convergence and Economic Policies", NBER Working Paper No 5039, February.

Shapiro, Carl and Varian, Hal R. (1998). *Information Rules: A Strategic Guide to the Network Economy.* Harvard Business School Press, Boston.

UNCTAD (2000). *Building Confidence: Electronic Commerce and Development.* UNCTAD/SDTE/Misc.11, Geneva.

United States (2001). *Annual Report of the Council of Economic Advisers.* United States Government Printing Office, Washington, DC.

Part Two

Impact of Electronic Commerce on Selected Sectors

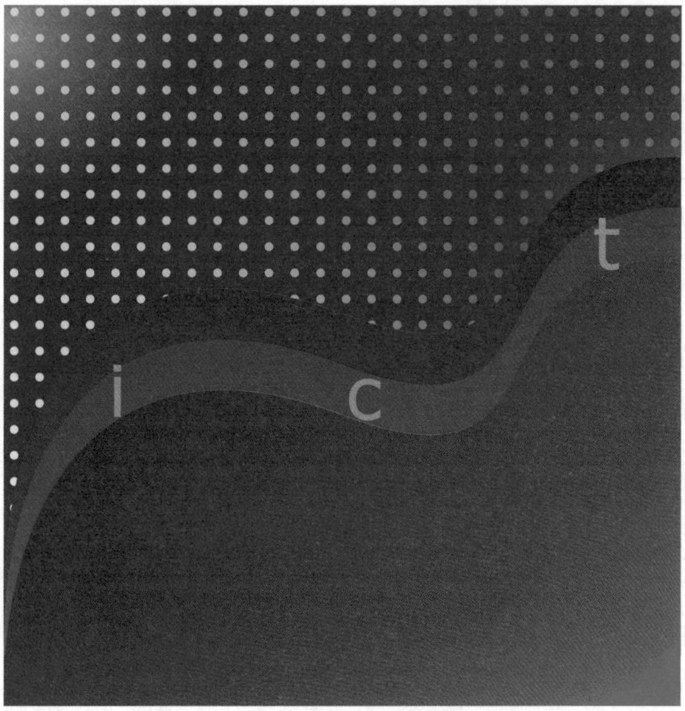

Chapter 3
ELECTRONIC COMMERCE AND TOURISM FOR DEVELOPING COUNTRIES

A. Introduction

Tourism and its Internet incarnation, often called "etourism", is regularly cited as one of the fastest growing e-commerce sectors. During 2000 online travel bookings in the United States and Europe rose to $15.5 billion from $8 billion in 1999. Online travel bookings now exceed online software and hardware purchases, previously the leading category in consumer electronic commerce. Estimates for online travel bookings for 2001 vary between $18 and 25 billion.[1]

Considering the importance of the tourism economy for many developing countries, and in particular its role as an employer and earner of foreign currency, the need to maintain and increase competitiveness through adopting e-commerce best practice is acute.[2] The use of the Internet and e-commerce, by tourism producers and consumers alike, raises a variety of issues regarding its impact on the tourism industry, in particular in developing countries where tourism is often an economic sector of primary importance. The main actors in the tourism industry include Governments, tour operators, distributors and wholesalers, hotels, airlines and other transport operators, and most important of all, the tourists themselves. Each of these actors has a stake in the development of the electronic market. Each expects to be affected in different ways by electronic commerce. Their concerns and interests need to be addressed comprehensively so that action that is realistic and relevant to all can be recommended.

Tourism is an interesting sector for appreciating the potential of electronic commerce for the economies of developing countries in several respects. Firstly, tourism is a sector in which a significant number of developing countries have established competitive advantages over the years. Secondly, tourism has remained largely a traditional service activity in which, until recently, buyers, sellers and intermediaries were well defined. Studying the relationship between tourism and e-commerce should provide an insight into at least two fundamental and broader questions, namely:

1. How do new information technologies and the Internet affect the structure of the global tourism industry and what are the effects on the competitiveness of developing countries?
2. How can the "old economy" (represented by tourism) combine with the "new economy" (represented by electronic commerce) in developing countries? How much room for manoeuvre does this combination create for local governments and enterprises to develop and maintain competitive advantages in global markets?

This chapter will discuss why tourism is an information product and a "confidence good" and its suitability for adopting e-commerce practice and tools. It looks at how business-to-business and business-to-consumer electronic commerce relationships are established and how these can improve customer service, reduce costs and promote market expansion. It identifies the roles that national tourism offices (NTOs) and destination marketing organizations (DMOs) may assume in developing countries in the movement to etourism as well as the technical and economic constraints that are likely to be encountered and the opportunities available. It suggests strategies that may be adopted to enable developing country tourism producers to set up and manage an Internet and e-commerce presence and operation. Finally, it proposes some conclusions that may form the basis for e-commerce policy in the tourism sector of developing countries.

Table 12
International arrivals and tourism receipts

	International Tourist Arrivals 1999 *(thousands)*	International Tourism Receipts 1999 *($ millions)*	Annual growth rate of receipts average 1990/1999 *(percentage)*	Share of world-wide receipts 1999 *(percentage)*
France	73 042	31 507	9.32	6.92
United States	48 497	74 881	11.73	16.45
Spain	46 776	32 400	11.75	7.12
Italy	36 516	28 359	11.50	6.23
China	27 047	14 098	44.76	3.10
United Kingdom	25 394	20 223	8.00	4.44
Canada	19 465	10 171	9.92	2.23
Mexico	19 043	7 223	5.73	1.59
Austria	17 982	12 533	-1.35	2.75
Germany	17 166	16 730	3.21	3.68
Hong Kong (China)	11 328	7 210	7.46	1.58
Switzerland	10 700	7 739	0.87	1.70
Netherlands	9 881	7 092	11.29	1.56
Thailand	8 651	6 695	9.13	1.47
Malaysia	7 931	3 540	16.26	0.78
Singapore	6 258	5 974	3.89	1.31
South Africa	6 026	2 526	20.55	0.56
Brazil	5 107	3 994	22.57	0.88
Tunisia	4 832	1 560	10.47	0.34
Indonesia	4 728	4 710	17.48	1.03
Republic of Korea	4 660	6 802	13.83	1.49
Egypt	4 489	3 903	28.83	0.86
Morocco	3 817	1 880	8.35	0.41
Argentina	2 991	2 812	19.98	0.62
Dominican Republic	2 649	2 524	22.90	0.55
India	2 482	3 009	14.74	0.66
United Arab Emirates	2 481	607	29.14	0.13
Israel	2 312	2 974	16.33	0.65
Philippines	2 171	2 534	14.18	0.56
Zimbabwe	2 103	202	27.48	0.04
Uruguay	2 073	653	20.04	0.14
Viet Nam	1 782	86	0.23	0.02
Chile	1 622	894	10.61	0.20
Bahamas	1 577	1 503	2.57	0.33
Cuba	1 561	1 714	47.80	0.38
Jordan	1 358	795	9.20	0.17
Iran (Islamic Republic of)	1 321	662	61.10	0.15
Jamaica	1 248	1 279	11.56	0.28
Costa Rica	1 032	1 002	29.51	0.22
Subtotal	**450 099**	**335 000**		**73.61**
World total	**650 200**	**455 100**	**2.90**	**100.00**

Source: World Tourism Organization.

B. Towards etourism

1. Developments and trends

In 1999, a total of $455 billion was generated by selling tourism services to international (foreign) tourists. This represents an average annual growth rate of 6.3 per cent when compared with the $263.4 billion generated in 1990.[3] However, if domestic tourism and all travel are included, global demand for tourism and travel services is expected to amount to $4,475 billion for 1999. Forecasts made for 2010 predict total international tourism receipts of $1,325 and a global tourism demand of $8,972 billion.[4]

In 1999, developing countries managed to capture 29 per cent of international tourism receipts, or $131 billion. However, this figure may be misleading since China, perhaps the largest tourism destination among developing countries, by itself accounts for a full $14 billion. Together with earnings generated by the Hong Kong Special Administrative Region (SAR) of China, this figure would exceed $20 billion and severely distorts any presentation of cumulative data for developing countries as a group.[5] Furthermore, China, the Republic of Korea, Thailand, Singapore and Indonesia together generated 35 per cent of all international tourism receipts accruing to developing countries in 1999.[6]

In contrast, the participation of least developed countries (LDCs) in the global tourism market is small and uneven. The United Republic of Tanzania, the Maldives, Cambodia, Nepal and Uganda together account for over half the total international tourism receipts of LDCs.

Table 12 shows the performance of a select group of important tourist destination countries. Growth rates of international tourism receipts were, on average, 50 per cent higher in the developing countries included in table 12, in comparison with those of developed countries. This is reflected in a general shift of tourism arrivals towards developing country destinations.

Developing countries have often used their natural and geographical endowments to achieve remarkable growth in their tourism sector. However, a number of circumstance that are common, but not exclusive, to developing countries work against their efforts to develop a strong tourism export sector:

- A generally weaker bargaining position *vis-à-vis* international tour operators and distributors;
- Long distances and less than strong or no competition, which result in high air fares;
- Global distribution systems (GDSs) and computer reservation systems (CRSs) that are owned by large international airlines;
- An increasingly competitive global tourism sector where natural competitive advantages are becoming less significant.

The tourism sector is profiting from globalization and liberalization, and it is important that developing countries position their national tourism industries to maximize any future benefits from these processes. The tourism product is an amalgam of a wide range of products and services. A strong national tourism industry can reduce a country's reliance on too few exporting sectors and thus tends to stabilize export earnings and foreign currency receipts.[7]

2. Information is confidence

The tourism product has a distinguishing feature that has thrust it into the forefront of the electronic commerce revolution: at the point of sale tourism is little more than an *information product.* A consumer obtains *product information* through the media, friends or a travel agent.[8] The *information* provided is often based on the consumer's queries and expressions of interest, i.e. *personal information.* Then the consumer pays up front, or provides *information* about how to be billed or gives *credit card information.* In return, he or she receives a ticket or a booking that confirms the details of the required travel, lodging and other services. Thus, in exchange for payment, the consumer receives yet again more *information.*

During the period leading up to the time when the product is actually consumed, consumers must be confident that the experience purchased will materialize and satisfy their expectations. We may therefore consider tourism to be a "confidence good".[9] While the price and customer service during the booking procedure are important competitive factors, tourism producers and intermediaries are increasingly competing on the confidence inspired in the customer directly through the *quality of the information* they provide.

At delivery, the actual tourism product may have several components that are particularly *information-intensive*, such as learning about local history and interacting with local communities and culture. It is often assumed that providing this type of *information* is the focus of DMOs and NTOs. Finally, a tourism product may be judged successful if it is unforgettable for the consumer, in a positive sense, and in particular when the consumer shares the *memories and impressions* — again more information — with family and friends, thus promoting the particular tourism product and destination. Thus the circle of *information* flows is completed.

Table 13
Ranking by type of company

Rank	Company URLs surveyed per category	Type	Composite unique visitors *(thousands)*
1	50	On-line agents	23 482
2	45	Airlines	21 586
3	61	Resources/reviews	14 624
4	97	Hotels/resorts	13 446
5	174	Destinations	10 079
6	51	Hotel booking	7 475
7	61	Transport	5 196
8	44	Vacations	4 895
9	14	Rental cars	4 198
10	13	Cruise lines	1 781
11	10	Timeshares	1 624
12	6	Travel adventure	1 320
13	7	Bed & breakfast	857

Source: Top9.com (Ferbuary 2001).

Table 14
Ranking of on-line agents

Rank	Overall web rank	Company name	Unique visitors *(thousands)*
1	56	travelocity.com	8 155
2	71	expedia.com	7 052
3	443	cheaptickets.com	1 906
4	497	lowestfare.com	1 706
5	854	hotwire.com	1 093
6	873	trip.com	1 073
7	1 524	travel.com	673
8	1 751	onetravel.com	599
9	3 426	sidestep.com	315

Source: Top9.com (February 2001).

Chart 2
Unique visitors per month at Travelocity and Expedia websites

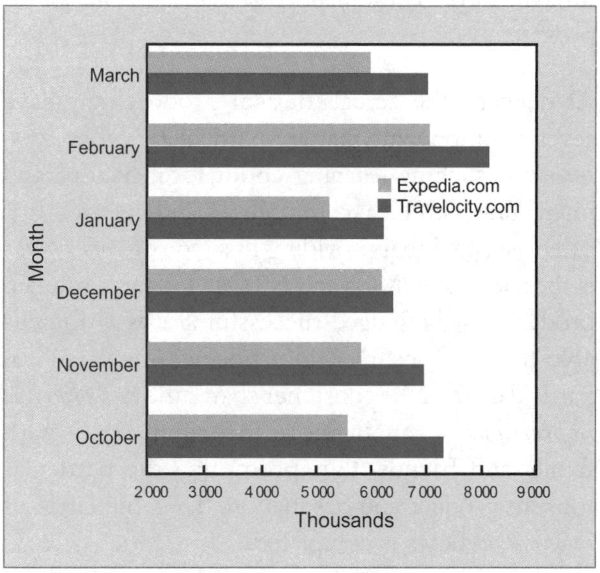

Source: Top9.com

The tourism industry is learning fast that the Internet can satisfy the acute need for information at all stages of the tourism product's life cycle far better than any other existing technology. The Internet and its inherent interactivity empowers people to find information quickly and precisely on any destination or activity that is arousing their interest. Consumers expect instant information and, increasingly, the possibility to design or customize the tourism product sought, and to pay for it on-line.

In response, the tourism industry has developed its on-line presence mostly following the traditional subcategories. Within each subcategory we can find businesses with varying levels of "click-to-brick ratios".[10] The basic structure of the on-line industry is presented in tables 13 and 14 and chart 2.

The table and chart rankings are based on the number of unique visitors[11] a particular on-line tourism producer has had. Because many on-line companies also have offline high-street operations, using unique visitors to measure e-commerce activity can bring a more focused insight regarding the relative size of on-line activity. At first glance, it is obvious that the category of on-line agents is the most prominent representative of etourism.[12] Unsurprisingly, the large global airlines are close behind in second place. Reflecting consumers' great thirst for information, on-line information resources rank third, ahead of several accommodation categories and car rental.[13] This is an indicator of the great challenge for DMOs in developing countries and will be discussed in section C of this chapter.

When we look at the category of on-line agents more closely, we find a very concentrated sector. Between themselves, Travelocity.com and Expedia.com capture about 65 per cent of unique visitors browsing the on-line agent category. The dominance of the two leading on-line agents may be explained by the resources made available to them during their initial period of set-up and market entry through their parent companies.[14]

The use of the Internet in developed countries for purchasing tourism products is increasing dramatically. Of the total e-commerce sales of $64 billion in 1999, travel, transport and hotel reservations as a group represented the largest category of Internet transactions, accounting for 38.5 per cent of all on-line sales. The major part of these transactions originated and materialized in the United States.

Almost half of Americans have booked either airfare, hotel reservations or car rentals online during 2001, up from barely more than one-fourth in 2000. Twenty percent of business travelers say they have made online bookings, up from 16 percent in 2000.[15] On-line sales in Europe are forecast to increase substantially. In 1999 only 0.1 per cent of the European travel market, worth GB£ 540 billion, was sold on-line and it is expected that Internet sales will have grown sixfold by 2002. For the United Kingdom it is estimated that by 2003, 30 per cent of flight-only bookings will be made on-line, as well as sales of 15 per cent of standard packaged holidays and 20 per cent of last minute and late packaged holidays.[16]

The changes which the tourism industry is experiencing present an opportunity for developing countries to improve their relative position in the international market, provided that they empower themselves to approach their customers and business partners on the Internet and build confidence. It is certain that embracing digital communication and information technology is no longer an option, but a necessity.

The hard reality in the tourism industry today is that "if you are not online, you are not on sale".[17] Destinations and businesses eager to have an impact on the market must be online. Small or remote destinations and products with well-developed and innovative websites can now have "equal Internet access" to international markets. This implies equal access to telecom infrastructure and financial services, as well as to training and education. It is not the cost of being there, on the on-line market place, that must be reckoned with, but the cost of not being there.

Chart 3
Tourism before the Internet

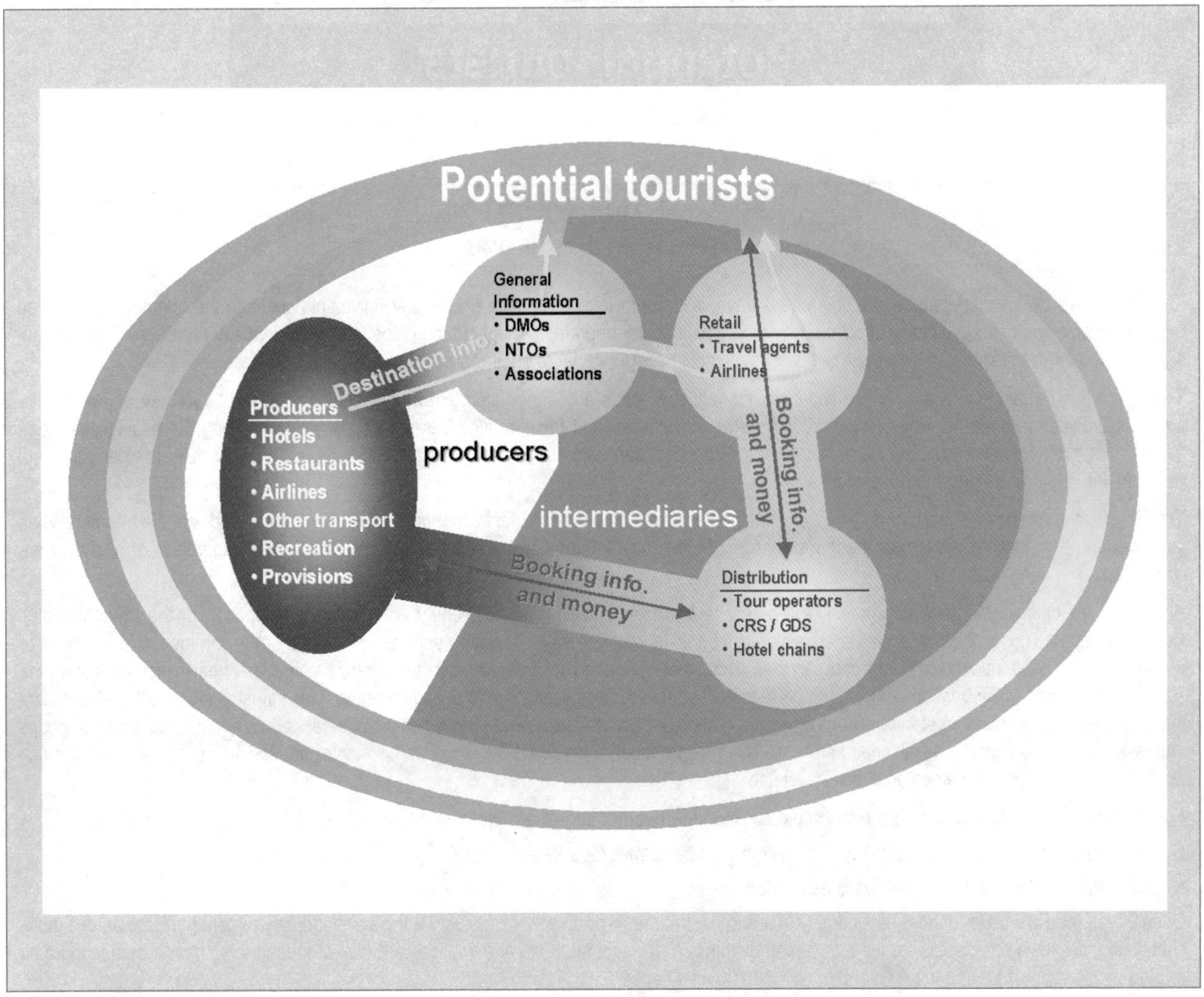

Chart 4
Internet-enabled tourism

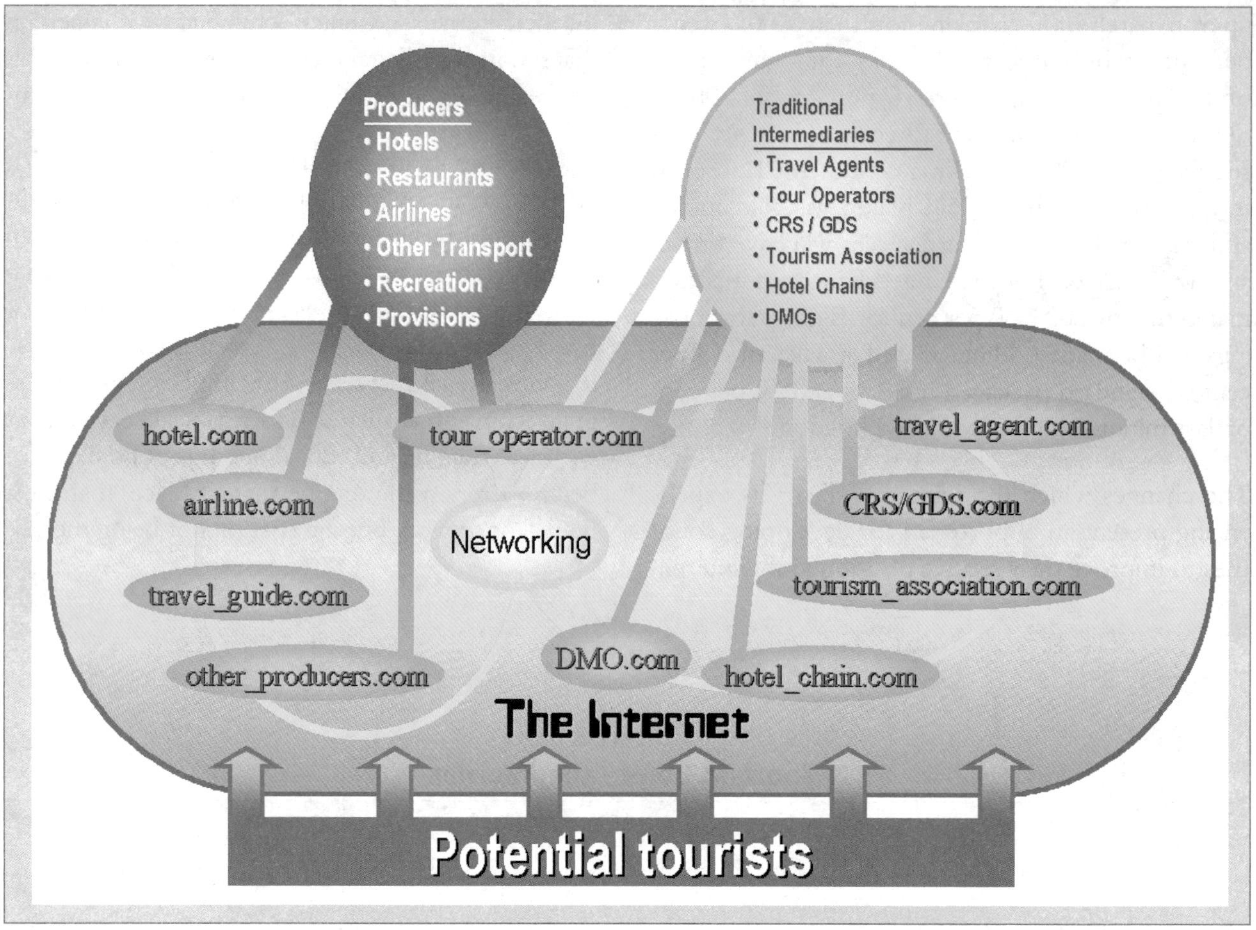

Box 7
OpenTravel Alliance

The OpenTravel Alliance presents a strategy for the travel industry to take advantage of the near universal access to the Internet. Internet and related technologies can significantly affect the way the travel industry operates throughout the global economy. Industry representatives responsible for product distribution can now transform the travel industry into one large supermarket of products and services.

To use the Internet along with established channels, the industry needs a common standard for the communication of information. An industry standard provides a format for communicating data between travellers and travel-related businesses, as well as among the businesses themselves. This standard will encourage development of systems that can help create new collections of services to better meet the demands and expectations of travellers and the travel industry.

The OpenTravel Alliance will produce a standard capable of exploiting the low-cost, fast communications that have arrived with the Internet. When implemented, the standard will encourage the exchange of trip-centric information between all industry participants, regardless of how they are connected.

Although developing a standard may look like a purely technical exercise, it actually requires the active participation of the travel industry. Communication across multiple channels offers significant benefits, thus the travel industry needs a well-defined set of common data elements or vocabulary. An OpenTravel vocabulary can serve as a common language for travel-related terminology and a mechanism for promoting the seamless exchange of information across all travel industry segments. Organizations that already represent the industry, along with key suppliers from all travel segments, have started taking ownership of the concept of OpenTravel. The OpenTravel Alliance has established working groups and task teams, and begun a development process. This has produced a version 1.0 dealing with customer profiles, however, there is still much work to be done. When implemented, OpenTravel can:

- Embrace the backbone of communication protocols on the Internet and elsewhere;
- Include UN and proprietary electronic data interchange travel message sets;
- Extend the OTA standard to new uses as needed.

OpenTravel, the Extensible Markup Language (XML) and the Internet provide an opportunity for the travel industry to communicate across multi-channels. Individuals responsible for the supply and distribution of travel products and services are invited to lead this change by offering their organization's support for and involvement in the OpenTravel Alliance.

The OTA membership list can be obtained at http://www.opentravel.org/opentravel/index.htm.

3. Restructuring the industry

The change in the structure of the tourism industry can best be appreciated by comparing chart 4, depicting Internet-enabled tourism, with chart 3 representing its pre-Internet structure.

When one looks at chart 4, it is immediately obvious that the Internet enables all the traditional players to become infomediaries.[18] Less obvious is the disappearance of the distinction between those intermediaries which only give destination information to travel agents and consumers, and those that both receive and give destination and booking information in all directions of the value chain and also receive, direct or forward payments.

This hierarchy of direction of information and payments is substantially disrupted with the advance of the Internet-enabled tourism industry. From the B2C[19] angle, a tourist may now book on-line any combination of tourism services with or through any combination of producers and inter- or info-mediaries. The B2B[20] dimension of tourism increases significantly when individual producers and inter- or info-mediaries start linking their proprietary booking systems with one another. When networked, they can provide a much greater variety of tourism products.

This linkage of diverse tourism capacity, or networking, as it appears in chart 4, can be achieved using the Internet as an information conduit. Before the Internet, networking was done by concentrating the capacity of individual tourism producers with one of the GDS or CRS computer systems using a privately owned or leased electronic data transfer network. The GDS and CRS would then provide retail agencies with computer terminals through which the agents could query and book the available capacity (rooms, flights, rent-a-car, etc.). Having each developed their own hardware specifications, software and information transfer protocol, the GDS and CRS systems are not good at talking to each other. Producers with proprietary booking systems also find it difficult, if not impossible, to share booking information. A detailed discussion of the GDS and CRS systems from the B2B perspective is presented in chapter 4 of this report.

The Internet may be used to network global tourism capacity with as yet unseen scope and detail. While its reliability and security are sometimes questioned, the benefits of its outreach as a public network and the relatively low cost of access far outweigh such perceived disadvantages.

The lack of broadly agreed data standards has, so far, impeded the development of online tourism. One industry initiative aiming at data interchange standardization is the OpenTravel Alliance (OTA).[21] Box 7 outlines OTA activities.

The proposed OTA standard is based on the XML Internet meta- or markup language.[22] XML enables the transfer of structured data. It consists of data definitions that can be embedded in the viewed website as needed and can be recognized by a software browser. These data definitions remain invisible to the viewer while the software browser "knows" what type of data it is handling. The actual data (e.g. flight number, date, type of vehicle) can then be presented coherently and exchanged in a more accessible and user-friendly manner using the public Internet. XML is licence-free and computer-platform-independent. It is important to note that working standards exist only when users embrace them, and not because any particular body or organization has decided to adopt or enforce them. On the other hand, the existing proprietary networks will not disappear overnight. The tourism industry will most probably witness the coexistence and assimilation of new XML/Internet systems and the old proprietary systems still being used by major GDSs and CRSs in an open network system.

Networked tourism businesses allow individual tourism companies to provide a much larger spectrum of tourism products to potential clients in addition to their core accommodation, travel or other products. This would empower the tourism business to act as a broker and agent, and possibly develop partnerships for referrals and commissions for business generated for third parties.

Making one's own reservation system accessible on the Internet may be technically more efficient in comparison with building a network together with existing systems offered by GDS operators or the new Internet-based infomediaries, as well as other tourism businesses in the locality or market segment. However, doing so defies the purpose of moving forward to websites that incorporate client profiling, personalized and dynamic information delivery and customer/enterprise relationship management. Knowing a customer's preferences, or enabling her or him to express a comprehensive and detailed product preference is useless if the owner of the web page offers only his own limited product (e.g. accommodation only), through an "Internet-enabled" reservation system, and cannot offer products and services from other providers (e.g. travel, rent-a-car, sports activities). The demand for a "one-stop shop" offering a complex tourism product that follows a consumer-customized itinerary of, say, accommodation, travel, car rental and recreational activities will promote B2B relations in the sector.

Having established online booking as a normal operation, the challenge facing the travel industry is bringing online the "travel consultant". The system producing the necessary consumer profiling and, most importantly, the relationship of confidence between consumers and the online automated virtual travel consultant must be of superior efficiency, if unavoidably less human than the relationship that a consumer would hope to develop with her or his travel agent.

With the majority of actors in the tourism market reinventing themselves as infomediaries it is not surprising that today there are more than 1,000 travel websites. However, some industry analysts expect this number to fall substantially, rather than increase, within the next three years.[23]

Not all tourism companies will necessarily become on-line travel agents or Internet-enabled wholesalers or distributors. Some may decide to become destination portals. Others may re-emerge as travel markets, handling bids and offers from many buyers and sellers. Those with strong technical proficiencies may choose to provide technology for running and connecting on-line tourism businesses: e-platforms and e-switching and networking. Each company or organization should pursue a business model that takes advantage of its own competitive strengths.

4. The demise of the travel agent

Much attention has been given to the predicted demise of the travel agent. The travel agent traditionally worked in collaboration with the other players in the tourism distribution chain that used its monopoly on booking information and payment transfers to impose terms and conditions on both tourism producers and consumers which often left much to be desired. The Internet revolution threatens to demonopolize information flows and is doing away with information bottlenecks.

The first and most obvious bottleneck for the prospective tourism consumer is her or his physical "brick and mortar" high-street travel agent community. The traditional wisdom was that it is worth "shopping around" as no one agent had the best price or product for every particular destination or activity. Such activities are increasingly being considered a waste of time and a source of frustration, in particular when a purchase has been made on the basis of the good selling skills of an agent and later the consumer finds the same or a similar product for less. In addition, the actual "shopping experience" is usually relegated to browsing through a colour brochure while waiting in a queue for a "travel consultant" to finish with another customer. Thus, the high-street travel agency is losing its advantage in comparison with the on-line experience. The Internet has the power to provide a comprehensive offer on the shopper's desktop, and consumers are more likely to take up the search for their perfect holiday from the comfort of their home or office, rather than visit and queue in high-street agencies. The agent's advantage of having direct contact with clients is fading rapidly with the improvements in Internet bandwidth and interactivity. Finally, there is a physical limit to how many clients a physical travel consultant can service per day.

From within the distribution chain, travel agents are being bypassed by GDS operators who see economic gains in putting their system on-line and making it directly available to consumers, while saving the costs of commissions and fees paid to agents. The pre-Internet position of travel agents is unsustainable, and agents are exploring their own online strategies as well as possibilities for creating their own CRS and GDS systems. As agents are often too small to pursue global ambitions, one solution may lie in forming business associations of agents. An example of this approach is the United States Travel Agent Registry (USTAR), established in 1996.[24] USTAR brings together 700 travel agents and its main objective is to deploy Genesis, its own CRS system. The advantages for consumers would be that Genesis will offer better diversified travel and tourism experiences. USTAR has been expanding the Genesis concept outside its national market and has grown its network to include Canada, Europe, Australia, India and Mexico.

In order to succeed, future infomediaries must establish themselves as a credible brand with positive consumer recognition. Companies that have a physical presence in the market and an established

Box 8
Asiatravelmart.com

Asiatravelmart.com describes itself as "Asia's number one on-line travel marketplace". It is an Internet-based booking engine platform for travel buyers and sellers around the world to meet, interact and trade travel-related products and services via a secure Internet connection. The company plays a dual role as an operator of an Internet Travel Reservation System and as a clearing house for secure e-commerce payment. Individuals and corporate customers from around the world can interact with over 43,000 travel suppliers and travel agents from more than 200 countries providing over 110,000 wholesale products.

Asiatravelmart.com SES (Secure Electronic Settlement) processes real-time credit card transactions based on both Secure Sockets Layer (SSL) and Secure Electronic Transaction (SET) protocols. Its main purpose is to provide Asiatravelmart.com's global clients with cutting-edge, credit card transactions that are secure and are able to support multiple currencies. Asiatravelmart.com acts as a facilitator to collect payments from buyers on behalf of the suppliers. Asiatravelmart.com SES supports multi-currency transactions over the Internet in Malaysian ringgit, Singapore dollars, Hong Kong dollars, US dollars, pounds sterling, Australian dollars, and Japanese yen.

Asiatravelmart.com offers a spectrum of customized solutions in various versions:

- Internet booking engines
- Internet Payment Gateway (supports multi-currencies)
- Business Travel Management System (BTMS)
- ePartners Engine
- Wireless technologies

More information is available from the company's website: www.asiatravelmart.com.

Box 9
Kalakbayan Travel Systems

Kalakbayan Travel Systems Inc. (KTSI) has created Lakbay.Net, an Internet-based national travel reservation system that primarily aims to provide travellers with accurate Philippine travel information and easy-to-use reservation and payment facilities.

The core commitment is to provide sustainable infrastructure and service to the Filipino people and its travel and tourism industry and the development of Filipino communities through sustainable, grassroots tourism initiatives. KTSI aims to being customer-focused and responsive to the challenges of convenience, accessibility, service excellence, and social responsibility. The Lakbay.Net Internet travel site is KTSI's virtual travel agency. It offers:

- E-commerce enabling services for network members on-line reservation and payment system;
- Various tour package offerings as well as special interests tourism;
- Travel stories by fellow travellers - peer-to-peer communication;
- Destination marketing - a travel information service featuring provinces, cities and municipalities.

The Lakbay.net is based on a community-based approach combined with private sector initiative, with a close partnership with non-governmental organizations (NGOs), and local governmental organizations (LGUs) and central government, using appropriate and diverse technology. Its e-business model brings together the website for B2C commerce, a B2B portal for tourism producers, e-services for the business community, consisting of a booking system and e-payment facilities, and off-line marketing through a dedicated television channel, Lakbay TV.

business, generating sales and earnings, have a double advantage. They should be able to build an online brand identity on top of their offline brand and real-world operations where they physically come into contact with and have immediate feedback from customers. Furthermore, they are in a position to establish and finance their online brand identity in parallel with existing marketing and public relations activities and with funds generated from existing activities.

However, pre-Internet players also have important disadvantages. Often, they are encumbered by a costly network of physical shops and long-standing arrangements, with varying degrees of exclusivity, with producers and agents. Moreover, "technologically challenged" high street agencies and retailers in developed countries often cannot provide comprehensive and detailed information on developing country destinations beyond distributing what is made available to them by the tourism industry wholesalers and distributors. Their knowledge of client habits and preferences is wasted if they cannot respond in an informed manner and provide more than clarifications on the content in the wholesaler's brochure.

Pure infomediaries, like many dot-com start-ups, initially may have to spend substantial funds on marketing campaigns designed to establish their brand from the ground up. Often sales and earnings do not provide enough funds and therefore they incur losses for what investors hope will be a limited time. The turnaround is supposed to happen when revenues increase and marketing costs decrease to a sustainable level.[25]

It is the ambition of every industry player embracing the Internet to become a dominant web point of entry, or "portal", for prospective tourism consumers. While the quality of the B2C relationship is crucial, it is unattainable without a fully developed B2B network, since only through extensive partnerships with other tourism companies can the on-line tourism company, or "etourism.com", offer a comprehensive but flexible and competitive product. For this reason it is very likely that the structure of the Internet-enabled tourism will not be static.

The inability to settle on a definite vision of the future is in itself a liberating feature that encourages entrepreneurial creativity and experimentation. Also, it does away with the common wisdom that all technical or managerial solutions must necessarily be imported from the developed world. Two different, yet equally interesting examples of possible directions to follow are Asiatravelmart.com and Kalakbayan Travel Systems. Their approaches are presented in boxes 8 and 9.

C. Destination organizations

1. Change, management and the Internet

Destination marketing organizations (DMOs), be they government bodies or business associations, can favourably contribute to modernizing the tourism industries of developing countries. It is imperative that the permanent advances in technology and best business practice be shared by all industry players across all categories and countries.[26]

The role of the DMO, an organization dedicated to a single destination, is fundamentally different from the role of an intermediary without a destination focus or responsibility. This particularity has led many DMOs to realize that promoting environmental and cultural sustainability is vital for maintaining their destination's touristic competitive edge. Thus, the term "marketing" seems no longer broad or suitable enough to describe the new responsibilities. The term "destination management organization" is often preferred as it speaks of a heightened level of accountability towards local communities and tourists alike. It also implies a realization that a destination's resources are not inexhaustible and that they need to be managed in order to maximize returns for both present and future generations.

The traditional DMOs are boards of tourism or tourism business associations. While many use the Internet to provide basic destination information, there is a general consensus that much more can be achieved given the existing technical possibilities of the web medium.[27] The usual explanation for underperformance is that the DMO's clients, its local or national tourism industry, are not the actual paying tourists. This inherent dualism can make it difficult to measure the effects of DMO activities, namely increasing the number of arrivals and improving tourists' perceptions of the quality of the tourism experience on offer and their willingness to pay accordingly.

A country's tourism industry usually finances its DMO through taxes or budget contributions. In return, the DMO communicates its country's touristic offer to the international market through various channels, including direct contact with the consumers, through physical offices in the world's major capitals, brochures, film and television and through being present at tourism trade fairs and similar "live" activities as well as through the Internet.[28]

An important objective of DMOs is to build a global brand for the destination and inspire credibility and trust among consumers. Providing information through a website is an attractive and convincing way to achieve this objective as the Internet is increasingly the information medium of choice for travellers worldwide. Dedicated travel portals and consumer communities and bulletin boards have become important sources of, what is assumed to be, unbiased and first-hand travel information.

The World Tourism Organization has focused a significant part of its activities on developing capacity with the local or national DMOs that would allow them to embrace Internet-based communications and e-commerce practice, assume a position of leadership and disseminate knowledge and best practice within their environment. Box 10 provides an outline of the approach used.

The structural changes in the tourism industry caused by the e-commerce revolution may encourage the appearance of a new type of private sector DMO. A tourism company may find it advantageous to broaden its on-line offer by including booking for

Box 10
Model of adaptation to new technologies in services

At each point on the pyramid is one of the three basic aspects of adaptation to the new technologies in services: training, acquisition and use. The "training in new technologies" aspect is at the top of the pyramid in order to underline its strategic importance in a knowledge-based society. The "acquisition of or access to the new technologies" and the "use or usage of the new technologies" aspects are at the base of the pyramid. The arrows connecting the different aspects illustrate how the relationships are organized. The pyramid is framed by four synonyms: "partnership, alliance, group, consortium" to illustrate the different types of associations in which more and more companies are evolving in the era of electronic commerce.

"Training" aspect

The term "training" is used here in a broad sense and also includes the activities aimed at increasing awareness, monitoring, and dissemination of the knowledge related to the new technologies. In a world in which the changes induced by the new technologies are constant, knowledge-acquisition and manpower-training activities occupy a strategic place in companies that want to remain competitive. Companies must at the same time integrate new qualified employees trained in educational institutions in the new technologies, as well as offer training programmes in the new technologies to the employees that they already have. Training and its related activities (e.g. awareness programmes, dissemination, technology watch), which are strategic aspects of a knowledge-based society, must be part of the companies' regular activities.

"Acquisition of new technologies" aspect

Another important facet of the adaptation pyramid involves the acquisition of new technologies. A number of questions can be asked in this regard. What portion of the budget must a company devote to the acquisition of new technologies? Which technologies really meet the company's needs? Which suppliers offer the best quality-to-price ratio for technological products and solutions? How often must the hardware be updated or replaced? Should generic technological products be purchased or should the products be custom-made? What are the advantages of being part of a group or a network that provides technological solutions? Such questions illustrate the problems involved in the acquisition of new technologies.

"Use of new technologies" aspect

The "use" aspect involves the uses that companies make of the new technologies. Specific technologies correspond to two main types of usage: technologies related to the company's internal operations (e.g. management, control) and those related to marketing activities (e.g. distribution, promotion, advertising, building customer loyalty). Internet-related technologies are considered the most strategic within the context of the new economy at the start of the twenty first century. It should be emphasized that tourism and travel products now rank first in purchases made by consumers over the Internet.

The pyramid of adaptation to new technologies illustrates the current trend in the companies in a given sector to join forces so that they can better face the challenges of the new economy.

Note: This model was designed by François Bédard, a special adviser in new technologies for the World Tourism Organization and a professor at the Université du Québec in Montreal.

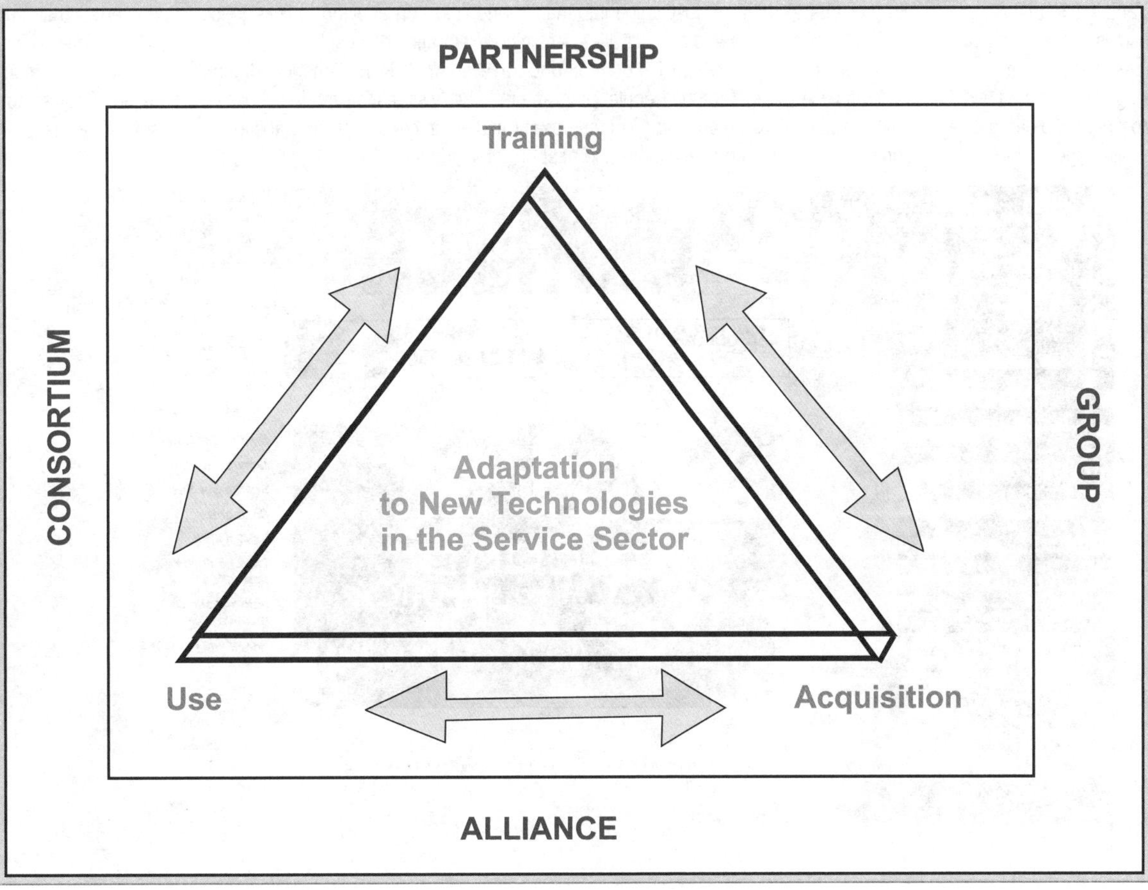

Box 11
Tanzania-web.com

While not using state-of-the-art technology, the Tanzanian Tourist Board has set up a very friendly and informative website which is easy to navigate and can be rapidly uploaded. It is comprehensive on destination information and provides a link to the official web pages of the Government of the United Republic of Tanzania containing useful but not exclusively tourism information. An e-mail link and a chat room provide a degree of interactivity. What could be added in future versions is a frequently asked questions (FAQ) page as well as some weather information. The page on climate is accessible through the info page but not directly from the home page. Travellers are strongly recommended to use verified tour operators. Some are suggested, including several with offices in the United Kingdom. The website does not handle commercial transactions. It is hosted and administered by a London-based company.

Box 12
Jamaicatravel.com

The Jamaica Tourist Board website provides exhaustive destination information and links. In addition to links to local and international tourism companies, there is an abundance of information on events and activities, including exploration of local history, culture and nature. The FAQ page provides interesting material, although it tends to be very specific or geared to travellers from North America. Interaction with local communities is strongly encouraged and the Board runs a special “Meet the People” programme. The “visitor’s forum” does not seem to be very frequented, the last posting being dated 25 April 2001, clearly not taking advantage of the possibilities of the medium. The website has two sets of navigation links on certain pages, which may be confusing. There is no indication of the host or administrator.

other tourism service providers. Its efforts to offer a comprehensive product will lead it to establish relationships with local tourism companies and promote and support their online capabilities. When its offer reaches a critical size and scope, it would practically become a DMO. As documented in table 14, the provision of destination information and reviews is the third largest generator of web page visitors in the on-line travel sector.

2. Internet leadership

Etourism presents a unique chance for traditional DMOs to promote their position in the global industry. In developing countries, their role is doubly important as they can assume a position of leadership in actively promoting the development of an Internet-enabled national tourism industry. DMOs are in a unique position because they can represent the national tourism potential with quality information that answers basic questions any visitor may have: how do I get there, where should I stay, what is there to do and how much will it cost? The Internet provides infinite possibilities for delivering exciting and entertaining information to consumers. Boxes 11 and 12 give examples of web pages from Tanzanian and Jamaican developing country DMOs.

Internet presence is no longer an option for any entity aspiring to be a DMO. Rather, it is an obligation and a question of determination to help develop and improve the national tourism industry that finally pays for the DMO's services. Destination, together with activity, is the first decision a potential tourist makes when looking for a suitable product online. If the DMO cannot produce "instant information gratification", another destination is only a few mouse clicks away. The opportunity to capture a client will be lost as web surfers are notoriously impatient.

The Internet enables the DMO to assume many of the functionalities of the new infomediaries already described. This is because they are, by definition, the focal point of a *de facto* business network. DMOs may spotlight the important domestic tourism companies, although this does not have to be a strict policy orientation, particularly since tourism is a multi-component export product that also contains value added from the broadest spectrum of destination tourism SMEs, non-tourism businesses and public utilities. The goal is to increase tourism revenues which may encompass more than just travel and accommodation earnings. Therefore, the battle for tourist dollars may possibly take precedence over the battle on behalf of the dominant domestic tourism industry players.

The developing country DMO is ideally placed to encourage and help its tourism industry to go on-line and compete in the on-line market. It can help individual companies market their websites. It may develop its own e-commerce applications and should promote consistency across e-commerce platforms that would enable synergetic B2B relations and therefore joint marketing of products and capacity.[29] An often voiced ambition is that the DMO website should become the destination's portal for prospective tourists. This ambition further underlines the need for extensive B2B partnerships in the sector. A destination portal would have to provide links and information on all tourism products offered that are of a reasonable quality and standard.

The DMO can also represent the industry and, if necessary, promote legislative and economic reforms that would reduce costs and technical barriers associated with telecom and Internet service provider (ISP) services, and enable online payments and finance. Individual tourism businesses are often not in a strong bargaining position when negotiating terms and conditions with banks: DMOs can negotiate on behalf of their members to reduce on-line transaction costs and commissions.

DMOs themselves should adopt what is often called a "total Internet strategy"[30] and should help and encourage all tourism companies in their destination to do the same. It consists of a number of elements that are presented in no strict order:

- Define the objectives of online presence;
- Conduct a competition overview;
- Study the consumer, his or her travel and tourism needs, preferences in acquiring product information and payment habits;
- Develop co-marketing strategies with tourism companies and other DMOs;
- Introduce information technology in everyday back-office operations;
- Plan for flexibility in the online development budget;
- Define success criteria and measurements;
- Define technical and design criteria;

- Integrate existing proprietary/legacy systems;
- Develop human resources;
- Focus on product quality;
- Establish online partnerships with all players with maximum data and content interface;
- Provide special assistance to small- and medium-sized enterprises (SMEs) and indigenous suppliers;
- Plan for third- and fourth-generation websites.

Several of these elements are of critical importance to developing countries, and are discussed in more detail below.

Define technical and design criteria

An overwhelming choice and complexity, together with a slow download, often result in consumers permanently avoiding a particular website. In website development, the following key success factors may be considered:

1. Ensure that the message and content of the website are appropriate for its audience; the use of the native language of the tourist is a definite advantage in attracting interest in the destination; DMOs should consider setting up non-English versions of their websites in the native languages of the most numerous visitors;
2. Create a lively design which maintains consumers' interest throughout the website, and reflects the nature of the destination and the DMO's corporate or promotional style; visual appeal and a website full of memory-gobbling graphics are not necessarily the same thing;
3. Do not compromise performance in order to exploit multimedia features; consider having two versions of the website, one being more suitable for low-tech users;
4. Ensure that the functionality of the website meets business objectives, such as awareness raising, information provision and transaction processing; pay constant attention to new user requirements and customer expectations;
5. Ensure that the content is current and accurate and that third-party information published on the website maintains a similarly high standard; do not publish information that cannot be updated;
6. Test the site thoroughly before launching it.

The design criteria may be influenced by the profile of incoming tourists. Learning about their Internet browsing, financial and touristic habits and aspirations is necessary, but this cannot be accomplished exclusively through on-line market research. Interviews and surveys, done "by hand", with tourists and tourism companies (hotels, car rental companies, etc.) may often be necessary.

Focus on product quality

It is important for DMOs to promote investment in developing and enhancing the quality of the tourism product and infrastructure. Neither marketing nor the Internet alone will guarantee success. Technology does not eliminate the need for quality and standards, but increases it as products can be transparently compared. It cannot replace credibility, quality control, knowledge, customer experience and contact. A lack of roads, airports, accommodation, facilities, guides and, most importantly, connection with local life and communities cannot be overcome through software.

However, the use of information technology for processing travellers and their documentation at exit and entry points and the streamlining of administrative procedure can virtually increase infrastructure capacity in multiples, in terms of throughput of travellers. It may also be more cost-effective than building additional arrival halls at airports and employing more migration and customs officers. Points of entry are the first contact that travellers have with a receiving destination. The good and positive experience of efficiency, or the lengthy discomfort of administrative procedures, necessarily becomes part of the destination experience and is an important element for judging product quality. Improving traveller throughput requires that the computers of DMOs, private sector tourism companies and various government offices are on a common network and run a software platform. Existing software solutions are increasingly turning to the XML standards and to the Internet.[31]

SMEs and indigenous enterprises

DMOs should promote and encourage small hotels and resorts to have websites with secure e-commerce capabilities. Funding may be provided for Internet training and technical workshops. The lack of third-party local websites is a major discouraging factor for expanding DMO Internet activities and leadership. E-commerce allows DMOs and local communities to communicate better and more directly with their clients with the aim of putting into practice full costing for the tourism services provided, including environmental and cultural depreciation and maintenance.

E-commerce legislation must be in place to protect consumers from fraud. A lack of trust is the main reason why many consumers are hesitant to buy goods and services on-line. International tour operators inspire consumer confidence by their mere size and physical presence in the tourist's high street. SMEs, by definition, are not global players and legislation for consumer protection must therefore be in place so that tourists do not shy away. Arbitration of conflicts and appropriation of remedies should be swift and efficient. The DMO website should inform consumers about legal details and direct them to the responsible government authorities if they need further clarification.

Plan for third and fourth generation websites

Vital marketing information about consumers can be collected passively while they are on-line, indicating, for instance, how many times a person visited a certain webpage, how long they spent viewing the information, etc., or by motivating them to volunteer information by filling in forms or querying a database. This information is then used to identify and communicate with travellers and explore their preferences for specific destinations and product niches. This in turn enables DMOs to track information on who buys what, goes where, how often and for how long.

Third-generation Internet sites allow for client profiling based on monitoring browsing activity. They can then produce dynamic and personalized content for the visitor. Fourth-generation sites incorporate active customer relationship management, and rely on a more extensive knowledge of the customers' professional or private needs, habits and lifestyles. It is, however, uncertain how far customers will want to go in giving such detailed information as fourth-generation websites are still uncommon.

In order to develop and nurture a one-to-one relationship with customers it is advantageous to communicate by e-mail wherever possible, as it is personal and immediate, but less intrusive than the telephone. Database-filtering tools may be used to ensure that proactive mail shots have a personal feel. Competitions, auctions, chat rooms, feedback forms and quizzes may be organized to encourage customers to tell more about themselves.

A first and fundamental step in moving to a third-generation website is to provide fast and accurate response to e-mail queries from prospecting customers. Monitoring and categorizing these queries will quickly provide the backbone for a useful FAQ page. Existing FAQs, set up in advance of a website going live, should be revised taking into account the substance of the first batch of e-mail queries.

3. Marketing

Website marketing is needed because merely having a website does not guarantee business. Having a website is like being listed in the Yellow Pages. The site still has to be promoted whether on billboards, in magazines, in the press, on television or at trade fairs.

Given the significant resources needed to advertise a website in the off-line media, DMOs, in particular from developing countries, may consider establishing regional and subregional portals that could be marketed jointly and that would direct Internet traffic towards their own websites. Private sector tourism companies should provide finance for such portals if these can improve sales.

A website should have clear and distinct strategies for micro- and macro-marketing. Micro-marketing, or marketing targeted at one particular person or client, is made possible with the Internet and its ability to provide interactive and customized messages to its users. The FAQ and e-mail response system described above are starting points.

Macro-marketing starts with choosing and promoting the website's name or its uniform resources locator (URL) (e.g. www.unctad.org). Provided that the chosen URL has an aural and verbal appeal, using a non-Internet medium for promotion may be worthwhile. Developing good relations with the NGO community and the Government can bring rewards.[32] An exchange of banners and links with other sites could also be beneficial.

Websites should also be listed with as many relevant search engines as possible so that they can be easily found when travellers are searching for information on-line. Getting listed usually requires an on-line submission of the website URL to a search engine (Yahoo, Alta Vista, HotBot, Excite, etc.). From the date of submission, it can take two or more months for the website to be included in the search engine's database and start appearing on query results. The registration service is often free of charge. However, if a website owner wishes to pay a fee, his or her URL can be listed within one or two weeks.[33] Registering with several search engines with one submission is another fee-based service.

A major concern has been how high a ranking a website can achieve on a given query or search. Attaining a high ranking requires a knowledge of how one's website is entered in a search engine's database and how the actual database is catalogued and indexed. Some search engines do manual reviews of websites submitted for listing, while others have automated this process. Several search engines require a submission of keywords along with the URL name, while others use the hidden text embedded in the page by the website owner ("meta-text") to generate searchable keywords, while still others ignore meta-text altogether and search for keywords within the visible text on the website itself. The choice of keywords by the search engine is also a process that can be manual or automated. The information most likely to be included in the keyword search is the website's full name and the contact information on the "home" or "index" page: the first page that opens when keying in the URL.

All search engines reserve the right to refuse inclusion as they are privately owned and are not a public service. The website owner should be informed of the different procedures and techniques for getting listed and attaining a high ranking for each and every search engine. Sufficient time and resources should be allocated to registering the website. If this not done properly, the investments in graphic design, functionality and offline marketing may not bring expected the returns. However, even the most pedantic registration cannot replace offline marketing.

D. Directions for action

The order of presentation should not be regarded as prejudging the importance of the conclusions outlined below. While there is an attempt at comprehensiveness, the speed of new developments and the competitiveness of the tourism sector will inevitably raise new issues and produce new modalities in the relationship between the new and old tourism industries that can only be guessed at. At present, the need for some practical recommendations supersedes the temptation to make futuristic predictions.

The particular role which DMOs can play is described, where relevant, within the particular conclusions. Because action and policy need to be implemented often by both government and businesses, and their associations, it is better to focus on what needs to be done, rather than on who should do it. Each and every developing country may find that it needs a different mix of participants to bring its etourism ambitions to fruition.

1. Improve competitiveness

Tourism producers and destination organizations in developing countries that adopt the Internet and e-commerce best practice have a chance to improve their competitiveness. There is, however, no unique recipe or formula for doing so. Competitiveness can be improved by producing better products, with greater tailoring to clients, more efficiently, faster to market with less waste and fewer inputs, and at better prices. A fundamental role of DMOs is to better the quality of destination information. Such improvements enhance the competitiveness of many, if not all, tourism producers in that destination.

2. Adopt appropriate technology

Infomediaries in developing countries should develop their e-business strategy having in mind the technical capacities of their national or regional tourism producers for using Internet technologies. Solutions must be appropriate for both consumers and producers. Technology adoption may be incremental. A producer may start with an "e-mail only with next day booking confirmation" system and work up to full on-line booking and payment. A third and fourth generation web presence may follow after the previous mode of operation has been mastered. If the confidence and resources are there, a tourism producer may wish to leapfrog several development phases. The national or regional DMOs and government offices should support the ambitions of such businesses and promote best practice.

It will rarely be possible to achieve a homogeneous e-commerce approach for a national tourism industry and all its players. Therefore, a diverse appropriate technology strategy is preferable to forcing "cutting edge" solutions. Broadband and wireless technologies of the "third generation" (3G) with sufficient bandwidth for Internet-based data transfer will soon be available. Devising a technology strategy should not necessarily consider existing fixed-line or terrestrial ISP and telecommunications capacity to be a permanently limiting factor.

3. Interface the traditional with the new economy

Early in this chapter we observed that tourism is an information-heavy product and thus suitable for treatment with information technology tools. The fundamental challenge is to take the traditional tourism product, delineate its information from its physical components, and selectively manage them using Internet and e-commerce technologies — without losing sight of the overall short- and long-term objectives of building competitiveness and sustainability.

4. Build the business web

The winner in the competitive etourism game will be the company or DMO that inspires consumer confidence, through quality data and physical product performance, and is able to offer a comprehensive yet tailor-made product. In the pre-Internet but recent past, providing a comprehensive tourism product meant integrating the different components of travel, accommodation, recreation, and so forth, within one business entity or structure, often with an almost complete reduction in tailoring flexibility. Internet-based information systems and e-commerce do away with this by allowing diverse producers to jointly offer their products and capacity without entering into structured and rigid hierarchical relationships and losing control over their capacity. The tourism business web may eventually take the place of the tourism wholesalers and distributors as the industry locus. This would be in line with the general consensus that B2B e-commerce, embodied in the business web concept, will be the dominant form of commercial Internet use for the foreseeable future.

Assisting the development of tourism business webs may become a priority activity for DMOs. Because of the great technological challenge and lethargic entrenchment in the disappearing pre-Internet vertical market structure, the development of local, national or regional tourism business webs or portals may need to be kick-started by DMOs, often in cooperation with international organizations active in this field. Among themselves, DMOs need to establish substantive cooperation, in particular to profit from one another's detailed knowledge of outgoing tourists' linguistic, touristic and Internet requirements and habits.

5. Know your customers, speak their language

When caught up in marketing campaigns and while negotiating and contracting capacity with distributors, tourism producers can easily lose sight of the need to closely interact with consumers and listen and learn about their needs, and to use this in refining and improving what is on offer. While Internet and e-commerce technologies offer unprecedented possibilities for interactivity and dialogue, traditional surveying and gauging tools estimating customer preferences and satisfaction are still very relevant. Footwork and face-to-face interviewing may be a necessary starting point for building a B2B network or business web. Market research, whatever the technology or even without technology, is a hugely important activity.

A fundamental factor for success is to speak the language of the prospective customers. A successful etourism strategy must assess the linguistic origins of its major client groups and replicate Internet content in their languages. Keeping in mind that etourism is to a great extent a retail business, English-only content will not satisfy, say, German or Japanese clients. But speaking the clients' language is not just a linguistic matter: it may also mean understanding their Internet habits and ways of learning, openness to on-line dialogue and attitudes towards privacy, as well as the underlying legal system. Data privacy and other legal implications are discussed in detail in chapter 6 which is devoted to legal and regulatory developments in electronic commerce.

Developing country DMOs, in cooperation with the DMOs of tourists' countries of origin, may be well placed to acquire and disseminate knowledge about how their tourism industry should adapt their Internet, as well as offline, client interaction in order to maximize competitiveness.

6. Provide clients with on-line payment possibilities

On-line payment facilities for retail clients using credit cards are an absolutely fundamental business tool that must be made available to the national tourism sector. The lack of such possibilities encourages tourism businesses to move their accounting and profit centres off-shore or to financially more advanced destinations. This results in leaving only the physical production of tourism services at the destination and thus decreases employment, reduces foreign currency inflows and encourages transfer pricing.

A lack of on-line payment facilities does not motivate developing country tourism producers to reduce their involvement with global distributors and take charge of marketing and selling their capacity themselves. While criticism of global distributors for unfair trade practices is not uncommon, providing on-line payment facilities for domestic tourism businesses must follow if such criticism is to be taken seriously.

DMOs can provide a voice to the fragmented industry producers in promoting their requests to the financial authorities and banks to provide them with on-line payment. When on-line payment is in place DMOs may, on behalf of the entire tourism industry, negotiate with domestic banks better terms and conditions for on-line payment than particular tourism companies would manage on their own. DMOs may be instrumental in informing their tourism industry about secure transactions and risk management techniques.

7. Enable etourism through training and education

Most of the above actions cannot be implemented without empowering and enabling people to take advantage of new Internet and e-commerce technologies. The quality of information provided and how it is structured depend, fundamentally, on the skills of tourism professionals in the particular destinations. The harvesting, analysis and interpretation of information about clients and their tourism wishes and habits, and its use to improve competitiveness also constitute a human effort.

E-commerce and Internet technology can improve communication and can make doing business easier. The ability of people at both ends of the message or transaction to use these technologies is a precondition for their wide adoption and impact. Persons and institutions in developed countries have had a head start in exploiting the newfound possibilities. Their counterparts in developing countries, and in particular in the tourism sector, may well appreciate the active involvement of an institution such as a DMO to kick-start or accelerate this process at the level of human resources development, training and education.

8. General government policy

The type of national information technology and telecom policy which a government wishes to pursue is a policy decision that typically takes into account national interests and commitments in multilateral trade negotiations. Maintaining certain restrictions on financial institutions and tourism producers (and not only on them), for the sake of stability and possibly at the expense of growth, is also a policy decision. Changing commercial legislation to promote healthy electronic commerce practice and to bolster consumer confidence is another policy issue and is subject to government decision as to its nature and extent. Finally, the level of leadership which national tourism boards and tourism business associations will exercise in embracing the digital age is also subject to decision. The scope for positive government influence is large and proactive decision-making will certainly help maintain, if not improve, a country's competitive advantage in the tourism industry.

Notes

1 http://www.emarketer.com/, "eTravel report cites estimates from 30 research organizations and studies", 4 April 2001; C. H. Marcussen, "Trends in European Internet distribution of travel and tourism services", http://www.rcb.dk/uk/staff/chm/trends.htm: All figures are estimates.

2 In anticipation of possible developments and in view of the timely need for policy debate and direction, the UNCTAD Expert Meeting on Electronic Commerce and Tourism was held in Geneva from 18 to 20 September 2000. It discussed the changes which the international tourism industry is experiencing by adopting the Internet as a business and economic medium. It analysed the change in the structure of intermediation, the breakdown of the traditional value chain and the opportunity given to destination marketing and management organizations. In its recommendations, attached as an annex to this chapter, the Exert Meeting proposed a number of elements for supporting the development of etourism.

3 World Tourism Organization, "Tourism market trends", Madrid, 2001.

4 World Travel and Tourism Council, "Travel and tourism's economic impact", Madrid, March 1999.

5 The Hong Kong Special Administrative Region (SAR) of China generated more than USD 10 billion in tourism revenues in 1999.

6 World Tourism Organization, "Tourism Market Trends", Madrid, 2001.

7 A detailed discussion of the economic relevance of tourism may be found in the UNCTAD publication "International trade in tourism related services: Issues and options for developing countries", TD/B/COM.1/EM.6/2, 8 April 1998.

8 Sometimes information can be first-hand. However, if information turns into a sense of familiarity, this seriously decreases the perceived value of the tourist destination because its primary quality may be its uniqueness and difference from the consumer's everyday environment or experiences. Familiarity erodes this quality.

9 H. Werthner and S. Klein, "ICT and the changing landscape of global tourism distribution", Electronic Markets, 1999, Vol. 9, no.4.

10 The "click-to-brick" ratio represents the proportion of orders generated online. Payment and physical delivery may be offline, however.

11 Unique visitors are counted using their unique Internet protocol address, as assigned by their Internet service provider. They are counted only once during a predetermined period (e.g. unique visitors per month or unique visitors per year), no matter how many times they visit the website throughout this period. Software that tracks and counts how many people have viewed a website can distinguish between visitors who visit the site only once and those who repeatedly return to the it. This is different from "hits" which indicate the number of requests for web pages from a website.

12 The category "on-line agents" refers to online only or Internet pure-play tourism agencies that do not own significant physical production capacities such as high-street retail outlets.

13 This category relates to websites that process few or no commercial transactions but serve as destination guides and destination information centres. They may consequently provide links and refer tourists to businesses that provide accommodation, travel and other services related to a particular destination and generate their own earnings in this way. In some cases they may qualify as DMOs, provided that their level of commitment is high and they promote sustainable destination management practice.

14 Sabre Holdings Corporation and USA Networks are the respective parent companies. Travelocity.com is a wholly owned subsidiary of Sabre, while USA Networks owns 75 per cent of Expedia.com. Sabre is a global leader in electronic travel distribution. USA Networks is a major cable television operator. For more information see http://biz.yahoo.com/p/t/tsg.html, http://biz.yahoo.com/p/t/tvly.html and http://biz.yahoo.com/p/e/expe.html.

15 http://www.thestandard.com/, "The net - more U.S. travelers don't leave home without it", 12 June 2001.

16 Genesys-The Travel Technology Consultancy, "The Battle of Brand" , Travel Trade Gazette, http://www.genesys-consulting.com/ttg/article000425.htm

17 World Tourism Organization, "Marketing tourism destinations online", Madrid, 1999, pg. 4.

18 For a more detailed discussion on disintermediation in e-commerce, and the growing role of infomediaries, see "Building confidence: Electronic commerce and development", UNCTAD/SDTE/Misc.11, United Nations publication, Sales No.E.0011D.16, 2000.

19 The expressions "B2C", "B2B" and "B2G" mean respectively to "business-to-consumers", "business-to-business" and "business-to-government", which are the three major forms of e-commerce. For a more detailed explanation, see "Building confidence" (note 18).

20 Ibid.

21 http://www.opentravel.org/opentravel/index.htm

22 http://www.w3.org/XML/1999/XML-in-10-points

23 http://www.wired.com/news/ebiz/, "T2: Budding travel monopoly?", 8 June 2000.

24. United States Travel Agent Registry, http://www.genesistds.com

25 Genesys - The Travel Technology Consultancy, "Online travel entrepreneurs" in Travel Trade Gazette, http://www.genesys-consulting.com/ttg/article000228.htm

26 The role of government or national institutions in creating an enabling environment has been dealt with in some detail in the UNCTAD publication "Building confidence" (see note 18).

27 A good overview can be had by going to http://www.towd.com, a portal that provides links to many DMO websites.

28 http://www.towd.com provides an exhaustive search of on-line and presence and contact details of most DMOs world-wide.

29 The Tourism Authority of Thailand has developed a "do-it-yourself" e-commerce kit for its members that allows a tourism company to create, on the basis of templates, an internet storefront, an on-line catalogue, an on-line reservation system, real-time secure payment, order tracking and an intelligent search system. UNCTAD, in its efforts to bring more least developed country DMOs online, has developed a Model Tourism Portal and a corresponding training programme in order to bring about local empowerment and ownership of web content, as well as sustainable and best practice website management and administration.

30 A total Internet strategy is often defined as using the web to unite and integrate in one's own website and previously disjointed applications such as e-mail, databases, third-party web content and payment transactions. The Internet becomes the top-level application providing a seamless fulfilment of client demands.

31 SITA (http://www.sita.org) is an e-commerce travel industry association that has developed several IT solutions for handling passengers and their documentation.

32 Kalakbayan Travel Systems Inc. (www.lakbay.net) has a dedicated travel channel on cable television which it uses to inform consumers and "push" them towards the Internet for more information and for bookings.

33 This is true at the time of writing but may vary considerably, with the registration delays likely to increase in the future because of the ever-growing number of applications for registration. Payment may also be required for for-profit entities in the business listings categories of the search engines' databases.

Annex

Recommendations of the UNCTAD Expert Meeting on Electronic Commerce and Tourism, Geneva, 18 - 20 September 2000

(Adopted by the Expert Meeting at its closing plenary meeting on 20 September 2000, and published in UNCTAD document TD/13/COM3/30 - TD/13/COM3/EMA/3)

1. Individual experts expressed their views on policies and strategies to be adopted by developing countries in order to increase their participation in electronic commerce in tourism and on the possible role of UNCTAI) and other international organizations in realizing the development benefits of those policies and strategies. The following is a summary of recommendations made by various experts. Not all the views were necessarily shared by all the experts; consequently, the summary reflects a wide diversity of views.

A. Recommendations to Governments and enterprises

2. Solutions for e-commerce in tourism should also address broader issues of electronic commerce in general, and their effects and benefits for development.
3. Ensure that etourism is considered alongside an appropriate multisectoral strategy for improved Internet access and telecommunications infrastructure, and use this strategy to influence investment in telecommunications.
4. Liberalize telecommunications and Internet services in order to attract new investment, reduce prices and improve the quality of service.
5. Create and continually update local content on the Internet in local languages and languages of the most important tourism consumers in order to provide information and databases on tourism experiences and attractions and general information about destinations.
6. Review available research, and conduct additional research when necessary, on e-commerce in tourism in order to provide information on market trends, consumer needs, website use, demographic profiles and the impact of non-availability of online payments and other information that may support the development of a sustainable tourism industry.
7. Implement appropriate mechanisms in developing countries for the safer use of electronic payments in tourism transactions at the local, regional and global levels.
8. Promote tourism that is sustainable in a social, cultural, environmental and economic sense. To this end, develop partnerships and links among all parties in the tourism supply chain, including government, destination management organizations (DMOs), local tourism service providers, travel agents and other intermediaries, global distribution systems (GDSs), travel portals and the information and communication technology (ICT) sector, as well as the local community and foreign suppliers.
9. Integrate new etourism channels into traditional and non-traditional distribution channels and foster the development of special-interest tourism websites, for example for eco-tourism and cultural tourism. These channels could be supported by the development of a common product database to share development costs and provide impartial information.
10. Develop a national vision, plans and policy guidelines on etourism and involve industry players and local communities in developing tourism strategies and products within the context of overall tourism marketing and development strategies.
11. Establish appropriate laws and regulations and service standards in order to build trust and consumer confidence and to ensure privacy and the protection of consumers and intellectual property rights. Also, cooperate in setting up an international framework to protect travellers conducting transactions on the Internet.
12. Call upon Governments to make joint efforts to ascertain whether the international e-tourism market is working in a way that does not promote unfair or anti-competitive practices which constitute barriers to the tourist industry for developing countries.
13. DMOs at all levels should be strengthened in order to be in a better position to coordinate the relevant public and private actors and thus be enabled to play a broader role. They will be essential for positioning developing countries

to be able to take advantage of new ICTs. In order to be effective, DMOs have to be representative of relevant stakeholders at the local level, institutionally established and provided with the necessary human, financial and logistical resources. Ultimately, this could allow developing countries to benefit from vertical cooperation and integration.

14. With respect to e-commerce, DMOs should play a broader role. They should promote destination markets in key tourism portals, search engines and gateways and also list destinations under as many links as possible so that descriptors are not limited to, for example, tourism or names of the country alone.

15. Build and enhance destination brand image in order to improve consumer awareness and confidence, and reflect this in any web strategy.

16. Develop capacity building through training and basic education in relevant fields, for example informatics and telecommunications, and conduct awareness campaigns about e-tourism.

17. Governments and donor agencies should stimulate activities in e-commerce through grants, tax incentives, special credit lines and other seed funding arrangements, and empower DMOs with technology and financial resources.

18. Online transactions must be combined with the development of physical tourist attractions, satisfactory product fulfilment and supply of support services, such as banking, insurance, transport and customs. Since not all suppliers will be ready for online transactions, destination strategy should include offline transactions support, local call centres and use of local knowledge.

19. Traditional travel agents and other intermediaries should transform themselves by adopting new information technologies and enhancing their expertise and creativity, so as to improve their efficiency and ensure their continuity.

B. Recommendations to UNCTAD

20. In cooperation with other appropriate bodies UNCTAD should:

21. Analyse the effect that tourism-related e-commerce has had or will have on development, and development policies. The objectives of this analysis should include identification of positive, negative or indifferent effects, as well as their causes, and formulation of recommendations for maximizing the development benefits of e-commerce.

22. Disseminate information to developing countries on approaches and elements of government policies on etourism, taking into account successful experiences in the developing and developed countries.

23. Give priority attention and support to the development of sustainable etourism in developing countries.

24. Stimulate exchanges of experiences among Governments and tourism enterprises of developing countries on the one hand, and Governments and enterprises of other countries on the other hand, and disseminate to developing countries information on experiences in e-tourism through website and periodic publications, inter-organizational cooperation, etc.

25. Signpost and carry out case studies and analysis of e-commerce in tourism, including problems of online payments, trust-building issues such as encryption and electronic certificates or signatures, and new technologies such as interactive television and cellphones that can support e-commerce; and collaborate with tourism research centres and academic institutions in order to promote capacity building and knowledge in etourism in developing countries.

26. Encourage the adoption of open data standards, e-signatures and new Internet developments (e.g. new top-level domains such as geo) where these would assist in opening up the etourism market place, taking into account in particular the development dimensions, of the sector; and ensure that e-commerce serves equitably the needs of developed and developing nations, and can contribute to social and environmental accountability within the tourism industry.

27. Promote exchanges on how to increase the effectiveness of DMOs.

28. Suggest possible arrangements for UNCTAD to act as an incubator for e-commerce and small and medium-sized etourism enterprises through appropriate United Nations programmes.

29. Examine ways to promote the visibility of tourism portals in developing countries and possible arrangements for the establishment of a global, central tourism portal for the benefit of developing countries.

30. Assist in the promotion of partnerships between DMOs in developing countries on the one hand, and intermediaries and origin country DMOs on the other hand, and encourage joint marketing within DMOs in developing countries.

31. Develop capacity building through training and basic education in relevant fields, for example informatics and telecommunications, and conduct awareness campaigns about e-tourism.

Chapter 4

BUSINESS-TO-BUSINESS ELECTRONIC MARKETPLACES: THEIR NATURE, IMPACT AND PROSPECTS IN DEVELOPING COUNTRIES

A. Introduction

This chapter examines business-to-business (B2B) electronic commerce.[1] In the last few years B2B transactions have witnessed a rapid growth in various types of market places (e-markets)[2] in which large numbers of buyers and sellers are connected to form online trading communities in order to exchange goods, services and information. The chapter provides an overview of the nature of and ongoing changes in e-markets, their economic impact and prospects for their growth in developing countries.

Some published sources show that Internet-based B2B e-marketplaces are becoming a dominant force in overall B2B e-commerce. It is predicted, for example, that by 2004 e-markets will be the single largest component of B2B e-commerce. Forrester Research, for instance, predicts that e-markets will account for 45 to 77 per cent of B2B e-commerce supply chains by 2004, while International Data Corporation (IDC) predicts that in 2004 e-markets will represent 56 per cent of all B2B e-commerce.[3]

The rapid growth of e-markets is attributed in part to technological developments that provide applications that can power e-market transactions, but more importantly it arises from the benefits that can accrue to sellers and buyers. Current trends show a number of important features that are emerging in e-markets. These include the growth of consolidations and a preference among large enterprises for using private e-markets as opposed to public or independent or third-party e-markets. Also, e-markets are increasingly being seen as a framework for promoting collaboration among trading partners across the entire supply chain.

Available data show that the bulk of e-market transactions take place in the United States, although there is a sizeable expansion of B2B e-market activity in Europe and to a lesser extent in the Asia-Pacific region. As a result, most of the published case studies and data relate to experiences of United States firms.[4] While the United States environment is significantly different from that of the majority of developing countries, it is nevertheless expected to provide a fair indication of the opportunities available, and the challenges faced by the developing countries.

B. The main features of B2B e-markets

B2B e-markets are a fast-growing component of e-commerce and are introducing a variety of new features and business models. This section outlines the major elements of those market places and how they compare with other forms of e-commerce.

1. Comparison with B2C e-commerce

There are a number of important differences between B2B and B2C e-commerce. The main comparisons between them are summarized in table 15. It is evident that the characteristics of B2B e-markets are considerably different from those of B2C e-commerce. Despite the existence of fundamental differences between the two, there are also important areas of convergence. This applies to the similarity of transactions for certain products or services and the existence of linkages between B2B and B2C transactions in the supply chain.

As regards products and services, certain transactions in B2B and B2C are not easily distinguishable. Good examples include online purchases of airline tickets, books and software. These tend to be purchased in small quantities and perhaps at similar prices both for businesses and consumers.

Table 15
Comparison between B2B e-markets and B2C e-commerce

Market characteristic	B2B e-markets	B2C e-commerce
Value/size of transactions	Very large value	Relatively small, including mini orders
Buyer-seller relationship	Usually long-term, based on contracts; personal, non-price factors important to buyer; market may be seller- or buyer-driven; integration between market place and traders' and third-party back-end systems	Mostly short-term and spot sales; transactions between strangers, price being the main consideration for the buyer; market predominantly buyer-driven; no integration with buyers' systems.
Participants	Many participants interacting in a given transaction - networks of suppliers; partners and buyers.	Many consumers dealing directly with single sellers (one supplier, many customers);
Functionality requirements	High degree of functionality required; factors other than price information essential	Less functionality required beyond price information
Pricing	Negotiated prices, long-term contracts, auctions, catalogue prices	Fixed prices, mainly catalogue
Payment system	Credit cards, bank credit, electronic account-to-account payments	Credit cards, electronic account-to-account payments
Order fulfilment	Stringent requirements regarding availability of products and particulars of fulfillment; global express deliveries	Fulfillment requirements more flexible and less stringent, global express deliveries
Infrastructure requirements	More complex, customized	Minimum requirement – a browser with Internet access
Entry conditions	Cost of technology and economies of scale may create entry barriers, especially for sellers	No major entry barriers
Network effects	Beneficial to both sellers and buyers	Beneficial to sellers and less to buyers
Intermediaries	Intermediaries are bypassed but also used in some cases	Intermediaries are bypassed
Product designation	Custom-made according to specification	Standardized
Sales procedures	On-line catalogues, tender	On-line catalogues
Security issues	Network security and corporate privacy	Protection of consumer information and needs

Source: Compiled from various sources; for example, see Sculley and Woods (2001), and Morgan Stanley Dean Witter (2000).

A development that has also contributed to this form of convergence is the growth of small, often one-person businesses that operate at home or in small offices. It is generally difficult to distinguish between the business owner and the consumer, and hence the type of transaction.

The second form of B2B-B2C convergence relates to the linkages on the supply chain. Some companies are integrating their Internet strategies straight from B2C retailing for their products to their internal information systems and on to external B2B supply orders with other companies. Thus orders from consumers may be electronically transmitted to contractor manufacturers that make the products and ship them directly to distributors and buyers. A number of initiatives are being undertaken by a number of technology companies to develop market-place applications that can integrate supply chains through e-market networks that include B2B and B2C transactions.[5]

2. Comparison with other B2B e-commerce

B2B e-markets differ from other forms of B2B e-commerce in that the e-markets involve a large number of buyers and sellers that engage in many-to-many transactions and relationships. They create a trading community in which buyers' orders are matched with sellers' offers and the trading partners benefit from other forms of collaboration. This is different from one-to-many B2B e-commerce models, in which single companies establish websites to sell or buy from other companies. It is only when single buying companies or single selling companies team up to create an environment of online multiple buyers and sellers that an e-market is established.

3. Comparison with traditional stock and commodity exchanges

There is also a distinction between the new types of Internet-based B2B e-markets on the one hand and traditional types of exchanges, particularly stock exchanges and primary commodity exchanges, on the other hand. Stock exchanges are places where businesses sell and buy shares, stocks and bonds (securities). They are owned by stockbrokers or members' firms, although some of them now include membership from the general public. They are auction markets that take place on the physical floor of the exchange and the transactions are conducted by public competitive bidding. Trading is done through brokers and specialists and the procedures are largely manual, although some degree of automation is being introduced.

Commodity exchanges, on the other hand, are organized markets for buying and selling such primary commodities as coffee, sugar, grain, cotton, rubber, crude oil and metals, for example gold, silver, copper, aluminium, tin and nickel. Commodities may be traded in (i) the spot market, where commodities are available for immediate transactions; (ii) in the forward market, where the transactions take place at some specified date in the future between specific contracting parties; or (iii) in the futures market. As in the forward market, in the futures market the parties agree to buy or sell a specific quantity of a commodity on a particular date in the future, but they try to reduce risk by hedging against fluctuations in commodity prices. By fixing the price of the commodity in advance, futures contracts enable buyers and sellers to hedge against spot price fluctuations. Also, through futures contracts participants may make a profit by speculating on price movements.

It is evident from the above that there are fundamental differences between traditional stock and commodity exchanges and B2B e-marketplaces. First, in B2B e-markets intermediaries do not play a pivotal role in the transaction processes to the same extent as they do in stock/commodity exchanges. Second, in the stock/commodity exchanges there may be no long-term contractual relationships between trading partners. By contrast, e-markets go beyond the matching of buyers and sellers by providing a trading community in which the whole range of activities on the supply chain are integrated, including the back-end functions of the trading partners. Third, goods and services traded on e-markets are priced using a variety of pricing models, including dynamic, negotiated pricing, while in stock/commodity exchanges auctions and public competitive bidding are the main pricing mechanism. Fourth, in e-markets trading is largely automated, while in the stock and commodity exchanges, transactions rely on "physical" auctions on the exchange floor.

Finally, in e-markets the Internet provides the backbone of the market activities. While in stock and commodity exchanges the Internet is being used to exchange information, the core functions take place physically on the floors of the exchanges. In recent years, however, a new form of security trading has emerged - the electronic communications network (ECN). ECNs are essentially small stock exchanges that provide an electronic marketplace in which buyers and sellers are matched automatically. Examples of companies that operate such markets include Instinet, Archipelago, Island, Tradepoint and Easdaq. These companies provide trading opportunities for institutional investors (B2B) as well as for retail investors (B2C).[6]

4. Main categories and ownership of B2B e-markets

E-markets may be grouped into various categories according to different criteria such as ownership, the types of products traded and the main groups of traders involved. Because of the multiplicity of these criteria, it may not be possible to fit them into single, non-overlapping categories. The main broad categories are described below.

Vertical and horizontal e-markets

Vertical e-markets are primarily industry-focused in that they provide exchange capabilities for sellers and buyers dealing in homogeneous products or in a particular industry that trades in direct goods, that is those goods that are a part of the final product created by the enterprise. They provide integrated exchanges in sectors such as health care, food, environment, manufacturing, communications and advanced technology[7].

Horizontal e-markets, on the other hand, are multi-industry and provide exchange capabilities for sellers and buyers in more than one industry to procure generic, indirect goods or services, that is goods that are not part of the final product of an enterprise. Such goods can be used in multiple industries, such as office furniture, office supplies and construction materials, financial accounting, human resources services and items that are referred to as MRO (maintenance, repair and operations).[8]

The distinction between vertical and horizontal e-markets tends to be blurred where companies try to attain scale economies by combining their purchasing of indirect goods with that of goods which are part of their core supply chain. Some horizontal e-markets have started to integrate with vertical e-markets, thus permitting traders in a vertical market to have access to horizontal markets, and vice versa.[9]

Independent, third-party B2B e-markets are owned and operated by enterprises that are not considered to be a trading partner. Their role is to provide a forum for buyers and sellers to find each other and complete online transactions. They rely on order matching and transaction fees for their revenue. A third-party e-market may be a propriety exchange owned and operated by a single large company functioning as a neutral intermediary[10] or operated by several independent companies that have no affiliation with buyers or sellers[11]. It may, however, also cooperate with leading firms in a given industry, in certain cases receiving equity investment from players in the industry. These include most of the early breeds of venture-backed e-markets.

Third-party exchanges are more likely to grow in markets that are characterized by fragmented demand and supply. They would tend to succeed in such markets because they can reduce transaction costs by aggregating and matching buyers and sellers. If, however, only the buy side is fragmented, the benefits for sellers would be reduced, and conversely the benefits on the buy side would be reduced if only the sell-side markets were fragmented.

Independent third-party e-markets are, in principle, attractive to both buyers and sellers, but their success would largely be dependent on whether they can actually attract sufficient numbers of buyers and sellers into the market place and generate cash flow from transaction fees. To achieve this, some third-party e-marketplaces have had to develop partnerships with bricks-and-mortar companies. However, independent e-markets that accept equity investments either from buyers or sellers may lose their neutrality and hence their attractiveness to one or other side of the market.

Industry consortia

Some existing bricks-and-mortar companies have come together to create their own independent e-markets. These may be organized either by buying companies or by selling companies.

Buyer-driven e-markets are formed by large enterprises dealing in large-volume purchases.[12] In these e-markets the traders are also owners. These may be private, with content and management being under the buyer, or they may be public with the management being placed under a separate venture such as a consortium. Having established the markets, sellers are either encouraged or forced to trade in the market place.

Supplier- or seller-driven e-markets are formed by large supply companies. They are less numerous than buyer-driven ones. Their creation may be for defence, aimed at pre-empting the possibility of their customers setting up buyer-driven exchanges. Alternatively, they may be set up in response to the presence of buyer-driven e-markets.[13]

In buyer- and seller-driven e-markets, the companies that establish the markets are likely to be the ones that are better placed to reap more of the benefits from the market. Thus in a seller-driven exchange the exchange acts as an aggregator of supplies and plays the role of an auction for buyers. On the other hand, in a buyer-driven exchange the e-marketplace aggregates a large number of buyers to create the force of a large single buyer and negotiate with suppliers on the buyers' behalf.

Industry consortia B2B e-markets have the advantage of secure support from large sellers or buyers. The buyer-driven e-markets in particular appear to be the easiest to create since in most trades the buyers seem to have the balance of power. Seller-driven exchanges may face difficulty in attracting large buyers that may already have access to volume discounts. Generally, industry consortia have faced a number of impediments that have limited their growth. These have included the fact that their members are commercial rivals, difficulties in creating a suitable ownership and corporate structure and in integrating their disparate back-end technologies, failure to provide a neutral trading environment and risks in sharing information.[14]

Private B2B e-markets

These are private or proprietary trading exchanges operated and owned by single owners as opposed to consortia. Their objective is to support or enhance their core businesses.[15] There is a growing consensus in the industry that private B2B e-markets will become the most preferred business model. For example, Deloitte Consulting found in a study that 73 per cent of firms surveyed said that private e-marketplaces would become the most important form of collaborative commerce for their business.[16] The study pointed out that the complex capabilities that public e-marketplaces have been struggling to implement were now being successfully implemented in private e-marketplaces.

Another study, by Boston Consulting Group, also predicts that private e-marketplaces will become dominant.[17] The study notes, however, that the ability of single sellers or buyers to set up their own e-marketplaces could be overestimated. The study showed that 54 per cent of sellers and only 13 per cent of buyers expected that single-seller sites would serve as their primary e-marketplace for any given product. Overall, however, private e-marketplaces are expected to play an increasing role in B2B e-markets.

5. Revenue sources

The creation, hosting and operation of B2B e-marketplaces are functions undertaken by a variety of companies. The sources of revenue of the operations of the e-marketplace are therefore varied, depending on whether a company is an application service provider or market-place operator or owner. The sources include transaction fees, auction service fees, sales of software, advertising, subscription fees and professional service fees.

Transaction fees

These are the principal source of revenue for many e-marketplaces. The fees are levied either as a fixed amount or as a percentage of the value of the transaction. In some cases different fees may be charged for individual components of a transaction, such as invoicing, payment services, cash transfers and transport documents. The transaction fee is often charged to the seller, but there are market places where they are charged to the buyer or to both sellers and buyers.

Software sales and licences

Companies that host market places or provide software used by sellers and buyers derive some revenue from software in the form of licence fees and maintenance of the installed system.

Advertising fees

Advertising fees may be an important source of revenue for some e-marketplaces, although some industry observers consider that the growth of Webvertising has been quite limited. A major move from advertising in other forms of media such as newspapers and television to the Web has not materialized. Consequently, for e-marketplaces, Webvertising is likely to remain a minor revenue source compared with other sources.

Subscription/membership fees

These are a common source of revenue and are imposed as flat periodic fees for example on a monthly or annual basis. A few e-marketplaces have tried to charge a subscription fee per transaction. However, this method appears to be unpopular with sellers or buyers as it tends to impose higher charges than flat periodical rates, and also tends to be confused with transaction fees described above.

Professional service charges

Providers of software that is used in e-marketplaces usually give training and other services to implement the installed applications. These services are charged to users. This applies particularly in user companies that do not possess their own internal professional technology departments and have to rely on third-party application service providers. There are a number of other revenue sources such as data mining charges and sponsorship income.

The relative importance of revenue sources will depend on the way the e-marketplace is structured in terms of ownership and service provision. In a market place where the bulk of the operations are provided by third parties that do not own the marketplace, user fees paid by buyers and sellers will be a critical factor in generating revenue. On the other hand, if the market place and the applications used are owned and operated by the trading parties, user fees may be less important. In this case, the owner/operator may attach greater importance to the market place as a promoter of trading relationships and transactions and for building customer loyalty rather than as a generator of user fees.

C. The market structure of e-markets and competition policy implications

This section examines the level of market concentration and entry conditions in B2B e-markets, both of which are essential to an understanding of the behaviour of markets and the degree of competition.[18] It may also help in the overall assessment of the opportunities available to developing countries to create e-markets. In addition, it describes issues of competition rules related to B2B e-markets.

1. Level of concentration

The level of concentration relates to the number of market places and the distribution of transactions over various market places. It also relates to the scope of the boundaries of markets within which e-markets operate. For example, the market boundaries of vertical e-markets could be defined in terms of the coverage of industries served by the e-markets, while for horizontal exchanges a much wider spectrum of exchanges would be included. Players in B2B e-markets tend to maintain links with traditional product and service trading channels, thus making the definition of their market boundaries complex.

Estimates of the number of market places in different types of e-markets vary widely. Chart 5 provides estimates of total B2B e-markets formed up to the year 2000. Table 16 shows the number of horizontal and vertical B2B exchanges worldwide in 2000. While most projections of future market places show that there will be an explosive increase in their number, there are no reliable figures on the exact number of e-markets actually in operation, as some estimates include e-markets that may have been announced but not yet commenced operation. Even some of those that may have established a physical presence may not have carried out any significant transactions yet.

Chart 5
Number of B2B e-markets formed up to the year 2000

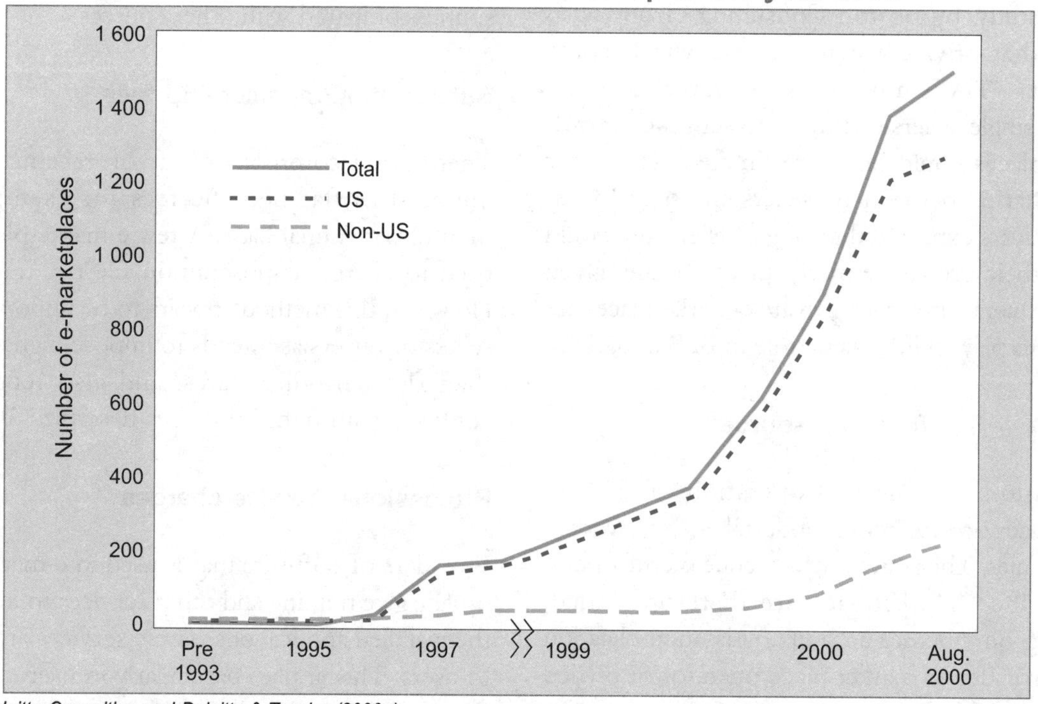

Source: Deloitte Consulting and Deloitte & Touche (2000a).

Table 16
Estimated number of vertical and horizontal B2B exchanges worldwide in the year 2000

Vertical exchanges	
Advertising and media	8
Agriculture	41
Automotive	20
Aviation	10
Chemicals and plastics	47
Construction	35
Electronic and IT components	26
Energy	26
Environment	8
Financial	32
Food and beverage	51
Forestry and wood	11
Health care	41
IT products and services	26
Machinery and vehicles	19
Marine	3
Metals	15
Packaging	6
Printing	26
Pulp and paper	14
Telecom	31
Textiles	10
Transport	48
Other	83
Horizontal exchanges	
Hospitality	9
MRO	24
Office	7
Services	20
Other	54
Total	**751**

Source: eMarketer (2001).

Equally important, the number of e-markets tends to vary between different industries or activities and therefore the levels of concentration and competition should be seen in terms of individual industries or market segments. Some small industries such as security services may have very few exchanges. Also, some niche markets such as fromage.com and e-instantcoffee.com involve one or two e-markets.

By contrast, large industries such as chemicals and financial services tend to have a large number of exchanges. In these cases, however, there are usually a few market leaders accounting for the largest share of the total market. The degree of competition in the larger e-markets may be restricted further by collaboration or inter-market integration arrangements. Examples of such arrangements include relationships established between Oracle and SciQuest and between Ariba and Chemdex.com that attempt to link up horizontal markets with specialized vertical markets. The growth of collaboration is increasingly being supported by technology companies, such as i2Technologies that are trying to promote systems suitable for creating co-operation between several e-markets. There are also a number of other factors that may influence the level of competition, such as differences in levels of functionality, type of ownership, specialization and availability of financial backing.

2. Entry conditions

The competitiveness of e-marketplaces can also be assessed in terms of the ease with which they can be set up. The ease of entry influences the number of e-markets that are actually established and hence the level of concentration. It also determines the presence of potential competition, which in turn is an important stimulus to actual competition. The factors that determine the ease of entry include the cost of establishing an e-market, the length of time it takes to establish it, the disadvantages faced by a new e-market when compared with already established markets, access to technology and the cost of winding up if the e-marketplace fails.

E-markets are generally characterized by low barriers to entry, and this tends to encourage the establishment of many market places. However, e-markets that attain critical mass[19] first tend to create a competitive advantage and erect significant barriers to entry by other exchanges. In this connection, analysts expect that the high rates of failure experienced in B2C e-commerce may be replicated in B2B e-markets. For example, in B2C e-commerce it has been relatively easy to establish online bookstores, and many have been created. However, only a few of them, for example Amazon, have achieved critical mass and have emerged as market leaders, thus providing them with commercial advantage over other potential online bookstores. In the B2B environment e-market operators do recognize the fundamental importance of critical mass and the role of market leadership. This has created a high degree of competition to gain leadership and in the process only the successful first movers are expected to survive.

Successful e-markets will be the ones that will become most attractive to buyers and sellers, and such an attraction tends to become self-sustaining. Also, major buyers and sellers are more likely to retain their membership in a successful e-market rather than move to newly established ones. There could, however, be exceptions to this tendency. In industries where buyers or sellers may be slow to accept e-markets, first movers may not necessarily be successful and become dominant. They may instead provide lessons to subsequent movers, who may introduce innovations through which they may attract buyers and sellers and thus achieve success and dominance.

Overall the situation as it stands may be described as one in which many B2B e-markets are still in their early stages of creation, and it is too early to assess the true degree of concentration and competition. The trend so far has shown the ability of first movers to establish market leadership, even though in some cases new entrants have been able to compete with first movers and succeed in attaining market leadership.

3. Competition policy issues

Governments and competition authorities have an interest in B2B e-marketplaces in so far as they have implications for competition policy. However, given that many B2B e-markets are still in their formative stages, competition authorities have only started to pay attention to the possible competition issues that such markets may raise. In the United States, for example, the Federal Trade Commission (FTC) has issued a report[20] in which it recognizes that B2B e-markets are likely to have pro-competitive attributes. So far, authorities have been applying existing antitrust standards to determine the presence of anticompetitive behaviour. The FTC, for example, has approved the establishment of Convisint.[21] However, the FTC's stance may change as more experience is gained about B2B e-market business models. In the case of Convisint, the FTC indicated that it reserved the right to re-examine its decision in order to reinvestigate possible antitrust concerns.

Chart 6
Projected growth of on-line B2B sales in the United States, by industry, 2000-2004
($ billions)

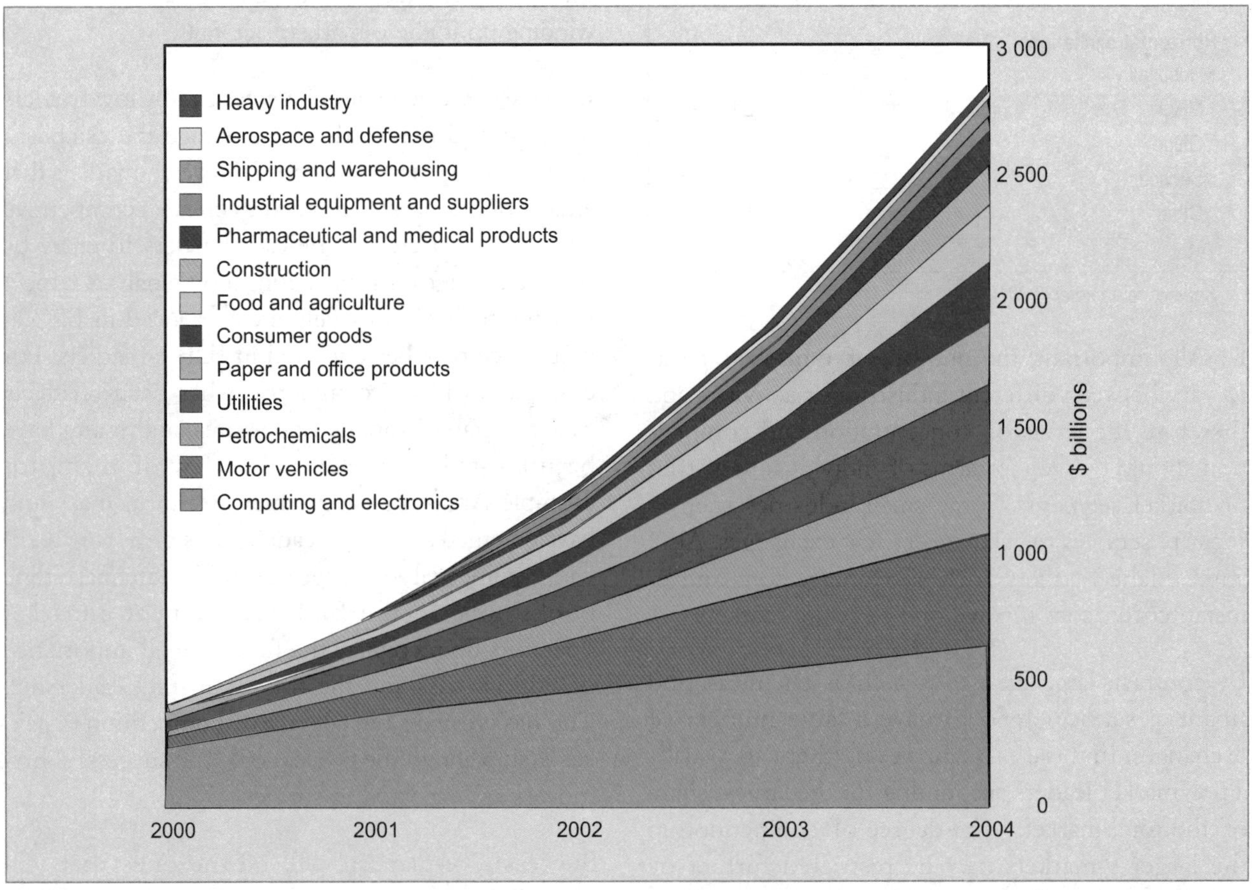

Source: Forrester Research, Inc. (2000).

Chart 7
Projected growth of on-line B2B sales in the United States, via e-markets, by industry, 2000-2004
($ billions)

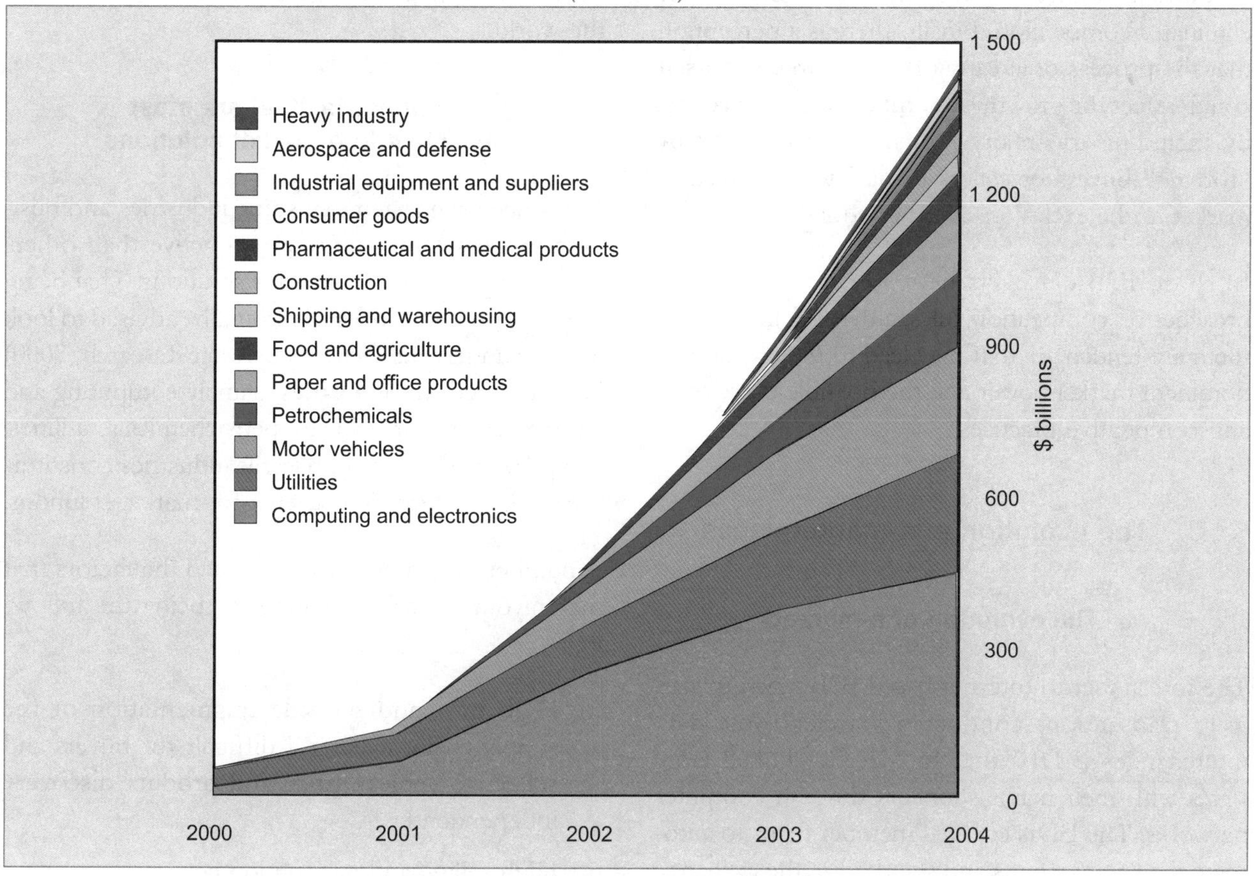

Source: Forrester Research, Inc. (2000).

Table 17
Projected B2B e-commerce by region, 2000-2004
($ billions)

	2000	2001	2002	2003	2004	As a % of worldwide B2B commerce, 2004
North America	159.2	316.8	563.9	964.3	1,600.8	57.7
Asia/Pacific Rim	36.2	68.6	121.2	199.3	300.6	10.8
Europe	26.2	52.4	132.7	334.1	797.3	28.7
Latin America	2.9	7.9	17.4	33.6	58.4	2.1
Africa/Middle East	1.7	3.2	5.9	10.6	17.7	0.6
Total	**226.2**	**448.9**	**841.1**	**1,541.9**	**2,774.8**	**100.0**

Source: eMarketer, (2001)

The possible antitrust concerns about B2B e-markets, for example as expressed in the FTC report, relate to three main areas, namely the sharing of price and other commercial information that may provide scope for collusion and price fixing, exclusionary behaviour among the market places and possible reduction of competition resulting from the creation of the market places.

Evidence of price fixing could be based on indications of price increases occurring after the creation of an e-marketplace. Also, indications of discussions relating to price or the sharing of information about costs and prices data could be considered to be evidence of collusion and price fixing. As regards exclusionary behaviour, the authorities may view a market place as a form of cartel with a potential to increase prices and also control the quantity of goods or services traded. Exclusionary behaviour also relates to companies that create e-markets and prevent competitors from becoming members. This becomes an antitrust issue if the exclusion limits or eliminates competition. Finally, there is a perception that the process of creating B2B e-markets in itself could affect the growth of competition in e-markets by including too many industry members or by "forcing" buyers or sellers to deal with a given e-market to the exclusion of other e-markets.

In short, B2B e-markets have so far not produced breaches of competition rules, although inherent in them are tendencies that may lead to the creation of dominant market power and the possible exercise of anti-competitive practices.

D. The evolution of e-marketplaces

1. The evolution of e-markets

The forerunner to Internet-based B2B marketplaces were transactions conducted via electronic data interchanges (EDIs) that for decades linked large firms with their major suppliers through computer networks. The EDIs enabled member firms to automate their transactions and standardize the exchange of business information, and thus achieve large cost savings through enhanced efficiency. Similarly, banks have been employing closed computer networks for the electronic transfer of funds. However, EDI required large capital expenses to establish and implement. As a result, their application was and is being limited mainly to large firms, since small firms could not afford the necessary capital and operational outlays.

The availability of the Internet provided an opportunity for the development of B2B transaction networks at much lower costs than EDIs. The initial impetus to form e-markets came mainly from independent exchanges dealing in individual industries such as electronics, chemicals, steel and telecommunications,[22] with standardized products and in which there were already advanced computer-based procurement systems. E-markets are now evolving into another stage of enhanced collaboration by adding new added-value services to the market place. Also, as mentioned earlier, in this stage large traditional bricks-and-mortar companies are coming together to create their own e-markets in competition with the independent exchanges. Chart 6 shows a forecast of the value of total B2B online trade in the United States by type of industry, and chart 7 shows a forecast of B2B sales in the United States via e-markets. Table 17 shows projected B2B e-commerce by regions of the world.

2. Industries that are most attractive to e-market solutions

It has been suggested that some industries and business processes may be more attractive than others for the application of e-market solutions. That being the case, potential investors would be advised to look into the underlying factors. Forrester Research (2000) has identified five industries, namely computing and electronics, motor vehicles, petrochemicals, utilities, and paper and office supplies, as industries constituting the largest group of users of e-market solutions.

A number of writers have suggested the factors that may favour e-market solutions as being the following:[23]

(i) High buy- and sell-side fragmentation of the supply chain, making it difficult for buyers and sellers to achieve price and product discovery independently;

(ii) High selling and distribution costs;

(iii) Highly variable demand for the transacted products or services;

(iv) Limited access to market information;

(v) High search costs;

(vi) Digital readiness of the companies operating in the industry.

3. Geographical scope of e-markets

The geographical scope of e-markets varies and includes (i) local e-markets servicing local areas within a country, (ii) national e-markets, (iii) regional e-markets servicing the trade of a group of countries, such as Europe and the Asia-Pacific region, and (iv) global markets. While the Internet eliminates physical geographical boundaries, in reality there may be a number of factors that may restrict the scope of an e-market in terms of its commercial value to users or the physical availability of the traded products and services. Some products or services such as security services, temporary employment bureaux and second-hand car sales tend to have localized markets for which a local e-market can be defined. Other factors such as language, local laws, commercial practices and currency convertibility could also set practical boundaries for e-markets. Some products such as electricity cannot be transported over long distances from their points of production. Thus B2B e-markets for electricity tend to be local or regional or national.

While an e-marketplace may find it beneficial to operate in a local or regional market that provides a niche, the main advantage of the Internet is that it provides sellers and buyers with global access. To this end, a major international initiative has been undertaken to facilitate the globalization of B2B e-commerce. An international commercial organization — the Global Trading Web (GTW) — has been established by Commerce One in cooperation with a number of other technology companies.[24] The GTW is a network of global and regional interoperable e-marketplaces that operate in inter-marketplace B2B e-commerce. It connects buyers and sellers through regional e-marketplaces located in all the regions of the world.[25] Within the framework of GTW local e-markets can be accessed in local languages and in accordance with local laws and business practices. Through it, businesses of all sizes around the world can source, buy and sell goods and services on a global basis. GTW can be accessed by a wide range of commercially available buying and selling applications.

E. The functionality and impact of B2B e-markets

1. Functionality of e-markets

Simply defined, the functionality of an e-marketplace refers to what capabilities it can offer. These capabilities fall into four main areas: (i) content or information made available to buyers and sellers, (ii) the ability to match buyers with sellers, (iii) the ability to handle online transactions, and (iv) the ability to support collaboration by integrating functions of trading partners. Functionality goes well beyond technological capabilities and includes all the core functions of a traditional commercial market. It is considered to be a key element in the overall operations, competitiveness and commercial success of an e-marketplace.

Not all participants in a market place will value different kinds of functionality in the same way. Similarly, the required functionality may differ in different types of markets or industries; for example, content that is useful in a metals e-market may be different from the one for energy or agribusiness trading.

Table 18
Elements of functionality of B2B e-markets

Type of capability	Details of functionality
Content/information	Directories listing companies, their profiles and ratings, aggregated catalogues, electronic brochures with product listings and trading participants' identity and background, information on products, their features, quality and prices, inventory listings, bulletin boards, on-line information browsing capability; ability to search information on order status and tracking; ability of buyers to pre-qualify vendors; databases on tariffs and transport charges; information about the site and customer services; buyer guides and news.
Matching buyers with sellers	Auctions, reverse auctions, on-line negotiations (bid/ask, RFP/RFQ), exchange, barter.
Commercial transactions management	Ability to process payments, credit financing, credit validation, tax laws, trade restrictions, integrating business accounting, on-line exchange of information and transaction-supporting documents, such as purchase orders, invoices and shipping documents; import/export compliance; providing on-line linkage to transportation and logistics and other third-party services linked to purchases, support for multi-currency and multi-language transactions; tariff and tax data collection and management; automated landed cost calculations, customs compliance and documentation.
Collaboration	Sourcing of products, order fulfilment, international trade customs, duties and tariffs, linking back-end systems of trading partners to the market place, fraud detection, digital certification, availability of authentication and encryption capability and digital signature, support for collaborative applications such as joint estimation and forecasting of demand, synchronizing production; optimizing order configuration, fulfilment and delivery, demand aggregation, inventory management, production planning and scheduling; research, customer and market intelligence, data mining and warehousing, service guarantees and contingency plans in case of collapse of market place during active trading, discussion forums, job postings.

Information/content

The provision of information is the most basic but necessary function of an e-market. The information provided by the e-market may range widely, including a listing of products, industry directories, prices and a variety of databases, such as databases of shipping terms and tax laws. By aggregating information and catalogues of different sellers, e-markets permit buyers to have access to a wide range of product or service information in one location, reduce search costs, make product comparison, and simplify choice. Some e-markets create virtual exhibits of vendors that provide buyers with detailed product information in the same fashion as a trade fair. Others are more dynamic, by being able to constantly update information, for example by listing new products as they become available or providing news of changes in currency exchange rates.

Matching buyers with sellers

The second functionality is the ability to connect buyers' needs with suppliers' offerings. This is provided through product postings, requests for proposals and requests for quotes (RFP/RFQ), auctions and online negotiating capabilities, as described earlier.

Transactions capability

The third functionality is the handling of actual transactions. Perhaps this is the most involved function, comprising such capabilities as handling payments, credit financing, credit validation, online exchange of information and transaction-supporting documents, and providing online linkage to transportation, logistics and other third-party services.

Collaboration

The fourth functionality is collaboration. It concerns the involvement of an e-market in the full range of B2B processes and support to members in such functions as quality assurance, production planning, forecasting and demand aggregation. Collaboration involves the exchange of vast amounts of information regarding products and services, and details of transactions. The information is exchanged through a number of channels within the market place, including discussion forums, virtual conferences, chat rooms and meetings, bulletin boards, newsletters, classified advertisements, industry and market reports, product reviews and directories. Through these channels market participants are able to make suggestions and comments concerning products and other matters of general interest. Thus suppliers can receive useful feedback from each other and from buyers. One of the possible outcomes of this is the building of confidence between market participants, something that has often been said to be lacking in e-commerce.

The various elements of B2B e-market functionality are summarized in table 18.

The role of technology in achieving functionality

It is beyond the scope of this chapter to provide details of technologies that power e-market processes. It is important, however, to mention that B2B e-marketplaces and the implementation of their business models rely to a very large extent on technology infrastructure. The market maker must posses or have access to a technology that is capable of handling the full range of commercial processes from ordering to order fulfillment and settlement. The technology must support transactions involving large numbers of users over the Internet and be capable of handling complex business practices, user relationships and integration with third-party commercial applications.

The central importance of technology infrastructure is borne out by the fact that the growth of B2B e-markets is closely correlated with a rapid growth in the number of e-marketplace solution companies. Also, most market makers have found it imperative to form alliances with companies selling or operating e-marketplace technology solutions.[26]

2. The impact of B2B e-markets

Research publications and the popular press show that B2B e-markets are likely to become hubs of B2B transactions. The following are a few quotations. Forrester Research notes that "Our interviews show the torrid pace with which firms are escalating their B2B plans. Fuelled by this widespread activity, online business trade has hit hyper-growth - moving even faster than our previous projections. Based on our analysis of supply chain characteristics and e-commerce readiness in 13 industries, Forrester projects that B2B sales over the Net will skyrocket to $2.7 trillion in 2004."[27] Gartener states that "Business-to-Business (B2B) e-commerce will grow at aggressive rates through 2004, causing fundamental changes to the way businesses do business with each other. The catalyst for B2B e-commerce is e-market maker activity. E-market makers are projected to facilitate $2.71 trillion e-commerce sales transactions in 2004, representing 37 percent of the overall B2B market." [28]

Other studies also provide an indication of the benefits of B2B e-markets.[29] It should be noted, however, that many e-markets are still in their formative stages and therefore have yet to provide sufficient data for study. In part, data on transactions in B2B e-markets tend to be inadequate since the final details of such transactions, including prices and transaction volumes, may not necessarily be known to the market place. This arises partly from the fact that some transactions initiated online are completed offline.[30]

The full impact of B2B e-markets goes beyond activities related purely to transactions and includes collaborative activities between members. The value of these non-transactional functions is hard to quantify. What is apparent, however, is that more and more companies around the world are participating or planning to participate in B2B e-markets, and a consensus seems to be growing to the effect that much of the existing traditional B2B trade is likely to migrate to the Internet and make use of B2B e-markets. The interest in B2B markets may in part be a defensive strategy by companies to retain their existing share of the market or as a move to capture business from other companies. There is also increasing pressure on companies not to be left behind and to adopt online transactions as a form of best practice. All this is happening rapidly, even before the real impact of the e-marketplaces is fully articulated and demonstrated.

The possible impact of B2B e-markets covers a wide range of factors, such as transaction costs, disintermediation, pricing transparency and the building of online trading communities, as outlined below.

Transaction costs

Transaction costs have received most attention in the discussion of the benefits of e-commerce, including B2B e-markets. There are a number of ways such costs can be reduced in B2B e-marketplaces. The first one is the reduction of search costs. In the traditional supply chain, buyers need to go through multiple intermediaries and spend a large amount of time in searching information about suppliers, products and prices. Being more efficient than traditional information channels, the Internet reduces search costs, which include effort, time and money. In B2B e-markets a large number of buyers and sellers, often engaged in similar lines of business, are brought together into a single trading community and this reduces search costs even further.

The second source of cost reduction is the ability of the Internet to reduce the costs of processing transactions, for example invoices, purchase orders and payment arrangements. These can be automated and implemented more quickly than through other channels such as telephone and fax. Improved efficiencies in trading processes can also be achieved through the ability of the e-marketplace to process sales through online auctions without buyers or the goods traded having to move to auction sites. Third, online processing adds value to other functions throughout the supply chain, for example improved inventory management and logistics costs, all of which are linked to transactions.

Disintermediation

One of the widely predicted changes resulting from B2B e-markets and e-commerce in general is the transformation of the traditional supply chain through suppliers being able to interact and transact directly with buyers, with the consequent elimination of intermediaries and distributors. This is largely because of the possible reductions in information and other transaction costs and increased market transparency that reduces the role of intermediaries as sources of information. Some observers have suggested, however, that by using information and communications technology (ICT), intermediaries can become more efficient and add value to their services, thus ensuring the continued demand for those services. It has also been pointed out that ICT expands the possibilities for companies to outsource some of their functions to other firms, thus expanding even further the need for intermediaries.

The experience in B2B e-markets shows that while the traditional middlemen may indeed be losing ground in some areas, new forms of intermediaries are emerging. The independent, third-party e-marketplaces themselves could be considered to be intermediaries by definition, as they are placed in between suppliers and customers in the supply chain.

On the other hand, the market places established by bricks-and-mortar companies are designed for the companies to link up directly with established trading partners, thus eliminating the role of intermediaries.

Pricing transparency

One of the most visible consequences of e-markets is increased price transparency. By bringing together large numbers of sellers and buyers an e-marketplace reveals market prices and transaction processing to participants. The Internet makes it possible to place information on each purchase into a common network and thus make the information readily available to all members of the market place. One result of price transparency is a reduction in price differences prevailing in the market place. Also, buyers are allowed more time to compare prices and make better purchasing decisions.

B2B e-markets also increase the scope for dynamic and negotiated pricing, in which multiple buyers and sellers participate in setting prices collectively by engaging in continuous two-way auctions. In such auctions, prices are arrived at though an automatic matching of bids and offers. In addition, B2B e-markets provide an effective framework for demand aggregation in which many buyers can cooperate to buy a single product or service and then sellers compete for the transaction. By aggregating their requirements, the buyers are able to obtain lower prices than if they had acted individually.

Economies of scale and network effects

The growth of e-markets provides scope for the creation of economies of scale. There are considerable upfront expenses in establishing an e-market, such as programming costs. This creates the traditional supply-side cost-based economies of scale. In addition, however, by linking large numbers of buyers and sellers, e-markets provide demand-side economies of scale or network effects. The latter do not relate to the supply side in the form of reduced average costs, but they relate to the fact that the addition of each incremental participant in a market creates value for all existing participants on the demand side. Large numbers of participants, i.e. critical mass, are a key factor that attracts users to an e-market since it promises benefits to both buyers and sellers.

F. Participation by developing countries in B2B e-markets

Participation by developing countries in e-commerce is limited owing to a variety of factors such as lack of infrastructure and awareness, high costs of Internet connectivity and inadequate skilled human resources.[31] While developing countries account for only a small share of B2B e-markets, the latter have grown significantly in the last few years, although there is no reliable data on the numbers of such markets that have been created. The bulk of this growth seems to have concentrated in a certain developing economies, notably Brazil, Mexico, Argentina, China, Hong Kong (China), Singapore, Malaysia and the Republic of Korea. The extent of the operations of e-marketplaces in developing countries must take into account the fact that e-marketplaces based in the United States and other developed countries have established international capabilities and are extending their reach to developing countries. Thus buyers and sellers from developing countries can in principle become participants in such markets.

Even though the growth of B2B e-commerce in developing countries is expected to continue to be limited, there is no doubt that enterprises in those countries will in the longrun establish a significant presence in B2B e-markets. In addressing this issue, it is important to distinguish between their participation as buyers and sellers in existing e-marketplaces and their participation as creators or operators of their own e-marketplaces.

1. Participating in existing B2B e-marketplaces

Many companies, and even some large ones in the United States, have yet to join e-markets. To sell or buy through e-markets, a company needs to make a conscious decision to do so. Such a decision is a strategic business decision and may be determined by a number of factors, for example profit expectations. Alternatively, buying or selling through e-markets may be a means of challenging competition, a necessary move to retain established trading partners who may have migrated to online transactions, or merely the result of pressure to follow market trends and practices. In other cases, the market places themselves take various measures to attract buyers and sellers to trade in their market places.[32]

Since the outcome of participation in an e-marketplace as a buyer or seller may be uncertain, companies need to develop an e-commerce action plan in order to maximize opportunities for ensuring competitiveness and commercial viability. The following is a range of possible questions that a company may consider in formulating an-e-commerce action plan:

(i) By joining an e-marketplace, will the company lower its transaction costs and ensure an increase in revenue? What methods will be used to assess these outcomes?

(ii) Does the company possess a basic online presence?

(iii) Does the company possess system applications and technologies that would be needed in order for it to integrate effectively with suppliers or buyers in the e-marketplace?

(iv) What knowledge does the company have about e-markets and how they work?

(v) Is the company a dominant player (buyer or seller) in the industry?

(vi) By joining an e-market, would the company expand its customer base by increasing the number of trading partners?

(vii) If the company is a supplier, does it have online product or service fulfillment and customer support service?

(viii) Are the company's competitors participating in e-market places?

(ix) Should the company join online trading while retaining traditional trading channels? How will joining e-markets affect relationships with existing trading partners?

(x) What is the added value of retaining existing trading relationships through participation in an e-market?

(xi) How long does a company have to wait before the benefits of participating in an e-market begin to be realized?

(xii) How many and which types of e-markets should the company join?

(xiii) If the company joins a number of e-markets, what are the requirements for ensuring compatibility between system applications?

(xiv) Will joining an e-market lead to the company losing its identity and brand image?

(xv) What would be the cost of technologies and infrastructure needed for the company to participate in an e-market?

(xvi) What type of e-market business model should a company adopt, taking into account its size and scope of its activities?

This type of checklist can help a company to plan proactively. A company may need, however, to go further and undertake a more detailed assessment of return on investment associated with joining a B2B e-market. Such an assessment would include an estimate of tangible variables such as increased revenue earnings, reduction in purchase and fulfillment cycles, transaction costs, inventory costs, and reduction in operational and administrative costs. The intangible variables would include such variable as improved integration and relationships with customers and increased competitiveness. The benefits and costs would then be compared in order to determine the value of the change-over to online trading. This is just one example of an approach that a company could use in arriving at a decision. Each company would of course employ a method that takes into account its own circumstances.

2. The promotion of online B2B markets in developing countries

In addition to participating in existing B2B e-markets as sellers and buyers, developing country firms could promote the growth of online B2B markets in activities that have potential for such markets. In particular, opportunities could exist in certain activities in which developing countries have a competitive advantage and the critical mass required for the success of e-markets. These may include traditional economic activities such as tourism and primary commodities marketing, and new activities such as teleservices.[33] This section attempts to assess opportunities that may be available to developing countries in creating B2B and other markets in tourism and primary commodities marketing. It is intended primarily to reflect the organizational structures or marketing practices of these sectors and how those structures and practices present opportunities or obstacles for entry by developing countries.

While the focus of this chapter is on B2B e-markets, both the distribution of travel/tourism products and primary commodities marketing have yet to develop business models similar to B2B e-markets of the type outlined earlier. The discussion here is therefore a more general one covering various forms of B2B and in some cases B2C transactions.

(a) Tourism and travel

Tourism and travel[34] are information-intensive activities that lend themselves well to Internet applications. Tourism is estimated to be one of the largest and fastest-growing industries in the world. Also, it is a key economic sector in the economies of many developing countries. The Internet is becoming the most effective channel for international tourism marketing, as more and more potential tourists use it to access information on travel, hotels and destination attractions.[35] Therefore, developing countries need to take measures to exploit the new Internet technologies in order to ensure that they are adequately involved in the supply and distribution of tourism/travel products. It is important, however, to understand the structure of the tourism/travel industry and, in particular, how products and services are distributed, both offline and online, and also how the main players in the industry relate to each other. Such an understanding may provide a basis for assessing the opportunities for tourism/travel service suppliers and intermediaries in the developing countries. An examination of e-commerce in tourism is presented in chapter 3 of this report. In this chapter the subject is treated for the sole purpose of assessing the scope for participation by developing countries in online B2B tourism/travel transactions.

Transactions in tourism and travel-related services are centred on a system of distribution channels that involve many players. These include suppliers of services, namely airlines, hotel operators, car rental operators, tour operators and travel agents, and global distribution systems (GDSs). The GDSs collect, maintain and distribute data and information on tourism and travel. Their core business is to connect buyers and sellers in the travel distribution channel. They evolved from computer reservation systems (CRSs), which are are databases that enable tourism/travel service operators to manage their inventories. The GDSs expanded from airline bookings by incorporating other forms of products such as hotel rooms, car rentals, cruises, tours, railway, bus and ferry tickets, travel insurance, theatre and sports tickets and foreign currency exchange.

Through integration of various CRSs and a range of tourism products, the GDSs are able to provide global distribution services for the travel industry. This in turn provides travel agents and other users with "one-stop shops" for all information and reservation matters that need to be covered in order to build a travel package. Travel agents are the main customers of the GDSs and at the same time they sell the largest share of all tourism and travel products. This obliges airlines, hotels and other suppliers to offer their products to the GDSs for distribution.

At present there are four main GDSs in international tourism distribution, namely Amadeus, SABRE, Galileo and WORLDSPAN. There are in addition smaller GDSs such as Axess, Abacus, Gets, Infini Travel Information and TOPAS. The reasons why a few GDSs are able to dominate the distribution system relate to the extremely high capital costs involved, and the technical skills and industry knowledge required to build the distribution systems. Another factor is the fact that most travel agencies are already linked to the existing GDSs, and a new entrant may find it extremely difficult to dislodge them from those linkages.

Table 19
Ownership and GDS affiliations of major on-line travel agencies

Site	Corporate	Consumer	Public company	Majority owner	Powered by
Expedia		X	Y	Microsoft	Worldspan
Travelocity		X	Y	Sabre	Sabre
Priceline.com		X	Y	Priceline	Worldspan
Trip.com	X	X	N	Galileo	Galileo
ETravel	X		N	Oracle	Various (choice of corporation)
BizTravel	X		N	Rosenbluth	Worldspan
SAP Travel	X		N	SAP	Amadeus
AmericanExpress.com		X	N	American Express	Sabre
Continental.com		X	N	Continental Airlines	Worldspan

Source: Global Aviation Associates, Ltd. (2001).

While traditional bricks-and-mortar travel agencies dominate the distribution of travel/tourism products [36], in recent years there has been a considerable increase in the use of the Internet as a tool for the distribution of tourism and travel products.[37] This development has resulted in the emergence of large online travel agencies, such as Travelocity, Expedia, Internet Travel Network, ORBITZ and Preview Travel. These travel agencies retail travel services on their own accounts and, in addition, provide information to other agencies and intermediaries. The online travel agency business is highly concentrated — for example, Traveocity and Expedia between them control over 70 per cent of Internet bookings outside those made online directly through airlines.[38]

The Internet has provided an opportunity for agencies and other intermediaries, even the smallest ones, to use alternatives to the traditional CRS/GDSs. It has also provided possibilities for new business models to the GDSs themselves, as some of them are responsible for a number of online travel/tourism ventures.

At least four types of online travel/tourism services have emerged. First, online services are offered by traditional bricks-and-mortar travel agencies that have built and maintained websites and booking tools, for example American Express and Carlson Wagonlit, and also smaller agencies. Second, there are direct online sales of inventory by travel/tourism service suppliers such as airline and hotel sites that have booking capabilities. Some airlines maintain such websites individually, while in other cases they operate joint websites. For example, a number of large airlines in the United States have set up a common Internet platform.[39] Similarly, in Europe a group of 11 airlines[40] have joined together to create a joint website that can provide services in competition to online travel agents and tour operators.[41] The online distribution of services by service suppliers using joint websites is also developing in the hotel sector, as exemplified by the joint website planned by Accor, Forte and Hilton.[42] Third, pure-play online travel agencies such as Travelocity and Expedia aggregate air, hotel, car and cruise options into a "travel supermarket". These agencies differ from the traditional agencies in that they are not bricks-and-mortar storefronts. Lastly, there are portals, such as Yahoo, Lycos, AOL and Excite that enter into agreements with online agencies or GDSs to distribute travel/tourism products on their behalf. An example of this is the agreement between Galileo International and Viajo.com, a large Latin American travel site.[43] Viajo.com will use Galileo's computerized reservation systems as its booking engines.

There are therefore complex interlinkages between the various players in the travel/tourism supply and distribution channels. The GDSs were originally owned by major airlines, although most of them are now public companies with varying degrees of airline ownership. In turn the GDSs have ownership interests in or affiliations with online travel agencies. For example, Worldspan's customers include Expedia and priceline.com. However, the GDSs also have purchased other agencies and entered into exclusive agreements with major Internet portals such as Netscape, AOL and Yahoo. Table 19 illustrates the types of ownership and GDS affiliations of major online travel agencies. While these affiliations may tend to change from time to time, they nevertheless illustrate the complexity of the linkages that exist between players in the industry.

The existence of a wide range of players offering online tourism/travel services has led to the growth of competition between them. Some suppliers and distributors have responded in different ways to the domination of the online agency business by a few firms.[44] For example, some airlines have reacted by attempting to reduce or eliminate commissions paid to online agencies. Others have created their own supplier-backed agencies to compete with the "independent" ones, and thus sell most of their products themselves. The case in point is the creation of ORBITZ by a group of United States airlines, namely United Airlines, Delta Airlines, Continental Airlines, Northwest Airlines and American Airlines. It was created largely as a reaction by the airlines, since they felt that their booking and ticketing business was being taken away by the large online travel agencies. A number of large airlines in Europe have also decided to create a joint online travel agency.[45]

(b) Assessment of opportunities for developing countries in the tourism/travel industry

The above discussion has shown that the supply and distribution of tourism/travel products has traditionally been dominated by a few GDSs that are linked on a global basis to service suppliers and distributors. The use of the Internet has not totally transformed the basic structure of the conventional distribution channels, as most players, including online distributors, continue to rely on GDSs for information and data.[46] However, the new technology is increasingly diminishing the role of GDSs since it enables suppliers to bypass them and thus create competition.

Developing country enterprises that supply and distribute tourism/travel services tend to be small and medium-sized enterprises (SMEs). They have to compete with large foreign-based suppliers or distributors that operate on a global scale. For example, major hotel chains have a presence in most developing countries, especially those with significant tourism activity. Similarly, major global airline service providers operate to most major tourist destination countries.[47] Not only are these global operators linked to the GDSs, but also many of them now make use of the Internet as well. This gives them a competitive advantage over developing country suppliers and distributors in their ability to reach suppliers and distributors as well as customers (tourists). Even where the developing country suppliers and distributors are not in direct competition with the global competitors, for example in local air travel, they tend to lack the channels for distributing their products to a wide international market. For example, although many suppliers and distributors have established websites, these are not interactive and are largely used for advertising only, without transaction capabilities such as booking and payments.

The use of the Internet for information, reservation, booking and marketing could help the developing country suppliers and distributors to reach wider markets and thereby increase their competitiveness. A number of developing country enterprises have been able to develop successful online distribution businesses. An example is the documented success of Asiatravelmart.com, which has been described in chapter 3 of this report. Other examples include Despegar.com, a Miami-based online travel site, which has launched online travel services in Argentina, Brazil, Chile, Colombia, Mexico and Uruguay.[48] Despegar.com is an interesting case in that it has the financial backing of major United States investment firms such as Hicks, Mus, Tate & Furst, Inc. and Merrill Lynch, as well as Accor, a major owner and operator of hotels worldwide.

Opportunities for online businesses also exist for small distributors through being affiliated to large players. A number of major online travel agents, for example, provide opportunities to small travel agents and tour operators through affiliation programmes or agreements.[49] Through the latter, a travel agent or operator or any small business that possesses an operating website links to the large agents' websites. This linkage allows the small travel agent or operator to have access to large databases and various functionalities provided by the large agent's Internet portal. Customers that book travel through the website of the affiliate agent's tour operator are considered to be customers of the large agent. The affiliate is paid a fee or commission for sales of air tickets, car rentals, hotel reservations and other travel services made on that website. In return, the affiliate agrees to place the large agent's promotions on its websites for the purpose of selling the agent's products.

Affiliate programmes are also used by online suppliers of tourism services. For example, World Choice Travel, an online hotel reservation website, operates an Internet-based programme in which it connects to large numbers of travel agents and companies around the world.

Generally, however, individual SMEs may not possess the know-how and resources required to develop, support and maintain websites. In part, this could be overcome by creating regional cooperation. Such cooperation has, for example, been initiated by a group of airlines in the Asia-Pacific region.[50] In cooperation with Travelocity, a leading online travel agent that will provide the technology, the airlines have established an online travel exchange intended to include a wide range of travel services such as airline and hotel reservations, and car and land tours. The travel website expects to become the Asian region's leading provider of B2C and B2B online products and services. Other types of suppliers and distributors, such as hotels and travel agents, could emulate this form of regional cooperation. In Peru, the Association of Peruvian Travel Agencies (Apavit) has established a partnership with a major GDS, Worldspan. Under the partnership, Apavit has made Worldspan its preferred GDS, and Apavit member agencies have access to Worldspan's products and services on preferential terms. Also, Apavit members get a direct connection to Worldspan's portal via Apavit's Home Page, when one is created.

One of the strategies that developing countries could use to overcome the individual weaknesses of their SME suppliers and distributors is to develop or strengthen the capability of tourist boards and other destination marketing organizations (DMOs) by using the Internet.[51] A number of DMOs, although not all from developing countries, provide examples that could be emulated by DMOs in developing countries.[52]

MySwitzerland.com is a website set up by the Swiss tourist board, Swiss Tourism. It has established a booking engine on its website where travel and other products are sold, including hotels, last-time hotels, apartments, chalets and rental cars.[53] Swiss Tourism intends to develop partnerships with other enterprises and specialty travel sites or large online travel agents in order to expand its reach to tourists worldwide.

The Caribbean Tourism organization, while not being involved as a business enterprise for selling travel, recognizes that often tourist boards provide destination information but the potential tourist is left without adequate channels for booking holidays. Therefore, it plans to develop partnerships with tourism/travel operators and sell products on its website.

The Australia Tourist Commission's website is a major source for tourists to locate information about Australian tourism. It contains a large database of Australian tourism/travel products and is linked to other Australian regional travel sites. It provides suppliers with a channel for marketing their products in several languages.[54]

The British Tourist Authority (BTA) is another example of an organization that recognizes that while many commercial websites provide destination information and sell tourism/travel products through the websites, a DMO can fulfil functions that a commercial website cannot fulfil. For example, the BTA, supported by a comprehensive search engine, provides comprehensive planning information and links to other searchable sites with more comprehensive details. The BTA's website maintains a large database on accommodation, visitor attractions and events throughout the country.[55]

The initiatives of DMOs at the local or national level could be complemented or enhanced through regional cooperation. An example of such cooperation is the e-ASEAN initiative taken by the member countries of the Association of South-East Asian Nations (ASEAN). The organization has agreed a number of pilot e-commerce projects for the region, including the development of a portal for tourism, the Asean eTourism Portal. It is planned that the portal will provide a comprehensive information hub which, through the Internet, will provide travel and tourism information from all ASEAN countries. The portal will create an integrated platform capable of providing various types of online transactions and payment methods.[56]

(c) Primary commodities marketing

Many developing countries, and especially the least developing countries (LDCs), continue to rely on primary commodities for their exports and overall economic performance. In order to improve their competitiveness in world trade these countries need to diversify their economies into other sectors. However, alongside such diversification, they need to improve the marketing of their primary commodities since these will continue to play an important role in their economies in the foreseeable future.

Most primary commodities in developing countries, particularly in agriculture, are produced by SMEs. The marketing and exports of the commodities have traditionally been channelled through a wide variety of middlemen, resulting in high transaction costs and reduced revenue for the producers. For example, many countries established public marketing boards that were a monopoly, to buy and fix prices for agricultural commodities. These boards bought the commodities from producers and auctioned them to licensed private exporters who in turn sold them to overseas buyers. However, private sector traders have now replaced many of the marketing boards.

The problem both with the marketing boards and with the private sector traders is that producers are not well informed about market prices. It has been suggested that in some cases the traders tend to use the producers' lack of price information to pay them prices that are considerably lower than those that the traders obtain in overseas sales.[57] This problem could be overcome if producers could develop the capacity to discover market prices. In this connection a number of developing countries have established commodity exchanges. These could introduce transparency and allow the dissemination of price information to producers.[58] Electronic trading through the Internet could play a role in this process to enable the producers not only to have better access to price information but also to reach a larger number of buyers.

There are a few examples of primary commodity exchanges that are moving away from the traditional commodity exchanges to new methods based on the same business models as B2B e-markets. This change includes the automation of the roles traditionally performed by human auctioneers, greater market transparency, booking and matching buy-and-sell orders on a first-come first-served basis, and the ability for communication to be made instantaneously. The following are examples.

Coffee exchanges

Several online coffee markets or exchanges have been established in recent years, while others are in the process of being created. Major examples include eGreenCoffee.com, InterCommercial Markets, Coffee-Exchange.com and CoffeeX.com. EGreenCoffee reports that it is already trading sizeable quantities of coffee from top producing countries such as Brazil, Indonesia, Guatemala, Uganda, Côte d'Ivoire, India, Costa Rica, Kenya and the United Republic of Tanzania.[59]

Most of the existing exchanges were founded by major players in the international commodity trade, backed by technology companies and partners in the coffee and food trade, as well as financial investors. InterCommercial Markets (www.intercommercial.com) is based in New York and its partners include Brown Brothers Harriman & Co., an American bank, the Colombia Coffee Federation; two multinational coffee traders — ED & F Man Holding and Mercon Coffee Corporation; and a number of other companies such as Kraft Foods, VOLCAFE Ltd., Procter & Gamble Company, Dreyfus Corporation and the New York Board of Trade.[60]

Coffee-Exchange.com is located in Costa Rica and was founded by an entrepreneur, Rodrigo Fernandez, in partnership with several private investors. EGreenCoffee was founded by a major coffee dealer. Its partners include a futures trading company (Sucden), a large bank (ABN AMRO) and a Swiss certification firm (SGS). The exchange has now been acquired by Tradax Group (TDMX) Company. It is evident from these examples that the ownership of the exchanges is predominantly in the hands of major coffee dealers and buyers. Membership of the exchanges is open to coffee producers of all sizes, exporters, dealers, roasters, brokers and traders in coffee futures around the world. Participation in other forms is also open to other parties associated with the coffee trade such as financiers and logistics management companies.

Internet-based commodity exchanges are also being created for other primary commodity markets such as tea and cotton. Teauction.com is an Indian-based B2B tea market that enables buyers and sellers worldwide to participate in tea auctions via the Internet. It also provides comprehensive information for the benefit of members and the tea trade at large.[61] A United States based venture has planned the formation of a B2B e-market for the cotton industry. Its objective is to create an independent electronic exchange for sellers and buyers of cotton and also for its products and supplies.[62]

The online commodity markets described here are all fairly new and information about their operations is still inadequate. Therefore, while in principle even SMEs that produce coffee or tea in developing countries can in principle participate in the markets, there are no data that show the numbers and profiles of producers or exporters from developing countries that participate. In the short run it is most likely that the brokers and intermediaries operating in traditional commodity markets will continue to play a major role, although the nature of their roles is bound to change.

While many of the exchanges have been created by enterprises located in developed countries, the examples of teauction.com and InterCommercial Markets show that enterprises in developing countries can also invest in such markets.

G. Future trends in B2B e-markets

E-commerce is characterized by rapid changes. B2B e-markets are a relatively new type of e-commerce and yet they have already undergone a number of business organizational changes during their brief existence. Analysts are predicting that further fundamental changes are underway and still others will occur.[63] This section outlines the main future developments in B2B e-markets.

1. Consolidation and strategic alliances between e-markets

It is predicted that B2B e-markets are likely to see a wave of consolidations or strategic alliances as market places attempt to achieve economies of scale and network effects. In the face of ongoing intense competition, e-markets will be obliged to adopt new strategies or business models in order to survive, and cooperation is the most likely strategy. By reaching wider markets through cooperation, the e-markets will be able to reduce their costs and increase value for trading partners. It is also expected that consolidation will be used as a means to acquire technology. Technology solutions are developing rapidly and becoming a major driving force of e-marketplaces. Therefore, e-markets tend to form alliances with leading technology companies as a business strategy.

There have already been important examples of consolidation, such as the creation of retailers Sears and Carrefour, the supplier-controlled e-market MetalSite, MAriba's acquisition of Tradex Technologies, Trading Dynamics and SupplierMarket.com, and the acquisition of Petrochem.com byCheMatch.purchase. It is not certain what sort of consolidations will prevail or dominate. They may, for example, be between horizontal and vertical market places, between several vertical market places or between buyer-driven and seller-driven markets.

2. Greater specialization or establishment of niche markets

In addition to using consolidation, e-markets will address competition by attempting to develop differentiated or specialized services and thus create niches for themselves. There are considerable benefits if firms select functions in which they can create their greatest competencies. Such a strategy hinges on the fact that because of cost and effort, individual exchanges would find it difficult to create the whole range of capabilities or functionality in the entire value chain. There will therefore be opportunities for e-markets to increase their competitiveness by focusing on specific services, functions or processes such as financing, logistics, order management, inventory and purchasing. These services may then be provided to other e-markets.

3. Movement towards industry-controlled and private e-markets

A significant development in B2B e-markets is the entry by traditional buyer-side or seller-side industries through consortium arrangements, in competition with independent third-party e-markets. It is expected that this trend will continue to dominate future developments, as these new entrants have strong backing from large firms with secure financial resources, providing them with the ability to mount long-term competitive strategies. However, the industry consortia are also likely to face increasing competition from private e-markets, namely those formed by individual firms. These trends may not, however, be totally clear-cut if the players in the various types of e-markets enter into strategic alliances.

H. Summary

B2B e-markets are expected to represent the largest share of global electronic commerce transactions. These markets bring together large numbers of buyers and sellers into single trading communities, thereby enhancing reductions in transaction costs and improving collaboration. They are distinguishable from B2C transactions, from B2B commerce that involves only one seller or buyer (one-to-many) and from traditional stock and commodity exchanges. They fall into various categories, the main ones being vertical markets, horizontal markets, independent third-party markets, industry consortia that are either buyer-driven or seller-driven markets, and private e-markets formed by single firms.

A large number of B2B e-markets have been established in different industries, and this has given rise to intense competition. While e-markets tend to have low barriers to entry, the attainment of liquidity and critical mass determines which of them will survive the competition. Generally, first movers tend to have the advantage in attaining critical mass, thereby creating barriers to entry for new comers. However, the structure of B2B e-markets has yet to reach a state of "equilibrium", as competition continues. Inherently, B2B e-markets have the potential for creating market dominance and anti-competitive behaviour. Competition authorities, however, have not so far established specific rules to address B2B e-markets.

B2B e-markets offer a wide range of capabilities or functionality concerning the content or information they provide, the handling of online transactions and support for collaboration, including linkages to members' back-end systems. Technology plays a critical role in the functionality of a B2B e-market. The impact of B2B e-markets includes reductions in transaction costs, reducing or changing the roles of intermediaries, enhancing pricing transparency, promoting economies of scale and network effects, and allowing trading communities to develop a wide range of collaboration activities.

Developing countries have so far accounted for a very small share of transactions in B2B e-markets. Before an enterprise decides to participate in e-markets as a buyer or seller, it must consider a number of strategic questions and assess the expected return on investment. Developing countries may find opportunities to participate in or create online markets in sectors where they have had a significant presence, such as travel/tourism and primary commodity marketing. The distribution of travel/tourism products is dominated by a few large players. The Internet has promoted competition and opened up alternative channels of distribution. A number of schemes, including regional cooperation and affiliation with major players, are available to enterprises in developing countries to enable them to participate.

Primary commodities play a key role in many developing countries. Traditional marketing and export channels can be improved and expanded by using the Internet. Online B2B exchanges are being created in trades such as coffee, tea and cotton. Some of these have been created by developing country enterprises. Many developing countries have established traditional commodity exchanges. These can provide foundations for the development of new online B2B commodity markets. Also, private sector buyers and export associations can be used to organize such online markets.

B2B e-markets have a relatively short history but have already undergone several changes. For the foreseeable future they are expected to experience consolidation and the formation of strategic alliances. Also, it is expected that they will tend to focus on the provision of differentiated and specialized products and services as part of their competition strategy. Furthermore, there is an apparent shift towards the development of industry-based or consortium-type B2B e-markets and also private B2B e-markets.

Notes

1 Other categories of e-commerce include business-to-consumer (B2C), where businesses sell to consumers; consumer-to-consumer (C2C), where individuals can buy and sell from one another in auctions; and consumer-to-business (C2B), where consumers post prices at which they are willing to buy goods and services from businesses.

2 They are also referred to as "exchanges" or "net markets".

3 See Forrester Research, Inc. (2000) and International Data Corporation (2000).

4 Throughout this chapter the names of specific firms are mentioned purely for the purpose of illustration, without implying any judgement on the legal and commercial status of the firms concerned.

5 For example, the alliance between Ariba and Dell is aimed at creating a B2B portal for Dell's SME customers powered by Ariba's B2B e-commerce platform and integrating Ariba's procurement software with Dell powerEdge services.

6 See Sculley and Woods (2001).

7 Specific examples include ChemConnect and e-Chemical (chemical industry) and e-Steel and MetalSite (metals industry). For more examples, see, for example, Legg Mason Wood Walker, Inc. (2000).

8 Examples include MRO.com, Ariba Network, SAP, Commerce One and Oracle.

9 For example, Ariba (a horizontal exchange) has established a relationship with SciQuest, while Ariba (horizontal) has linked up with Chemdex.com (chemical industry).

10 For example, Wal.Mart's RetailLink.

11 For example, WorldOil.com.

12 An example of a buyer-driven exchange is Covisinst, which is an auto parts e-market created by GM, Ford, DaimlerChrsler and Renalt/Nissan. Other example include Trade Ranger (oil refining), eHitex and e2Open (electronics/high-tech sectors), Aerospan and MyAircraft, Exostar and e2open.

13 Examples of these include Works.com and Grainger.com.

14 See Brown (2000).

15 Examples of these include Nypro and e-Exchange. For a discussion see King (2000).

16 Deloitte Consulting (2001).

17 Boston Consulting Group (2000).

18 B2B e-markets are in reality markets for markets, in the sense that they bring together players who are already operating in markets.

19 Critical mass is the number of participants in an exchange that would ensure that the operation of the exchange can at least breakeven.

20 See United States Federal Trade Commission (2000).

21 See, for example, UNCTAD (2000).

22 The initial market places were established by independent companies, such as E-steel (steel industry), SciQuest (life sciences), Chemdex (chemicals industry), Freemarkets (industrial goods) and GoCargo (logistics services).

23 See, for example, Morgan Stanley Dean Witter (2000).

24 See www.commerceone.com/news/us/gtw_association.html.

25 At the end of 2000, GTW comprised a total of 80 global e-marketplaces. See Raisch (2001).

26 See, for example, eMarketer (2000b) and Raisch (2001).

27 Forrester Research Inc.(2000).

28 Gartner Group (2000).

29 See, for example, Raisch (2001).

30 For an extended discussion of statistics on e-commerce, see chapter 3 of this report.

31 For an extended discussion of participation by developing countries in e-commerce, see UNCTAD (2000) and chapter 9 of this report, which discusses a survey of e-commerce in selected least developed countries.

32 For examples of such measures, see Wilson (2000).

33 For an examination of teleservices in LDCs, see chapter 9 of this report.

34 Tourism and travel are closely interrelated activities and their transactions or the distribution of their products are largely handled through the same channels.

35 For a comprehensive discussion of e-commerce in tourism, see chapter 3 of this report.

36 It is estimated that traditional travel agencies account for over 75 per cent of all airline tickets. See Global Aviation Associates (2001).

37 It is estimated, for example, that travel reservations constitute the largest consumer and business purchases on the Internet (see www.phocuswright.com/research/index.html).

38 Global Aviation Associates (2001). Also see chapter 3 of this report.

39 See "eTourism marketplaces – a major revolution", http://www.etourismnewsletter.com/archives/3105200/efocus.htm.

40 See "eTourism marketplaces – a major revolution", http://www.etourismnesletter.com/archives/31052000/efocus.htm.

41 The joint websites set up by the airlines are intended to distribute products related to air travel as well as other related products such as hotel reservations and car rentals.

42 This site was launched in April 2001. However, the Forte Hotel Group brands have now been purchased by various other companies.

43 See www.webtravelnews.com/archive/article.html?id=363.

44 See for example, "Travelocity.com and Expedia.com's globalisation strategies challenged", at www.etourismnewsletter.com/archives/2000-2/ecommerce.htm, Serious threats for the future of online and offline agencies", at www.etourismnewsletter.com/efoc.htm, and "eTourism market places – a major revolution", at www.etourismnewsletter.com/archives/31052000/efocus.htm

45 The participating airlines are British Airways, Air France, Lufthansa, Alitalia, KLM, Iberia, SAS, Aer Lingus, Austrian Airlines Group, British Midlands and Finnair. The joint airline travel agencies created by airlines should be distinguished from joint websites that are operated directly by the airlines themselves.

46 The availability of standard XML interfaces means that data sources such as the GDSs or other distributors can be accessed by users on the Internet.

47 Penetration by large multinational enterprises into developing countries has been part of the wider trend of the globalization of the world economy in all sectors and particularly in services.

48 See www.webtravelnews.com/archive/article.html?id=492.

49 See for example, www3.travelocity.com/about/about_main…:EN/AFFILIATEAGREEMENT,00.htm.

50 See http:// www3.travelocity.com/pressroom/pressrelease/0,1090,1631/TRAVELOCITY,00.htm/26/03/01.

51 The role of DMOs has been outlined in greater detail in chapter x of this report.

52 In addition to public bodies, DMOs can be associations of private tourism operators.

53 See Rice (2001)

54 See Australia Tourist Commission – Resources for the Australian Tourism Industry, http://www.atc.net.au/market/intnet/intnet.htm.

55 See Quarmby (2000).

56 See Asean e-Tourism Portal, eASEANtravel.com.

57 See, for example, Lovelace, (1998).

58 Commodity exchanges exist or are planned in many developing countries, such as Argentina, Brazil, Mexico, El Salvador, Honduras, Nicaragua, Costa Rica, Panama, Colombia, Ecuador, Peru, Bolivia, India, Sri Lanka, Thailand, Malaysia, Singapore, Zambia, Zimbabwe and Kenya.

59 http:/www.egreencoffee.com/public/sundry/headline.asp?id=211lang=e.

60 www.intercommercial.com/Icpublic/AboutUsEnglish.asp.

61 See www.teauction.com/home/aboutus.asp and www.teauction.com/home/faq.asp.

62 See www.cargill.com/today/release/00_5_24cotton.htm and http://memphis.bcentral.com/memphis/stories/2000/07/17/story2.html.

63 See, for example, Kendrick (2000), Covill (2000) and Konicki (2000).

References and bibliography

Australian Tourist Commission

Boston Consulting Group (2000). "The B2B opportunity: Creating advantage through E-marketplaces", 21 December, ttp://www.ebizchronicle.com/backgrounders/dec00/b2bsnapshot.htm.

Brown, D. (2000). "B2B bricks-and-mortar: All bark, no bite," 15 June, News.com, *Tech News First.*

Covill, R. (2000). The future of e-markets, 17 December, http://b2b.ebizq.net/exchange/covill_1.html.

Deloitte Consulting and Deloitte & Touche (2000a). *The future of B2B: A new genesis.* New York.

Deloitte Consulting and Deloitte & Touche. (2000b). *B2B Darwinism: How e-Markets Survive (and succeed).* New York.

Deloitte Consulting and Deloitte & Touche (2000c). *B2B Antitrust: Opening Moves in the Game.* New York.

Deloitte Consulting (2001). *Collaborative Commerce: Going Private to Get Results.* New York.

Deutsche Bank Alex.Brown (2000).*Revolution 2.0: The rire? Of the B2B e-Hub-Pre-Launch Teaser,*1 March.

Emarketer (2000a). *The eCommerce: B2B Report, Executive Summary*, July, www.emarketer.com.

Emarketer (2000b). *The ASP Report, Executive Summary*, 2000, www.emarketer.com.

EMarketer (2001). *The eCommerce: B2B Report, Executive Summary*, February.

Forrester Research, Inc. (2000). E*Marketplaces boost B2B trade*, February.

Gartner Group, (2000). " *Triggering the B2B electronic commerce explosion",* 26 January, www.gartnergroup.com/public/static/aboutgg/pressrel/pr012600c.html.

Ghosh, S, (2000). "The Antitrust implications of B2B electronic marketplaces", March, http://www.internetnews.com/articles/2001/ghosh-2001-01-p4.html.

Global Aviation Associates, Ltd. (2001). *The History and Outlook of Travel Distribution in the PC-Based Internet Environment.*

Gossain, S. (2000) "Building successful net markets, *Nervewire*, April.

Gossain, S and Kenworthy, R. (2000). "Winning the third wave of e-bBusiness: Beyond Net Markets, *Nervewire*, December.

International Data Corporation (2000). Publication # 22501, June.

Kaplan, S. and Sawhuey, M. (2000). "E-hubs: The new B2B marketplaces," *Havard Business Review*, May-June, pp. 97-103.

King, J. (2000). "Quietly, private e-markets rule", *Computerworld News and Story*, 4 September.

Konicki, S. (2000). *Exchanges got private*, http://www.informationweek.com/790/private.htm.

KPMG Consulting, (2000). *Business Exchanges.*

Legg Mason Wood Walker, Inc. (2000) *B2B eCommerce, Industry Analysis*, Spring.

Lipis, L. et al. (2000). "Putting markets into place: An emarketplace definition and forecast", IDC, Document # 22501, June.

Lovelace, J. (1998). *Export Sector Lberalisation and Forward Markets: Managing Uncertainty During Policy Transition*, http://www.afbis.com/analysis/financial_markets.htm.

McKendrick, J. (2000). *Old Economy players step up*, http://ecomworld.com/html/novcov00.htm. 4 December.

Mercer Management Consultants, (2000). *Beyond the Exchange: Promising Business Models for the Next Round of B2B E-commerce, A Commentary.*

Morgan Stanley Dean Witter (2000). *The B2B Internet Report: Collaborative Commerce.*

Quarmby, D. (2000). "Net gains for NTOs", http://www.asiamaya.com/travel-asia/04_14_00/stories/net.htm.

Raisch, W. (2001). *The e-marketplace: Strategies for Success in B2B ecommerce*, McGraw-Hill.

Ramsdell, G, (2000) *The real business of B2B*, www.mckinseyquarterly.com/electron/rebu00.asp.

Rice, K. (2001). Breaking the Barrier: Tourist Boards Move into E-commerce, http://www.webtravelnews.com/archive/article.html?id=707.

Sawhuey, M. and Kaplan, S. (1999). "Let's get v ertical," *Business 2.0*, September.

Sculley, A .and Woods, *W*. (2001). *B2B exchanges*, Harper Business.

Seybold, P. et al. (2000). *Exploring B2B E-markets,* Patricia Seybold Group, October.

Singh, B. (2000) "Beyond transactions: The value of data within the e-marketplace", http:/dmreview.com/mastersponsor.cfm?NavID=193&EdID=2540

Sterling Commerce (2000). *A First Look at Next Generation E-marketplaces*, www.sterlingcommerce.com.

Tapellini, D. *Negotiating B2B Exchanges: A quick Tour through Online Marketplaces*, http:// dmreview.com/master_sponsor.cfm?NavID=193&EdID=2540.

United States Federal Trade Commission (2000). *Entering 21st Century: Competition Policy in the World of B2B Electronic Marketplaces, A Report by the Federal Trade Commission*. Washington, DC.

UNCTAD (2000). *Building Confidence: Electronic Commerce and Development*. United Nations Publication, Sales No. E.00II.D.16.

Wilson, T (2000). "Hubs hunt for buyers, sellers", *Internet Week Online*, 11 September, www.internetweek.com/lead/lead091100.htm.

Chapter 5
TOWARDS DIGITAL GOVERNMENT

A. Introduction

Just as e-commerce is creating a new business environment for most sectors, including many traditional ones, so it is expected that the Internet will introduce deep changes in the organization, management and provision of government services in the next few years. Although e-government is still in its infancy, its effects on the way some Governments are performing some of their core functions, such as tax collection, law enforcement or even defence, are already discernible. On a smaller scale, but with potentially equally important long-term implications, the Internet is also beginning to influence the political process and the interaction between citizens and their representatives.

Although the Electronic Commerce and Development Report is not directly concerned with many of the above-mentioned matters, there are several reasons why it could not leave out e-government. The first one is that in most countries the public sector (broadly defined, and including regional and local Governments) is the largest economic actor, whether this is measured in terms of employment, expenditure or revenue.[1] The changes that the Internet will bring about in the way Governments manage these vast resources, especially as they interact with businesses, will have a deep impact on the overall efficiency of an economy, the competitiveness of its enterprises and its ability to attract foreign investment. The implications for a country's development prospects are obvious.

A second reason why e-government matters for e-commerce is that by embracing the Internet, Governments can accelerate the change in mentality that is needed for e-commerce practices to spread among private sector enterprises, particularly the mass of small and medium-sized enterprises in developing countries. Just as some large corporations have forced their suppliers and distributors to adapt to e-commerce in order to keep doing business with them, so Governments can stimulate the introduction of e-commerce by demonstrating the potential of the Internet and by encouraging the private sector to adopt e-practices in their dealings with government agencies.

The sections that follow will present a broad picture of the main recent developments in the area of e-government, the key elements of e-government strategies and the prospects for the immediate future. A more in-depth examination of these matters, including case studies of e-government projects around the world, will be included in the next issue of the Electronic Commerce and Development Report.

B. A revolution biding its time

Broadly speaking, e-government could be defined as the use of information and telecommunication technologies, especially the Internet, to enhance access to and delivery of government services to benefit citizens, businesses and the staff of the public sector. In itself, the application of information technologies to government business is nothing new; on the contrary, government agencies have been among the earliest and largest users of information technologies. But operating a large number of mainframes to manage payrolls or tax collection, or even putting a personal computer on the desk of every civil servant, does not transform a traditional bureaucracy into an e-government. It is the Internet, with its capacity to break the barriers of time and distance and to bring together a wealth of information from a virtually unlimited number of sources, that is creating the possibility of reorganizing and networking government services to make them more user-centred, transparent and efficient. However, the pace at which Governments in general are adapting themselves to the Internet is considerably slower than the pace at which the private sector is adapting itself. The reasons for this are varied.

First, the size and complexity of government operations can explain the relative slowness in the spread of e-government practices. Many government agencies deliver services that affect large numbers of people (pension benefits) and/or are politically and socially sensitive (education), or involve several levels of government that are accountable to different constituencies (law enforcement). These agencies cannot afford the disruption in service which they fear, sometimes with reason, is an inevitable part of the re-engineering of their operation that is required in order to become an e-government service provider.

Secondly, the inequality of access to the Internet is a matter of serious political concern. Governments cannot choose their customers: their services must be available to all. Today, even in those countries where Internet access is more widespread, only about half of the population has an Internet connection at home. Since government services must be equally accessible to all citizens, government agencies will not be able to become full-fledged online operators until Internet access reaches a significantly larger part of the population. Policies aimed at improving the access of the public to the Internet are therefore inextricably linked to the establishment of e-government services, particularly in developing countries.

Thirdly, there are fundamental differences between the incentives and deterrents faced by government agencies and commercial operators. For a company facing competition from dot.coms or from more traditional competitors who have been quicker in becoming "bricks-and-clicks" businesses, to ignore the Internet is not an attractive option. This is rarely the case of government agencies, which generally have a captive customer base. The exception, of course, is public sector operators (for instance, some railways and airlines) that face direct or indirect commercial competition and have been as rapid as their rivals in setting up commercial (and sometimes remarkably effective) online services.

Finally, organizational and cultural factors also matter. The typical hierarchical structure of government agencies is much less "Internet-friendly" than the more flexible, flatter structures now common in the private sector. The increased transparency and accountability that are inherent to the transition from the traditional to the digital organization can be perceived as dangerous in a government environment, either for legitimate reasons (such as security or privacy) or because they represent a risk for the bureaucratic establishment. Competing claims among departments and/or various levels of government about responsibilities for e-government projects are not uncommon. Civil service values that stress respect for authority, rules and precedent are not necessarily the most attractive ones for the kind of employee that may bring with him or her the skills and preference for innovation that are so relevant in an Internet environment. Compensation packages in the public sector are also less likely to reward risk-taking and innovation than those of companies at the forefront of the digital economy. And resistance to change can often more easily find support in the generally more organized workforce of the public sector.

While all the reasons mentioned above are equally valid for developed and developing countries, in most of the latter the difficulties are compounded by the lack of telecommunications infrastructure, poor computer and general literacy, lack of awareness of the potential of the Internet and regulatory inadequacy that hinder other applications of the Internet there. Also, the investments required are perceived as too high for the budgets of many Governments of developing countries, even though the application of the Internet (and of information and communication technologies in general) to public management often results in significant net financial gains. The experience of the introduction of UNCTAD's Automated System for Customs Data (ASYCUDA) computerization programme[2] provides an interesting example in this regard.

In spite of all these reasons, the rise of e-government in the years to come will be as unstoppable as that of e-commerce. For instance, in August 2000 a report by Forrester Research estimated that by 2006 the Government of the United States would collect about 15 per cent of its tax and fee revenue online.[3] This represents a three-fold increase compared with figures for the year 2000. The same report calculated that by 2006, Governments at all levels in the United States would receive 333 million online filings. In April 2000, the Gartner Group predicted that total government spending in the United States (including federal, State and local) in e-government projects would grow from $1.5 billion in 2000 to $6.2 billion in 2005.[4] It is reasonable to expect that this trend will be reproduced in the rest of the world, in the same way as e-commerce has spread mainly from the United States to other advanced economies and more and more to developing countries. The next section will explore why.

C. The incentives to go online

Growing public expectations will be among the main factors behind the move towards e-government in most countries. As e-commerce becomes more and more a part of the everyday life of people, it will be harder for public sector service providers to lag behind in terms of the availability and the quality standards of services offered by private e-businesses. As the public grows accustomed to the convenience of round-the-clock, customized online services without the inconvenience of physically going to a public office and then wasting time in queues, public sector managers will be confronted with mounting pressure from users expecting to receive the same treatment as citizens as they receive as consumers.

The same organizational complexity that was mentioned earlier as a factor contributing to the slow development of e-government provides a good reason for public demand for more sophisticated online government services. The large number of government agencies that affect the activities of people and businesses in one way or another — each of them with its own regulations, practices and formal requirements — makes the relationship between citizens and government an ideal candidate for the efficiency gains provided by the Internet. For instance, a change of residence may require contacting agencies involved with, for example, tax, utilities, education, health care, driving licences and vehicle registration and voting registration. Each will ask for very similar but not necessarily identical information, provided in different forms and within various deadlines. In an ideal situation (and a quite unrealistic one for the time being), a fully operational e-government would allow users to log on to a secure website from which they could provide all necessary information which would then be checked and transmitted to all agencies concerned in a matter of minutes.

A second, strong incentive for Governments to go online is the political pressure for the public sector to "do more with less". In the private sector, one of the clearest benefits for companies that have re-organized themselves to become e-businesses has been cost reduction at every stage of their value creation chain. Given the vast amount of financial and human resources handled by Governments, the potential savings in areas ranging from public procurement to personnel management are considerable. In the case of procurement, for instance, savings of the order of 20 per cent are common among private companies that have moved their procurement operations to the Internet.[5] It is true that Governments may not be able to automatically reap the same benefits as are now available to the private sector. For example, while the Internet makes it easier for private firms to outsource part of their activities to cheaper overseas contractors, many defence contracts are unlikely to be awarded to a foreign company. But even allowing for these kinds of differences, the savings in procurement costs derived from the widened scope of suppliers, lower administrative expenses and reduced need for financing stocks can be high.

Enhancing the overall competitiveness of the economy is another reason for Governments to embrace the Internet. Apart from helping in the more efficient use of a significant share of the nation's resources (public consumption represents about 15 per cent of GDP worldwide), e-government will provide an example and an incentive for firms to adopt e-business practices, thus spreading the efficiency gains to the economy as a whole. And if in the "old economy", an efficient Government was a key factor for successful development strategies, a good e-government will be equally important for the "new economy". A well-run e-government will also help make a country more attractive to foreign investors and the mobile, highly skilled talent that can be crucial in enabling the new digital economy to take off.

These and other reasons have contributed to a change of perception among public sector decision-makers. Until recently, the most pressing concern for many Governments in the area of e-business was how to create the right environment for private e-business to prosper. It remains true that Governments have a crucial responsibility in areas such as the regulatory framework for e-commerce (including rules for e-contracts, consumer protection, taxes or privacy), ensuring the competitiveness of telecommunication services or equipping the population with Internet skills. However, public sector managers are now realizing that this is not enough. Governments (mainly, but not exclusively, in developed countries) are putting in place strategies to transform themselves into e-governments, and setting targets to measure progress.

Table 20 provides some information about the targets that the Governments of the G-7 and a few

Table 20
E-government service delivery targets of selected countries

Country	Electronic service delivery target
Australia	All appropriate Federal Government services capable of being delivered electronically via the Internet by 2001.
Canada	All key government services fully on-line by 2004.
Finland	A significant proportion of forms and requests can be dealt with electronically by 2001.
France	All administrations to provide public access to government services and documents by the end of 2000.
Germany	No high-level targets. Some departmental targets have been set.
Ireland	All but the most complex of integrated services by the end of 2001.
Italy	No high-level targets. Some departmental targets have been set.
Japan	All applications, registrations and other administrative procedures involving the people and the Government will be available on-line using the Internet or other means by the fiscal year 2003.
Netherlands	25 per cent of public services delivered electronically by 2002.
Singapore	Where feasible, all counter services available electronically by 2001.
Sweden	No high-level targets. Some departmental targets have been set.
United Kingdom	100% of government services carried out electronically by 2005.
United States	Provide public access to government services and documents by 2003. Provide the public with an option to submit forms electronically.

Source: Central IT Unit (2000).

other countries have set themselves as part of their e-government strategies.

D. Delivering e-government

A search for government sites in any popular Internet search engine will return thousands of governmental websites, with practically every country in the world represented. They can be roughly classified into five categories:

(i) Those that merely provide Internet visibility. Sites from many developing countries fall into this category, but governmental websites from developed countries are also present. These sites usually include a few pages with basic information on the agency concerned and tend to be updated on a rather irregular basis. The business process of the agency remains unchanged.

(ii) Sites that provide a one-way channel for information are also quite numerous. They may include a large volume of information on issues such as laws and regulations, procedures, objectives and policies of the agency concerned and institutional and contact information. When they are regularly updated, well organized and focused on the needs of the user rather than on the structure of the agency, these websites can provide a valuable service. However, they are not e-government tools because they cannot support formal transactions. As in the previous case, setting up a website does not, by itself, change the way the agency operates.

(iii) Sites which combine the content of the previous category with the possibility for users to interact with the staff of the agency, usually through e-mail. They may also include downloadable forms that can be later submitted offline. Complex transactions are not supported, but users can in theory provide information such as a change of address or ask questions. According to some surveys, a common problem is that a significant amount of these e-mail queries remain unanswered.[6] This reflects the fact that it will take time to put in place a new customer-oriented organizational culture, which is a prerequisite for successful e-government (see below).

(iv) A fast-growing number of sites, concentrated in developed or advanced developing countries, support formal transactions that involve either payments or the creation or transfer of legal rights (for instance, paying taxes, renewing a driving licence or claiming social security benefits). Some also allow users to check online the status of a request, or may use the information they accumulate about a citizen's particular circumstances to remind him or her of the need to renew a licence or the deadline for submitting a tax declaration. These sites may include tools to help users complete online transactions, but they normally need to be combined with more traditional support systems, such as a telephone "hot-line".

(v) A handful of sites aim at providing services not on the basis of the way the agency entrusted with their delivery is organized, but according to the needs of the user. This implies that they must integrate a wide range of governmental services, normally under the same overall political responsibility (integrating the services of different levels of government raises complex political issues). Ideally, operating sites in this category should be the ultimate target of e-government efforts: a comprehensive government portal through which users could interact with their Government by asking simple questions such as "What do I need to do to set up a new business?" The system would ask the user to provide all relevant information and process it through the interlinked systems of the various agencies concerned without the user noticing it. Eventually, the user would receive in his e-mailbox legally valid e-documents reflecting all the actions taken by the agencies involved.

The list of Governments that have launched, or announced plans to launch, comprehensive Internet portals is long and not limited to developed countries. The list of those that are actually using them to provide e-transaction services is much shorter and mostly comprises local or State-level Governments, or countries with a highly centralized political system. Even at the government portals that are considered to be the most advanced only some selected services are operating fully online.

Even though government portals are crucial to most e-government strategies, their implementation is fraught with difficulties. They require change on an unprecedented scale, both in the processes of government agencies (to make them more user-centred and less hierarchical, to redesign procedures, to learn how to work better with other agencies) and in their management of information technology (for instance, to adapt legacy systems so that they can handle payments and e-signatures, or to adopt common approaches to issues such as data collection and processing).

Technology itself is not the main problem. First, what makes the Internet such a powerful force for change is that, at least in theory, it allows people using different information technology platforms to communicate and work together thanks to a set of open standards and protocols. Second, in many applications of the Internet to government, the difference between e-government and e-business will be one of scale more than substance. This means that solutions that are already available for the private sector — from public key infrastructures for identification to Internet procurement software — can, with only relatively few changes, be applied to many government activities.

Organizational aspects are a more serious concern. Successful e-government agencies need to see the citizen as their customer, which represents a cultural revolution for many organizations. Becoming a user-centred organization may require a change in resource allocation priorities (for instance, from internal administration to customer service) and, as indicated earlier, a thorough review of the business processes of every agency. This means more than just streamlining or digitalizing forms: it involves deciding how many of the tasks an agency performs will remain relevant after the change. A user-centred agency will also need to give credible answers to concerns about the integrity and confidentiality of the sensitive data that government agencies often collect.

Agencies must upgrade the skills of their staff: technology without people will be useless. Motivating public employees to support the change to e-government can be challenging if the move is perceived to be motivated by cost-cutting (i.e. job-cutting) considerations rather than by the will to provide better value to citizens. The change in mentality must reach all levels in the government structure. Government decision-makers who feel uncomfortable using e-mail or who rarely surf the web cannot credibly lead the move to e-government.

Finally, some degree of inter-agency coordination needs to be ensured. This should not be confused with a preference for large, centralized projects. On the contrary, financial, technical and political reasons make this approach likelier to fail than one that gives priority to smaller projects with short, well-defined time frameworks and relatively modest objectives. There is, however, a need to ensure that a common vision of e-government exists and that consistent policies are applied in addressing issues such as security or privacy protection.

It seems therefore likely that in most countries the move towards e-government will tend to be incremental. The current phase can be considered an experimental one, with Governments concentrating on limited, relatively low-risk applications of the Internet that do not pose too hard questions in areas such as security and privacy. As the demand for e-government grows, and agencies feel more secure in their handling of it, e-government will enter a second phase in which portals integrating a wider range of online transactions in a secure environment will be more widespread.

For most Governments the issue today is how to identify the areas where their first forays into e-government can be more productive. The experience so far points to procurement, self-service websites for the processing of relatively simple transactions (where business services should have priority) and intranets that allow agencies to share and exploit data more efficiently as the types of Internet applications in which early success is more likely.

E. A few starting points

The step-by-step approach that most Governments are likely to follow as they adapt their services to the Internet does not mean that ambitious long-term objectives should be abandoned. On the contrary, it is the success of focused, realistic e-government projects that will lend legitimacy to far-reaching visions of change. The final section of this chapter sets out a number of points that need to be kept in mind when launching e-government projects.

- **E-government requires reliable, fast technology.** Demand for e-government services is expected to grow at a rapid pace. But a web page that is frequently inaccessible at peak demand times can be extremely frustrating no matter how well designed the page is. Reliability problems in a widely used online service can damage the credibility of a whole e-government project. Untested technologies should be avoided and standard software solutions adopted as much as possible. In developing countries, technology choices should also be made keeping in mind that Internet platforms designed for use in a context of high-quality telecommunications infrastructure will not be a viable option for their e-government projects. And the personal computer need not be the only means of access to e-government services: m-commerce (e-commerce through cellular phones) is an example of a cheaper alternative that may be more adapted to the conditions of developing countries.
- **Start small and build on success stories.** Large, complex projects are more likely to fail and thus undermine e-government initiatives than modest, self-contained projects. On the contrary, the success of small but scalable projects boosts staff morale, provides valuable lessons that can be applied in more ambitious undertakings and will help create a critical mass of e-government users.
- **Digital government is not just digitized forms.** E-government is an opportunity to rethink the business process of governmental agencies, following a logic that places the user at the centre of every task performed.
- **Remember that not everyone will be online.** The Internet adds a new channel for the delivery of government services; in some areas it will eventually become the most popular one. But because of concerns about social inclusion, traditional channels such as counter service and the telephone will retain an important role. The special needs those categories of people who may find it harder to use the Internet in their dealings with the Government (for instance, illiterate people) must also be taken into account.
- **Recognize and address privacy and security concerns.** Government agencies handle and store a great deal of confidential information about people and businesses. An e-government project will not take off if people are not convinced that dealing with the Government online provides the same level of data protection as more traditional methods.
- **Prioritize government-to-business services.** E-government services aimed at the business sector are those in which efficiency gains are more likely to translate into improved competitiveness for the economy as a whole. Examples of such services include Customs, business taxation and government procurement.
- **Build up critical mass.** The success of an e-government project will be measured mainly by the number of users it can attract. For this, citizens and businesses need to be made aware of the availability and advantages of e-government services. Marketing campaigns may be complemented with financial (lower fees) and non-financial incentives (guaranteed faster

processing of tax returns filed online) for e-government users.

- **Ensure leadership and political commitment.** E-government will bring about profound changes in the relationships among government agencies, and between them and government, citizens and public employees. This complex challenge calls for political commitment and a clear strategic vision at the highest possible level. This should be accompanied by strong project leadership at the operative level, with the capacity to arbitrate between different departments.
- **Explore partnerships with the private sector.** Implementing e-government will require significant investment. Budgetary resources may need to be complemented with alternative sources of funding, including the possibility of joint private–public financing of concrete e-government projects. These partnerships may also allow e-government projects to benefit from the experience accumulated by the private sector in the area of e-business.

Notes

1 For instance, according to the World Bank (2001), in 1998 the current revenue of the central Governments of the world amounted to 26.4 per cent of global gross domestic product (GDP) and the total expenditure was 27.9 per cent of GDP. With regard to procurement, Eurostat (2001) data show that for the fifteen countries of the European Union, openly advertised public sector procurement (which amounts to just 13.1 per cent of all public sector procurement) represented 1.83 per cent of GDP, or almost $155 billion.

2 See www.asycuda.org.

3 Forrester Research Inc., "Sizing U.S. e-Government", quoted in E-commerce Times (2000). www.ecommercetimes.com 31 August 2000.

4 Gartner Group Inc (2000).., press release available at www4.gartner.com

5 The Economist (2000).

6 According to a study of 81 government sites in the United States carried out by Jupiter Communications in April 2000, as much as 52 per cent of e-mail queries received no response, and only 12 per cent were answered within one day. See remains eThestandard.com (2000).

References

Central IT Unit, Cabinet Office (2000). Benchmarking Electronic Service Delivery, London. Available at www.e-envoy.gov.uk/publications/int_comparisons.htm.

Eurostat (2001). Structural Indicators, European Communities, Brussels and Luxembourg. Quoted data available at www.europa.eu.int/comm/eurostat.

E-Commerce Times (2000). "Report: E-government becoming a reality", 31 August, www.ecommercetimes.com.

Gartner Group Inc. (2000). "Gartner says U.S. e-government spending to surpass $6.2 billion by 2005", press release dated 11 April, available at www4.gartner.com/5_about/press_room/pr20000411c.html.

The Economist (2000). "Survey: Government and the Internet", 22 June.

Thestandard.com (2000). "E-government services elusive", 6 November, www.thestandard.com.

World Bank (2001). World Development Indicators 2000, World Bank Publications, Washington, DC. Quoted data available at www.worlbank.org.

Part Three

Electronic Commerce Environment and Practices

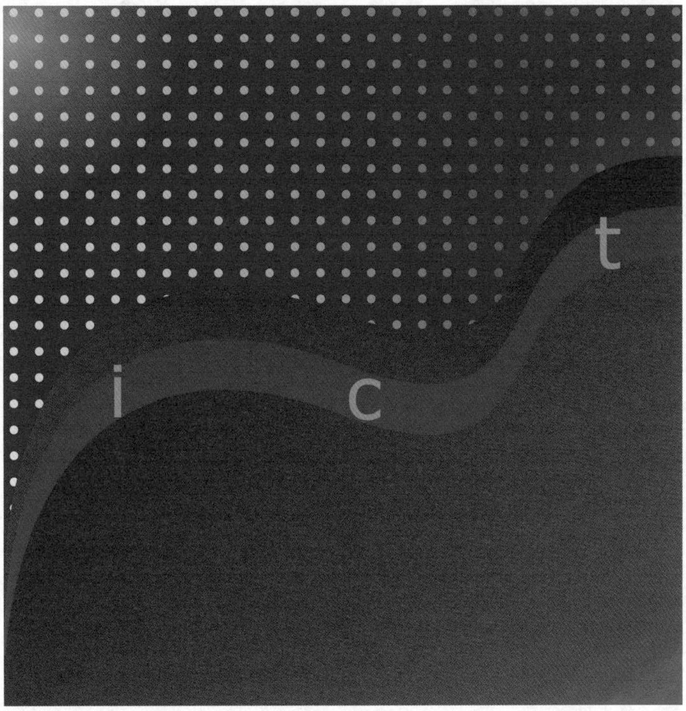

Chapter 6

OVERVIEW OF SELECTED LEGAL AND REGULATORY DEVELOPMENTS IN ELECTRONIC COMMERCE

A. Introduction

The present chapter reviews some of the most pressing e-commerce issues, such as dispute resolution, applicable law, privacy and data protection, and provides an overview of other relevant legal and regulatory developments in the field of e-commerce, including e-commerce taxation. By e-commerce we mean not only contracts or transactions (both business-to-business and business-to-consumer),[1] but also torts. In addition, issues pertaining to applicable law, as well as to dispute resolution through courts and through alternative techniques, are analysed here. An attempt is made to explain both the status of the solutions currently available, as they may be applied by courts in some countries,[2] and the evolution of international negotiations on these matters.

However, first of all, the current discussion on whether the Internet constitutes only a space by and of itself which could be called "cyberspace" needs to be explained. This discussion is important because if the conclusion is positive, a number of consequences will follow. If the Internet is a space, it is a space without borders in which private international law does not have any meaning since the rules of private international law are made in order to deal with different legal systems and borders. As a result, the Internet should have its own uniform legal system specifically applying to it. Finally, there is no reason why private operators cannot be accepted as the source of norm together with, or in lieu of, States. Indeed, claims that the Internet is a specific and separate space leads to the assertion that States should not be trying to legislate on Internet issues.[3] However, most agree nowadays that States do have an important role to play even though an increased role is to be given to the private sector. Let us consider for a moment the most evident feature of the Internet — the one which gives cyberspace its very original nature — the domain name system.[4] It is true that the way in which Internet operators are allowed to access and operate on the Internet, i.e. through the domain name system, transforms the nationality question which is traditionally important for private international law. The generic top-level domain names (the .com, .net, .org, etc.) do not give any indication about the nationality or location of the "site" or the person who owns or operates it. Therefore, expressions such as "a foreign site" or "a domestic site" are without any meaning in the present context. Even national top-level domain names (e.g. the .fr for France, .us for the United States, .ch for Switzerland and .cm for Cameroon) are no longer meaningful. Indeed, most registrars in charge of the registration of national domain names do not block registration by domain name owners that are not domiciled in the country in question.[5] For example, a national or resident of the United States can register a domain name in France and vice-versa. In other words, the domain names are of no help for private international law issues. But, in our view, this is not enough to conclude that cyberspace is a space.

It is also said that the Internet is a space because it is an entirely decentralized system with absolutely no inherent control since it is a network of networks, linking two techniques — computers and telecommunication means. However, this description is purely a technical one and does not automatically mean that the Internet is a space. In fact, this technical description shows one thing: the Internet is a means of communication between human beings, or entities composed of human beings. Whether this communication is partially or entirely automated and software-driven does not alter the fact that the use of a software is possible only through the will of a human being or an entity.

The fact that the Internet is a means of communication does not mean that it does not have its own specific characteristics which will have an impact on private international law. Those characteristics will be rapidly reviewed here, first in order to determine whether the Internet is international or transnational. Whoever sends data via the Internet, even to a local correspondent, may well be dealing with operators located in different countries, sometimes without knowing it. Therefore, the use of the Internet may mean that a transaction will be international even though both parties to the transaction are located in the same country. Thus, it may mean that a new concept of internationality is born, that of "electronic transaction". As soon as the electronic communication system is used, the transaction is an electronic transaction and may necessitate the application of specific rules.[6]

Cyberspace is also characterized by its ubiquity and multiplicity since the Internet allows a person to reach out to a multitude of persons at the same time. This has an immediate consequence. At first sight, because the Internet covers the whole world, each of the 200 or so countries around the globe may have a claim to apply its own legal system to an Internet transaction. Instead of there being the vacuum of which some may have warned a little too quickly,[7] there are in fact too many potentially applicable legal rules. Because this result is impossible to accept, there must be a shift in the analysis. We need to recognize that there are only two relevant contact points: the places where the parties to the transaction are located.[8] With the Internet, it is necessary to accept that the place of conclusion or the place of enforcement of a transaction, traditionally used in private international law analysis, is no longer pertinent.

A third characteristic of great importance is the extreme rapidity of Internet communications. This is particularly crucial for torts. Indeed, harmful actions in cyberspace may have more damaging effects than in real life, just because of this factor. One immediate consequence for dispute resolution follows from this: courts must act more quickly and international judicial cooperation is absolutely essential.

A fourth characteristic is the very low cost of market entry. It is therefore very easy for a one-person shop to start a multinational activity as long as that person organizes his or her logistics carefully with independent partners. Nowadays, the expression "transnational enterprise" or "multinational enterprise" has another, completely different meaning. As well as referring to the traditional giants with a bricks and mortar presence in many States, it can refer to very small entities dealing via the Internet. This will necessitate a new analysis of the concept of "consumer". This aspect of the problem will be discussed in Section B, paragraph (c) (i).

Finally, a new phenomenon is starting to spread through Internet activities which is of a major concern particularly for torts. Although the Internet was initially created as a transparent network in which each and every participant was identified and identifiable, many claim nowadays that they enter cyberspace and deal on the net with full anonymity.[9] Again, this is contrary to the original philosophy behind the Internet but does not yet seem to cause much concern in international forums. This will be discussed mainly in Section B, paragraphs (d), (e) and (f).

In the preparation of this chapter the work done by a number of organizations (either intergovernmental or non-governmental) was taken into consideration: the preliminary draft Hague Convention on Jurisdiction and Foreign Judgments in Civil and Commercial Matters[10] and other work done by the Hague Conference;[11] discussions and proposed texts adopted under the auspices of UNCITRAL; discussions and recommendations adopted under the auspices of the OECD; work done by the European Union and studies prepared by the American Bar Association (ABA), discussing a range of legal issues associated with jurisdiction in relation to the needs of electronic commerce.[12] In addition, we have studied declarations released by professional interest groups such as the Global Business Dialogue in Electronic Commerce (GBDe)[13] and the Internet Law and Policy Forum (ILPF).[14]

B. Dispute resolution

When legal relations are essentially based on contracts, the role of dispute resolution mechanisms is absolutely crucial. Traditional means of dispute resolution include recourse to national courts, but arbitration and mediation have always had their role to play in different cultures and at different times. Arbitration has had a renewed preponderant role in international trade, at least for the past half-century. Since e-commerce is based on party autonomy (at least in business-to-business (B2B) transactions), arbitration may be the preferred means for dispute resolution[15] in this area as well. However, there are cases in which arbitration or other alternative dispute resolution (ADR) mechanisms are not suitable[16] or may not be working. Thus, it is important that courts of law be available and clear rules of jurisdiction be offered to private operators. This is usually known as the "last resort rule".

1. Court jurisdiction

In the last few years, attention was focused on a major project undertaken by the Hague Conference on Private International Law to propose a worldwide convention on jurisdiction and foreign judgements in civil and commercial matters.[17] This project tried to use the very successful experience of a number of European countries with the Brussels[18] and Lugano[19] Conventions on the same issues. Although the Hague draft[20] did not fully take into consideration potentially specific e-commerce needs, several subsequent meetings discussed them. The following discussion will draw both on the work done at The Hague and on the work subsequently done in a number of other forums.[21]

(a) Choice of court

Since e-commerce has increased the need to rely on party autonomy, choice-of-court clauses become central to any discussion of court jurisdiction. It is essential that national legal systems clearly provide for rules on which parties can rely in order to ensure that their choice-of court-clauses will be deemed valid. Uncertainty in this respect is detrimental to the trust which private operators will have in the judicial and legal systems of a particular country. This is why it is so important that countries develop rules. The best way would be to develop them collectively, in an international forum. But if this is not possible, countries should at least develop a set of rules of their own.

An example of a possible rule to be adopted by States is the proposed Article 4 of the preliminary draft Hague Convention, which reads as follows:

> "1. If the parties have agreed that a court or courts of a Contracting State shall have jurisdiction to settle any dispute which has arisen or may arise in connection with a particular legal relationship, that court or those courts shall have jurisdiction, and that jurisdiction shall be exclusive unless the parties have agreed otherwise. Where an agreement having exclusive effect designates a court or courts of a non-Contracting State, courts in Contracting States shall decline jurisdiction or suspend proceedings unless the court or courts chosen have themselves declined jurisdiction.
>
> 2. An agreement within the meaning of paragraph 1 shall be valid as to form, if it was entered into or confirmed -
>
> a) in writing;
>
> b) by any other means of communication which renders information accessible so as to be usable for subsequent reference;
>
> c) in accordance with a usage which is regularly observed by the parties;
>
> d) in accordance with a usage of which the parties were or ought to have been aware and which is regularly observed by the parties to contracts of the same nature in the particular trade or commerce concerned.
>
> ...."

The important features of this rule are as follows:

1. The jurisdiction conferred on the court chosen by the parties to the agreement is exclusive unless the parties have expressly provided otherwise. This rule, which is not yet accepted all over the world,[22] seems to be preferred by practitioners since it provides more predictability and certainty.
2. The effect of a court selection clause on non-contracting States is relevant only when the rule is inserted in an international treaty. Obviously, if the rule is adopted by a national legislative body, this part of the rule will have to be deleted. It may be replaced by a direction given to national courts that in the event that it is seized of a dispute when a choice-of-court clause grants jurisdiction to a court of a foreign country, the court seized suspends the proceedings unless the court of the foreign country has declined jurisdiction.
3. As far as the formal validity of the clause is concerned, subparagraph (b) is the most relevant for e-commerce purposes since it accepts the validity of electronically formed agreements. This provision is in conformity with the most advanced state of the art in this respect. This was the conclusion of the Geneva Round Table,[23] and it did not give rise to any criticism in the forums where jurisdictional rules were discussed. The language

is that adopted by the UNCITRAL Model Law on Electronic Commerce, of 1996.

4. Finally, it should be noted that the provision does not include a rule on the substantial validity of the choice-of-court clause.[24] This is due to the fact that in B2B transactions there is an assumption that the contract is executed by equal partners. Thus, the protection of one partner against the other may not be necessary. This is different in relations between a professional and a consumer, as will be discussed below. However, in electronic commerce there may be a need to reassess the notions of "equal partners" and "consumers". This will also be dealt with below.

(b) Business-to-business contracts

This is one of the most difficult issues in international jurisdiction. Before we look at potential provisions relating to it, it is important to stress why a specific business contract jurisdiction has been considered necessary in the past (in addition to the defendant's domicile or habitual residence).[25] When deciding on court jurisdiction rules, legislators try to find the most suitable court with regard to the parties and to the claim, taking into consideration in particular the location of the evidence. In the real world, the most frequently used contract, that of sale of goods, may lead to disputes involving most of the time defective or non-conforming products. Thus, very often, it is easier to grant jurisdiction to the court in the location where these products are located, which is usually the court where the contract was performed or was to be performed.

The preliminary draft Hague convention reflects this kind of thinking, since it provides as follows in Article 6:

> "Article 6. *Contracts*:
>
> A plaintiff may bring an action in contract in the courts of a State in which:
>
> (a) in matters relating to the supply of goods, the goods were supplied in whole or in part;
>
> (b) in matters relating to the provision of services, the services were provided in whole or in part;
>
> (c) in matters relating both to the supply of goods and the provision of services, performance of the principal obligation took place in whole or in part."

This rule is slightly different from the rule in the Brussels and Lugano Conventions and in the European Regulation of December 2000. But it stems from the same reasoning as that explained above. It is important to reassess this rationale in view of the specificity of electronic commerce. But before doing so, it should be understood that any contract jurisdiction is a jurisdiction by default, i.e. a jurisdiction for all contracts in which the parties have not taken the precaution of including a valid choice-of-court clause.

Recent discussions show that three fundamental issues arise in e-commerce. The first is need to distinguish between contracts which are concluded electronically but performed offline (see (i) below), and contracts which are both concluded and performed electronically (see (ii) below). The second issue is the identification and location of the parties to the contract ((iii) below). The third issue is the distinction traditionally made between products and services. As this will be raised during the discussion about contracts which are to be concluded and performed online, it will be discussed here in that context.

(i) Contracts concluded online and performed offline

Although it is customary in many e-commerce discussions to stress that, as far as possible, rules for online dealings must not be different from those applied to real-life dealings, there is one exception which seems to be accepted: special rules are needed when the contract is performed entirely online. Indeed, in the latter case, the link of the contract (and the potential dispute arising out of it) to a specific territory does not exist separately from the location of the parties to the contract. This will be discussed below, together with the identification of parties.

For the time being, the present discussion is limited to one very important consensus: any analysis of a potential jurisdictional rule for contracts must separate contracts performed offline from those performed online. A rule such as the one in Article 6 of the draft Hague Convention may be satisfactory when the contracts in question are concluded electronically, although performed offline.[26] In that case, it seems to be agreed that no special provision is necessary because the traditional approach defining jurisdiction, with a focus on the place of performance, is still pertinent. However, for contracts which are concluded and performed online, the question of a potential supplementary clause arises. It may be considered, at the end of the analysis, that the defendant's forum coupled with the forum chosen by the parties may be sufficient for the needs of e-commerce. However, before this conclusion is reached, a thorough analysis of the needs must be conducted.

(ii) Contracts concluded and performed online

The question that arises with regard to these contracts is whether the traditional distinction between products and services is a realistic one for electronic transactions. This is a subject that is still debated in the World Trade Organization. In the European Directive on Electronic Commerce,[27] however, it has received an answer. For the European Community, the subject matter of an electronic exchange is primarily information, and this information has to be treated as equivalent to services. However, it is not entirely clear whether the description of an online contract is absolutely necessary for the definition of a jurisdictional rule. In any case, whether one accepts that an online contract is one for "services" or that no description is necessary, it may be said that the distinction proposed by Article 6 of the draft Hague Convention is not pertinent for contracts performed online.

One should focus on finding the most appropriate court, taking into consideration all the specific factors mentioned above which make the Internet a specific means for conducting business. With this in mind, it is clear that the place where the contract is performed is not relevant in the online world. Many "places" have been proposed, for example where the server's computers are located or where the Internet service provider (ISP) is located. But none of them are relevant when the contract in question does not involve the server or the ISP. In fact, the analysis leads us back to a fiction: the contract is deemed to be performed where either of the parties is located. This is why the identification and the location of the parties are of such importance in an Internet transaction.

(iii) Identification and location of the parties

All documents published in the past two years or so emphasize the crucial importance of the identification and location of the parties when one is dealing over the Internet.[28] As far as the identification of the parties is concerned, it is assumed that no request for anonymity can seriously be made when the transaction in question is a commercial one. Whoever takes the risk of dealing anonymously over the net runs the risk of not having access to the courts on a favourable basis. Dealing under cover of anonymity may be a preferred way of protection for some operators. However, it cannot be used afterwards to claim court jurisdiction detrimental to the other party.

The location of the parties must be defined as the place where the party has its bricks and mortar location. All agree nowadays that a site is not a location per se.[29] The discussions under the auspices of the Hague Conference seem to show that a preferred approach could focus on the concept of presumption. This could be summarized as follows:

(a) Maximum use should be made of freedom of contract (party autonomy);

(b) Statements by the parties to the contract concerning their identification and location, during the negotiation and in the contract itself, should be used for jurisdictional purposes;

(c) If a provider of services[30] wants to know in advance which court may have jurisdiction to settle any disputes he may have with his co-contractor, he will have to ask him for details of his location;

(d) The co-contractor will then be bound by the information he supplies concerning his location, and the jurisdictional rule will apply in respect of this information;

(e) In the event of difficulties due to false information, error or lack of information, the specific jurisdictional rule will no longer apply. In such a case, the traditional defendant's forum or the branch forum will be the only jurisdiction available.

A system which is based mainly on statements made by the parties may present some disadvantages, particularly the abuses which may arise from it. It is quite conceivable that one of the parties to the contract may declare that he or she is situated on the territory of a given State, solely in order to confer jurisdiction on the courts of that State for reasons entirely unconnected with the contract itself, such as the way in which those courts operate, the rules of procedure they follow or the rules of evidence or conflict of laws used in them. Of course, this danger is not entirely absent from the system proposed. However, it is the role of any co-contractor to be vigilant and to check, if necessary, that the information supplied by the other party matches the true situation.

In the unlikely event that the prudence of the co-contractor has not been sufficient, the court seized of the dispute may still have the possibility to use its discretion to refuse jurisdiction if it finds that it is not the most appropriate forum. It is true that not all systems in the world provide for a *forum non conveniens* theory to be applied by their courts. But it seems that there is a consensus nowadays for some kind of *forum non conveniens* to be applied in international cases.

(c) Consumer contracts

(i) A new concept of "Consumer"?

One of the most difficult issues in e-commerce discussions is the definition of a consumer. In most legal systems, a consumer is defined as an individual acting for personal or family purposes, and thus any enterprise, undertaking or company and any person having a business purpose[31] is excluded from the definition.

The characteristic feature of the Internet is that it greatly lowers the cost of entry into the market. Thus the size of an undertaking which may start an Internet activity has been reduced to an unprecedented level. An individual is now able to conduct a multinational business from a one-man shop as long as it has secured the proper contracts for goods and delivery. Thus, two questions must be asked. First, does this very small undertaking deserve protection in the online world? Secondly, when dealing with its own consumers, is this small undertaking at arms length or do those consumers still deserve protection?

Another factor also is adding some complexity to the discussion. Consumers now have at their disposal software products by which they can search the web and find the best offer for a service or a product they are looking for. These are known as BOTs (short for robots). Some argue that using a BOT gives the consumer a sophistication transforming him or her into a much more powerful contractor. Thus, the cyber-consumer, using a BOT, would not need any more protection.[32]

It is impossible to give an answer to these questions for the time being, as the debate is still raging. Consumer protection groups around the world claim the same protection in the online environment as in the real world,[33] whatever the size of the business.

At an early stage, many Governments declared that consumers must be protected in the same manner whether dealing over the Internet or in the real world. However, interest groups representing corporations have argued that if consumers are protected by the possibility of their suing from home and by the application of the relevant rules of their domicile, Internet operators on the other hand are not at all likely to be knowledgeable about all the laws in the world and to be able to defend themselves in all the courts in the world. Their conclusion therefore is that we should do away with the rules protecting consumers.

Although it is not claimed that it is easy to give an answer, a few guidelines may be kept in mind for further reflection. First, it may be possible to agree on a new definition of a sophisticated consumer who may need less or no protection in the online world. In Europe, in the financial service sector, a concept of "sophisticated investor" has been used for a number of years[34] which may be used as a starting point for a definition of the cyber-consumer. Second, Internet operators make considerable savings when they start their business over the net and could be asked to use part of those savings to buy some special insurance coverage for their Internet dealings.[35] Third, operators may define their price policy in order to offer different prices to consumers and to professional buyers. Knowing that it is more costly to sell to a consumer (if current rules still apply), the buyer would be able to buy at the price he prefers: either he saves money immediately knowing that he will not have much protection if something goes wrong, or he pays a higher price in order to be better protected.[36]Fourth, operators should make use of jurisdiction avoidance. This means that if they feel unable to sell in one jurisdiction, when a consumer declares that he/she is located in that jurisdiction, a notice should appear on the site to the effect that no sale may be concluded in that jurisdiction. If the consumer decides to make a statement that he/she is located in a different jurisdiction, he/she will not be able to claim, later on, protection of his/her real jurisdiction.

(ii) Any place for party autonomy?

Referring to the Hague project is not the best way to discuss the potential place for party autonomy in business-to-consumer transactions. As it stands now, the rule in Article 7[37] does not leave room for party autonomy except under very strict conditions which are not pertinent to online dealings. In fact, the whole rule was prepared without taking into account the issues relating to electronic commerce.

The same applies to the new European Regulation which will replace the Brussels Convention.[38] That was why, before the text could be finally adopted and published in the *Official Journal of the European Communities*, an agreement was reached between the Council and the Commission so that work would continue to develop ADR systems within the European Union. This shows the importance currently given to ADR in business-to-consumer relations even in a system traditionally unfavourable to ADR such as the European legal system.[39]

Almost all international meetings held over the past two years or so have shown that ADR or online dispute resolution (ODR) could solve many disputes at an early stage without use of the court system. Once this has been said, all the rest needs to be defined. How will the ADR/ODR system be linked with the court system? What procedural rules will be applied by the ADR/ODR service providers? Will the consumer be able to choose an ADR/ODR system? If not, how will the system ensure that the ADR/ODR system chosen by the company, co-contractant to the consumer, is independent and fair? These are only a few of the numerous questions to be asked.[40]

As regards the validity of the choice-of-court clauses in business-to-consumer contracts, it is as controversial as the use of ADR. The traditional European attitude towards such clauses in consumer contracts has always been very restrictive.[41] Similarly, a number of courts in the United States have recently refused to uphold choice-of-court clauses in Internet contracts.[42] However, it is still too early to say that a trend has already been established in that country. During the Hague discussions, several proposals led to a solution whereby choice- of- court clauses would be valid if the State of the consumer's habitual residence accepted them as valid. There would be an express statement by the relevant country in its legislation. This solution might be a means of achieving consensus by maintaining the status quo but does not solve the actual issue.

(iii) The present solutions

Whatever the place of ADR/ODR, there will always be some role for courts. Whether it is a last-resort role if the ADR system does not work, or whether it is the "juge d'appui" role in aid of the ADR system, there must be a definition of a jurisdictional rule for courts in business-to-consumer contracts. At present the systems applied in various countries differ.

In the United States, the definition of jurisdictional rules specifically for consumers is rendered unnecessary by two factors. Indeed, rules on jurisdiction are very flexible in that country. They assume, as a starting point, that the plaintiff's choice of a forum must be respected unless it is unfair to the defendant. From that point, courts have developed an ever-increasing body of case law defining what set of circumstances is fair or unfair to the defendant. In that context, they do not need a specific starting point for consumers, and it is only the set of circumstances acceptable from the defendant's point of view that is different. But the reasoning is the same in B2B and B2C contracts.

In Europe, because the starting point is just the opposite, i.e. the plaintiff's forum is used only in exceptional circumstances as a derogation from the "normal" forum — that of the defendant — special rules have developed for consumers. This was true in the Brussels and Lugano Conventions. It is also true in the new Regulation, although the content of the rule has been slightly amended to include some kind of "targeting".

The present wording of Article 7 of the Hague draft requires all the conditions in its subparagraphs (a) and (b) to be fulfilled in order for the consumer to initiate proceedings in the courts of his or her habitual residence. Those conditions are:

(a) The conclusion of the contract must be linked to the activities of the business in the State of the consumer's residence, or directed at that State in particular by soliciting business through means of publicity;

(b) The consumer must have taken the necessary steps to conclude the contract in his or her State of residence.

The main question is whether placing material on an Internet site is regarded as advertising by the business. If so, the first condition will always be met. Thus, it does not seem to have any further relevance for the purposes of electronic commerce. As for the second condition, present-day means of telecommunication enable a consumer to conclude the contract in a place other than his/her habitual residence, but this does not have any particular implications for the purpose of deciding which courts have jurisdiction.

In order to solve these difficulties there must be a clear assessment of the interests at stake. States want to encourage electronic commerce, especially in the area of consumer contracts. Enterprises which offer goods and services via the Internet may be very small businesses, which need to be encouraged. From another point of view, it is clear that in the context of trade with consumers, the Internet will take off only if consumers themselves have confidence in it. And one of the essential points for consumers is to make sure that if a problem arises in their relationship with a business, they can obtain redress both rapidly and cost-effectively.

Would the inclusion of targeting be of some help? If the enterprise has specifically targeted consumers in a particular country, it would be logical to decide that the courts of that country have jurisdiction for consumers residing on its territory. On the other hand, if the business uses an unsophisticated site, i.e. one which does not make it possible to target certain consumers, the result will be that no particular conclusion can be drawn as regards jurisdiction. This development is not unanimously endorsed as yet.[43] In fact, we find the concept of targeting somewhat inconsistent with the fact that the Internet allows any service provider or seller to propose services and goods all over the world with no restriction except possible filtering of accessibility by local authorities. Therefore, it seems not "natural" in the cyber context to require some targeting. In addition, the circumstances usually considered in order to assess whether there is targeting or not may not be very determinative.[44]

In any event, even if the rule of default jurisdiction is kept for the consumer's habitual residence, the same principle as the one discussed for relationships among businesses would apply to the identification and location of the parties to the contract. The consumer would be required to identify his or her habitual residence in order to bring the jurisdictional rule into play.

(d) Torts

The major difficulty with tort[45] committed via the Internet is twofold: (i) it is very difficult to discover who committed the tort; and (ii) it may have had an immense impact on the victim before the latter was able to stop it. Thus, tort jurisdiction, even if needed, may have little impact unless ISPs[46] provide cooperation.

The difficulty is also that the tort impact or effect may be all over the world as some recent cases have demonstrated. Although they concern criminal matters, the recent Italian Supreme Court decision[47] and the French Yahoo case are interesting for our analysis.[48] The latter is particularly important since after defending fully in the French case and deciding to discontinue the harmful acts which were the very core of the French action, Yahoo! Inc. nonetheless decided to continue the action filed in a San Jose (California) court. The core of the United States action was to ask the United States court to rule that France did not have jurisdiction in that particular dispute. This cross-Atlantic battle over jurisdiction shows how urgent it is to have an international agreement on jurisdictional rules.

Italy and France have asserted jurisdiction against a foreign corporation on the basis of the harmful effect felt in each of those countries through websites owned by that foreign corporation. In each case, the remedy sought was an injunction to stop the harmful acts. Although the remedy was one that could have also been sought equally in a civil or commercial action, it is important to note that the harmful acts did violate criminal law in both countries. It is not certain whether the French and Italian courts would have asserted jurisdiction for a similar injunction if the dispute had been purely civil or commercial, unless some other links than the pure accessibility of the site was demonstrated between the circumstances and the forum.[49] At any rate, these two cases do pose the very questions which need to be answered when dealing with Internet tort jurisdiction.

Although it has been the subject of some criticism, Article 10 of the Hague draft could be taken as a starting point for discussion of what could be an internationally agreed rule.[50] The major feature of the rule is that it grants jurisdiction to the court of the place where the act takes effect (the place where the injury occurs), unless it can be shown that the perpetrator could not reasonably foresee that or a similar consequence. The courts of the place where the injury occurs will also be competent to rule on all the injury suffered anywhere in the world by an injured party, provided that party is a habitual resident of the State in which the court seized is situated. In all other cases, the jurisdiction of the courts of the place where the injury occurs is limited to injury suffered on their territory.

It may be pointed out that in the cyberworld the proof required in Article 10.1(b) can never be adduced. Internet sites, it is true, operate somewhat like newspapers which are distributed worldwide. A person who uploads defamatory information onto a site can reasonably foresee that it may be read anywhere in the world. The only unknown factor is the number of "copies" distributed (to pursue the analogy of the printed press).

Another criticism has been voiced about the use of the place of the wrongful action since that place specified in Article 10.1 a) is very difficult, if not impossible, to identify with the Internet. Thus, we may need to equate that place with the place where the perpetrator is located. However, in a tort action this would lead automatically to the defendant's forum which is otherwise made available in the Hague draft. Thus, it is questionable whether, in this context, we need a separate rule also pointing to the defendant's forum but through a different route. The second inconvenience resides is that it is very easy for a defendant to locate in a friendly jurisdiction with a judicial system which is not functioning well. This may be of concern in the drafting of such a rule.

In consequence, it appears that offences committed through the Internet make it necessary to have an alternative forum to the defendant's forum, but one which also has general jurisdiction (i.e. a court which can deal with injury suffered everywhere). The rule in Article 10, paragraph 4, of the preliminary draft was therefore welcomed by some as a particularly important one in the electronic context.

Since discussions on the Hague draft are still continuing, it is difficult to predict at this stage whether a common understanding and agreement will emerge.

(e) Branch offices

Jurisdiction based on a branch or business office is present in many legal systems. It is assumed that a corporation that uses a branch office in a country other than the one in which it conducts its main business or in which it is incorporated must be answerable in the courts of the country where the branch is located for disputes arising out of the activity of the branch. The same idea underlies some of the jurisdictional rules applied in the United States on the principle that a corporation which avails itself of the economic environment and the rules of a State has implicitly agreed to be accountable in the courts of that State.

There are two main questions regarding branch office jurisdiction in the context of electronic commerce:

1. Can an Internet site be regarded as a branch office?
2. Does the reply to the previous question depend on the level of interactivity of the site?[51]

It can be said that on the first question a clear consensus has already been reached which seems to cover a broad range of stakeholders. At a regional level, the European Union has clearly stated that a website is not a branch or establishment for any legal purpose.[52] This conclusion was also reached by experts, meeting under the auspices of the Hague Conference.[53] More recently, the OECD stated that a website is not a permanent establishment within the context of the model tax convention.[54]

The answer to the second question is also clear: whatever level of interactivity of the website, it will not change the conclusion reached above. However, if a site is an interactive one, it may lead countries which apply a doing-business concept for court jurisdiction to assert jurisdiction as long as the interactivity could be seen as a clear link with the State whose court asserts jurisdiction. On this issue there is a long line of cases in the United States showing how jurisdiction is asserted on the basis of an interactive site. This line of reasoning is difficult to apply in practice. It necessitates a very sophisticated reasoning both for the judge and the parties. Because of its casuistic nature it may not be predictable for parties. It involves an appreciation of the targeting concept. But it is difficult to agree on what targeting is and how much targeting is necessary in order to justify a court's assertion of jurisdiction.

(f) Is a domain name a real property?

This question is posed directly because of the Anticybersquatting Consumer Protection Act adopted in the United States on 29 November 1999.[55] It is not our aim to analyse all the provisions of the Act[56] but only to show how its jurisdictional provisions were recently interpreted and the difficulties in applying it in international cases.

The Act is mainly aimed at providing a forum and an action to a plaintiff whose intellectual property rights are violated by a domain name. Although the Internet Corporation for Assigned Names and Numbers (ICANN) has established a quasi-arbitration system to resolve such disputes[57] and many cases have already been decided under it by one of the three accredited dispute resolution service providers, the

United States thought it was not sufficient and adopted the above-mentioned Act.

The Act provides that in a case where the defendant cannot be found, the plaintiff may file a request for an injunctive relief before the court of the place where the domain name is registered. The court jurisdiction is purely *in rem*. In order to provide for this jurisdictional ground, the Act proceeds with two legal fictions: (i) a domain name is a property; and (ii) the location of that piece of property is deemed to be at the place of registration.[58]

This legislation is well intended in principle since it specifies that the *in rem* jurisdictional ground can be used only if the defendant cannot be found, i.e. if no personal jurisdiction (*in personam*) can be asserted. The American legislators wanted to combat trademark infringement by anonymous cybersquatters who, in bad faith, register a domain name that violates a valid trademark but then prove to be beyond the reach of an action. However, one of the first decisions rendered under this Act in an international context is worrying, and it may be of interest in the context of this chapter to discuss it in a little more detail.

The case involved two Internet domain names "Technodome.com" and "Destinationatechnodome.com" which the plaintiff, Heathmount A.E. Corp, claimed infringed its trademarks.[59] Both the plaintiff and the defendant (the owner of the domain names) were Canadians having places of business in Canada. There was no doubt that, under Canadian jurisdictional rules, there was *in personam* jurisdiction in Canada. However, the court in Virginia asserted *in rem* jurisdiction under the Act for two main reasons: (i) there was no *in personam* jurisdiction in the United States; and (ii) Canadian law did not provide a body of law similar to the United States Act.

It appears that the Virginia court interpreted the Act without taking into consideration the fact that *in personam* jurisdiction was available in Canada for a dispute between two Canadian citizens or legal persons. In addition, the second reason offered by the court for asserting jurisdiction was based on the lack of equivalent legislation in Canada. The court never considered the possibility that a Canadian court would apply the United States law. This lack of international perspective when dealing with Internet issues might lead to confusion and more forum shopping.

As a general and practical principle, *in personam* jurisdiction must always be preferred to an *in rem* jurisdiction since it allows the court to solve the entire dispute between the parties. Usually, it also facilitates enforcement of the decision.

2. Alternative dispute resolution

Because the judicial systems around the world face new challenges at a time when they have not entirely resolved old ones, private sector operators call for an increased role for alternative dispute resolution offered by private enterprises. We have already mentioned the discussion about the potential role of ADR/ODR in a business-to-consumer relationship. We will now explain briefly the type of services which are already offered and the ongoing discussions on a potential international legal framework for these services.

(a) Developments in different organizations

Numerous meetings have already taken place in various forums to develop alternative dispute resolution mechanisms with an emphasis on online techniques.[60]

(i) Meeting on alternative methods of dispute resolution, Brussels, March 2000

At the initiative of the European Commission, a meeting was held in Brussels on 21 March 2000 to deal with the alternative methods of resolving online disputes between consumers and businesses. The documents made available to the participants, and the report of the meeting, are available on the site dedicated to this Working Group.[61]

The main conclusions of the meeting can be summarized as follows:

1. Confidence in e-commerce will be achieved only if clear sets of rules are approved by all stakeholders at a European level, if not at an international level;
2. Any ADR/ODR system must be regarded as visible and transparent, accessible, affordable and efficient for users;
3. The decision taken or the transaction concluded after an ADR process must be fair;
4. The finality of the decision or transaction remains to be discussed, particularly with regard to the consumer;

5. ADR systems must be independent and impartial; and
6. Any work in this area must promote cooperation and coordination between consumers, companies and public institutions.

After the meeting, the European Commission launched the ECODIR project, which is an attempt to define a complete framework for a European ADR system. The project, which includes technical, legal and policy aspects, should be completed in the spring of 2001.[62]

(ii) Meeting organized by the United States Federal Trade Commission and the Department of Commerce, Washington DC, June 2000

The aim of this meeting was to identify the interests involved in electronic commerce when the transaction is concluded between a business and a consumer. Many ADR service providers attended the meeting. The participants discussed which avenues should be explored in the future to give confidence to consumers, and the incorporation of alternative methods into a complete dispute resolution system, specifically in relation to court proceedings.[63]

The meeting was a unique opportunity to gather first-hand information on the services which are already available and the principles on which they act. The conclusions of the meeting may be summarized as follows: (i) the ongoing process of trying to find global solutions must be favoured and emphasized with all stakeholders present (private and public sector alike); (ii) the technological innovations which were presented during the meeting must be developed further since they will help a more user-friendly set of systems to be offered; (iii) "one size won't fit all", i.e. ADR/ODR systems to be developed must be tailored to deal with certain types of disputes so that they are best adjusted to their specific needs; and (iv) fairness and effectiveness are the two main features which any ADR system must aim at.

(iii) Joint meeting between the OECD, the Hague Conference and the ICC

In December 2000, a meeting was held at The Hague under the joint auspices of the OECD, the Hague Conference on Private International Law and the International Chamber of Commerce (ICC).[64] It allowed stakeholders to present progress made in the course of the year regarding ADR/ODR services from different angles: cultural, political, economic, legal and policy. Issues were discussed from the point of view of consumer contracts and privacy protection. The role of ADR/ODR was again emphasized, but no firm conclusion could be drawn from the discussion about the actual place of ADR/ODR as a sole recourse or as part of a more complete system including recourse to courts.

(b) The potential place of ADR in the global system

In our view, there is quite a pressing need to develop ADR/ODR systems adapted to Internet dealings both for business-to-business contracts and for consumer contracts. Several important statements have been released by some countries on this issue. The United States–European Union joint statement is an important one and represents the strong influence of private sector interests.[65] It focuses essentially on consumer confidence and will therefore be dealt with in paragraph (ii) below, after a few words have been said about ADR/ODR in B2B relations (paragraph (i)).

(i) Business-to-business contracts

In business-to-business contracts, it is not difficult to see how ADR/ODR will continue to have a major role to play. Mediation and arbitration had already become preferred means of dispute resolution in the B2B context long before the Internet was used. The Internet will only increase the need to use ADR.

The legal norms applicable to ADR all over the world have developed and are firmly established thanks to the considerable work done by the United Nations Commission on International Trade Law (UNCITRAL).[66] In addition, arbitration is well established around the globe. What is needed is some adaptation work to use increasingly electronic means for the arbitration process. This will be done in the course of time. It is already clear that the writing requirement of Article 2 of the New York Convention can be met by an electronic functional equivalent. Also, there is a consensus that the place of arbitration may be used as a legal fiction and does not need to be purely a geographical place.[67]

However, there is one aspect which has not been developed so far in the area of mediation. The result of successful mediation is a settlement. In most legal systems, a settlement is considered to be a contract. Therefore, if the settlement needs to be enforced outside the country in which it was reached, the rules applicable to arbitral awards or court decisions are not applicable. In addition, since the settlement is a contract, no automatic enforcement can be obtained. A court procedure may be necessary. This seriously impairs the value of a settlement. Thus, we think that work is needed on unified rules for transborder enforcement of settlements obtained through an out-of-court mediation system.

(ii) Consumer contracts

As explained above, the most controversial aspects of ADR/ODR concern consumer contracts. The joint statement by the United States and the European Union may set an important framework for further discussion at an international level. Part of the statement reads as follows:

"We now reaffirm these important goals and objectives, including the agreement to provide "active support for the development, preferably on a global basis, of self-regulatory codes of conduct and technologies to gain consumer confidence in electronic commerce". We also reaffirm our commitment to the OECD Guidelines on Consumer Protection in the Context of Electronic Commerce issued in December 1999.

Our common aim is to help generate consumer confidence, which is necessary for open, competitive, and cross-border electronic commerce. Ensuring consumer protection and generating consumer confidence requires a combination of private sector initiatives and a clear, consistent and predictable legal framework.

The means of building consumer confidence and consumer protection in shopping online is good business practice and enforceable self-regulatory programmes such as codes of conduct and trust marks. Key elements to building consumer confidence and consumer protection also include security and confidentiality, respect for privacy, high standards of customer service, timely delivery, full and fair disclosure of information, and responsiveness to complaints.

We recognize that consumers should have meaningful access to redress, consistent with the applicable legal framework and should be protected from fraudulent, deceptive, and unfair practices.

The Internet, which can support the growth of cross-border consumer transactions at unprecedented levels, poses challenges to the existing legal framework. The issues of applicable law and jurisdiction will be difficult to resolve in the near term, but solutions at the international level would help to achieve our shared goals of global electronic commerce growth, consumer confidence and predictability."

Most agree that any ADR/ODR system proposed for consumer disputes must be independent and impartial, transparent, efficient, legal, fair, and embody a procedure which fully respects the principle of contradiction.[68]

Some propose that the systems should be taking as a model the system embodied in the Uniform Domain Name Dispute Resolution Policy (UDRP)[69] of ICANN.[70] We do not deny that the UDRP rules may be of interest when reflecting on ODR. However, we think that these rules can only be a starting point and cannot be considered to be a model. The main reasons for that assertion are as follows: (i) the UDRP system covers a very limited area of substantive law, namely cybersquatting, i.e. the violation of trademark rights by domain names, whereas consumer disputes are much more diverse and may relate to different kinds of damages and different kinds of actions; (ii) the UDRP contains specific rules of evidence, whereas it is not possible to set in advance rules of evidence in a context where actions are diverse; (iii) the UDRP includes a limited sanction if the violation has been recognized, whereas sanctions in consumer disputes may be monetary and hence present specific difficulties of enforcement; and (iv) the UDRP contains its own enforcement rules, whereas such rules will need to be different depending on the type of sanction.

Disagreement is still strong on the following aspects: (i) How costly should the process be for consumers? (ii) Who will choose the ADR/ODR system? (iii) Would the consumer be obliged to go first to an ADR/ODR system before having recourse to court? (iv) If so, would the ADR/ODR process be limited in time? (v) How binding would the result of the ADR/ODR process be? Would it be binding only on the business? Or on both parties?

Most of the systems available in Europe, do not preclude the consumer from having recourse to the court system if the consumer disagrees with the decision rendered or the solution proposed by the ADR system. However, it should be noted that two systems propose an arbitration mechanism which is binding on the consumer. At an international level, the discussion is still going on in order to answer the questions posed in the preceding paragraph.

C. Applicable law

In comparison with dispute resolution, not much has been done at the international level to address the issues of applicable law. However, because in some countries, particularly common-law countries, the issues of court jurisdiction and applicable law are dealt with together, it can be said that a large part of the same controversies triggered by the proposed court jurisdiction rules also relates to applicable law rules. For example, work was started in the European Union, to revise the Rome Convention of 1980[71] in order to transform it into a new Regulation and to prepare another Regulation (called Rome II) on extra-contractual obligations. Both projects, however, have been halted for the past year or so because Internet operators claimed that these texts were unfair to them, obliging them to know all the laws in the world.[72] The present status of the conflict of law rules will therefore be described briefly, in the knowledge that much more work is needed at an international level on this issue.[73]

1. Business-to-business contracts

The main feature of the debate is the renewed interest in codes of conduct. It is not necessary to recall the details of the controversy, which are well known and have agitated international lawyers for the past half century at least. The Internet has simply put the role of codes of conduct once again in the forefront of international negotiations. That is why this aspect of the subject matter will be discussed briefly before mentioning a few words about party autonomy and default conflict rules.

(a) The place of codes of conduct

It would seem indisputable that, in a business-to-business context, parties to a contract may decide either to adhere to a pre-existing code of conduct or to create one of their own. After all, most States have been keen on giving as much freedom to businesses as possible and codes of conduct are considered to be a large part of the *neo lex mercatoria* which developed all over the world in the 1960s. It is thus understandable and acceptable that operators over the Internet develop their own codes of conduct.[74]

That said, however, States must not think that their role ends there. On the contrary, because the effect of codes of conduct stops where States' public policy starts, States are confronted with an ever more pressing duty to define carefully the limits of their public policy. It is arguable that a special effort should be made to set the scene at an early stage, perhaps as early as at the domestic legislation stage. It has always been said in international law that, except in extraordinary circumstances, national legislators legislate only for their own domestic needs without regard for the international aspects of a question. This may not be possible any more, at least to some extent.

Another consequence of the Internet may be the need for States to agree internationally on a minimum standard of public policy. This idea is contrary to the tradition whereby States are recognized to be the masters of their public policy and to have the sovereign right to decide unilaterally on these matters. It is not at all our intention to suggest that States will not be able to continue to define their public policy for themselves (particularly for reasons of cultural specificity). It would, however, facilitate access to and use of the Internet if some common international ground was to be found.

(b) Party autonomy

In the conflict of laws, the expression "party autonomy" reflects the freedom for operators to choose the law which will be applicable to their transactions. Party autonomy is clearly the rationale behind the codes of conduct studied above, but it does not stop at that. In all international contracts, parties may include a choice-of-law clause which is normally upheld by all countries around the world. The limit of that freedom is again, as for codes of conduct, the public policy of each State. The discussion above is pertinent here and we will not repeat it.

Party autonomy is limited in two ways in respect of regulated professions such as doctors, security brokers and lawyers. If the professional uses the Internet to render services in the jurisdiction in which he is located, professional regulations will continue to apply to him as before and the extent of his freedom will not be different from that in the period before the Internet. If the professional uses the Internet to provide services in a different jurisdiction he may still be obliged to respect the regulations of his own jurisdiction and will also be obliged to respect professional regulations in the jurisdiction in which its clients are located. Therefore, a lawyer would not be free to offer legal services via the Internet to clients located in a different jurisdiction, unless he or she respected the rules of the profession in that jurisdiction.[75] This result is not different from the one in real life.

As far as the validity of the choice-of-law clauses included in electronic contracts, i.e. contracts negotiated and drawn up over the Internet, is concerned, the rules to be developed will be very similar to those already developed for choice-of-court clauses. This aspect of the question has been discussed above,[76] and what we said then can apply *mutatis mutandis* to choice-of-law clauses.

(c) Default conflict-of-laws rules

If the parties have not included a choice-of-law clause in their contract or if the choice was held to be invalid, the contract will be considered to be subject to the law defined by the conflict of laws rules of the country in which the court seized of the dispute is located.

A preliminary remark is necessary at this stage. The way in which conflict-of-laws rules work obliges parties to a contract, who have not used the freedom granted to them to choose the law to be applied, to first assume which court will hear the dispute in order to be able to discover what conflict rules are to be applied. In the European Union the inconvenience is not so great since several member States apply the same conflict rules.[77] Outside Europe, however, the problem remains.

Many countries have codified their conflict rules.[78] In consequence, these rules are more readily accessible to operators. It is not possible, in the context of this chapter, to analyse in detail all rules available around the world even in codified legislation. Briefly stated, to the best of our knowledge, most rules take into consideration the main obligation which characterizes the contract in question and look at the location of the party which must provide this main obligation. The law of that country is deemed applicable. This is also the basic principle used in international conventions adopted under the auspices of the Hague Conference on Private International Law.[79] In electronic commerce, the link with the location of the party which must provide the contractual obligation does not seem to trigger difficulties in the B2B context.

2. Consumer contracts

Because of the specific nature of consumer contracts, in countries where consumers are protected, the law applicable to those contracts — among the laws which may apply to such a contract — is almost always that which is more favourable to the consumer. Therefore, if the law of the location of the consumer is the most favourable, it will apply; but if, on the contrary, it is not, the law of the professional who supplied the service or the goods will apply.

This is the main reason why Internet operators have been so keen on blocking adoption of rules of the same sort for the Internet. The controversy mentioned above with regard to dispute resolution is also relevant here.[80] Discussions are going on in the international sphere. The joint United States-European Union statement mentioned above calls for the use of codes of conduct including for consumer relations. The use of such codes in a field where partners are not equal may pose difficulties. If this course of action was to be favoured, public authorities would have a clear role to play in ensuring that the process of elaboration is a fair one and the result takes into consideration the specific needs of consumers.

This discussion shows that there is a clear need for an international agreement on common rules of protection for consumers. Before the Internet, it was commonly said that a consumer contract was rarely international. Indeed, a consumer contract was usually formed and performed locally (the proximity principle). This is why the Internet has changed the nature of the consumer contract dramatically.

3. Torts

Anyone studying legal systems around the world will discover that basically two conflict rules for tort cases coexist: that of the country where the tort was committed and that of the country where the effect is felt. Some countries apply both rules, allowing the victim to choose the law that is more favourable to its interests.

The rationale behind the first conflict rule takes into consideration the fact that in order for a tort to be committed, there must be a violation of a norm. Thus, it is only fair to impose on the offender respect for the norms in force in the place where the act occurred. This clear policy, however, has been undermined by the evolution of liability rules around the world and the increase in insurance coverage. Increasingly strict liability systems have been put in place which require a person whose acts have adverse effects to repair the damage.

The rationale behind the second conflict rule stems from the observation that a victim of a tort must be protected at least up to the point allowed by the law where that victim feels the effects. In the application of this rule, one difficulty stems from the fact that a victim may be injured in one place but returns to the place where it has its habitual residence, where it continues to suffer damage. It is usually considered that the law to be applied is the law of the country where the first damage was experienced.

The terms are slightly different with the Internet. Indeed, as mentioned above for the place of conclusion and performance of a contract, the place where the wrongful act was performed over the Internet is not easy to locate. In fact, the only sensible answer is to say that this place coincides with the place where the offender is located. However, an immediate objection comes to mind: if this rule were to become the international standard it would be an incentive for potential violators to locate in digital havens. Thus, the conflict rule cannot lead to that law since it would be all too easy to commit torts without ever having to face their consequences.

This is why most decisions which have been taken by national courts around the globe apply the law of the place where the effect was felt.[81] The limitation in most of these cases was that plaintiffs asked only for compensation of the damages suffered in that particular country. Again, this is the usual limitation applied in international tort cases. This rule has to be reassessed against Internet specificity. Recent discussions, notably on torts dealing with intellectual property, show that the plaintiff must have one forum where it can consolidate all the claims for all the damages suffered in as many jurisdictions as exist.[82] Indeed, the court would have to apply several different laws. But this is not an absolute obstacle in practice. Courts in many countries around the world are accustomed to applying foreign law. In addition, Internet-based information may ease the findings of the content of foreign law.

The other difficulty stems from an injunctive relief. Some Internet operators claim that it is technically not feasible to filter the web so that certain sites or pages cannot be accessed in a specific country, while others claim the contrary.[83] If the first group is right, an injunction decided by one court would have effects all over the world. If the second group is right, it would be possible for a court in one State to decide on an injunction with limited effects.

D. Privacy and data protection

The Internet has rendered the question of privacy and personal data protection acute. This is due not only to the very nature of the Internet itself, with its special technical features which allow data banks to be set up with a large amount of information to be retrieved in many different ways, but also to the fact that the value of many Internet corporations depends on the amount of data they have been able to gather. Thus, personal data about consumer habits, tastes and the like are of great value to any corporation wishing to operate over the net.[84] The problem is not new; what is new is its scale.[85] This is why an attempt to unify substantive law has been made, with the European Union in the forefront (para. (1)). However, the difficulty in completely unifying substantive law leaves some role for the conflict of laws rules (para. (2)).

1. Attempts to unify substantive law

The explanations given below are essentially on the work done in Europe, since it seems to be the most advanced on these questions. The European system of data protection is based on the European Convention on Protection of Personal Data of 1981 (Convention No.108).[86] In 1995, the European Community adopted a Directive on the protection of personal data and their freedom of circulation within the Community.[87] However, the Directive is considered not sufficient in view of the specific features of Internet communications and this is why a new Directive is being proposed for this field.[88] The new Directive will not replace that of 1995, which remain in force, but will complement it.

The main features of the protection proposed by these two Directives may be summarized as follows: (i) the confidentiality of communications must be guaranteed; (ii) legal persons must be protected, as well as individuals, in the context of electronic communications; (iii) this protection is necessary in order to increase confidence in electronic communications, which is crucial to the effective development of this economic sector; (iv) ISPs must take appropriate measures to provide security for their services and inform their clients of the limits of that security; (v) data banks containing personal data must be collected and maintained only to the extent necessary for the services provided and for a limited period of time; (vi) any other use of those data may be made only with the express consent of the person whose data are collected; (vii) persons must be able, without difficulty, to require deletion of personal data and to have access to courts for their protection; (viii) member States may limit the use of anonymity or other filtering processes in order to combat criminal activity.

Before entering into an agreement with a foreign country to allow free circulation of personal data outside Europe, the European Community must evaluate the adequacy of data and privacy protection in that country. This has been done with regard to a number of countries, for example Switzerland,[89] Hungary,[90] the United States[91] and Canada.[92] Other countries may follow when their data protection system has evolved.[93] It took a long time to reach the decision concerning the United States since it related to the specific system applied in that country, known as the "safe harbour" principle. This system is based on a proactive attitude by operators themselves (self-regulation), as there is no preventive legislation in the United States. The system was criticized by the European Parliament and by some privacy groups (including American privacy groups) during the hearings held by that body before the final approval of the Commission's decision. Experience will show whether the system is viable or not.[94]

Another organization that has been very active in the field of privacy protection is the OECD. As early as 1980, it drew up "Guidelines on the Protection of Privacy and Transborder Flows of Personal Data".[95] These lay down principles for the collection and processing of personal data, to apply at both the national and international levels. Member countries are called upon to implement these principles internally, by introducing legal, administrative or other provisions, or setting up institutions to protect privacy and personal data.

Similarly, in 1985 the Governments of the OECD member countries adopted a declaration on transboundary data flows, emphasizing their intention of seeking to achieve transparency in the rules and policies affecting international trade, and developing common approaches or harmonized solutions for dealing with the problems associated with this trade.

The OECD continued its work in an expert group on security of information and privacy, which in 1997 issued a report on "Implementing the OECD Privacy Guidelines in the Electronic Environment: Focus on the Internet".[96] This report discusses the growing importance of data protection, especially in an electronic online environment. As several surveys have shown, the fears of Internet users concerning the collection and use, even for commercial purposes, of their personal data, are tending to hold back the development of electronic commerce. The report also describes the complaints recorded in certain OECD member countries about problems such as the use of electronic addresses and the right of employers to inspect the electronic mail of their employees; inaccurate information and fraudulent activities on the Internet; and the ease with which personal information, especially electronic addresses, can be derived from activities conducted on the Internet and then used in the compilation of commercial marketing lists without the knowledge of those concerned. The report describes certain methods of data collection on the Internet, and mentions some initiatives taken by the private sector to protect privacy on websites. According to the group of experts, solutions have to be found through dialogue between Governments and the private sector. The report highlights the role of Governments, and reaffirms that the guideline principles must be implemented through law or through self-regulation, and that remedies must be available for individuals if they are breached. The report also encourages Governments to support private sector initiatives to find technical solutions for implementing the Guidelines. In conclusion, it recommends collaboration among all players on the Internet, emphasizing the important role of the OECD.

In February 1998 the OECD organized in Paris, with the support of the Economic and Industrial Consultative Committee of OECD (BIAC), an international conference on "Privacy Protection in a Global Networked Society".[97] This conference was an opportunity to bring together representatives of Governments, the private sector, consumer organizations and the authorities responsible for data protection. At the end of the conference, its Chairman noted that there was a broad consensus on the need to strike a proper balance between the free circulation of information and the protection of privacy. In order to evaluate the current situation on the web, an "Inventory of Instruments and Mechanisms Contributing to the Implementation and Enforcement of Privacy Guidelines on Global Networks"[98] was drawn up in September 1998. This inventory comprises the laws and mechanisms of self-regulation which have been adopted at the regional, national and international levels.

At the OECD Ministerial Conference held in Ottawa from 7 to 9 October 1998, the OECD Ministers adopted a Declaration on the Protection of Privacy on Global Networks, reaffirming their commitment to achieving effective protection of privacy on these networks and their determination to take the necessary steps for this purpose, and recognizing the need to cooperate with industry and businesses. They also agreed that the OECD should provide practical guidance for implementing the guidelines on the protection of privacy, based on national experience and examples.[99]

In the light of the undertaking by Ministers at the Ottawa Conference, the OECD decided to devise, in collaboration with industry, specialists in the protection of privacy and consumer associations, an experimental "html" tool, a generator of OECD policy declarations on the protection of privacy. This tool is addressed to public organizations and private sector enterprises, to encourage them to draw up policies and declarations on protecting privacy. It is presented in the form of a detailed questionnaire which will enable the organizations concerned, after an internal review of their privacy protection practices, to draw up a policy declaration on the protection of privacy which will appear on their site. The generator is currently available in English, French, German and Japanese, and is accessible on the OECD Internet site. The questions posed in the generator are very similar to those included in the "safe harbour" analysis annexed to the European Commission decision concerning the protection of personal data in the United States.

2. What role for conflict-of-law rules?

The unification of substantive law is certainly the best solution for international protection of privacy and personal data. However, it is not always possible to unify all aspects of the law; and, therefore, the question of applicable law is still pertinent in that context.

In preparing the guidelines mentioned above, the group of experts paid great attention to the problems of conflicts of law and of jurisdiction raised by transboundary flows and the protection of privacy, but did not offer any specific detailed solutions. However, the guidelines do contain one general recommendation, that "Member States should work towards the development of principles, domestic and international, to govern the applicable law in the case of transborder flows of personal data".[100]

Although paragraph 22 of the guidelines was never repeated in the subsequent work of the OECD, identification of the applicable law, in the context of establishing modes of dispute resolution which will be readily accessible and efficient, is still one of the possible techniques for bringing about the effective protection of privacy in a transnational framework.[101] This was the aim of the Joint Conference organized in The Hague in December 2000 which explored online dispute resolution mechanisms as potentially applicable to privacy protection.[102]

What could be the conflict rule? If we look at the aim of personal data protection, it is clear that it leads us to favour the law of the location of the person whose data have been collected. It is the law which that person would be deemed to know. He or she is probably going to act in accordance with the level of protection which that law provides. However, this conflict rule clashes with the economic needs of Internet operators. This is why if it is the rule that may be adopted, it must remain a default rule to be applied only if substantive unification is not possible.

E. Other legal and regulatory issues

1. Electronic signatures

The enforceability of e-commerce transactions is the most basic and fundamental issue to be addressed by e-commerce legislation. Moreover, it is the subject that has seen the most activity during the past year, generally in the form of electronic signature legislation.[103] Thus, it has been recognized in many instances that electronic signature legislation can provide the predictability which businesses require in order to engage in e-commerce transactions.[104] Governments wishing to promote e-commerce are urged to identify and remove legal barriers that hinder the recognition of electronic authentication.[105] In this regard, electronic signature legislation might accomplish two important goals: to remove barriers to e-commerce, and to enable and promote the desirable public policy goal of e-commerce by helping to establish the trust and the predictability needed by parties doing business online.[106]

There are at present three main functions attached to electronic signatures:

(1) **Data origin authentication**: This can provide assurance that a message came from its purported sender;

(2) **Message integrity**: This enables the recipient of a message to verify that a message has not been intentionally or accidentally altered during transmission;

(3) **Non-repudiation**: The sender cannot deny that the message was sent.

At the moment, several methods are available for carrying out the above functions.[107] However, one type of electronic signature, the so-called digital signature technology based on public key cryptography, is today regarded as the most common and reliable technique. For digital signatures to achieve authenticity functions it is necessary to use a trusted third party called a certification authority (CA), which, given satisfactory evidence, is prepared to certify the identity and attributes of the parties.

A review of legislative and regulatory activities reveals three basic approaches to electronic signature legislation.[108]

(1) **Minimalist approach**: The primary motivation is to remove existing legal obstacles to the recognition and enforceability of electronic signatures and records. Legislation is limited to defining the circumstances under which an electronic signature will fulfil existing legal requirements for tangible signatures. This kind of legislation does not address specific techniques and is, therefore intended to be technology-neutral. The minimalist approach focuses on verifying the intent of the signing party rather than on developing particularized forms and guidelines. The UNCITRAL Model Law on Electronic Commerce (see Article 7) [109] and a number of common-law countries (e.g. Canada, the United States,[110] the United Kingdom, Australia and New Zealand) have adopted such an approach.

(2) **Digital signature approach** (prescriptive approach): This establishes a legal framework for the operation of digital signatures (PKIs), whether or not other forms of secure authentication are included or permitted. Legislation and regulations enacted under this approach share the following characteristics: adoption of asymmetric cryptography as the approved means of creating a digital signature; imposition of certain operational and financial requirements on certification authorities (CAs); prescription of the duties of key holders; and definition of the circumstances under which reliance on an electronic signature is justified. The prescriptive approach has been adopted by a number of civil-law countries (e.g. Italy, Germany and Argentina).

(3) **A two-tier approach**: This represents a synthesis of the two previous approaches. The laws enacted prescribe standards for the operation of PKIs and take a broad view of what constitutes a valid electronic signature for legal purposes. This approach achieves legal neutrality by granting minimum recognition to most authentication technologies, while at the same time it incorporates provisions for an authentication technology of choice. The two-tier approach has been followed, by, among others the European Union (1999 Directive on Electronic Signatures), the UNCITRAL Model Law on Electronic Signatures, 2001 and the 1998 Singapore Electronic Transactions Act.

Some recent samples of regional legislation and international model law legislation on electronic signatures that might guide States wishing to enact legislation in this field are as follows:[111]

- **EU Directive of December 1999 on a Community Framework for Electronic Signatures:**[112] The aim of the Directive is to establish a harmonized Community-wide legal framework for electronic signatures and electronic certification services. This means in particular that electronic signatures cannot be denied legal effect just because they are in electronic format, but are recognized in the same way as handwritten signatures relating to paper-based data. The Directive does not apply to closed systems, such as a corporate Intranet or banking network, although electronic signatures used within closed systems benefit from legal recognition. In an effort to ensure that the Directive will not soon become obsolete a technology-neutral approach is adopted, one which is based on an open electronic signature concept that includes digital signatures based on public-key cryptography as well as other means of authenticating data.[113] In addition to providing a definition of electronic signature (article 2 (1)), the Directive refers to the "advanced electronic signature" that is designed to provide a higher level of security.[114] Although member States are prohibited from making the provision of Certification Services subject to prior authorization, they are entitled to set up voluntary accreditation schemes to provide consumers with a higher degree of legal security as regards certification service providers (CSPs).[115] Furthermore, they are required to ensure the establishment of an appropriate system that allows for supervision of CSPs which are established on their territory and issue qualified certificates to the public.[116] The Directive does not preclude the establishment of a private-sector-based supervision system or oblige CSPs to apply to be supervised under an accreditation scheme. It establishes common requirements for qualified certificates (annex 1), CSPs (annex 2) and secure signature-creation devices (annex 3). As regards liability, the CSP is liable for damage caused to any entity or legal or natural person who reasonably relies on the certificate unless the CSP proves that he has not acted negligently. Under certain conditions, the CSP is entitled to set limits regarding the use of a certificate and the value of transactions for which the certificate is valid.[117] Article 7 of the Directive addresses the international dimension of electronic commerce by ensuring that certificates issued in a third country are recognized as legally equivalent to certificates issued by a CSP established within the Community under certain precise conditions. Article 8 of the Directive, which refers to data protection, provides for the application to CSPs and national bodies responsible for accreditation/supervision of Directive 95/46EC of 24 October 1995 on the protection of individuals with regard to the processing of personal data and on the free movement of such data. Furthermore, it is specifically provided that CSPs may collect personal data directly from the data subject only, or after the explicit consent of the data subject, and only insofar as it is necessary for the purposes of issuing and maintaining the certificate. The data may not be collected or processed for any other purposes without the explicit consent of the data subject.

- **UNCITRAL Model Law on Electronic Signatures, 2001**: Following the adoption in 1996 of the Model Law on Electronic Commerce and in particular of Article 7 concerning "signatures",[118] UNCITRAL requested the Working Group on Electronic Commerce to develop further rules on electronic signatures (the original mandate read "digital signatures and certification authorities"), so as to help provide more certainty through implementation of the said provision. The Working Group began its work in February 1997 and finished it at its thirty-seventh session in September 2000. The Model Law on Electronic Signatures (MLES),[119] together with the Guide to Enactment,[120] was adopted by UNCITRAL on 5 July 2001. The MLES three main parts: on criteria for reliable electronic signatures; on the duties of the three potential functions involved in an electronic signature (signatory, certification service provider and relying party); and on the recognition of foreign certificates and electronic signatures.[121] In addition, the Guide to Enactment, much of which is drawn from the preparatory work on the Model Law, is intended to assist States in considering which, if any, of the MLES provisions should be varied in order to be adapted to any particular national circumstances. Furthermore, a number of issues not included in the MLES are referred to in the Guide so as to provide guidance to States enacting the Model Law.[122] The MLES applies only to commercial activities (Article 1) in a wide sense that includes the supply or exchange of goods or services, distribution agreements, agency, factoring, leasing, investment, financing, banking, insurance and carriage of goods. Article 6 constitutes one of the main provisions of the MLES, since it provides guidance in paragraph 3 as to the test for reliability of electronic signatures. The criteria are as follows:[123]

"(a) The signature creation data are, within the context in which they are used, linked to the signatory and to no other person;

(b) The signature creation data were, at the time of signing, under the control of the signatory and of no other person;

(c) Any alteration to the electronic signature, made after the time of signing, is detectable; and

(d) Where a purpose of the legal requirement for a signature is to provide assurance as to the integrity of the information to which it relates, any alteration made to that information after the time of signing is detectable."

Article 6 (4) emphasizes that there is no need to meet all the above-mentioned criteria for a signature to be reliable but that reliability could be established in any other way. Furthermore, and in accordance with article 7, any person, organ or authority, whether public or private, specified by the enacting State as competent, may determine which electronic signatures satisfy the provisions of article 6. Any such accreditation must be consistent with recognized international standards. Article 8 sets out what the signatory must do and article 9 describes the conduct of the CSP. Concerning the recognition of foreign certificates and electronic signatures article 12 establishes the general principle of legal equivalence between foreign and domestic signatures and certificates if the system in the State of origin offers a level of reliability "substantially equivalent" to that in the receiving State. Although the MLES does not constitute a comprehensive set of rules on the subject, its rules are consistent with international practices and it provides an important international model for countries wishing to enact legislation on electronic signatures.

2. Electronic contracting

Following the adoption in 1996 of the UNCITRAL Model Law on Electronic Commerce,[124] which is intended to remove legal barriers to the use of electronic communications and provides "functional equivalents" to the use of paper-based documents, a number of countries, including developing countries, have enacted legislation based on the Model Law.[125] Although the Model Law offers national legislators a set of internationally acceptable rules that could be used to overcome some of the main obstacles when conducting legal transactions in cyberspace, it seems that, at least in some jurisdictions, a problem might arise in order to overcome references to "writing", "signature" and "document"[126] in conventions and agreements relating to international trade.[127] It is precisely for this reason that the Centre for the Facilitation of Procedures and Practices for Administration, Commerce and Transport (CEFACT) of the United Nations Economic Commission for Europe (ECE) recommended[128] to UNCITRAL that it "consider the actions necessary to ensure that references to writing, signature and document in conventions and agreements relating to international trade allow for electronic equivalents". In a note[129] of 20 December 2000 entitled "Legal barriers to the development of electronic commerce in international instruments relating to international trade: ways of overcoming them", the UNCITRAL secretariat included the advisory opinion of a law professor as to the "adaptation of the evidentiary provisions of international legal instruments relating to international trade to the specific requirements of electronic commerce". The note was submitted to the thirty-eighth session of the UNCITRAL Working Group on Electronic Commerce in March 2001. The Working Group agreed to recommend to the UNCITRAL Commission that it undertake work towards the preparation of an international convention to remove legal barriers that might result from international trade law instruments.[130]

At the regional level, the European Union adopted a "Directive on certain legal aspects of information society services, in particular electronic commerce, in the Internal Market" (Directive on electronic commerce),[131] which lays down a general framework to ensure the free movement of information society services in the EU. The Directive covers all information society services, B2B and B2C, as well as services provided free of charge to the recipient. It establishes rules in various areas, including the following: definition of where operators are established; transparency obligations for ISPs; transparency requirements for commercial communications; conclusion and validity of electronic contracts; liability of Internet intermediaries; and online dispute settlement. Although the Directive does not apply to services supplied by service providers established in a third country (outside the EU), the solutions provided for some of these issues may serve as a model for countries wishing to regulate this area.

Other recent work of a related nature that focuses on contractual matters is the Electronic Commerce Agreement (the E-Agreement), developed by the UN/CEFACT.[132] The E-Agreement is intended to serve the commercial needs of B2B electronic commerce partners. It contains a basic set of provisions which can ensure that one or more electronic commercial transactions may be concluded by commercial partners within a sound legal framework. Although the E-Agreement could also be used in the B2C relationship, it does not include provisions relating to consumer protection. Thus, businesses wishing to use the E-Agreement in the B2C sector must be aware of the need to comply with mandatory consumer protection laws. Furthermore, parties must ensure compliance with other mandatory national and local laws, such as tax regulations and data protection legislation.

In addition to the above-mentioned contractual solutions, the UN/CEFACT has recommended a Model Code of Conduct for Electronic Commerce as a means of facilitating e-commerce transactions. The Code of Conduct, which is a self-regulatory instrument, can work in parallel with other measures to facilitate electronic commerce, such as trustmark schemes. The Recommendation that requests States, for the promotion and development of self-regulation instruments for electronic business, includes as an example the "Model Code of Conduct for Electronic Commerce developed by the Electronic Commerce Platform of the Netherlands", which is annexed to the Recommendation.[133]

F. Fiscal and customs regulations

1. E-commerce taxation

The question of taxing e-commerce has increasingly been of concern to Governments and tax authorities in both developed and developing countries. Fears about revenue losses resulting from uncollected taxes on Internet transactions, coupled with the substantial growth of Internet commerce in the past years and predictions for the next few years, have prompted Governments and international organizations to set up committees to evaluate the implications of e-commerce for national and international tax systems and provide recommendations on how to change existing legislation to take account of e-commerce.

The main players in the debate on e-commerce taxation have been the United States, the European Union (EU) and the Organisation for Economic Co-operation and Development (OECD). The United States and the EU member States are primarily concerned with how their respective tax systems will be affected by e-commerce (see below). The OECD secretariat, whose Model Tax Convention serves as a basis for most bilateral tax treaties (including between non-OECD member countries), has been asked by its member States to take the international leadership role in e-commerce and taxation, a mandate that was confirmed at the 1998 OECD Ministerial Meeting in Ottawa. It has prepared a number of taxation principles that should govern e-commerce and has worked closely with the EU on consumption tax issues.

Developing countries have participated little in these debates and the proposals and papers so far produced by the OECD countries have given scant consideration to developing countries' concerns.[134] While it is true that developing countries' shares in e-commerce are still modest, the international rules and regulations that are adopted now will impact on e-commerce in many countries in the future, including in the developing countries. In addition, the increasing number of small and medium-sized enterprises (SMEs) that will be drawn in by e-commerce from the developing countries have little experience in international taxation issues. It is therefore crucial to include their concerns as early as possible. This section will briefly introduce two key issues currently debated as regards Internet taxation: consumption taxes and income taxes. It will present proposals put forward on how to change existing tax regulations in the light of e-commerce and discuss possible implications for developing countries.

(a) Consumption taxes: Which jurisdiction applies?

Consumption taxes usually include value added taxes, sales taxes and turnover taxes. Traditionally, they are borne by the consumer and collected by the seller; different rules apply depending on the product or service sold, the location of consumer and seller, and the type of consumer (business or individual). With e-commerce, the number of foreign online suppliers, who are often subject to different taxation rules, has increased considerably. Research carried out in the United States on the impact of taxation on Internet commerce and consumer online purchasing patterns found that consumers living in high sales tax areas are significantly more likely to buy online than those living in low sales tax areas (Goolsbee, 1999). Hence, differentiated Internet taxation rules among countries could have a significant impact on the purchasing behaviour of consumers, with the latter shifting from domestic to foreign suppliers.[135]

This raises several problems for tax authorities. First, it leads to the gradual elimination of traditional intermediaries (so-called disintermediation) such as wholesalers or local retailers, who in the past have been critical for identifying taxpayers, especially private consumers. Second, foreign suppliers may be tax-exempted, whereas local suppliers are normally required to charge value added tax (VAT) or sales taxes. Third, direct orders from foreign suppliers could substantially increase the number of low-value shipments of physical goods to individual customers. These low-value packages now fall under so-called *de minimis* relief from customs duties and taxes in many countries, basically to balance the cost of collection and the amount of tax due. A substantial increase in these shipments as a result of e-commerce (where foreign suppliers replace domestic ones) could pose an additional challenge to tax as well as customs authorities.

(i) European Union vs. United States proposal

Major differences exist between the EU and the United States in the way taxes are redeemed and hence in their approaches to international taxation rules on e-commerce. The EU countries derive about 30 per cent of government tax revenue from taxes on domestic goods and services (mainly VAT). In addition, VAT extra charges contribute 45 per cent to the EU Community budget (in addition to customs duties and GNP contributions) (European Commission, 1998). Their main concern is the increasing import of digital content and services from outside the EU, which would be exempted from VAT payments in the EU. The United States Government, on the other hand, derives most of its tax revenues from personal and corporate income tax and social security contributions; revenues from taxes on domestic goods and services are extremely low (3.6 per cent) (although individual States depend significantly on local sales taxes, see below). The United States is currently both a net exporter and the main exporter of e-commerce worldwide. Hence, it has a great interest in encouraging business (including e-commerce business) to locate in the United States and pay direct taxes to the United States tax authorities.

Therefore, the issue of consumption taxes on international e-commerce has received most attention in the OECD and the EU. In particular, the EU feels very strongly about maintaining VAT duties and is likely to modify tax rules in a way that will ensure a continuation of VAT contributions, rather than lowering or eliminating them. A closer look at current VAT regulations in the EU will explain the growing concern among EU tax authorities and Governments.[136]

Goods. Imported goods from non-EU members are subject to (import duties and) VAT of the importing country. Sales within the EU are subject to the VAT of the receiving country in the case of business-to-consumer trade. Businesses selling to businesses in another member State are tax-exempted; the receiving or importing business is required to pay VAT locally (i.e. in the country of final consumption).[137] Exports to non-EU countries are zero-rated.

Services. Services differ according to the type of services traded. In the case of information (currently the majority of e-services), imports from non-EU businesses to EU consumers are not subject to customs duties and are VAT-exempted (except in Denmark, France and Italy). Sales from non-EU businesses to EU businesses are subject to self-accounted VAT at the local rate (a so-called reverse charge). Intra-EU service suppliers are required to charge VAT in the country in which they are established (location of the seller), if selling to private consumers. EU business-to-business services trade is subject to VAT in the country of the final consumer. Sales to customers outside the EU are subject to VAT in the location of the seller (European Commission, 1999; Kerrigan, 1999).

The challenges to EU tax authorities that arise from e-commerce therefore lie in non-EU supplies of e-services to EU customers (and in an increase in non-EU customers not subject to EU VAT). Under current tax law, these are exempted from VAT, while at the same time their share is increasing, in direct competition with EU suppliers who are subject to VAT payments. Furthermore, the VAT exemption provides incentives for suppliers to locate outside the EU, a fairly easy undertaking in e-commerce, which no longer requires the presence of human and technical resources.

Even though the United States Government has been less concerned about VAT regulation, the potential loss in sales taxes as a result of e-commerce has caused major concern among local Governments. Within the United States, individual states have autonomy with regard to determining and collecting State tax and local sales tax, which are often their largest source of revenue. Sales taxes differ substantially among States, ranging from 0 to 7 per cent. United States-based online suppliers selling to out-of-State (including foreign) customers do not currently have to charge local sales tax. States are therefore becoming increasingly worried about how to secure their sales tax revenues in the light of Internet commerce, and estimates of revenues lost due to Internet sales range from $ 1.2 billion (1999) to 10.8 billion (2003) (University of Tennessee, 2000).

In 1998, the United States Congress created the Advisory Commission on Electronic Commerce, under the Internet Tax Freedom Act, to study a variety of issues involving e-commerce taxation, including international issues. The Commission collected proposals from the public and private sectors for consideration, which contributed to the final report and recommendations submitted to Congress in April 2000. At its final meeting in March 2000 (Dallas, Texas), the Commission voted *inter alia* to extend a three-year moratorium on domestic "new" Internet taxation imposed by the Internet Tax Freedom Act and due to expire in October 2001, until 2006. The moratorium essentially bans taxes on Internet access fees. However, owing to a disagreement among the Commission's members, no solutions have been provided on the question of State and local tax collection.

The National Governors' Association has therefore initiated the Streamlined Sales Tax Project (SSTP), an ad hoc group composed of 30 States whose aim is to simplify and harmonize State sales tax systems in the light of e-commerce. Model legislation was approved in December 2000, providing for a Uniform Sales and Use Tax Administration Act and Streamlined Sales and Use Tax Agreement, which are expected to simplify the collection of sales taxes on online transactions. The group hopes that other states so far not participating will follow suit.

(ii) A multilateral framework?

At the Ottawa Ministerial Conference, the OECD proposed a number of "framework conditions", including on consumption taxes, which since then have been adopted by a large number of countries, including OECD non-member countries (OECD, 1998a). These conditions include:

- Cross-border trade should be taxed in the jurisdiction where consumption takes place;
- The supply of digitized products should not be treated as a supply of goods for consumption tax purposes (differences in the definition among countries may lead to uncertainties about the tax treatment of products from outside suppliers);
- Where services and intangible property (i.e. goods) from suppliers outside the country are acquired, countries should examine the use of reverse charge, self-assessment or other equivalent mechanisms;
- Appropriate systems should be developed to collect tax on the importation of physical goods.

On the basis of these conditions, the EU has proposed changes to its current VAT legislation taking into consideration e-commerce (European Commission, 2000a). Under this proposal, non-EU suppliers with annual sales to the EU exceeding □ 100,000 would be required to apply taxes on the same basis as an EU operator when transacting business in the EU. This would follow the Ottawa framework condition whereby taxation is applied in the jurisdiction where the consumption takes place.[138] In order to facilitate compliance, the European Commission proposes that non-EU e-commerce operators be required to register in one EU member State only and have the possibility of discharging all their obligations by dealing with a single tax administration. This has been a controversial point among members States who are concerned that Luxembourg, the State currently with the lowest VAT rate (15 per cent), would be the preferred country of registration and collect taxes without having to compensate other member States. EU suppliers, on the other hand, would not be obliged to levy VAT on products sold to customers outside the EU. Business-to-business transactions would not be affected by the proposed new Directive: as in the past, the tax would be accounted for in the EU under the reverse charge system whereby traders assess their own VAT liability.

The proposal has prompted a strong reaction from non-EU suppliers (notably businesses in the United States), who have little interest in collecting VAT for EU tax authorities, arguing that this would impose an unnecessary burden on their overseas transactions and, in general, restrict e-commerce. The VAT Directive is to be implemented on 1 January 2001, but it is unlikely that it will become law for another few years.

A key problem for tax authorities will be to identify the customer and the location of the jurisdiction responsible for collecting the tax. Because of the process of disintermediation, apart from the seller and the customer there are no other parties involved in the transactions (which could collect the tax). Credit card companies, ISPs, banking and payment systems providers and telecommunications companies have all been mentioned as potential new intermediaries in verifying the location of a customer and the respective tax jurisdiction ("trusted third parties" – TTPs). This, of course, raises privacy issues and could lead to abuses of information. It could also lead to an increasing use of foreign credit cards or digital cash; needless to say, the customer's location may differ from the billing address. In addition, how can an Internet seller determine whether the customer is a business or an individual consumer, each of which is subject to different VAT rules? An increasing number of e-commerce businesses are small entrepreneurs operating from home who may receive services for business or personal purposes.

Following the OECD framework conditions, the EU also proposed that for VAT purposes trade in digitized goods be treated as a supply of services and that VAT rates on all e-services be harmonized into a single rate. This could result in tax losses since consumption taxes are lower on services than on goods. It could also lead to losses on tariffs and import duties on digitized goods that were shipped physically in the past and which would now be subject to much lower duties. This would impact in particular on the developing countries, whose reliance on import duties as a government revenue source is much higher than that of the developed countries.

At the Ottawa Conference, the United States took a different position on this issue: digital products should be characterized on the basis of the "rights transferred" in each particular case. It argued that some goods which are now zero-rated (such as books and newspapers) would be subject to VAT if treated as a service. Customers may therefore prefer to buy local zero-rated books rather than digitally imported (and taxed) services, many of which could be supplied by United States online providers. As an alternative, the United States has proposed an origin-based consumption tax for intangibles (e-services), which would be collected from the supplier and not from the consumer. It argues that it is easier to identify the supplier than the customer on the basis of the permanent establishment rule (see below), and since businesses are subject to audit. The United States as a net exporter of e-commerce would benefit from an origin-based tax, although such as tax may further erode the tax base in e-commerce-importing countries. On the other hand, it disadvantages domestic producers in their export sales since they would have to pay the tax on the exports, instead of the final consumer. This may encourage business to set up shop in countries with no origin-based taxation. Finally, it needs to borne in mind that most e-commerce will be business-to-business (currently 80 per cent of e-commerce), which is often tax-exempted or subject to voluntary compliance.

(iii) Implications for developing countries

How does consumption tax legislation affect developing countries? Most of them rely heavily on consumption taxes for their government budgets (Teltscher, 2000). Given that many developing countries will be net importers of e-commerce in the medium term, they would have a strong interest in not eroding their tax bases by switching to an origin-based tax system. They need to be aware, however, that tax collection on e-commerce activities will require access to the latest technologies by tax authorities. Thus, developing countries need to catch up on modernizing their tax administration systems in order not to lose important tax revenues on the collection of consumption taxes. In this context, the OECD, in cooperation with four regional tax organizations, is organizing a conference on "Tax administrations in an electronic world", to be held in Canada in June 2001. The OECD expects the conference to be attended by participants from 106 countries (including many developing countries) and eight international organizations.

To avoid double taxation, some multi- or bilateral agreements have to be adopted on where consumption taxes are to be collected: in the country where the supplier is established, the country where the customer is established or the country of consumption. The proposal by the EU to require non-EU suppliers to register for and charge VAT in a EU country would not favour providers from developing countries, thus placing an additional burden on their e-commerce exports.

(b) Income taxes: "Permanent establishment" in cyberspace?

The taxation of income, profits and capital gains is another major source of government revenue, especially in the developed countries. There are two basic concepts of how countries tax income. First, source-based taxation is applied in the jurisdiction where the economic activity takes place, for example the sale of the service or digital good traded. Foreigners who do not reside in the jurisdiction where their economic activity takes place are still taxed on their profits earned in that jurisdiction. Second, residence-based taxation takes place in the jurisdiction of the place of residence of the person/business earning the income. In other words, taxpayers are taxed on their worldwide income by the country in which they live. Among the OECD countries, it is agreed that if a "permanent establishment" has been determined, source-based taxation applies; if not, residence-based tax principles apply (Lukas, 1999). The usual practice among OECD countries is to tax residents on their worldwide income and non-residents on the income they earn in the relevant country.[139] To avoid double taxation, countries enter into bilateral treaties, for example to reduce or eliminate source tax. Treaties are normally based on the OECD Model Tax Convention, which defines residence-based taxation according to where the management takes place. If no treaty exists, domestic tax legislation governs the taxation of non-resident businesses carrying on business in the country. In this case, the source principles generally apply.

Traditionally, direct taxation of income has employed the "permanent establishment principle" used in the OECD Model Tax Convention (Article 5) to determine in which country income has been generated and is therefore taxed. Accordingly, business profits of non-resident enterprises may only be taxed in a country to the extent that they are attributable to a permanent establishment that the enterprise has in that country, which must also be a "fixed place of business". However, the principle was drafted in 1963 and is not fully compatible with e-commerce as it relies on physical presence. For example, the source-based concept of income taxation could lead to a substantial erosion of the tax base since the link between income-generating activity and a specific location becomes blurred in e-commerce. In particular, the question of whether a website or web server can constitute a permanent establishment or fixed place of business has been at the centre of the debate. In December 2000, the OECD reached consensus on the following important changes to the Commentary on Article 5, which would be applied to e-commerce (OECD, 2000):

- An Internet website does not constitute a "place of business", as there is "no facility such as premises or, in certain circumstances, machinery or equipment". Hence, a website in itself cannot constitute a permanent establishment. On the other hand, the server operating the website is a piece of equipment which needs a physical location and may thus constitute a "fixed place of business" of the enterprise that operates it.
- A distinction between the enterprise that operates the server and the enterprise that carries on business through the website is necessary. If the website is hosted by an Internet service provider (ISP) and a different enterprise carries on business through the website, the server cannot be considered a fixed place of business. The server and its location are not at the disposal of the enterprise and the enterprise does not have a physical presence in that place since the website does not involve tangible assets. However, if the web server is owned or leased by the business which carries on business through a website located on that server, the place where that server is located could constitute a permanent establishment.
- A server constitutes a "fixed" place of business if it is located in a certain place for a sufficient period of time.
- In the case of ISPs, even though they own and operate the servers (i.e. a fixed place of business), they cannot be considered to constitute permanent establishments of the businesses whose websites they host, because they will not have the authority to conclude contracts in the name of the enterprises they host and thus are not agents of those enterprises.
- Whether computer equipment used for e-commerce operations may be considered to be a permanent establishment needs to be examined on a case-by-case basis, depending on whether the equipment is used for activities that form an essential part of the commercial activity of an enterprise (as opposed to being used for merely preparatory or auxiliary activities). In this case, and if the equipment constitutes a fixed place of business, it would be a permanent establishment of the enterprise.[140]

What would be the possible implications for tax revenues of these amendments to Article 5? For example, if a web server constitutes a permanent establishment of a business, and since few resources are needed to set up and maintain a server, it could encourage the migration of servers and computer equipment to low-tax countries, including some of the developing countries. Currently, the United States has the highest concentration of web servers in the world;[141] should these be considered permanent establishments and thus be subject to direct taxation, the United States may take a minimalist position on income tax to prevent servers from migrating across the border. One problem that needs to be addressed is tracing the legal entity operating a business through a website and identifying the business and its physical location.[142]

Because of the difficulties in defining permanent establishment (and because of its large tax base), the United States has favoured residence-based taxation over source-based taxation. However, residence-based taxation may not favour developing countries, given their small number of residents with e-businesses. In the short run, they are primarily net e-commerce-importing countries; hence, they would have an interest in source-based rather than residence-based taxation. Also, a move to residence-based taxation may shift tax revenues from developing to developed countries once developing countries' share as consumers of e-commerce increases. On the other hand, residence-based taxation favours tax havens, which are often developing countries. Here, developing countries could be attractive to foreign investors looking for certain, low-skilled activities in the production of digital content.

If Article 5 were not amended, countries that are net importers of technology would face significant revenue losses because businesses would close down branches and replace them with Internet communications and e-commerce, which would not be regarded as permanent establishments and would thus be tax-free. Hence, the main business activity would not take place in the country any more, and the country's source-based tax would decrease.

The amendments to Article 5 refer to the definition of permanent establishment as it currently appears. Another OECD group is examining the more important issue of whether any changes should be made to that definition or whether to abandon the concept of permanent establishment altogether. Given that today's technology allows a company to base itself in one or more places and outsource all activities which require physicality, the concept of permanent establishment may become obsolete.

On a related issue, the OECD has discussed whether income from the sale of digital products or services should be characterized as business profits or royalties (OECD, 2001b). While business profits are taxed in the country where the business has permanent establishment, royalty income is taxed by the country from which the royalties arise. A minority of countries argued in favour of classifying digital sales as royalties, arguing that the payment is only for the right to copy.[143] This would allow e-commerce-importing countries to capture tax on sales to their residents, if permitted under their treaties. Developing countries, however, often do not have tax treaties and are net importers of e-commerce. They could, therefore, still tax digital sales to their residents, whether these were classified as royalties or business profits.

(c) A need for global coordination

No matter what changes to the existing tax legislation are adopted, without a certain degree of international cooperation and harmonization of existing tax rules, the expansion of e-commerce will be hampered. Traditionally, tax collection has been based on the belief that individual countries have the right to set their own tax rules; thus, there has been little international cooperation and few multilateral agreements have been concluded. Unless this approach changes and countries agree to enter into multilateral tax agreements, tax competition will intensify with e-commerce. This is a likely scenario since, even within the OECD, individual countries implement domestic tax rules that give them a competitive edge.[144] This is also why it is unlikely that countries will collect taxes for other countries, for example in the case of VAT, where the EU has suggested that VAT be collected from the supplier of the non-member country. On the other hand, if rules are not harmonized internationally, the risk of double taxation may keep foreign suppliers/competition out; and non-taxation may distort competition against local suppliers.

With a few exceptions, developing countries will not be part of an OECD agreement on Internet taxation. Nevertheless, they can use the principles and rules agreed upon as a basis for adjusting their own legislation. One of the first developing countries to develop national legislation on e-commerce, including on taxation, has been India. In December 1999, the Ministry of Finance set up a technical committee on e-commerce taxation, which was expected to submit its report, including recommendations on e-commerce taxation in India, by the end of 2000.

Developing countries have used tax legislation in the past to attract private foreign direct investment (FDI). Multinationals increasingly operate in countries that have low taxes or are willing to negotiate favourable tax regimes to attract foreign business. In fact, fiscal incentives are the most widely used type of FDI incentives (UNCTAD, 1996). Depending on the agreements adopted in the OECD, developing countries could negotiate specific bilateral treaties for e-commerce taxation, which would give them a competitive edge.[145] For example, the transaction costs of setting up or moving a web server are low; hence, e-commerce allows companies to respond quickly to tax incentives offered by Governments and move their web servers to a developing country.

However, any decision that developing countries may take on modifying their tax legislation to accommodate e-commerce, will have to take into account the significant role of tax revenues in their national budgets. Until new international agreements on e-commerce taxation have been defined, an increasing number of goods and services will be traded online, largely tax-free. In the short to medium term, developing countries will be net importers of e-commerce and will therefore run a greater risk of losing revenues if traditional imports are replaced by online delivery. Therefore, the development of efficient tax collection systems for e-commerce should be a priority for all developing countries.

2. Customs duties

Compared with the debate on e-commerce, where countries in principle agree that e-commerce should be taxed, the debate on whether to levy customs duties on electronic commerce has been more controversial. A number of countries have advocated a tariff-free environment for e-commerce, while others have expressed concern about possible revenue losses if products that have been subject to customs duties in the past are now imported duty-free.

The World Trade Organization (WTO) addressed this issue at its second Ministerial Meeting (Geneva, May 1998), when Ministers agreed to ban the imposition of customs duties on electronic transmissions until the 1999 WTO Ministerial Meeting in Seattle. The Seattle meeting, however, failed to address electronic commerce and a decision on whether to extend the customs moratorium was deferred; it may be considered at the next Ministerial Meeting, to be held in Doha in November 2001.

In the meantime, the discussions in the WTO in the area of e-commerce continue. One of the most controversial points in the debate has been the question of how to define or "classify" digitized products, i.e. products than can be shipped both physically and digitally. These include software, books, printed material, and sound and media products. Traditionally, they have been shipped physically, via carrier media such as CDs, tapes or cassettes. They were physically moved across borders, where they were subject to customs duties. Today, and increasingly so in the future, these products are being sent via data files through virtual networks, thereby crossing numerous (often-unknown) borders. How should these data or their content be classified? Are they equivalent to a hard copy of a book or catalogue, a CD or a videotape and therefore to be classified as a "good"? Is the transmission of the data itself a service, and thus should the "data" fall withing the "services" category? Or should there be a third category of electronic transmissions, some mixture of goods and services - but in that case, which would be the governing multilateral rules?

Within the WTO context, there are important political and regulatory implications associated with the electronic delivery of goods and services. Depending on the classification, the trade is subject to different multilateral rules: goods are subject to the General Agreement on Tariffs and Trade (GATT), the Agreement on Technical Barriers to Trade, the Agreement on Customs Valuations, or rules of origin; while services would be subject to the General Agreement on Trade in Services (GATS).

In general, the multilateral rules for services are still far less elaborate than the multilateral rules for trade in goods, providing countries with substantially more leeway for national policy discretion in the services trade. One important difference between the GATT and the GATS relates to general obligations. While the GATT's general obligations include most favoured nation (MFN), national treatment and a general prohibition on quantitative restrictions, the GATS includes the national treatment principle only in negotiated specific commitments and specific services. For example, WTO member countries have defined in their national schedules whether, for a certain services trade, foreign suppliers will be given national treatment, i.e. whether they are subject to the same rules as domestic suppliers of the equivalent service. In other words, if a country grants national treatment, and if the WTO members decide to include electronic transmissions in the GATS framework, no additional taxes can be imposed on foreign suppliers by that country. If no national treatment is specified, on the other hand, imports could be subject to higher taxes than domestically supplied services.

A second important difference between the GATS and the GATT relates to the possibility of imposing quantitative restrictions or quotas. While the GATT (in general) prohibits the use of quotas, they are allowed under the GATS (depending on the market access commitment specified in a country's schedule). Thus, theoretically, this could mean that a country could impose (in principle) a limit on, say, the number of books transmitted electronically via the Internet. Although it is not clear how this could be enforced, it is a question that has to be solved in the discussions on how to include e-commerce in the WTO agreements.

3. Fiscal implications of digitized goods trading

Until WTO member States have agreed on whether to (i) extend the customs moratorium, and (ii) classify digitized products as goods or services, discussions will continue on the question of potential tariff revenue losses resulting from the ban on customs duties. As a contribution to the debate, this section will briefly present UNCTAD calculations on tariff and tax revenues currently collected from the import of digitized goods. This will provide countries, in particular in the developing world, with concrete numbers for potential fiscal implications of digitized goods imports.

For this purpose, a number of commodities have been selected, which traditionally have been shipped physically and been subject to border tariffs, but which today can be transformed into a digitized format and sent through the Internet. More specifically, these "digitized products" are here defined as goods, identifiable by Harmonized System (HS) headings, that can be sent both physically via carrier media and electronically via networks. They comprise five product categories: (i) printed matter, (ii) software, (iii) music and other media products, (iv) film and (v) video games.[146]

The calculation of fiscal revenue is based on two types of customs duties: first, the MFN applied tariff; and second, additional duties such as customs surcharges and consumption taxes levied on imports.

Table 21 shows fiscal revenue resulting from the MFN tariff levied on digitized products, per country. The majority of countries that are most affected by tariff revenue losses come from the developing world. Given their higher levels of MFN rates applied to these products, this should not come as a surprise. What is remarkable, however, is the magnitude: despite the developing countries' import share in digitized products of only 18.5 per cent, their *absolute* tariff revenue (loss) is almost double that of the developed countries, amounting to 64.5 per cent of world tariff revenue losses for these products (chart 8). This clearly shows that, as far as potential fiscal losses are concerned, developing countries would be much more affected by the proposed ban. The top ten countries affected by fiscal loss are the EU, India, Mexico, Malaysia, Brazil, Canada, China, Morocco, Argentina and Israel.

These losses now need to be placed in the context of total government revenues. Table 22 compares tariff revenues from digitized products with total revenues and revenues from import duties. As has been shown elsewhere,[147] the percentages are relatively low: for all countries, tariff revenues from these products amount to only 0.14 per cent of total government revenues and 1.7 per cent of revenues from import duties. Nevertheless, there are some significant differences between countries, with shares ranging from 0 to 1.1 per cent of total revenue and from 0 to 20 per cent of revenues from import duties. Generally, customs duties as a source of government revenue play a more important role in many developing countries than in developed countries. Hence, a reduction in customs revenues as a result of e-commerce would be felt more strongly in the developing countries.

Chart 8
DP imports and tariff revenues

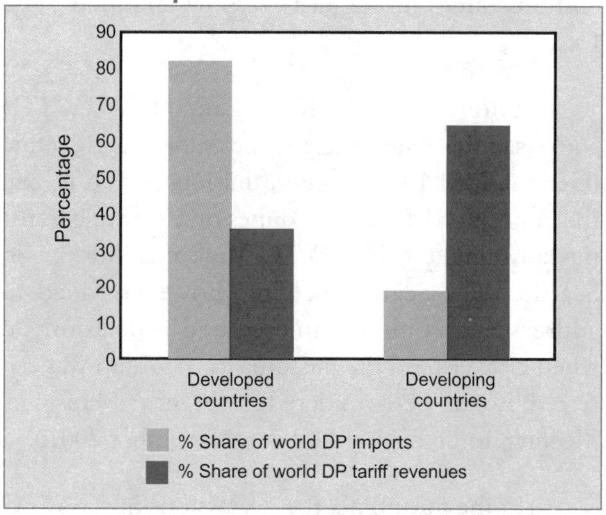

Apart from the MFN tariff, many countries collect a number of additional duties on their imports, such as customs surcharges and fees and consumption taxes. These additional duties would also be lost if products were "imported" electronically and duty-exempted. Therefore, it is important to consider the amount of those revenues (table 23). Calculations show that, compared with the tariff rates, the rates for additional duties are significantly higher. They account on average for 23.2 per cent (all countries), with a wide range between 0 and 120 per cent. The (on average) high rates are largely due to the relatively high consumption taxes levied on imports, in particular in the developed countries. Consumption taxes on imports of digitized products account for 15.2 per cent (all countries), 17.3 per cent (developed countries) and 14.4 per cent (developing countries).

Given these relatively high rates of additional duties collected on digitized products, revenues resulting from the collection of these duties ought to be high as well. As far as absolute numbers are concerned, table 23 shows that while total tariff revenue from digitized products was $977 million, total revenue from both tariffs and additional duties is now more than $8 billion. A large proportion of this is explained by consumption taxes levied on developed countries' imports ($6.2 billion). The shares of these duties in government revenue now account on average for 0.5 of total government revenue, up from 0.1 per cent (tariff only), an increase of 400 per cent. Shares in import revenues have also changed considerably. The combined tariff and customs surcharges (excluding consumption taxes) amount now to 3.6 per cent of total import revenue, up from 1.7 per cent (tariff only), an increase of more than 200 per cent.

To summarize, fiscal losses from customs duties are small compared with total government revenue, but significant in absolute terms and if additional duties are taken into account. Developing countries suffer higher losses from tariff revenues, while developed countries would mainly be affected by forgone consumption taxes on the import of digitized products. The significant amount of lost consumption taxes highlights the importance of addressing taxation in cyberspace and the need to find an agreement at the international level.

G. Policy recommendations

A legal and policy infrastructure that is supportive of and conducive to electronic commerce is an important prerequisite for the growth of the latter. Thus, the existence of a predictable and supportive legal framework has been singled out as an essential tool to increase the much-needed confidence of both business and consumers in international transactions.[148] As pointed out in a report[149] prepared by the UNCTAD secretariat, the key for developing countries may be to identify: (i) those areas in which an international consensus has emerged on how to treat electronic commerce issues; (ii) those areas where domestic action is absolutely necessary in order to foster an environment favourable to electronic commerce; and (iii) those areas where it is possible for developing countries to resolve the legal issues expeditiously. On that basis, it is suggested that developing countries wishing to accommodate e-commerce might wish to give consideration to the following:

- To ensure that e-transactions are given the same legal effect as traditional paper-based transactions, Governments are urged to examine their legal infrastructure to ascertain whether paper-based form requirements prevent laws from being applied in an e-environment.[150] They might consider using UNCITRAL's Model Law on Electronic Commerce as a basis for preparing new laws or adjusting current ones.
- As regards encryption and electronic signatures, there seems to be a consensus that a mechanism for secure authentication of electronic communication is critical to the development of e-commerce. Such a mechanism must provide for confidentiality, authentication (enabling each party to a transaction to ascertain the identity of the other party) and non-repudiation (ensuring that the parties to a transaction cannot subsequently deny their participation). The new UNCITRAL Model Law on Electronic Signatures and the Guide to Enactment, together with some recent examples of regional legislation on electronic signatures described in this chapter, might guide developing countries wishing to prepare legislation on electronic signatures.
- As pointed out in this chapter, a key element in building trust is to ensure that users and consumers have effective redress for disputes arising from transactions online. Since traditional dispute

settlement mechanisms do not provide effective redress in e-commerce transactions, there is a need to consider ADR/ODR mechanisms that would provide speedy, low-cost redress for a large number of the small claims and low-value transactions arising from consumers' online interactions. It is assumed that the adoption of rules and standards concerning consumer protection, resolution of disputes online and choice-of-court clauses will significantly increase consumer confidence in e-commerce.

- International cooperation is absolutely essential, because of the very nature of e-commerce. It is important in this regard that harmonized rules based on international standards be adopted in order to combat criminal activities, and that judicial cooperation be strengthened.
- In the area of e-commerce taxation, developing countries are encouraged to follow the international debates closely and adjust their own legislation using as a basis the rules and principles agreed upon. Furthermore, they could negotiate specific bilateral treaties for e-commerce taxation, which would give them a competitive edge. Any decision that developing countries may take on modifying their tax legislation to accommodate e-commerce will have to take into account the significant role of tax revenues in their national budgets. In the short to medium term, developing countries will be net importers of e-commerce and will therefore run a greater risk of losing revenues if traditional imports are replaced by online delivery. Therefore, the development of efficient tax collection systems for e-commerce should be a priority for all developing countries.
- Governments of developing countries are encouraged to participate in helping shape the emerging international consensus and to contribute to the preparation of various legal instruments being considered in international forums. To this end, cooperation and coordination among countries with similar problems and concerns are critical in order to ensure that, ultimately, all voices are heard in the various international forums.

Table 21
Applied MFN rates and tariff revenue on DP imports, 1999

Country/Economy	Ave.MFN %	W.MFN %	Tariff revenue ($ 000)	Country/Economy	Ave.MFN %	W.MFN %	Tariff revenue ($ 000)
European Union	1.8	1.5	165 277	Sri Lanka	4.6	8.5	1 462
India	23.1	27.1	110 503	Tanzania, United Rep. of	14.9	12.6	1 358
Mexico	15.6	12.2	104 037	Zambia	16.4	9.5	1 323
Malaysia	7.3	10.5	53 331	Iran, Islamic Rep. of	6.0	2.8	1 320
Brazil	13.3	9.7	43 386	Papua New Guinea	13.4	15.4	1 311
Canada	1.9	0.9	42 776	Bangladesh	16.9	5.4	1 297
China	8.8	7.5	40 138	Barbados	12.1	12.8	1 284
Morocco	30.7	30.7	24 159	Gabon	16.2	10.1	1 268
Argentina	13.6	6.8	22 677	Jordan	19.7	10.7	1 211
Israel	5.9	8.0	21 800	Malta	5.3	3.8	1 192
Thailand	11.3	11.8	21 311	Jamaica	9.7	5.1	1 173
Pakistan	38.7	30.2	20 533	Honduras	7.9	4.7	935
Australia	1.5	1.7	19 639	Costa Rica	5.9	2.0	867
Czech Republic	4.2	4.7	19 534	Belize	12.1	17.5	805
Korea, Republic of	4.0	3.7	18 529	Uganda	7.3	6.3	799
Russian Fed.	12.0	6.9	18 472	Cuba	8.0	6.3	779
Venezuela	9.8	7.9	15 726	Oman	5.0	5.0	725
Poland	5.9	3.1	14 412	Saint Vincent	11.2	18.4	675
Nigeria	11.5	20.6	14 123	Nepal	8.8	7.9	603
Hungary	5.2	5.0	13 886	Mozambique	19.6	13.4	564
Asia (other)	2.7	1.9	12 627	Malawi	13.0	4.9	488
United States	0.3	0.2	12 050	Mali	14.2	17.0	476
Colombia	8.6	8.7	12 023	Maldives	17.5	16.9	419
Philippines	7.1	5.1	11 109	Belarus	12.0	5.9	406
Chile	9.0	9.0	10 817	Bahrain	5.2	2.7	361
Paraguay	11.4	10.9	9 540	Norway	0.1	0.0	352
Egypt	16.7	10.3	8 856	Seychelles	20.4	14.3	349
Peru	12.0	12.0	8 811	Albania	14.7	12.5	326
Saudi Arabia	10.4	8.1	8 574	Georgia	9.9	11.6	318
Algeria	15.3	15.9	8 085	Ethiopia	21.2	8.2	312
Tunisia	23.8	16.3	6 864	Madagascar	3.8	5.3	298
Dominican Republic	14.7	15.3	6 695	Chad	16.2	12.0	293
Romania	12.2	6.9	5 537	Antigua, Barbuda	11.1	8.5	290
South Africa	2.6	1.5	5 414	Nicaragua	3.6	2.2	276
Ukraine	8.0	8.7	5 229	Cent. Afr. Rep	16.2	9.8	266
Uruguay	13.5	8.3	5 120	Saint Lucia	10.9	6.6	242
Latvia	7.4	8.1	5 077	Dominica	11.8	9.1	144
Cote d'Ivoire	16.3	13.6	4 370	Suriname	11.6	8.5	142
Indonesia	9.4	8.2	4 305	Moldova	3.2	2.5	129
Turkey	2.6	2.4	4 297	Saint Kitts and Nevis	11.1	10.6	112
Lebanon	14.7	8.4	4 137	Eq. Guinea	16.2	9.1	105
New Zealand	1.4	1.5	3 981	Grenada	11.2	4.7	102
Libya	23.7	14.3	3 173	Brunei Darussalam	1.3	0.6	84
Panama	6.8	5.1	3 152	Solomon Islands	27.0	5.4	57
Slovenia	5.5	2.8	2 698	Guyana	12.1	1.5	32
Rwanda	45.6	23.4	2 433	Montserrat	12.2	17.4	28
Viet Nam	16.7	17.0	2 371	Bhutan	16.5	16.0	27
Zimbabwe	22.5	18.3	2 349	Sudan	1.5	0.3	12
Ecuador	10.8	4.5	2 209	Bahamas	0.0	0.0	4
Kazakhstan	6.9	9.4	2 124	Hong Kong (China)	0.0	0.0	0
Guatemala	6.7	5.1	2 120	Estonia	0.0	0.0	0
Mauritius	9.7	10.2	2 014	Japan	0.0	0.0	0
Kenya	16.2	9.9	2 004	Kyrgyzstan	0.0	0.0	0
Ghana	12.8	7.8	1 995	Lithuania	0.0	0.0	0
Burkina Faso	29.6	31.5	1 990	Singapore	0.0	0.0	0
Bolivia	8.9	7.1	1 798	Switzerland	0.0	0.0	0
Iceland	3.9	4.4	1 717	Turkmenistan	0.0	0.0	0
Lao, People's Dem.Rep.	9.3	11.8	1 715				
Congo	16.0	15.7	1 512				
El Salvador	5.4	4.1	1 480	**World**	**10.7**	**8.5**	**1 036 973**
Trinidad and Tobago	12.0	9.1	1 480	**Developing countries**	**15.3**	**13.1**	**689 767**
Cameroon	16.2	9.6	1 476	**Developed countries***	**3.6**	**2.9**	**347 206**

Sources: Comtrade, TRAINS.
Note: Excludes intra-EU trade. Excludes imports which are subject to specific tariffs.
* Includes economies in transition.

Table 22
Tariff revenue losses from DP imports per country

Country	DP tariff revenue ($ 000)	DP tariff revenue as % of total rev.	DP tariff revenue as % of imp.rev.	DP tariff revenue as % of tax rev.
European Union	165 277	0.01	1.06	0.01
India	110 503	0.19	0.96	0.27
Mexico	104 037	0.18	4.30	0.21
Malaysia	53 331	0.22	2.00	0.26
Brazil	43 386	0.02	0.91	0.03
Canada	42 776	0.03	2.15	0.03
China	40 138	0.07	1.06	0.07
Morocco	24 159	0.24	1.69	0.30
Argentina	22 677	0.06	0.87	0.06
Israel	21 800	0.05	7.20	0.06
Thailand	21 311	0.11	1.21	0.12
Pakistan	20 533	0.21	1.74	0.28
Australia	19 639	0.02	0.79	0.02
Czech Republic	19 534	0.11	5.74	0.11
Korea, Republic of	18 529	0.02	0.29	0.02
Russian Federation	18 472	0.05	1.06	0.06
Venezuela	15 726	0.09	0.97	0.13
Poland	14 412	0.03	1.06	0.03
Hungary	13 886	0.08	2.47	0.09
United States	12 050	0.00	0.07	0.00
Colombia	12 023	0.10	1.39	0.12
Philippines	11 109	0.09	0.52	0.10
Chile	10 817	0.07	0.98	0.08
Paraguay	9 540	1.01	8.13	1.57
Egypt	8 856	0.04	0.36	0.07
Peru	8 811	0.11	1.10	0.13
Algeria	8 085	0.06	0.42	0.06
Tunisia	6 864	0.12	1.00	0.13
Dominican Republic	6 695	0.25	0.71	0.26
Romania	5 537	0.06	1.17	0.07
South Africa	5 414	0.01	0.55	0.02
Uruguay	5 120	0.09	2.80	0.10
Latvia	5 077	0.24	18.77	0.28
Côte d'Ivoire	4 370	0.19	0.57	0.20
Indonesia	4 305	0.01	0.72	0.02
Turkey	4 297	0.01	0.81	0.01
Lebanon	4 137	0.13	0.45	0.18
New Zealand	3 981	0.01	0.40	0.01
Panama	3 152	0.14	1.40	0.20
Slovenia	2 698	0.04	1.15	0.04
Rwanda	2 433	1.19	3.73	1.30
Viet Nam	2 371	0.05	0.21	0.06
Zimbabwe	2 349	0.14	0.86	0.16
Ecuador	2 209	0.08	0.81	0.10
Kazakhstan	2 124	0.14	4.05	0.18
Guatemala	2 120	0.12	0.89	0.12
Mauritius	2 014	0.22	0.85	0.26
Kenya	2 004	0.08	0.54	0.09
Ghana	1 995	0.27	1.35	0.35
Bolivia	1 798	0.12	2.15	0.15
Iceland	1 717	0.07	5.49	0.08
Congo	1 512	0.25	2.56	0.78
El Salvador	1 480	0.11	1.00	0.11
Trinidad and Tobago	1 480	0.10	1.71	0.11
Cameroon	1 476	0.11	0.42	0.13
Sri Lanka	1 462	0.05	0.38	0.06
Zambia	1 323	0.26	1.56	0.27
Iran, Islamic Rep. of	1 320	0.00	0.03	0.00
Papua New Guinea	1 311	0.03	0.10	0.03
Jordan	1 211	0.06	0.30	0.08
Malta	1 192	0.11	2.64	0.13
Costa Rica	867	0.03	0.62	0.03
Belize	805	0.57	1.93	0.64
Oman	725	0.02	0.35	0.07
Saint Vincent & the Gre.	675	0.67	1.69	0.78
Nepal	603	0.12	0.45	0.14
Maldives	419	0.24	0.76	0.49
Belarus	406	1.37	20.66	1.49
Bahrain	361	0.02	0.23	0.07
Norway	352	0.00	0.10	0.00
Seychelles	349	0.13	0.33	0.20
Albania	326	0.05	0.34	0.07
Georgia	318	0.08	2.20	0.10
Ethiopia	312	0.03	0.14	0.04
Madagascar	298	0.09	0.17	0.09
Nicaragua	276	0.06	0.29	0.06
Moldova, Republic of	129	0.04	1.35	0.05
Saint Kitts and Nevis	112	0.17	0.48	0.21
Guinea	105	0.01	0.03	0.01
Grenada	102	0.13	0.80	0.16
Bhutan	27	0.03	2.65	0.09
Bahamas	4	0.00	0.00	0.00
Estonia	0	0.00	0.00	0.00
Japan	0	0.00	0.00	0.00
Kyrgyzstan	0	0.00	0.00	0.00
Lithuania	0	0.00	0.00	0.00
Singapore	0	0.00	0.00	0.00
Switzerland	0	0.00	0.00	0.00
Total	**977 532**	**0.14**	**1.70**	**0.17**
Developing countries	**630 326**	**0.16**	**1.44**	**1.44**
Developed countries	**347 206**	**0.04**	**2.70**	**0.05**

Sources: As for table 21.

Table 23
DP revenues from tariffs, additional customs duties and taxes, 1999

Country	DP tariff revenue ($ 000)	DP cons. tax revenue ($ 000)	DP tariff and cust. surch. revenue ($ 000)	DP all imp. duties revenue ($ 000)	DP tariff and cust. surch. as % of imp. rev.	DP all imp. duties as % of imp. rev.	DP all imp. duties as % of tax rev.	DP all imp. duties as % of total rev.
Albania	326	326	326	653	0.3	0.7	0.1	0.1
Algeria	8 085	10 656	49 773	60 429	2.6	3.2	0.5	0.4
Antigua and Barbuda	290	410	376	785	..	..	..	..
Argentina	22 677	69 609	42 348	111 957	1.6	4.3	0.3	0.3
Australia	19 639	436 773	19 639	456 412	0.8	18.3	0.5	0.5
Austria	1 452	185 834	1 452	187 286	0.6	71.8	0.3	0.3
Bangladesh	1 297	3 598	3 216	6 814	..	..	..	..
Barbados	1 284	1 511	1 284	2 795	..	..	..	..
Belarus	406	1 032	467	1 499	23.8	76.3	5.5	5.1
Belgium (Belg./Lux.)	2 606	238 981	24 040	263 021	1.9	20.5	0.2	0.2
Belize	805	691	805	1 496	1.9	3.6	1.2	1.1
Bolivia	1 798	3 809	6 079	9 888	7.3	11.8	0.8	0.7
Brazil	43 386	36 772	87 057	123 829	1.8	2.6	0.1	0.1
Burkina Faso	1 990	946	2 621	3 567	..	..	..	..
Cameroon	1 476	2 872	1 476	4 348	0.4	1.2	0.4	0.3
Canada	42 776	710 261	504 405	1 214 665	25.3	60.9	1.0	0.9
Chad	293	0	523	523	..	..	..	..
Chile	10 817	16 281	10 817	27 098	1.0	2.5	0.2	0.2
China	40 138	80 731	44 968	125 699	1.2	3.3	0.2	0.2
Colombia	12 023	21 406	12 023	33 429	1.4	3.9	0.3	0.3
Congo	1 512	0	5 441	5 441	9.2	9.2	2.8	0.9
Costa Rica	867	5 871	1 368	7 239	1.0	5.2	0.3	0.2
Côte d'Ivoire	4 370	6 414	5 171	11 585	0.7	1.5	0.5	0.5
Cuba	779	0	779	779	..	..	..	..
Czech Republic	19 534	80 702	19 534	100 235	5.7	29.5	0.6	0.6
Denmark	1 336	160 268	1 336	161 604	0.4	51.1	0.3	0.2
Dominica	144	221	238	459	..	..	..	..
Dominican Republic	6 695	18 352	12 902	31 254	1.4	3.3	1.2	1.1
Ecuador	2 209	3 027	2 665	5 691	1.0	2.1	0.2	0.2
Egypt	8 856	12 945	11 445	24 390	0.5	1.0	0.2	0.1
El Salvador	1 480	2 889	1 480	4 369	1.0	2.9	0.3	0.3
Estonia	0	7 793	0	7 793	..	..	0.6	0.5
Ethiopia	312	182	4 679	4 861	2.0	2.1	0.6	0.4
Finland	1 038	51 541	1 038	52 578	0.7	33.5	0.1	0.1
France	8 265	390 312	8 265	398 577	0.5	22.7	0.1	0.1
Gabon	1 268	1 884	1 268	3 152	..	..	..	..
Germany	16 274	405 459	16 274	421 733	0.4	11.5	0.1	0.1
Ghana	1 995	4 147	1 995	6 142	1.4	4.2	1.1	0.8
Greece	685	27 957	685	28 642	0.3	14.2	0.1	0.1
Grenada	102	437	211	649	1.7	5.1	1.0	0.9
Guatemala	2 120	4 399	2 120	6 519	0.9	2.7	0.4	0.4
Guinea	105	0	187	187	0.1	0.1	0.0	0.0
Guyana	32	0	32	32	..	..	..	..
Honduras	935	1 389	1 034	2 423	..	..	..	..
Hong Kong (China)	0	0	332	332	..	..	..	..
Hungary	13 886	73 333	17 379	90 712	3.1	16.2	0.6	0.5
Iceland	1 717	9 515	1 717	11 232	5.5	35.9	0.5	0.4
India	110 503	0	216 547	216 547	1.9	1.9	0.5	0.4
Indonesia	4 305	5 649	4 305	9 954	0.7	1.7	0.0	0.0
Ireland	2 139	102 528	32 469	134 997	12.8	53.1	0.6	0.5
Israel	21 800	80 857	203 695	284 552	67.3	93.9	0.8	0.7
Italy	2 868	262 541	2 868	265 409	0.2	19.3	0.1	0.1
Jamaica	1 173	3 431	1 173	4 604	..	..	..	..
Japan	0	189 482	0	189 482	0.0	2.1	0.0	0.0
Kazakhstan	2 124	7 183	13 418	20 601	25.6	39.2	1.7	1.3
Kenya	2 004	3 244	2 004	5 247	0.5	1.4	0.2	0.2
Korea, Republic of	18 529	49 182	18 529	67 711	0.3	1.0	0.1	0.1
Kyrgyzstan	0	863	1 849	2 712	23.5	34.5	2.2	1.6
Latvia	5 077	11 226	45 615	56 841	..	..	3.1	2.7
Lithuania	0	6 805	0	6 805	0.0	14.1	0.3	0.2
Luxembourg	241				..	..	..	..

Table 23 (contd.)

Country	DP tariff revenue ($ 000)	DP cons. tax revenue ($ 000)	DP tariff and cust. surch. revenue ($ 000)	DP all imp. duties revenue ($ 000)	DP tariff and cust. surch. as % of imp. rev.	DP all imp. duties as % of imp. rev.	DP all imp. duties as % of tax rev.	DP all imp. duties as % of total rev.
Madagascar	298	3 937	1 985	5 922	1.1	3.3	1.8	1.7
Malawi	488	0	1 536	1 536	..	..	..	..
Malaysia	53 331	50 667	53 331	103 998	2.0	3.9	0.5	0.4
Mali	476	0	476	476	..	..	..	..
Malta	1 192	0	1 192	1 192	2.6	2.6	0.1	0.1
Mauritius	2 014	1 742	2 014	3 756	0.8	1.6	0.5	0.4
Mexico	104 037	143 359	111 873	255 232	4.8	10.9	0.5	0.5
Moldova	129	1 061	144	1 206	1.5	12.6	0.5	0.4
Montserrat	28	32	44	77	..	..	..	..
Morocco	24 159	15 742	36 162	51 904	2.5	3.6	0.6	0.5
Mozambique	564	1 755	878	2 633	..	..	..	..
Nepal	603	1 149	603	1 752	0.5	1.3	0.4	0.3
Netherlands	15 684	267 177	15 684	282 861	0.8	14.5	0.2	0.2
New Zealand	3 981	0	37 491	37 491	3.7	3.7	0.1	0.1
Nicaragua	276	3 759	276	4 035	0.3	4.2	0.9	0.9
Nigeria	14 123	2 084	19 608	21 692	..	..	..	..
Norway	352	180 595	0	180 595	0.0	53.3	0.4	0.3
Oman	725	0	725	725	0.3	0.3	0.1	0.0
Pakistan	20 533	8 508	20 533	29 041	1.7	2.5	0.4	0.3
Panama	3 152	3 226	6 877	10 103	3.1	4.5	0.6	0.4
Papua New Guinea	1 311	0	5 045	5 045	0.4	0.4	0.1	0.1
Paraguay	9 540	18 414	9 540	27 954	8.1	23.8	4.6	3.0
Peru	8 811	40 793	8 811	49 603	1.1	6.2	0.7	0.6
Philippines	11 109	19 653	11 109	30 762	0.5	1.4	0.3	0.3
Poland	14 412	99 579	85 998	185 577	6.4	13.7	0.4	0.4
Portugal	555	50 351	555	50 906	0.3	25.2	0.1	0.1
Romania	5 537	18 956	9 963	28 919	2.1	6.1	0.4	0.3
Russian Federation	18 472	67 200	63 524	130 723	3.6	7.5	0.4	0.3
Rwanda	2 433	1 561	3 047	4 608	4.7	7.1	2.5	2.2
Saudi Arabia	8 574	0	12 262	12 262	..	..	..	..
Singapore	0	20 355	0	20 355	0.0	7.5	0.2	0.1
Slovenia	2 698	17 988	5 005	22 993	2.1	9.8	0.3	0.3
Solomon Islands	57	215	57	272	..	..	..	..
South Africa	5 414	56 315	5 414	61 730	0.5	6.3	0.2	0.2
Spain	2 138	152 878	2 138	155 016	0.3	21.7	0.1	0.1
Sri Lanka	1 462	0	9 464	9 464	2.4	2.4	0.4	0.3
Saint Kitts and Nevis	112	157	143	301	0.6	1.3	0.6	0.4
Saint Lucia	242	1 448	443	1 892	..	..	..	..
Saint Vincent & the Grenadines	675	0	767	767	1.9	1.9	0.9	0.8
Sudan	12	0	12	12	..	..	..	..
Suriname	142	0	175	175	..	..	..	..
Sweden	2 690	159 782	2 690	162 471	0.6	38.9	0.2	0.2
Switzerland (Switz/Licht)	0	163 230	0	163 230	0.0	26.5	0.3	0.2
Tanzania, United Rep. of	1 358	3 039	1 358	4 398	..	..	..	..
Thailand	21 311	12 359	21 311	33 670	1.2	1.9	0.2	0.2
Trinidad and Tobago	1 480	2 667	1 480	4 147	1.7	4.8	0.3	0.3
Tunisia	6 864	30 316	6 864	37 180	1.0	5.4	0.7	0.7
Turkey	4 297	42 491	4 297	46 788	0.8	8.8	0.2	0.1
Uganda	799	2 155	799	2 954	..	..	..	..
Ukraine	5 229	13 050	5 229	18 279	..	..	..	..
United Kingdom	25 266	492 775	25 266	518 041	0.9	17.5	0.1	0.1
United States	12 050	0	12 050	12 050	0.1	0.1	0.0	0.0
Uruguay	5 120	14 159	10 969	25 128	6.0	13.8	0.5	0.4
Venezuela	15 726	32 655	17 705	50 360	1.1	3.1	0.4	0.3
Viet Nam	2 371	1 392	2 371	3 764	0.2	0.3	0.1	0.1
Zambia	1 323	2 444	1 323	3 767	1.6	4.4	0.8	0.7
Zimbabwe	2 349	0	6 198	6 198	2.3	2.3	0.4	0.4
Total	**928 922**	**6 037 696**	**2 140 561**	**8 178 257**	**3.6**	**13.3**	**0.6**	**0.5**
Developed countries	**265 167**	**5 102 676**	**1 144 248**	**6 246 924**	**4.9**	**26.9**	**0.4**	**0.4**
Developing countries	**663 755**	**935 020**	**979 784**	**1 914 803**	**2.9**	**6.5**	**0.7**	**0.6**

Sources: As for table 21.

Notes

1 We will not deal in this chapter with business-to-government transactions. See chapter 5 on digital government.

2 We are not in a position to give a full picture of all national case law, but we will try to explain the most important decisions rendered so far in Europe, the United States and a few other countries.

3 This refers to the famous "Declaration of independence of the Internet" , to be found at http://www.eff.org/~barlow/declaration-final.html. This clearly marks a new attack on State-made law in the erroneous belief that the "market" will regulate the Internet by itself.

4 A domain name is a commercial comprehensible alternative to an address Internet Protocol (IP),which web servers use to identify each other on the Internet. The domain name system is the hierarchical system by which easy-to-remember, human-friendly names are associated with Internet locations.

5 The notion of "domicile" in international law is defined as follows: (i) for individuals, it is mostly equated with habitual residence, i.e. a place where the individual presents most of the contact points for his/her personal, family and professional lives; (ii) for corporations or other legal entities, legal systems vary in their definitions. Thus, in some systems, a corporation is domiciled at the place of incorporation and in others the main centre of activity or principal establishment is the essential contact point. A third category would also accept the place where a branch or another establishment is situated. So far, all attempts to agree on a single definition worldwide have failed, and international agreements usually respect the different variations described above. For an example of this, see Article 3 of the Hague preliminary draft Convention on Jurisdiction and Foreign Judgements in Civil and Commercial Matters (accessible on www.hcch.net, work in progress).

6 This does not mean that specific rules are automatically needed. In fact, as demonstrated below, existing rules may very often be enough to deal with questions posed by the use of the Internet.

7 This is the conclusion reached in 1997 at the Utrecht Colloquium, reproduced in Boele-Woelki and Kessedjian (1985, p. 143).

8 That is to say, where they are domiciled (see note 5 above).

9 The issue of anonymity is a difficult one. It is linked with the responsibility which Internet service providers (ISPs) have to disclose the names of persons using their services. This is a major controversy, partially addressed in national laws adopted recently for Internet activities. In summary, it can be said that ISPs are not responsible for content when their role is only one of transport. However, no law directly addresses the potential obligation of ISPs to disclose information they possess. This is a question which will have to be addressed sooner or later at the international level.

10 Work was initiated by the United States in 1992. After a few years of preliminary studies, negotiations started in June 1996 and culminated in October 1999 with the adoption of the preliminary draft convention to be found on the Conference's website (www.hcch.net) under the heading "work in progress". On the site can also be found all preliminary documents drafted to help the negotiations and the explanatory report written by Mr. Peter Nygh and Mr. Fausto Pocar, co-rapporteurs for the draft.

11 The Hague Conference organized a colloquium in 1997 Boele-Woelki and Kessedjian, 1998. In September 1999, the Hague Conference organized a round table in cooperation with the University of Geneva, to review all aspects of the private international law of the Internet. The report of that round table is included in a more general report on the information society available on the Hague Conference site, under the heading "Special Commission on General Affairs and Policy", as Preliminary Document No.7, (ftp://hcch.net/doc/gen_pd7e.doc).

12 In the ABA project, the word "jurisdiction" stands for both adjudicatory jurisdiction and applicable law. The report on the study was released in public in New York and London in July 2000. It is the product of a Working Group on Cyberspace, set up by the ABA in 1998, entitled "Transnational issues in cyberspace: A project on the law relating to jurisdiction". The Working Group consisted of sub-groups, dealing respectively with (i) advertising and consumer protection, (ii) data protection, (iii) intellectual property, (iv) payment systems and banking, (v) public law gaming, (vi) sale of goods, (vii) sale of services, taking tele-medicine as an example, (viii) securities and (ix) taxation. The report may be accessed at www.kentlaw.edu/cyberlaw.

13 The GBDe has a website at www.gbde.com.

14 The ILPF has a website at www.ilpf.org.

15 We will not deal at length with arbitration in this report. The literature on arbitration, is considerable and the specific problems with arbitration and e-commerce are not so complicated that they need extensive discussion. The one question which was debated at length was the writing requirement in the New York Convention of 1958. But as in the case of all writing requirements in international conventions or national law, the solution is to be found in the authentication and electronic signature systems which are now admitted by an ever increasing number of legal systems. The second question

posed by online arbitration relates to the "place of arbitration". However, this is also being solved by the consensus achieved on the fact that the place of arbitration is a legal fiction which is useful for the law applicable to the arbitration process and, potentially, to the procedure. Thus, favouring online arbitration does not mean that a place of arbitration must not still be chosen by the parties. See the debate at the Geneva Round Table in September 1999 (Hague Conference on Private International Law, 1999).

16 In the present discussions, it is customary to attack the judicial systems for being inefficient, too slow and too expensive and, therefore, not suitable to e-commerce disputes. Even though it is true that judicial systems around the world need some reform, it is dangerous to give the impression that societies can do without them. The increasing privatization of justice has its limits, particularly because, as mentioned earlier, if society increasingly relies on contract, the justice system cannot also rely only on contract. A contractual relationship is first and foremost, a relation of force. The justice system must be able to restore the balance when necessary.

17 All preliminary documents for this project are available at http://hcch.net/, under the heading "work in progress.

18 The Brussels Convention of 27 September 1968 is in force between all members States of the European Union and will be replaced by a European Regulation owing to the entry into force of the Amsterdam Treaty amending the Treaty on the European Community. The new Regulation was adopted on 22 December 2000 (published in OJEC L12, 22 December 2000) and will enter into force on 1 March 2002.

19 The Lugano Convention of 16 September 1988 was negotiated between the EU member States and the States party to the EFTA Agreement. The Lugano Convention can also be adhered to by non-EFTA countries. This is the case of Poland, which became a party to it in 1999.

20 It was adopted by the Special Commission in October 1999. The draft can be accessed at the following address: http://www.hcch.net/e/conventions/draft36e.html.

21 These forums are too numerous to be cited *in extenso* here. However, mention must be made of the work done at informal meetings within the Hague framework; by the European Union both for the revision of the Brussels and Lugano Conventions and for the electronic commerce Directive; the numerous discussions in the United States with non-governmental organizations such as ILPF and the ABA and with government bodies (see particularly the Federal Trade Commission (FTC) and Department of Commerce workshops (http://www.ftc.gov/bcp/altdisresolution/index.htm).

22 For example, in some common-law countries the jurisdiction conferred on the chosen court is not exclusive unless the parties have so indicated.

23 See note 15 above.

24 For this notion, see, for example, C. Kessedjian (in Hague Conference on Private International Law, 1999).

25 In all jurisidictional discussions, it is assumed that the defendant's forum is always available even though, in some countries, flexible theories such as that of *forum non conveniens* may apply to the defendant's forum.

26 See the Report on the Ottawa Expert meeting at ftp://hcch.net/doc/jdgmpd12.doc. The Geneva Round Table reached the same conclusion (see Hague Conference on Private International Law, 1999).

27 Directive 2000/31/EC of the European Parliament and of the Council of 8 June 2000 on certain legal aspects of information society services, in particular electronic commerce, in the Internal Market (Directive on electronic commerce' OJ L 178 17.07.2000 p.1.*)*.

28 They are too numerous to be cited. Suffice it to say that they emanate both from international governmental organizations such as the OECD and from NGOs such as the ICC.

29 See the discussion below in paragraphs 2.1.5 and 6.1 (A).

30 For the purposes of this chapter, the word "services" is a term of convenience; it has no legal implications.

31 For a thorough analysis of legal provisions applying to consumers or currently proposed by a number of countries and some international organizations, see Andrews (2000).

32 For further details on BOTs, see the ABA report cited in note 12.

33 See, for example, the discussions at the FTC/Department of Commerce Seminar in Washington, DC, in June 2000, http://www.ftc.gov/bcp/altdisresolution/index.htm.

34 This concept is found in Article 11 of the EU Investment Directive (93/22).

35 Insurance companies have started to offer special coverage for some judicial and legal protection when doing business over the net.

36 This is already what some sellers on the net do. The potential buyer is asked to state, before he/she starts shopping, whether he is buying for his/her personal use or for professional reasons. In the latter case, the price offered is lower.

37 The text of Article 7 reads as follows:

"*Article 7 Contracts concluded by consumers*

1. A plaintiff who concluded a contract for a purpose which is outside its trade or profession, hereafter designated as the consumer, may bring a claim in the courts of the State in which it is habitually resident, if

a) the conclusion of the contract on which the claim is based is related to trade or professional activities that the defendant has engaged in or directed to that State, in particular in soliciting business through means of publicity, and

b) the consumer has taken the steps necessary for the conclusion of the contract in that State.

2. A claim against the consumer may only be brought by a person who entered into the contract in the course of its trade or profession before the courts of the State of the habitual residence of the consumer.

3. The parties to a contract within the meaning of paragraph 1 may, by an agreement which conforms with the requirements of Article 4, make a choice of court

a) if such agreement is entered into after the dispute has arisen, or

b) to the extent only that it allows the consumer to bring proceedings in another court."

38 See note above 18.

39 This is attested by the fact that, at present, in Europe, not few than eight Directives apply to the protection of consumers which are said to be equally applicable to Internet dealings. See the answer given by Mr. Bolkestein on behalf of the European Commission to the European Parliament on 17 November 1999 (OJEC C303E of 24 October 2000, p.10).

40 See section 2 below.

41 See Articles 13 to 15 of the Brussels and Lugano Conventions and Articles 15 to 17 of the new Regulation replacing the Brussels Convention. This attitude was confirmed by the European Court of Justice on 27 June 2000 in the joint cases C-240/98 to C-244/98. The Court said in point 24: "It follows that where a jurisdiction clause is included, without being individually negotiated, in a contract between a consumer and a seller or supplier within the meaning of the Directive and where it confers exclusive jurisdiction on a court in the territorial jurisdiction of which the seller or supplier has his principal place of business, it must be regarded as unfair within the meaning of Article 3 of the Directive in so far as it causes, contrary to the requirement of good faith, a significant imbalance in the parties' rights and obligations arising under the contract, to the detriment of the consumer."

42 See, for example, *Mark Williams et al vs. America Online Inc*, a Superior Court decision rendered in February 2001. The court was seized of a class action against America Online for problems that appeared after AOL 5.0 was installed on clients' computers. The court refused to transfer the case to Virginia, which was the chosen forum in the contract.

43 The report published by the Working Group of the American Bar Association in July 2000 (cited above in footnote 12) discusses this development and its limitations. See also the discussion in Kessedjian (2000).

44 For example, some would use the language as a criterion for targeting, while others would use the currency. But would the use of English or the dollar be really meaningful?

45 We define "tort" as an "act which causes harm to a determinate person, whether intentionally or not, not being the breach of a duty arising out of a personal relation or contract, and which is either contrary to law, or an omission of a specific legal duty, or a violation of an absolute right". Burke, J., "Osborn's Concise Law Dictionary", Sweet & Maxwell, London, 1976, p. 327.

46 The questions posed by ISP's responsibility will not be developed here.

47 We had access only to the English translation prepared by the office of Steptoe and Johnston. The document is available at http://www.steptoe.com/webdoc.nsf/Files/ItalySupCt/$file/ItalySupCt.doc. The case involved defamation and insults on a site, owned by a foreign resident, against an Italian resident. The Italian Supreme Court decided that Italy had jurisdiction since end-users connect to the site from Italian territory.

48 After the French decision was rendered, German courts began to reconsider asserting jurisdiction in similar cases. See Reuters News, 19 February 2001.

49 In a civil case, a Canadian Appellate decision refused to enforce a Texas judgement rendered between two Canadian residents (*Braintech, Inc. V. Kostiuk (1999)* 171 D.L.R. (4th) 46). Texas asserted jurisdiction on the basis of the fact that the defamatory data were accessible in Texas. The Canadian court decided that the link was too tenuous and that Texas did not have jurisdiction. One must add, to fully understand this decision, that the Texas decision was rendered *ex parte* since the defendant did not appear in the proceedings in that State.

50 The text of Article 10 reads as follows :

"*Article 10* *Torts or delicts*

1. A plaintiff may bring an action in tort or delict in the courts of the State :

a) in which the act or omission that caused injury occurred, or

b) in which the injury arose, unless the defendant establishes that the person claimed to be responsible could not reasonably have foreseen that the act or omission could result in an injury of the same nature in that State.

2. Paragraph 1 *b)* shall not apply to injury caused by anti-trust violations, in particular price-fixing or monopolization, or conspiracy to inflict economic loss.

3. A plaintiff may also bring an action in accordance with paragraph 1 when the act or omission, or the injury may occur.

4. If an action is brought in the courts of a State only on the basis that the injury arose or may occur there, those courts shall have jurisdiction only in respect of the injury that occurred or may occur in that State, unless the injured person has his or her habitual residence in that State."

51 A third question arises in the context of the draft Hague Convention: What level of interactivity must a site be shown to possess, or what level of targeting must it comprise, for it to be regarded as a "regular commercial activity" within the meaning of Article 9? This question will not be discussed in this report since the notion of "regular commercial activity" is a very controversial one and has not yet been defined with enough precision to be considered as reflecting a general consensus.

52 See the Electronic Commerce Directive, cited in footnote 27 above.

53 See the Report of the Ottawa meeting, cited in footnote 26 above.

54 See "Clarification on the application of the permanent establishment definition in e-commerce: Changes to the commentary on Article 5 of the model tax convention", OECD, January 2001. For further details, see paragraph 6.1 (B).

55 The Act amends Section 43 of the Trademark Act of 1946 (15 U.S.C. 1125) and is cited as 15 U.S.C. §1125(d).

56 On 20 February 2001, Law.com reported that more than 700 lawsuits had been filed in the United States using the Act.

57 For an analysis of the ICANN arbitration rules and their relations with court jurisdiction, see Kessedjian (2000b, pp. 69-96).

58 It may be noted that for all generic Top Level Domains (TLDs,) such as .com and .net, there is a concentration of litigation in Virginia since the registrar is located in that State.

59 United States District Court for the Eastern District of Virginia, December 2000.

60 Only three meetings are mentioned here because it is not possible to mention all of them.

61 Http://dsa-isis.jrc.it/ADR/workshop.html.

62 The variety of ADR systems within the European Union is best illustrated in a document prepared by the European Commission in the financial services area. Accessible via the Internet at http://europa.eu.int/comm/internal_market/en/finances/consumer/intro.htm, it allows access to pages for each country, indicating the main features of the ADR system proposed in that country together with the addresses of the authority responsible for maintaining the system.

63 The complete documentation for this meeting can be consulted at www.ecommerce.gov/adr.

64 The documents are available at http://www.oecd.org/dsti/sti/it/secur/act/online_trust/presentations.htm.

65 The statement was released on 18 December 2000. It is available at http://www.ecommerce.gov/joint_statements/EU_ADR1-5-01.html.

66 The first result of this work was the New York Convention of 1958 on the enforcement of foreign arbitral awards. The Convention is now in force in 125 States and is applied satisfactorily in the great majority of cases. The list of States Party to the New York Convention may be accessed at http://www.uncitral.org/en-index.htm. The UNCITRAL rules of arbitration are also very useful for ad hoc arbitration. The 1985 UNICTRAL arbitration model law has also helped harmonize arbitration laws around the globe.

67 This is particularly important when the arbitration process takes place entirely online.

68 See, for example, the seven principles included in the EU Recommendation No. 257/98. Also the joint statement by the United States and the European Union cited above gives some guidelines on common basic principles. A very thorough study of the ODR systems already existing and how they apply the common principles mentioned in the text was released by Consumers International in December 2000 (Consumers International, 2000).

69 The full text of the Uniform Domain Name Dispute Resolution Policy, adopted on 26 August 1999, and the Rules of Procedure are available at http://www.icann.org/udrp/udrp-rules-24oct99.htm.

70 Establihed in October 1998, ICANN is a non-profit, private sector corporation formed by a broad coalition of the Internet's business, technical, academic and user communities. It has been recognized by the United States Government as the global consensus entity to coordinate the technical management of the Internet's domain name system, the allocation of IP address space, the assignment of protocol parameters and the management of the root server system. See http://www.icann.org.

71 Convention on the Applicable Law to Contractual Obligations. See consolidated version OJEC C027 of 26 January 1998.

72 It must be noted that although the Rome Convention and the future Regulations are European texts, they apply to all cases coming before European courts even though no European member States, domestic law is involved. The rationale behind this solution is to unify all conflict rules within the member States so that there are not two sets of conflict rules, one for European cases (how to define those?) and one for non-European cases.

73 This matter was discussed at length at the May 2000 meeting of the Hague Conference on Private International Law. It was decided that applicable law is one of the topics to be kept on the agenda for the work done on legal norms adapted to the information society. See ftp://hcch.net/doc/concl e.doc.

74 Practice is not uniform in this respect. Some contracts refer to Internet usages (see, for example, contracts proposed by UUNET, Prolink or Strato) or to what is known as "netiquette" (contracts proposed by Club Internet or Exceed).

75 In the security brokerage market, regulators such as the Securities and Exchange Commission (SEC) in the United States and the Commission des opérations de bourse (COB) in France have warned Internet brokers that they may have to comply with security-offering laws in the country where the client is located.

76 See paragraph 2.1.

77 As mentioned earlier, the Rome Convention of 1980 unifies the conflict rules in ten member States of the European Union for all cases where there is a question of applicable law. The parties to the Convention are Austria, Finland, France, Germany, Greece, Luxembourg, the Netherlands, Portugal, Spain and Sweden. Because of the Amsterdam Treaty, the Convention should be transformed into a Regulation which will then apply directly to all member States.

78 For a list of all codified rules as of 1986 see Vassilakakis (1987). Since then, many other countries have codified their private international rules, e.g. Tunisia.

79 Two main conventions may be cited here. The 1955 Convention on the Law Applicable to Sales of Goods (http://www.hcch.net/f/conventions/text03f.html) and the 1978 Convention on the Law applicable to Agency (http://www.hcch.net/e/conventions/text27e.html).

80 See paragraph 2.1.3 above.

81 See the Yahoo! case in France. For case law in the United Kingdom, see Vick et al. (1999, p. 58).

82 The latest meeting held in this regard took place at the World Intellectual Property Organization (WIPO) in Geneva on 30 and 31 January 2001.

83 See the Yahoo! case in France.

84 Everyday information collected over the net brings new stories about inappropriate sales of data banks containing personal data.

85 For example, courts which previously worked under legal norms allowing for public access to court documents are now wondering whether this rule can still be applied without any limitations, in view of Internet techniques (see Groner (2000)).

86 This Convention may be found at http://www.coe.fr/dataprotection/edocs.htm. It is a Convention adopted under the auspices of the Council of Europe which is a different organization from the European Union. The European Community became a party to that Convention with effect from 1999 (http://www.coe.fr/dataprotection/Treaties/amend108e.htm). The European Council has also adopted a Recommendation No.R(99)5 for the Protection of Privacy on the Internet (23 February 1999).

87 Directive 95/46/CE of the European Parliament and Council of 24 October 1995, OJEC L 281, 23 November 1995, p. 31.

88 Proposed Directive of the European Parliament and Council presented by the Commission on 25 August 2000, OJEC C365E, 19 December 2000, p .223.

89 OJEC L215 of 25 August 2000, p. 1.

90 OJEC L215 of 25 August 2000, p. 4.

91 OJEC L215 of 25 August 2000, p. 7.

92 http://europa.eu.int/comm/internal_market/en/media/dataprot/wpdocs/wp39en.pdf.

93 See the Australian Privacy Amendment Act 2000, finally approved on 22 December 2000 (www.privacy.gov.au).

94 For concerns over corporate actions not respecting principles of privacy see Krebs (2001). See also Weber (2001). Mention should be made of an attempt by Senator John Edwards (Democrat, North Carolina) for the United States Congress to legislate on privacy. He introduced a bill on 29 January 2001, even though in 2000 Congress had considered more than two dozens bills on privacy but had failed to enact laws.

95 Recommendation by the OECD Council of 23 September 1980. See http://www.oecd.org/e/droit/doneperso//ocdeprive/priv-en.htm.

96 This document is published under the reference DSTI/ICCP/REG(97)6/FINAL, accessible on the OECD website, www.oecd.org.

97 DSTI/ICCP/REG(98)5/FINAL, accessible at www.oecd.org.

98 This inventory is published under the reference DSTI/ICCP/REG(98)12/FINAL.

99 This Declaration is included in the Conclusions of the Ottawa Conference, published under the reference SG/EC(98)14/FINAL.

100 See paragraph 22.

101 In this connection, it is important to note that the Geneva Round Table (Committee IV) concluded in similar fashion. See the document mentioned in note 26 above.

102 See http://www.oecd.org/dsti/sti/it/secur/act/online_trust/presentations.htm.

103 For a survey of digital signature law, see http://rechten.kub.nl/simone/ds-lawsu.htm and http://www.mcbridebakercoles.com/ecommerce/international.asp.

104 Already in 1996 the Commission of the European Communities noted: "for e-commerce to develop, both consumers and businesses must be confident that their transaction will not be intercepted or modified, that the seller and the buyer are who they say they are, and that transaction mechanisms are available, legal, and secure. Building such trust and confidence is the prerequisite to win over businesses and consumers to e-commerce." A European Initiative in Electronic Commerce, (COM (97) 157 final, 16 April, 1997); http://www.spa.org/govmnt/govnews.htm.

105 The Internet Law and Policy Forum proposed the following additional principles : respect for freedom of contract and parties' ability to set provisions by agreement; making laws governing electronic authentication consistent across jurisdictions; preventing discrimination and erection of non-tariff barriers; allowing for the use of current or future means of electronic authentication; and promoting market-driven standards. See http://www.ilpf.org/digsig/intlprin.htm.

106 See Smedinghoff and Hill Bro (1999).

107 See OECD (1999).

108 See Kuner and Baker (2000) and Aalberts and van der Hof (1999).

109 Available at http://www.uncitral.org.

110 The United States Electronic Signatures in Global and National Commerce Act follows the minimalist approach. It gives e-signatures the same legal validity as traditional paper signatures and explicitly forbids the denial of an electronic agreement simply because it is not in writing. To prevent conflicting State-level approaches, the law further forbids any State statute or regulation that limits, modifies or supersedes the Federal Act in a manner that would discriminate for or against a particular technology.

111 A number of international organizations, such as the OECD and the ICC, have also been involved in electronic authentication issues. See http://www.ocde.org/dsti/sti/it/secur/ and http://www.iccwbo.org/home/menu_electronic_commerce.asp.

112 The Directive was published on 19.January.2000 in the *Official Journal of the European Communities*. According to article 13, Member States should implement it not later than 19 July 2001. For the full text of the Directive, see http://europa.eu.int/ISPO/ecommerce/legal/digital.html.

113 See Schlechter (1999).

114 See Article 2 (2).

115 See Article 3 (1) and (2).

116 See the Commission Decision of 6 November 2000 on the minimum criteria to be taken into account by member States when designating national bodies responsible for the conformity assessments of secure signature-creation devices. *Official Journal of the European Communities* L 289/42 of 16 November.2000. Available at http://europa.eu.int/comm/trade/index_en.htm.

117 See Article 6.

118 Article 7 provides that where the law requires a person to sign a document, that requirement is met if a method is used to identify the person and indicate his or her approval of the document, and if that method is as reliable as appropriate in the light of all the circumstances, including any relevant agreement.

119 "The MLES was prepared on the assumption that it would be directly derived from Article 7 of the UNCITRAL Model Law on Electronic Commerce and would be considered as a way of providing detailed information about the concept of a reliable "method used to identify" a person and "to indicate that person's approval" of the information contained in a data message. UNCITRAL document A7CN.9/WG.IV/WP.71, paragraph 49.

120 The UNCITRAL Model Law on Electronic Signatures and the Guide to Enactment, as well as the background documentation, can be found at http://www.uncitral.org/en-index.htm.

121 See Gregory (2001).

122 See the preamble to UNCITRAL (2001).

123 The UNCITRAL criteria coincide with the requirements set out in the EU Directive for defining "advance electronic signature".

124 The UNCITRAL Model Law on Electronic Commerce with Guide to Enactment (1996), with additional article 5 *bis* as adopted in 1998, can be found at http://www.uncitral.org/en-index.htm. A discussion of many of the provisions of the Model Law may be found in UNCTAD (1998). paras. 15-23 and 93-179.

125 According to the information provided by UNCITRAL, as of 17 January 2001, the following countries or territories have adopted legislation based on the Model Law: Australia, Bermuda, Colombia, France, Hong Kong Special Administrative Region of China, Mexico, Ireland, Republic of Korea, Singapore, Slovenia, the Philippines, and the States of Jersey (Crown Dependency of the United Kingdom of Great Britain and Northern Ireland), as well as, within the United States of America, the State of Illinois. See http://www.uncitral.org/en-index.htm.

126 See survey conducted by the Economic Commission for Europe (ECE) published on 22 July 1994 (TRDE/WP:4/R.1096), as revised on 25 February 1999 (TRADE/CEFACT/1999/CRP.2). Available at http://www.unece.org/cefact/ .

127 See Articles 39, 40 and 41 of the Vienna Convention on the Law of Treaties, 1969, concerning "amendment and modification" of treaties.

128 See document TRADE/CEFACT/1999/CRP.7 of 26 February 1999. Available at http://www.unece.org/cefact/.

129 See United Nations document A/CN.9/WG.IV/WP.89. Available at http://www.unece.org/cefact/.

130 See the Report of the Working Group at its 38th session, A/CN.9/484, April 2001, pp. 81–86.

131 Directive of 8 June 2000, *Official Journal of the European Communities*, 17 July 2000. The full text of the Directive is available at http://europa.eu.int/ISPO/ecommerce/legal/legal.html#frame. See footnote 27 above.

132 See Recommendation No. 31 of March 2000 (ECE/TRADE/257). The full text of the E-Agreement is available at http://www.unece.org/cefact/. See also "The Model Interchange Agreement for the International Use of Electronic Data Interchange", adopted by UN/ECE WP.4 in March 1995 as Recommendation No. 26.

133 See Recommendation No.32 on E-Commerce Self-Regulatory Instruments (Codes of Conduct), ECE/TRADE/277, March 2001. Available at http://www.unece.org/cefact/.

134 An earlier OECD proposal on basic principles of international e-commerce taxation made reference to developing countries, stating that "any tax arrangements adopted domestically and any changes to existing international tax principles should be structured to ensure a fair sharing of the Internet tax base between countries, particularly important as regards division of the tax base between developed and developing countries" (Owens, 1997). However, this principle was not included in the final set of basic principles agreed upon in 1998 (OECD, 1998a).

135 There are, however, also barriers that could prevent this shift, such as other regulatory obstacles (besides taxation), delivery problems, or cultural and linguistic barriers. To circumvent these, some United States suppliers have started to buy local competitors in Europe (*The Economist*, "A survey of e-commerce", 26 February 2000).

136 For details and facts about EU VAT rules, see European Commission (1997a). The complexity of the existing EU VAT system is considered by business to be a major barrier to developing e-commerce in Europe.

137 This regulation was put in place in 1993 under the "transitional VAT arrangements", with the objective of removing border controls for tax purposes inside the European Community.

138 Guidelines for defining "place of consumption" have been prepared by the OECD Working Party on Consumption Taxes (OECD, 2001a) and are currently being discussed by OECD member States.

139 The United States is again a different case: United States citizens are subject to taxation on their total global income in the United States, no matter whether they are resident in the United States or in any other country. United States taxation law allows them, however, to offset the taxes paid in their country of residence against their United States tax liability.

140 OECD member countries have not yet agreed on what the "core functions" of an enterprise could be.

141 According to *The Economist* ("A survey of e-commerce", 26 February 2000), the United States currently accounts for 90 per cent of commercial websites.

142 For example, if Amazon.com posts its link on another business' website/server, this does not constitute a permanent establishment.

143 In their final conclusions, however, OECD member countries agreed that payments related to transactions that "permit the customer to electronically download digital products for the customer's own use or enjoyment" do not constitute royalties. On the other hand, if the downloaded product is commercially exploited (i.e. reproduced and sold), the payments would be classified as royalties (OECD, 2001b).

144 And even within the EU, VAT differs among member States.

145 Bermuda is currently examining how to attract foreign business in the light of e-commerce, on the basis of its previous success in attracting the insurance industry through its "no tax" policy (Storie and Green, 1999).

146 Detailed information about the products included here (such as their corresponding HS headings), the methodology employed in the data collection and analysis, as well as tables on trade flows, tariff levels and revenues, are provided in Teltscher (2000).

147 Perez-Esteve and Schuknecht (1999).

148 In many of the joint statements which the United States has signed with other countries, it has been underlined that «The role of government is to provide, where necessary, a clear, consistent and predictable legal framework, to promote a pro-competitive environment in which electronic commerce can flourish and to ensure adequate protection of public interest objectives.»

149 UNCTAD (1999).

150 As pointed out by some commentators, the traditional paper-based rules governing the form of legal transactions could be extrapolated by national courts and other national authorities to cover paperless trade. The difficulties of such an approach stem not only from the time needed to extrapolate them but also from uncertainty about its consequences and from the lack of harmonized solutions at an international level.

References and bibliography

Aalberts, B.P. and van der Hof, S. (1999). *Digital Signature Blindness, Analysis of Legislative Approaches toward Electronic Authentication*, November, http://cwis.kub.nl/~frw/people/hof/ds-fr.htm.

American Bar Association (2000)."Transnational issues in cyberspace: A project on the law relating to jurisdiction", www.kentlaw.edu/cyberlaw.

Andrews, S. (2000) *The Consumer Law Sourcebook 2000: Electronic Commerce and the Global Economy*, Washington DC, Electronic Privacy Information Center.

Australian Privacy Amendment Act 2000, 22 December 2000, www.privacy.gov.au.

Bleuel, J. and Stewen, M. (2000). "Value added taxes on electronic commerce: Obstacles to the EU Commission's approach ", in *Intereconomics*, July/August 2000, pp. 155-161.

Boele, K. and Kessedjian, C. (1998). "Internet, which court decides, which law applies?" The Hague, Kluwer Law International, p. 143.

Consumers International (2000). "Disputes in cyberspace – Online dispute resolution for consumers in cross-border disputes – An international survey", http://www.consumersinternational.org.

Economic Commission for Europe (ECE) (1995). *The Model Interchange Agreement for the International Use of Electronic Data Interchange*. Recommendation No. 26, UN/ECE WP.4, March.

Economic Commission for Europe (ECE) (2000). *E- Agreement.* Recommendation No. 31 of March 2000, ECE/TRADE/257, http://www.unece.org/cefact/.

Economic Commission for Europe (ECE) (2001). *Draft Recommendation on E-Commerce Self-Regulatory Instruments (Codes of Conduct)*, TRADE/CEFACT/ 2001/14, 15 January, http://www.unece.org/cefact/.

European Commission (1995). *Directive 95/46/CE of the European Parliament and Council of 24 October 1995*, OJEC L 281, 23 November 1995, p. 31.

European Commission (1997a). *VAT in the European Community*, XXI/541/97, EC, DGXXI, January.

European Commission (1997b). *A European Initiative in Electronic Commerce* (COM (97) 157 final, 16 April, http://www.spa.org/govmnt/govnews.htm.

European Commission (1998). *Financing the European Union. Commission Report on the Operation of the Own Resources System*, DGXIX, October, www.europa.eu.int/comm/dg19/agenda2000/ownresources/html/index.htm.

European Commission (1999). *Indirect Taxes and E-commerce*, Working Paper, Working Party No. 1, DG XXI, June.

European Commission (2000a). *Proposal for a Regulation of the European Parliament and of the Council amending Regulation (EEC) No. 218/92 on administrative co-operation in the field of indirect taxation (VAT) and Proposal for a Council Directive amending Directive 77/388/EEC as regards the value added tax arrangements applicable to certain services supplied by electronic means*, COM (2000) 349 final, 7 June.

European Commission (2000b). Directive 2000/31/EC of the European Parliament and of the Council of 8 June 2000 on certain legal aspects of information society services, in particular electronic commerce, in the Internal Market, *Official Journal of the European Communities* L 178, 17 July, http://europa.eu.int/ISPO/ecommerce/legal/legal.html#frame.

European Commission (2000c). Decision of 6 November 2000 on the minimum criteria to be taken into account by member States when designating national bodies responsible for the conformity assessments of secure signature-creation-devices, *Official Journal of the European Communities* L 289/42, 16 November, http://europa.eu.int/comm/trade/index_en.htm.

European Commission (2000d). Proposed Directive of the European Parliament and Council on the protection of personal data, *Official Journal of the European Communities* C365E, 19 December, p. 223.

Federal Trade Commission/Department of Commerce Seminar (2000). *Joint Workshop on Alternative Dispute Resolution for Online Consumer Transactions*, 6 and 7 June 2000, Washington, DC, http://www.ftc.gov/bcp/altdisresolution/index.htm.

Goolsbee, A. (1999). *In a World without Borders: The Impact of Taxes on Internet Commerce*, National Bureau of Economic Research Working Paper No. 6863, Cambridge, MA.

Gregory, J. (2000). "UNCITRAL meeting on electronic signatures", October, http://rechten.kub.nl/simone/gregory.htm.

Groner, J. (2001) "Court consider privacy perils of electronic filing", *Legal Times*, 16 January.

Hague Conference on Private International Law (1999). *Geneva Round Table on the Questions of Private International Law raised by Electronic Commerce*, September, http://hcch.net/doc/gen_pd7e.doc.

ICANN (1999). *Uniform Domain Name Dispute Resolution Policy and Rules of Procedure*, 26 August, http://www.icann.org/udrp/udrp-rules-24oct99.htm.

Kerrigan, A. (1999). "Taxation of e-commerce. Recent developments from a European perspective", in *Wirtschaftspolitische Blätter*, 5/1999, pp. 439–447.

Kessedjian, C. (2000a). "Aspects juridiques du e-trading: règlement des différends et droit applicable", in Thévenoz, and Bovet, *Journées 2000 de droit bancaire et financier*, Bern, Stämplfli 2001, pp. 65–97.

Kessedjian, C. (2000b) "Internet et le règlement des différends", in Grosheide, F.W. and Boele-Woelki, K. (eds.), *Molengrafica* 1999/2000, Koninklijke Vermande, pp. 69–96.

Krebs, B. (2001) "Self-regulation champions dig own graves", *Newsbytes*, 30 January.

Kuner, C. and Baker, S. (2000). "An analysis of international and digital signature implementation initiatives". Study prepared for the Internet Law and Policy Forum, September, http://www.ilpf.org/digsig/analysis_IEDSII.htm.

Lukas, A. (1999). *Tax Bytes: A Primer on the Taxation of Electronic Commerce*, Cato Institute for Trade Policy Analysis No. 9, Washington, DC.

OECD (1980). *Guidelines on the Protection of Privacy and Transborder Flows of Personal Data*, 23 September, http://www.oecd.org/e/droit/doneperso//ocdeprive/priv-en.htm.

OECD (1997). *Implementing the OECD Privacy Guidelines in the Electronic Environment: Focus on the Internet*, DSTI/ICCP/REG(97)6/FINAL, Paris.

OECD (1998a) *Electronic Commerce: Taxation Framework Conditions*, DAFE/CFA(98)50, www.oecd.org/daf/fa/e_com/ottawa.htm.

OECD (1998b). *Electronic Commerce: A Discussion Paper on Taxation Issues*, 17 September, http://www.oecd.org/daf/fa/e_com/discusse.pdf.

OECD (1998c). *International Workshop on Privacy Protection in a Global Networked Society*, DSTI/ICCP/REG(98)5/FINAL, Paris.

OECD (1998d). *Inventory of Instruments and Mechanisms Contributing to the Implementation and Enforcement of Privacy Guidelines on Global Networks*. DSTI/ICCP/REG(98)12/FINAL, Paris.

OECD (1999). *Inventory of Approaches to Authentication and Certification in a Global Networked Society*, October, http://www.olis.oecd.org/olis/1999doc.nsf/linkto/dsti-iccp-reg(99)13-final.

OECD (2000). *Clarification on the Application of the Permanent Establishment Definition in E-commerce: Changes to the Commentary on the Model Tax Convention on Article 5*, December.

OECD (2001a). *Consumption Tax Aspects of Electronic Commerce*. A Report from Working Party No. 9 on Consumption Taxes to the Committee on Fiscal Affairs. Draft for public comment, February.

OECD (2001b). *Tax Treaty Characterisation Issues Arising from E-Commerce*. Report to Working Party No.1 of the OECD Committee on Fiscal Affairs, February.

Owens, J. (1997). "What chance for the virtual taxman?" in *OECD Observer*, No. 208, October/November 1997, pp.16-19.

Perez-Esteve, R. and Schuknecht, L. (1999). *A Quantitative Assessment of Electronic Commerce*, WTO Working Paper ERAD-99-01, September, Geneva.

Schlechter R. (1999). "Electronic Signatures: The European Community Approach", paper submitted to the UNCTAD Expert Meeting on Capacity Building in the Area of Electronic Commerce: Legal and Regulatory Dimensions, 14-16 July, Geneva.

Smedinghoff, T. and Hill Bro, R. (1999). "Moving with change: Electronic signature legislation as a vehicle for advancing e-commerce", *John Marshall Journal of Computer and Information Law,* vol. XVII, no. 3, Spring 1999, p. 723.

Storie, B. and C. Green (1999). *Will E-commerce succeed in Bermuda?* Discussion paper, Bermuda, William R. Storie & Co. Ltd.

Teltscher, S. (2000). *Tariffs, Taxes and Electronic Commerce: Revenue Implications for Developing Countries*, UNCTAD Study Series on "Policy Issues in International Trade and Commodities", No. 5, UNCTAD/ITCD/TAB/5, Geneva.

UNCITRAL (1996). *Model Law on Electronic Commerce with Guide to Enactment (1996), with additional article 5 bis*, http://www.uncitral.org/en-index.htm.

UNCITRAL (2001). *Draft UNCITRAL Model Law on Electronic Signatures and the Draft Guide to Enactment*, http://www.uncitral.org/en-index.htm.

UNCTAD (1996). *Incentives and Foreign Direct Investment*, UNCTAD/DTCI/28, Current Studies, Series A, No. 30, Geneva.

UNCTAD(1998). "Electronic commerce: Legal considerations", SDTE/BFB/1.

UNCTAD (1999). "Legal dimensions of electronic commerce", TD/B/COM.3/EM.8/2, para. 53.

University of Tennessee (2000). "E-commerce cuts into State tax revenues". Press Release, 27 January, University of Tennessee, Knoxville, Tennessee.

Vassilakakis, E. (1987). "Orientations méthodologiques dans les codifications récentes du droit international privé en Europe", Paris, LGDJ.

Vick et al. (1999). "Universities, defamation and the Internet", *Modern Law Review*, 1999, p. 58.

Weber, T. (2001). "Network solutions offer for sale of its database of domain-names", *Wall Street Journal*, 16 February.

Chapter 7

MANAGING PAYMENT AND CREDIT RISKS ONLINE: NEW CHALLENGES FOR FINANCIAL SERVICE PROVIDERS

A. Introduction

E-finance or e-payments or online payments are interchangeably used to describe the process of finance and payments mainly using the medium of the Internet. At the onset of e-commerce in 1994, the Internet population had at its disposal approximately 3 million host computers around the world. By the end of 2000 the number of hosts worldwide had risen to 93 million. Yet online retail sales still represented volumes equal to only 1 per cent of consumer spending in the United States. However, the rapid growth of online sales as well as online payments suggests that we are witnessing the beginning of possibly revolutionary changes in the world economy.

The main Internet-based payment methods are credit cards, regardless of the fact that even wealthy online consumers from most developed countries are not comfortable with communicating their credit card numbers over the Internet. Although there have been many candidate systems offered to fill the payments gap for business-to-consumer (B2C) e-commerce, not many have been adopted to any significant degree, and it may take some years before the industry converges on a standard in this area. It is really only since 1999 that the private sector in OECD countries and some emerging economies have started to get very interested in the area of business-to-business (B2B) e-commerce, and the jury is still out as to what will be the payment method of choice in this environment.

At the same time the main "bricks & mortar", i.e. traditional, banks, in facing up to the challenge of the newly emerging "clicks only", i.e. Internet banks, have developed considerable e-banking activities and have become "bricks and clicks" banks. Moreover, as a result of a crisis of trust vis-à-vis purely Net banks, consumers' preference has been for the "bricks and clicks " banks. According to one estimate, the banking industry in developed countries will grow at a rate of 3 per cent till 2003, while the Internet banking segment will grow at a rate of 25 per cent annually. Other projections suggest that, in the coming five years, half of the banking and 80 per cent of the brokerage in the developed countries will go online. The share of e-finance in developing countries might vary between 20 and 35 per cent for e-banking and between 15 and 40 per cent for e-brokerage, with higher projections in the event of a better policy, regulatory and institutional environment.

The banks of developed countries are expecting this exponential growth of online banking for both households and corporations and are actively preparing themselves. The e-commerce preparedness of various groups of developing and transition economies, especially within the financial sector, will also depend on their policy environment, their institutional set-up, and the determination of both private and public financial institutions to build up their e-finance capacities. Many of them take the Internet as a chance to catch up with the developed financial services providers, thus combating the international digital divide. However, well coordinated international co-operation will be needed to help the developing and transition economies to achieve this goal.

This chapter is mainly devoted to online payments and hence to the problems of developing secure payment techniques and technologies and risk management on the Internet. It also tries to identify the problems of current and future participation of developing country operators in online payments. For greater understanding of the modes of payment that can be used on the Internet, the chapter briefly highlights the conventional payment methods, including physical or electronic transfer of money, within existing electronic bank transfer systems, with or without use of the various credit, debit and other cards or checks, etc. The overview of conventional payment systems also makes it possible to identify the similarities and differences between offline and online payments. The purpose of this is to draw policymakers' and practitioners' attention to issues involved in developing various online payments systems in the Internet, with particular emphasis on problems specific to the developing and transition economies.

B. Conventional and electronic payments prior to Internet

1. Cash

Cash currently represents 80 per cent of day-to-day transactions. Being versatile, its use does not require a financial intermediary, and it can be converted at a rate close to its announced value as long as it has a serious central bank, Government and developed economy behind it. The dollar, as the most usable and accepted cash in the world, sometimes even pushes out local currencies from circulation — the well known phenomenon of dollarization seen in many third world economies. In the latter, cash is used in all domains, including inter-enterprise payments, predominantly within the framework of the informal economy. Lack of trust and propensity to hide incomes from tax authorities could keep cash for quite some time as an important traditional payment method servicing both traditional and Internet-based commerce in those countries. In more transparent developed economies, cash continues to be an important payment instrument in business-to-consumer and person-to-person low-value transactions.

Cash is not without its problems, however. The costs incurred by central banks to produce and maintain the national stock of notes and coin greatly exceed the seigniorage revenues for the right of issuing them. It is open to attack from counterfeiters. It can be stolen. Its anonymity makes it attractive to citizens who wish to keep their transactions private, it is equally attractive to organized crime, and its use in large value transactions is often associated with tax evasion or money laundering.

2. Money orders, checks, drafts, notes, bills of exchange

Higher value transactions need more security than cash can provide. Hence the importance of modern financial intermediaries transferring value mainly for their clients through proprietary electronic means of communications or so called Intranets. These modes of payment involve money orders, i.e. bank transfers on the orders of clients, or documents issued in paper and electronic forms, mainly by banks, such as checks, drafts, bills of exchange, promissory notes, documentary collections and credits. Drafts and notes might be issued for immediate payment (sight draft) or represent a promise to pay at some future date and hence giving a financing opportunity to the debtor (term draft). Drafts, including bills of exchange (instructions to pay) and promissory notes (promises to pay), are negotiable, i.e. they are transferable instruments where the beneficiary (normally a company) might through the secondary market (acceptance market) discount the instrument and pass the right to collect to another beneficiary (normally a financial intermediary). The latter might then opt to resell the portions of an underwritten risk to other financial intermediaries (forfaiting market). Afterwards the debt instrument might have its own autonomous life, i.e. change hands in the secondary market until the payee honours the debt.

Drafts and notes are instructions to the payer's bank or a promise to transfer funds to the payee. They are fundamentally dependent on the presence of financial intermediaries, usually banks, as well as clearing and settlement mechanisms created by the latter. In its most simple form involving two banks, a check clearing process is as portrayed in chart 9. The bill of exchange is a similar instrument and is widely used to finance trade in so called documentary collection.

The check and other negotiable money instruments can be used as payment vehicles to transfer values of any amount. They involve at least one financial intermediary and might be associated with a considerable amount of paper processing, i.e. elapsed time and transaction costs. This effectively makes them impractical for very small transactions. The check, as a promise to pay, depends on quite a degree of trust being established beforehand between the two parties. The seller in this case might demand evidence of an asset, collateral or surety from the buyer and will try to include the right to realize the collateral in a contract. It is important also to mention the risk associated with "not sufficient funds" (NSF) or a "returned-item" or bounced check. Even though the incidence of checks being returned is very small, the fact that it can happen at all makes the risks associated with checks rather high for many transactions, particularly where goods are delivered immediately and to high risk destinations.

Chart 9
Check clearing process

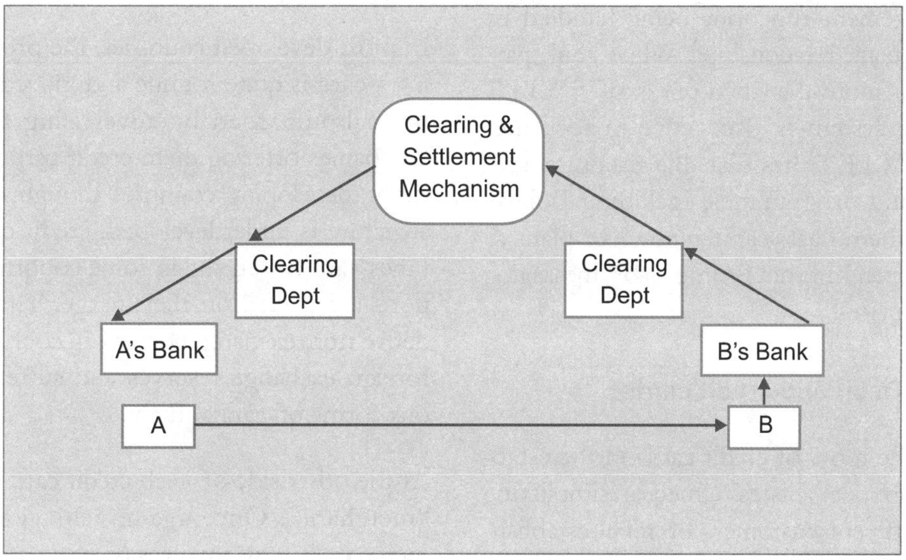

Another way to pay is to use a credit transfer or giro payment. Whereas a check represents a "pull" payment with the paper check pulling funds from the source account through the clearing network into the destination account, the giro does the reverse. Funds are "pushed" from the source account to the destination account. The credit transfer cannot be initiated unless the funds are available and this greatly reduces risks associated with the payment. Post offices are usually the key players in giro payments. They have their own accounts system and in this case they play a role of financial intermediary between the payer and the payee. While checks are very popular in the United States, the giro payments are particularly characteristic for Europe. Among the reasons for giro payments is consumers' desire to keep control over their bank accounts and plan their payments schedule in light of their own preferences. However, by "disintermediating" banks as direct payers, retail consumers tend to be late in their payments.

Where the bank details of the payee are known in advance, it is possible to make electronic transfers between bank accounts using the so-called automated clearing house (ACH) networks. In fact in the United States and Canada funds can be "pushed" as well as "pulled" by ACH debits and credits. These organizations grew out of the systems that were developed to process checks clearing and are now used by consumers for recurrent payments to regular service providers (utilities, telephone, residential charges, etc) in the form of direct debits. They are also used extensively by businesses to pay their regular suppliers and by Governments to issue all kinds of payments to individuals and corporations. In the United States, the system is operated by the National Electronic Payments Association (NACHA), and most countries in the developed world have a similar system. Indeed, it is quite common to have multiple systems of this sort operating in a single country – some operated by the central bank, and others by consortia of leading banks.

In 1999, the average value of a payment made through the ACH system was approximately $1,500 and settlement was made overnight. Where the value of the transaction is significantly larger, a different class of payment method is typically used which is referred to as a 'wire transfer'. One example of this is the FEDWIRE system operated by the Federal Reserve in the United States. This offers the facility to make immediate payments, with settlements performed by transferring funds between accounts maintained by the member banks with the Federal Reserve. In 1999, the average value of each transaction in the FEDWIRE system was $4.3 million. It is thus used principally for major business-to-business and also business-to-Government transfers.

When such payments are to be made internationally, the messages relating to wire transfers are typically carried on the networks of the Society for Worldwide Interbank Financial Telecommunications (S.W.I.F.T.), a huge bank cooperative including 7,000 financial institutions from 190 countries. The magnitude of payment and transfer traffic in the S.W.I.F.T.

proprietary electronic system or Intranet is impressive, exceeding $5 trillion daily, with the settlement and risk management functions being handled by correspondent bank relationships. While bank payments represent more than two-thirds of S.W.I.F.T operations, the system is also active in securities settlements. S.W.I.F.T. has also big e-commerce-related plans and programmes, including Bolero, TrustAct and others. Last year it announced plans to move to more open Internet Protocol (IP) messaging and network services.[1]

3. Debit and credit cards[2]

One can find the roots of credit cards in the establishment of 'shoppers' plates' aimed at simplifying payments for affluent customers of retail establishments. The possibility of transmitting communications electronically gave a huge boost to the card industry in recent decades.[3] As a result, an enormously popular, globally acceptable payment instrument has emerged embodied a plastic card with a magnetic strip making it possible, through various electronic devices, to identify the card number and receive authorization from the bank to make the payment. For the system to operate, the potential cardholder must approach a 'card issuing' bank or company and get a physical card that will allow transactions to be made. In some cases it involves opening a related bank account. Without appropriate restrictions, the possession of a card confers unlimited spending power on its owner. In the majority of cases, though, the card-issuing bank will assign a 'credit-limit' to the cardholder based on an examination of his creditworthiness. The cardholder can either retrieve cash using automatic telling machines (ATM) at banks or card associations or purchase goods and services from merchants electronically linked either with the authorizing card association or the bank. While a debit card involves direct pulling of money from an account and is limited by the availability of money in the account, a credit card gives the possibility of a credit limit and hence short-term financing for a cardholder. Hence credit card fees are much higher than those for debit cards. To some extent, a debit card is similar to an electronic version of a check. Typically, the debit cardholder needs to enter a pin (his individual code) at the point of sale, verifying at least that the card is not stolen and whether sufficient funds are available. In the case of credit cards, merchants demand a written signature from a cardholder, which they normally compare with that on the card. So far, the more popular card-related payment mode is the credit card.

In most developed countries, the process of acquiring a card is quite routine and indeed customers are often bombarded by advertising from different companies offering them credit cards. In the majority of developing countries though, the card infrastructure is underdeveloped, credit cards are sometimes hard to get, and in some countries tight restrictions are placed on their usage. Those restrictions derive from exchange controls in countries with scarce foreign exchange reserves and suffering from various forms of capital flight.

At the other side of each credit card transaction is a "merchant". Once again, achieving "credit card merchant" status involves opening an account with a bank that will 'acquire' transactions on behalf of the business. Once the account is set up, the merchant has the ability to charge arbitrary amounts to any credit card that has been issued anywhere in the world. Clearly, this represents a major opportunity for fraud in the short term, and acquiring banks will often subject a business to strict checks before permitting them to operate as a merchant, particularly if they intend to carry out business across the Internet. In the United States, these checks are not very stringent, but they are much more so in most European countries, whilst in some developing countries, companies may have extreme difficulty in gaining credit-card merchant status. In developing countries or regions where telecommunications facilities are not available or where dial-up telephone connections are very expensive, the authorization step may just be a simple check of the credit card number against a periodically updated blacklist. Often merchants operate under quite complex policies to balance the risk of fraud against the cost of verifying the transaction. This may involve going through authorizations only where a transaction value exceeds a 'floor-limit' or carrying out an online authorization randomly for one in every 10 transactions. The costs involved in processing credit card transactions are considerable. Typically, these are recovered by a per-transaction levy on the merchant. The charges depend on the acquiring bank and also on the level of risk associated with the business.

Chart 10 shows the information flow when a credit card transaction is made. The cardholder presents the card details to the merchant. The merchant can authorize the transaction prior to actually making it.

Chart 10
Information flow in a credit card transaction

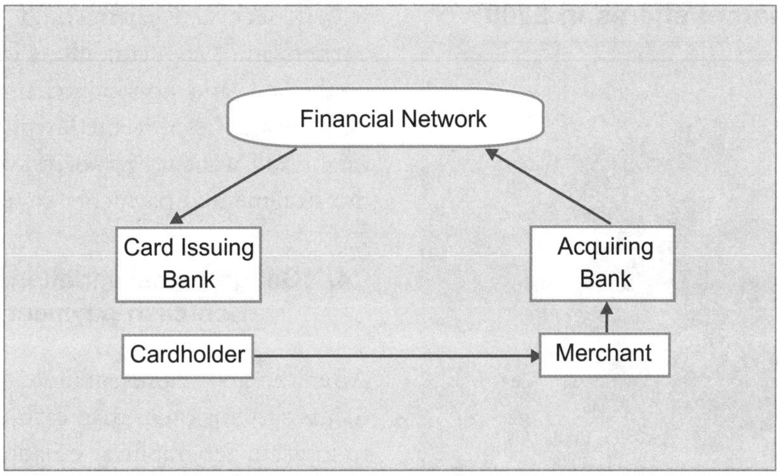

This is done through a connection either directly to the merchant's acquiring bank or to a technology provider acting on its behalf. The acquiring bank can authorize this transaction using a financial network which has access to the data of card-issuing banks worldwide. The transaction can have two steps – an authorization step (this is used frequently by hotels at the beginning of a guest's visit) and a later 'capture' step where the previously authorized transaction is completed. Alternatively an authorization-and-capture step can do everything in a single action.

One credit-card usage scenario that is interesting because it serves as the background for Internet credit card transactions is the so-called Mail Order Telephone Order (MOTO) transaction. Under this scenario, merchants are allowed to accept orders by post or over the telephone, with the customer simply quoting the credit card details verbally. Under this scenario — also called "Card-Not-Present" — the merchant is unable to tell if the customer has the card in his or her possession, nor can the signature be verified. Some simple safeguards are put in place regarding the address to which the goods can be dispatched and, in the event of the customer later disavowing the transaction, the merchant must bear the cost.

The costs involved in processing credit card transactions are considerable. Typically, a merchant that has been trading profitably for years will be able to negotiate a better rate than a start-up company. Any company that trades on the Internet is regarded as being 'risky' and is typically subject to higher charges. Generally there is a fixed fee of around \$0.10–0.50 and a percentage of the transaction of around 1–5 per cent. This effectively means that credit card transactions are not worthwhile for transactions less than \$10.

The great strength of credit cards is their global acceptability. Since the processing of transactions across the financial networks takes care of the currency conversion, merchants will receive funds in their local currency while the cardholder is levied in his own currency. Naturally the country of a cardholder should accept currency convertibility at least on current account. The global recognition of the two major brands (Visa and MasterCard) and also others such as American Express, Diners Club, Europay and Discover reassures merchants that the payment will be honoured. On the downside, rogue cardholders and rogue merchants quite easily perpetrate fraud, particularly where the authorization process does not go online to verify each transaction with the issuing bank.

The two leading brand names are Visa and MasterCard, which account for 75 per cent of the general–purpose credit and charge cards market. Like S.W.I.F.T. they are associations involving mainly banks. At the same time they have very strict procedures for accepting a bank as a Visa or Mastercard issuing member bank. In 1970, Visa was confined to the United States, with 243 members, and was covering payments worth \$3 billion with 30 million cards. In 2000, it was accepted by 19 million brick and mortar locations in virtually all countries and territories and was servicing payments traffic of around \$1.6 trillion with more than 1 billion cards, of which the overwhelming majority were credit cards[4]. One of the principal reasons for the success of these two 'card associations'

Chart 11
Major international credit cards companies market shares in 2000

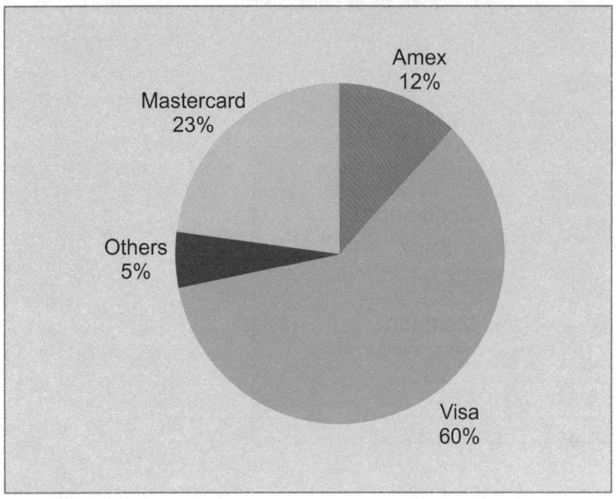

Source: www.visa.com

Chart 12
Global distribution of VISA cards in 2000

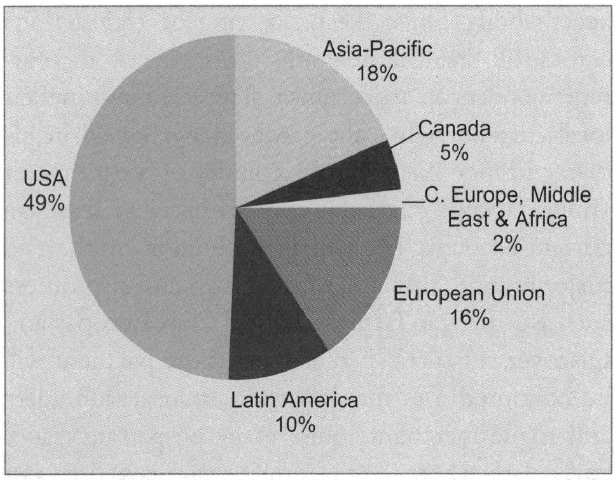

Source: www.visa.com

is that they are owned and operated by banks from all over the world. It is these local banks that manage the relationship with the cardholders, while the card associations provide the global branding and also the common infrastructure that registers the payments traffic and links the banks that operate the system with the merchants and consumers. Other card issuers with much smaller shares of the market include American Express, Diners Club (owned respectively by American Express Bank and Citibank), Discover and others. In mid-2000 American Express initiated a United States antitrust lawsuit, considering Visa and Mastercard to be monopolies. The latter were blamed for collusive practices preventing their bank members from issuing rival cards. It is too early to draw conclusions on this matter, as the legal ruling has yet to be made. The propensity of consumers as well as merchants to go for the most widely accepted cards could explain high entry barriers and tough conditions for smaller players. So on the one hand monopoly charges and collusive practices should be prevented, while on the other users might still want to go for universally accepted and non-fragmented payments systems.[5]

4. Geographical variations of conventional non-cash payment systems

After the above presentation of conventional payments systems other than cash, it would seem useful to indicate geographical variations in their use.

As the table 24 shows the degree of adoption of different payment systems differs markedly between countries. In the United States, for example, checks represent 70% of all non-cash payments, payment cards come next with 25 per cent while the use of credit and debit transfers is quite infrequent. 84 per cent of all checks in the United States are issued by enterprises. This is almost the reverse in Germany, where payment card usage is extremely low compared with other developed countries and giro credit transfers are used for more than half of non-cash transactions.

When comparing developed countries, many of the differences can be explained by the historic evolution of payment systems over time. For example, the popularity of giros in many European countries can be explained by the involvement of post offices in providing payment services over many years. In considering the developing countries, however, the overall financial infrastructure tends to be poor. Since checks are perhaps the most basic payment instrument that a bank can offer, these tend to be available everywhere and attract widespread usage. Moreover, for example in Latin America, a check might be endorsed many times thus becoming a pseudo currency note. In such countries payment cards are used only in particular industries or they are not issued at all. Thus out of the 1 billion Visa cards that have been issued throughout the world, Central Europe, the Middle East and Africa account for just 2 per cent. And finally unusual local factors often lead to a payments situation that is anomalous compared with other, similar countries. For example, Turkey has embraced the use of payment cards almost to the exclusion of other forms of payment.

Table 24
Geographical variations of consumer preferences in non-cash payment methods by country in 1998
(Percentage)

Country	Use of checks	Use of credit tTransfers (Giros)	Payment cards	Direct debits
United States	70.0	3.7	24.3	2.0
Netherlands	1.9	45.0	24.5	28.5
United Kingdom	28.0	19.3	33.1	19.4
Germany	4.8	50.6	5.1	39.5
Turkey (1997 figures)	6.9	2.6	83.9	-
Namibia (1996 figures)	75.0	14.0	Not provided by local banks	9.0
Angola (1996 figures)	75.0	25.0	Not provided by local banks	-

Source: Bank for International Settlements.

5. Payments protection by financial intermediaries: secured notes, documentary credit, credit insurance, factoring, and others

Where trust is a problem, a planned transaction or project may be at risk, and delays or even defaults may occur in dispatching goods and services as well as in reciprocal flows of payments. In such a case, the parties may have to resort to various systems of third party protection by banks, credit insurers, factors and others. The financial services sector has developed an array of risk management instruments including bank, insurance, derivative and combined products. Some typical examples are described below.

A basic example of bank-related protection could be check guarantee cards, which indemnify the payer against risks as long as the transaction size is small and some fairly rudimentary security checks are made at the time of the transfer. For larger transactions, a customer's bank will often sign the check itself, converting a simple check into a cashier's check (drawn on itself) or teller's check (drawn on another bank). Those instruments are also called bank drafts.

In more risky situations, sellers accept only the so-called letter of credit (L/C), which is an obligation of the buyer's bank to pay to the seller's bank on condition of scrupulous adherence by the seller and its bank to the related documentary requirements (bill of lading, cargo insurance, other certificates, etc). That is why the L/C is also called documentary credit. The L/C is stricter in its requirements than documentary collection based on instruments like bills of exchange. In a similar arrangement called factoring, the factor (usually a specialized department of a bank) discounts sellers' receivables, mainly without recourse to the seller. Meanwhile the correspondent and related to the buyer factor handles the payment and related risks. This technique is reminiscent of a mix of a L/C with the acceptance or discounting business.

The money order or so-called open account payments can be protected by a technique called credit insurance – a good instrument to encourage and diversify exports and bear the risk of going for new markets. After receiving goods, the buyer should normally give a money order to his bank to pay against the seller's invoice. The main credit insurance products are short-term policies protecting the supplier from default on the part of the buyer in paying his trade debt due to commercial (related to the buyer himself) and political (related to the buyer's country) risks. Credit insurance thus creates sufficient security for sellers to dispatch their goods and services to mainly foreign buyers on open account, *inter alia* providing the latter with short-term trade credits.

Various arrangements have been developed to pre-finance suppliers and structure performance related risk, including pre-shipment financing, structured financing, warehouse receipts financing, etc. In the majority of the above cases, the promise to pay comes from or is guaranteed by a much more trusted third party, i.e. a bank or a credit insurer and hence greater risks can be taken by the payee to ensure that transactions and related payments are completed successfully. It is important to stress here that the same third parties have also developed instruments to protect risks related to non-performance of the seller, thus making sure that the good payer will not suffer from failure to deliver according to the terms of the sales contract or that of a project. Bonding is the most accepted means of protecting the buyer.

Recently the world financial community witnessed a phenomenal growth of financial instruments called derivatives. The global daily turnover of counter and exchange-traded derivatives reached $2.7 trillion in 1998.[6] On an annualized basis this is 20 times more than the world GDP. According to the Bank of International Settlements (BIS) these instruments comprise mainly financial contracts "the value of which depends on the value of one or more underlying reference assets, rates or indices" and are in the form of so-called "forward contracts, options or combinations thereof".[7] Being basically bets designed to protect the contracting party or make a gain for him from fluctuations in future prices they can exist if there is enough appetite to ensure the opposite bet is made and thus balance supply and demand in the derivatives markets. So while other instruments protect parties to financial contracts from non-payment or non-performance risks, derivatives were designed to manage the risks related to price fluctuations, including the exchange rate risk in cross-border operations. In other words, decisions related to the prices, choice of the currency and the timing of its real conversion are very important.

C. Making payments online

The term online payment is now part and parcel of e-commerce terminology. However the scope of the term varies depending on whether the reference is made only to the Internet or whether it also includes electronic payments made through the proprietary electronic networks or the so called Intranets described above.

Some experts define online payments in a technology neutral manner and would include in it all payments where the transaction information is transmitted electronically, the payer and the payee are directly involved in the transaction, and the necessary information to authorize the payment is part of the transaction information exchange between the payer and the payee. In this case, the technical channels, as well as the format and the payment instrument are not essential to characterize online payments. Thus in the United States and some other countries, electronic transfer of money described above is considered online. In other countries and primarily in the developing world, the term online payments relates only to the electronic transfer of funds over public or private networks based on the Internet and related technologies (for more details on e-commerce definitions, see chapter 1).

The main purpose of this chapter is to help developing and transition economies to identify Internet based online payment mechanisms and networks. So, without going into the debate on the definition of online payments, this report, limits the scope of the analysis in this section to the payments involving the Internet.

The survey of conventional payments presented in the previous section is based on the sequence of their historical evolution, moving from cash to negotiable money orders and then cards, including many proprietary electronic payments networks such as S.W.I.F.T, credit card associations' networks and others. The short history of the Internet has rather shown a reverse movement: online payments started with credit card related consumer purchases online and then went into a variety of electronic checks and other documents with the use of electronic signature and combined instruments such as smart cards. At the same time the cash function migrated to the stored value or prepaid cards (electronic purses) and software products (digital cash)[8]. In smart cards the stored value is still one of its main functions, as the multipurpose chip still needs some time to become popular. One might presume that, as in the case of conventional payments, different kinds of online payments will evolve, with considerable geographical variations in their usage.

According to numerous surveys, consumers so far prefer solid financial institutions with combined online and offline skills, and the leading banks are taking the challenge of online payments very seriously. For the moment the industry lacks standard online payments technologies and is still in the stage of choosing between competing models and solutions. Many solutions did not live up to expectations, while others needed development and marketing efforts. Thus according to a GartnerGroup survey, electronic wallets represent less than 1 per cent of online payments. Equally, smart cards were announced as the future device for online payments due to the ability of their chips to combine high security, storage of much more information, specific risk management tasks and other characteristics. However for the moment they are used more as prepaid card devices than as multifunctional applications.[9]

Thus this section will first look into business to consumer (B2C) online payments and will then analyse business to business (B2B) online payments mechanisms. The presentation of those methods under either the B2C or the B2B heading does not preclude their applicability for any purpose but merely reflects their main area of use at present.

1. Business to consumer (B2C) online payments

B2C e-commerce, which started from just a trickle in 1995, grew dramatically to somewhere between $23 billion and $109 billion in 2000[10]. Some of the sectors that proved popular include books (e.g. amazon.com), apparel (Land's End, Gap, Victoria's secret), computer products (Dell, Gateway) and travel (Expedia, Priceline).

Starting from credit card payments through Internet, online payments are evolving into a system where payers might use smart cards combining the functions of all cards and electronic cash or electronic checks, with encrypted electronic signatures or other modes of secure identification of the payer and payee. These systems are used both in B2C and B2B payments. However credit cards were the first online payment instruments and the security in Internet was challenged when credit card holders giving credit card numbers on the Internet were subjected to serious risks from hackers and fraudsters. In fact the analysis of various modes of online payments in this section contains detailed descriptions of different systems defending the security of the payer.

(a) Online payments by credit and debit cards

For various reasons, the most natural way for a consumer to make a purchase over the Internet in the absence of other widely accepted alternatives is to use a credit card. A precedent had already been set over a number of years by catalogue shoppers. Business rules, including the MOTO rules referred to earlier, had been developed to handle transactions where card details were given to the merchant either on a printed order form or over the telephone and there was no possibility to identify the cardholder by at least asking him to sign in the presence of the merchant. For the majority of international shoppers, the currency convertibility problem was solved, and there were already large numbers of people worldwide who could make and accept payments without the need for any sign-up procedure.

The earliest web purchases were made either by insecurely transferring the credit card details in a web dialogue or by resorting to a separate e-mail exchange to complete the payment. The credit card companies were not happy about this method of conveying the details, and the advice they issued to consumers and merchants was not to use credit cards on the Internet until new technologies were developed to allow it to be done securely. However the market largely ignored that advice.

(i) Secure Socket Layer (SSL)

A stop-gap solution arrived in1995, when Netscape incorporated support in its Internet browser software for a technology standard called the Secure Socket Layer (SSL). SSL is still the dominant mode of online payments, especially by credit cards.

A merchant wishing to use SSL to protect credit card transactions must apply to a recognized X.509 Certification Authority (described later) to be issued with a certificate. All Internet browser software comes preconfigured to trust the 20 or so most common certification authorities operating worldwide.[11] A user browsing the merchant's site will interact normally until it comes to the point where the credit card details are to be transferred across the link. At this point, the user's browser will be directed to a web page that starts with HTTPS rather than the usual HTTP. This is a signal to the browser to start a special security dialogue with the browser in which two things happen. First, the merchant proves that he represents the business to which the X.509 certificate is issued, and secondly he agrees on a session encryption key that is used to protect the credit card details and any other financially sensitive information from being intercepted by attackers as they travel across the Internet.

Thus the cardholder is afforded some protection in terms of confirmation that the merchant to whom he is giving his card details exists as a bona fide business, or at least did at the time the certificate was issued. Both the cardholder and the merchant are also protected from eavesdroppers capturing the credit card details from an insecure Internet link. For the merchant there is no protection in terms of ensuring that the card is not being used by someone other than the cardholder, and if the latter denies making

Chart 13
The Secure Socket Layer protecting a credit card payment

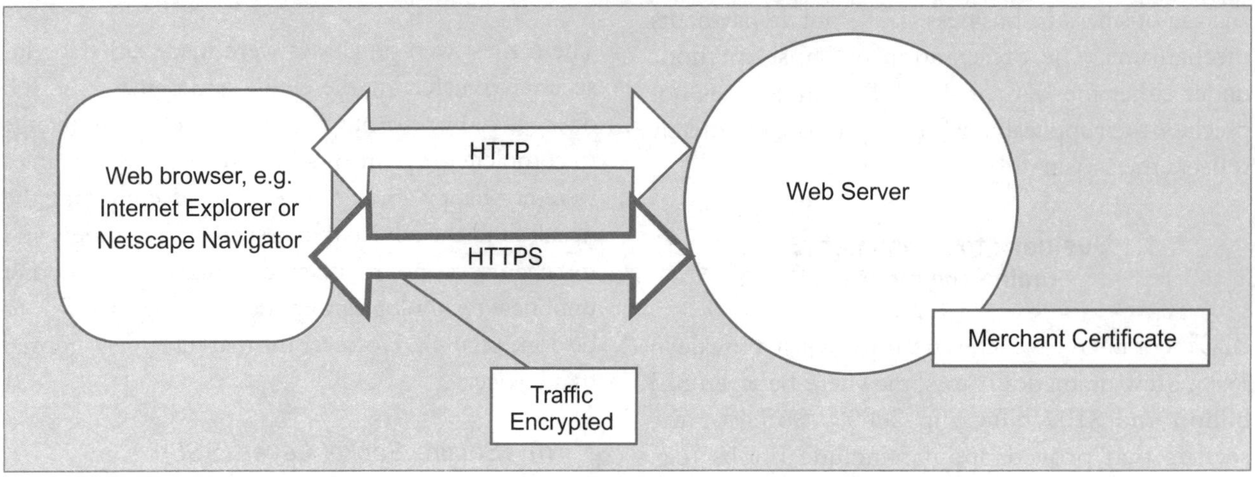

Chart 14
Online authorization of a credit card transaction

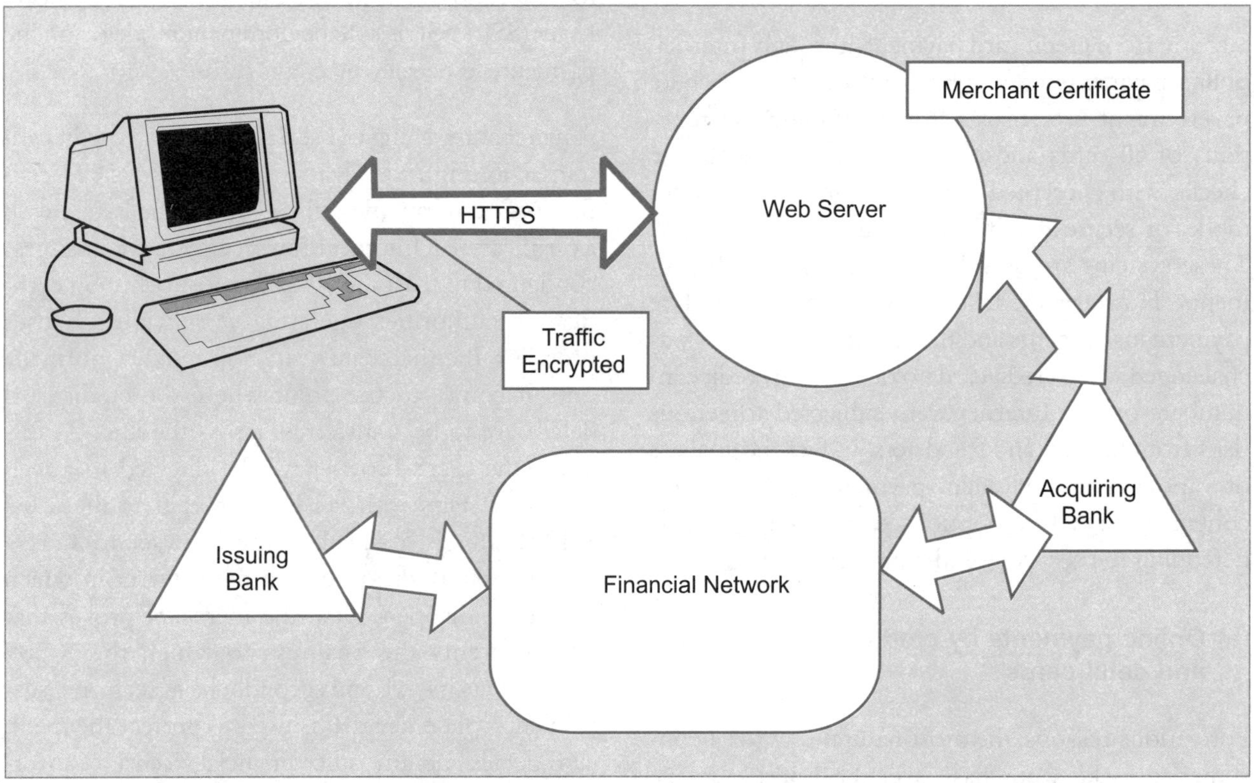

the transaction, there is way of proving otherwise. The cardholder has no protection against a merchant who may retain the card details and subsequently charge multiple transactions against the account. If the merchant site stores the card details online, they make themselves vulnerable to attackers breaking into their site to gain access to those details[12].

In order to streamline the process of making credit card transactions and also to allow each individual transaction to be authorized, merchants generally equip themselves with an online connection to their acquiring bank or to an entity operating on its behalf.

This process has been taken further by companies such as iTransact, which operate links to the financial network on behalf of many hundreds of online merchants. Using their services, the B2C merchant can interact with iTransact's web site during the purchase to get authorization and complete the transaction in real time. Merchants are required to hold accounts in developed country banks, and transactions are denominated in US dollars or other leading hard currencies. Every other component of the system, including the merchant web site, can be located elsewhere.

(ii) Secure Electronic Transactions (SET)

Although the use of SSL, with or without online authorization, is for the moment the most common means of making credit card transactions, a more advanced technology is available in the form of a security standard called Secure Electronic Transactions (SET). This was developed principally by the two major credit card companies, Visa and Mastercard, in 1996, with the support of many major technology providers, including IBM, and other card brands including American Express. It is a comprehensive solution to all the practical risks that are encountered in any credit card transaction. SET was introduced primarily to prevent rogue merchants from misusing credit card information. It hides the credit card number from the merchant but leaves him with the important ability to verify that the card is good and that the authorization is good.

Special wallet software is used by the cardholder that is partially or totally integrated into the web browser's software. The wallet software is loaded with the card details and also with a certificate that is issued to the cardholder by the issuing bank. When a credit card transaction is to be made, the wallet software composes an encrypted payment request which is sent via a SET module running on the merchant's web site and from there to an SET payment gateway run either by each acquiring bank or by the credit card company itself. The SET standard underwent a one year public review period and is thought to be highly secure and efficient at guarding against all anticipated risks due to stolen cards, rogue merchants and rogue cardholders.

The main problem with SET lies in its complexity. Three independent pieces of software need to be in place and working together well before a single transaction can be carried out, and certificates must be issued to each of the three parties (buyer, seller, bank) to allow them to securely identify each other. Banks began to pilot SET at the beginning of 1997, but this was done mostly on a regional basis (which does not fit well with the global way in which the Internet operates) and these pilots achieved limited success in terms of persuading large populations of users and merchants to change over to the new system. As of early 2001, SET has still achieved little market penetration and its proponents are beginning to experiment with so-called 'light' versions of the standard that involve less complexity.

Chart 15
The Secure Electronic Transactions Protocol

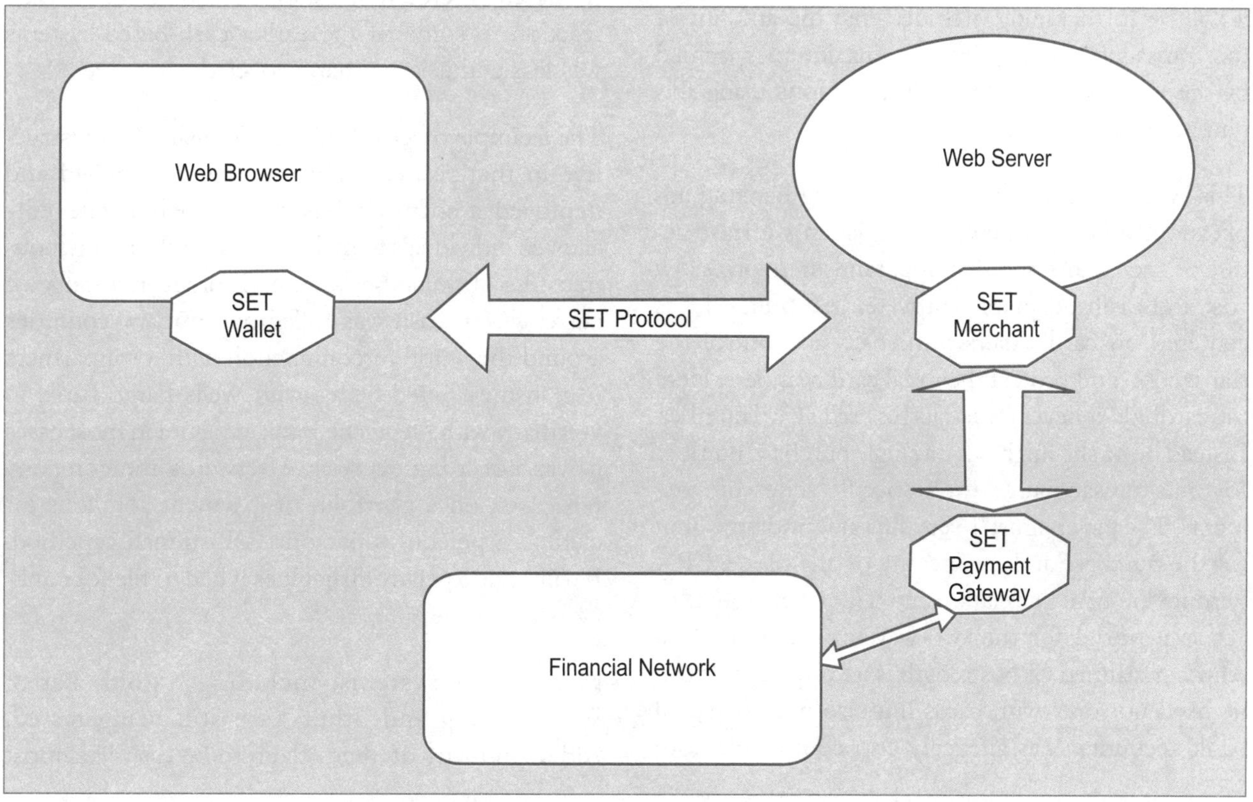

(iii) Controlled Payment Numbers (CPN) and other systems of securing card-based payments

There are also several transaction processing systems which add security and do not require merchants to keep separate transaction terminals or processing software. For example, one system that offers extra security over SSL is a technology referred to as a Controlled Payment Number (CPN) or One-Time Credit card Number. In a normal web based credit card transaction secured by SSL, the user supplies credit card details to the merchant, allowing the latter to make a charge against his account. The problem is that if an attacker gains access to this information, he can use it to make bogus transactions. The cardholder also has no protection against rogue merchants who make multiple transactions or charge amounts other than those agreed.

Users of CPN can gain some protection against this kind of fraud. The system works by cardholders installing an application on their local workstation, which they invoke whenever they do an online purchase. This software asks them for a maximum value and a time period for payment and then contacts their bank online. The bank generates a number that looks like a normal credit card number, but in fact is not associated with a real card. This number is given to the merchant in place of the normal number. The merchant is unaware that there is anything unusual about the number, and when authorization is sought, it will be forthcoming provided that the amount of the transaction is less than the maximum specified by the user. Any subsequent transactions using this number will be refused.

This system is compatible with existing banking applications and in particular the payments infrastructure of merchants' servers. Apparently it involves low cost and easily adaptable software. In a nutshell it is centered on cardholders propensity to control the transaction and protect their real card numbers. Here the cardholder never transmits his credit card number. Instead he or she might give a single purchase number for one transaction or for a specific series of payments. The payer himself sets the value and time limit for the purchase and the identity of the payee. CPN permits the bank in relationship with its customer to act as a portal for the two-way information flow. Another claimed CPN strength is its versatility. It can be used not only with cards but also with personal bank accounts. It is allegedly also compatible with emerging biometric and voice activated identification systems.[13]

The downside is that it requires cardholders to install special software, to register with their bank to use the CPNs and then to have online dialogues with their bank every time a purchase is made. This technology was first brought to the market by Orbiscom in early 2000 and their system has been deployed by Discover Card and MBNA (a major international credit card issuer) among others. Somewhat similar systems have also been announced by American Express for their United States cardholders and by Cyota Inc in Israel.[14]

(b) Electronic money or cash-like systems

According to a recent publication of the Committee on Payment and Settlement Systems of the Central Banks, members of the BIS, electronic money refers to "prepaid products in which a record of funds or value available to the consumer is stored on a device in consumer possession".[15] Prepaid cards, sometimes called electronic purses, as well as prepaid software products, also called digital cash, are examples of electronic money, which uses the Internet as a medium for a transfer.

Since cash is used for approximately 80 per cent of retail consumer transactions, one would expect that there would be great demand for this service in electronic commerce transactions. However the market reaction to some of the earlier cash-based systems was less enthusiastic than expected.

The example of eCash from Digicash BV is instructive in that respect. This company launched and deployed a software-based system that allegedly allowed individuals to make arbitrary fully anonymous transfers of value between each other in a range of currencies. E-cash was rolled out in many countries around the world in conjunction with local partners (e.g. in the United States with Wells Fargo bank, in Germany with Deutsche Bank, etc), but in most cases it was not a big success. Afterwards the company refocused on a portfolio of payment solutions including a person-to-person (P2P) transfer method. Finally, due to many difficulties it had to file for bankruptcy.

Many other systems, including e-gold, Papal, Webmetering and others, are still being tested. Although many of them claim to be cash-like, most of them fall into the category of account-based systems, where the payment is simply a transfer between identified accounts on the provider's system. Most of them still lack convenience and hence general acceptance.[16]

The future of digital cash might lie in combined solutions where a prepaid or charged device is a part of a smart card which includes also the roles of credit and debit cards. The following paragraph explore smart cards further.

(c) Smart cards: combining e-cash, e-cards and more

In conventional bank-mediated transactions, the trend for retail point-of-sale systems is away from paper-based instruments such as cash and checks and towards electronic payment effected with a card. Most of the cards in use today are based on magnetic strip technology with some rudimentary account identifying information recorded (insecurely) on a magnetic strip on the back of the card. The banking industry is in the process of transitioning to the next generation of payment cards based on the smart card or chip card technology. The main catalyzers of this process include the card associations such as Visa, Mastercard and Europay who are actively pushing their bank members towards the adoption of smart cards. At the same time equipping the merchant with a combined magnetic strip and smart card reader device incurs additional expenses. There is also the risk factor that is peculiar to each country or region. The nature of the customer/merchant base or the availability of an inexpensive network or telecom services to enable online authorization strongly influence the credit card associations' plans to introduce new non-magnetic strip i.e. smart card technology.

The smart card is a plastic card with a chip securely embedded in the card. When inserted into a card reader, this chip powers up and is able to have electronic dialogues with the card reader device. One advantage of the chip is that it can carry 100 times more information than the traditional card in a form that cannot be copied. The chip on the card encrypts data before sending it to the card reader, making it very difficult to break the security, while secret quantities like cryptographic keys never leave the card. Another advantage which partially derives from the first is the possibility to have various functions in one chip, including the functions of credit, debit and prepaid cards, as well as the functions of secure Internet shopping, mass transit applications, identification services, merchant loyalty programmes etc. Thus, by having just one smart card, the client can run multiple operations with his bank and third parties. On the down side, the cards are more expensive to produce and are vulnerable to attacks from card reader hardware that has been subverted.

The electronic purse is related to electronic money or prepaid card related applications and could be a part of chip-card technology. Here value is loaded into the smart card for later spending. There are two main efforts ongoing in this area, the first by Mondex International and the second by a consortium led by Visa called the Common Electronic Purse Specification (CEPS). The difference between the Mondex system and the Visa/CEPS initiative is that Mondex does not require overnight transaction bank clearing. The value is immediate and saves the banks from processing a massive volume of petty cash transfer transactions. Of the two, the Mondex effort is more mature and has been in common use since 1992. The Mondex system offers a means of transferring value from one card to another. A person can transfer value from his card to that of his friend by simply inserting both cards into a hand-held value-transfer terminal. Similarly bricks-and-mortar merchants can use a point-of-sale terminal containing a merchant card into which the buyer inserts the Mondex card to allow the transfer to take place. The Mondex card is currently licensed in over 80 countries around the world, including several in Sub-Saharan Africa. Pilot experiments have been conducted on the use of this system to purchase across the Internet, but no large-scale scheme has yet been attempted.

In 2000, all major credit card associations rushed to announce their new smart card initiatives. It is interesting to note that the strength of Mondex pushed Mastercard, which normally cooperates with Visa, to strike up a partnership with the former and thus promote Mastercard's own new chip operating system platform called Multos or the Complete Chip Solution. The Multos operating system, referred to in the technical press as "the Windows of smartcards", was developed by Mondex International in London. It is currently the base operating technology of the Mondex Purse smart card and the American Express Blue (smart) Card. Multos is an "open" technology and is owned by Mondex but is governed by the Maosco Consortium that has 14 industry members.[17] The partnership also includes American Express, EMV Credit/Debit Chip programmes and others.[18]

Meanwhile American Express and Compaq have linked their smart card programmes by using American Express blue cards together with the Compaq Smart Card Keyboard suitable primarily for individuals and small businesses.[19] In December 2000, Visa in turn launched together with IBM and Phillips Semiconductors, its low-cost smart cards supported by four major smart card manufacturers. The so-called Visa Price Breakthrough is proposing to its member banks open platform multi-application smart cards for a price of three dollars instead of the average price of a microprocessor chip card of around six dollars. Based on Java Card 2.1 and the Open Platform 2.0 specification, the card initially proposes credit/debit functions and other applications. The latter could be loaded in the read-only memory (ROM), while there will also be room for other multiple applications in the so-called erasable memory compartment (EEPROM), giving issuer banks the possibility of proposing secure Internet access, loyalty programmes and other options.[20]

One of the difficulties of using smart card based payment methods for e-commerce is that each user terminal must be equipped with a smart card reader. Although many thought that this hardware would become part of a standard specification PC, this has not yet happened. Nevertheless Visa has announced that smart cards will represent more than 30 per cent of its cards in five years and 70 per cent in 10 years. Although that statement seems for the moment to be a bit strong, the pace of technological advance and the pressure to address the issue of fraud might create smart card momentum.[21]

(d) Internet banking

In many OECD countries, bank customers are more and more encouraged to use the Internet for all their bank related operations. A client operating through a PC linked to Internet opens the special e-banking site of his bank and then, using a set of special secure numbers, gets access to his bank accounts and has the opportunity to consult them, as well as to make all necessary payments and transfers from his personal accounts. For example, in the case of UBS e-banking, the client enters his e-banking contract number, the password in numbers (PIN) and an individual number for each transaction. When the transaction numbers are exhausted the bank sends him a new set of numbers for his individual transfer sessions.The downloaded bank software programme can also be utilized offline, for example for preparing the payment orders offline and then making the actual order online. The client receives all numbers separately, mainly by mail. The bank also provide clients with similar facilities in its premises so that clients can use bank equipment such as an ATM or a special facility linked to the main terminal facility called Multimat, permitting them to effect the same account examination, payment and transfer operations without consulting the bank staff.[22] Variations of above model are proposed to their clients by many banks in OECD and some emerging economies.

(e) Other systems

(i) Electronic Mobile Payments Systems (EMPS)

A variant of smart cards may play a role in the emerging area of mobile commerce (m-commerce). Since all GSM digital phones contain a smart card (referred to as a Subscriber Identity Module or SIM), and there are expected to be billion mobile phone subscribers in the world by 2002, this represents a huge user base. Yet it is far too early to say what form the mobile Internet will take and whether the presence of a SIM will be influential in determining consumers' modes of payment in this environment.

One example of this approach concerns the pilot project of Meritanordbanken, Nokia and Visa aimed at making payments from a mobile phone. The system uses the Wireless Applications Protocol (WAP) to access Internet sites and the smart card based SIM to assist in securing payment. Mobile phones can also be used to get online financial news, especially on forex and share prices, besides making basic online payments and transfers. Supporters of this model from Nordic countries believe in the future of m-commerce as a main vehicle of e-commerce. Some call it me-commerce (mobile e-commerce).

(ii) Interactive television (iTV)

iTV is considered to be one of the future channels for bringing e-commerce, including simple forms of e-banking and e-finance, to households. Linked to the Internet through digital TV packages, iTV involves a simplified screen and remote control and is easy to use. However, it might be limited to services proposed by a given ISP. Given the relaxed position approach of TV viewers, financial service providers would most probably choose iTV for basic financial advice rather than for complex interactive financial transactions. However, the success of TV sales channels suggests that TV-e-marketplaces will grow in popularity and might present merchants and buyers with value transfer opportunities that compete with PC based channels of e-commerce. As a result, companies supplying iTV technology and services might have unique opportunities to supply an exponentially growing market.

(iii) Shared account based systems

Most of the technology involved in a credit card transaction is required because the merchant and buyer have accounts with different banks (possibly in different countries) and each transaction involves both a check for funds availability and ultimately a transfer between banks. Pooling big groups of users so that they hold accounts with the same entity greatly simplifies transfers. When a transaction is to be made, this one entity is contacted and requested to transfer the funds from the buyer's account to the seller's account. There are numerous systems of this type available on the Internet, most of which are operated by companies that are not banks or financial institutions. Two that are worth mentioning due to their substantial customer bases are Yahoo PayDirect[23] and PayPal[24]. These systems all have links to conventional payment systems, e.g. bank accounts or credit cards to inject or withdraw money from the system, but conceptually any method can be used. Indeed some systems, e.g. PocketPass[25], allow the account to be primed with cash by buying a prepaid card in a store.

The difficulty these systems have in succeeding is that they essentially create relatively closed pools accessible only to people who have registered to use their service. Since, initially, only a few merchants accept those circuits, it makes them less attractive for buyers. This chicken-and-egg problem has caused many companies to fail in providing payment services. Nevertheless, for countries where the existing financial infrastructure is poor and the alternatives are few, such account-based systems may be highly practical, provided that the common system is under adequate regulatory control to ensure protection of the account holder's money.

(iv) Charging to the telephone account

The regulatory changes permitting telecommunications (telco) providers to charge customers for services unrelated to telecommunications has opened a possibility for telco companies to compete or co-operate with financial service providers in rendering payments services. The charges for goods and services go to the authorized telco account in a way similar to a credit card related process and then the telco enters those charges into the monthly telephone bill presented to the customer. The simplicity of charging for consumer goods through telephone bills and the fact that more people have telephone than a banking relationship adds to the competitive pressure on banks and credit card companies as providers of retail payments services. In fact history has already shown a working model — the Minitel in France.

(f) Considerations for credit card and other online B2C payments for developing countries

One lesson that has been learnt from the early years of e-commerce is that merchants must adopt a method of payment that is easy for their customers to employ. Many payment methods have failed due to the need for complicated signup procedures or the need to set up accounts.

Where the customer base for a given product or service already uses credit cards for conventional commerce, cards serve as an ideal method for online transactions. Although there is widespread unease about the security of typing credit card details into web forms, the use of SSL on a merchant site seems to allay most people's fears and the prospect of SET becoming available in the medium to long term should significantly reduce both the perceived and real risk of fraud.

In a scenario where companies and individuals located in developing countries are selling products and services to those in developed nations, the credit card may prove to be extremely effective. Although the transactions do demand financial infrastructure, this can be provided by third parties in countries with developed and robust financial systems and no limitations in respect of currency exchange. Moreover, given the competitive exchange rates proposed by credit card companies to their customers, the latter do not worry too much about the currency denomination of the sales contract, although for the buyers convenience, the currency used in the transaction should be that of the customer rather than that of the merchant.

Wire transfer can be used to transfer aggregate amounts back to domestic bank accounts at regular intervals. Similarly, the provision of the web site that offers the goods for sale can also be outsourced to a global data center provider close to the core Internet with its content being managed by personnel from the originating country.

Where transactions are intra-country, it is important to choose methods of payment that are appropriate to the local population. In countries where the local banks do not issue credit or debit cards, these would be a very poor choice as an online payment method.

A major impediment to B2C e-commerce and online payments is the system of informal relations between local traders and the retail customers in developing countries. Being used to personalised relations, those clients would have to overcome more psychological hurdles than their Western counterparts when resorting to the Internet. Only price differences and a sort of personalised after sales service could help to overcome that hurdle. As the informal economy might persist as a considerable share of national economies in many developing and transition economies, large amounts of unregistered cash balances with consumers could still be used to effect offline payments for goods and services ordered through Internet.

2. Business to business (B2B) online payments

B2B and B2G transactions differ from B2C transactions in that they involve a more limited and stable number of participants in a given business chain or a given government procurement operation. However, in one-to-one transactions, the use of cards or checks as a means of online payment for the delivery of goods and services is generally based on the same type of procedures as in B2C transactions. The reason for considering checks under the B2B heading is that commercial checks represent the bulk of checks, they involve large sums and might have long-term future in B2B e-commerce.

The similarity of B2B and B2G transactions is also based on the use of common contractual relations and payments instruments, as well as on the fact that parastatals act as common corporates or contractual parties within a framework of similar contractual rights and obligations. Differences arise only in the legal treatment of defaults and bankruptcies and have little to do with online payment techniques per se. As far as procurements of government agencies are concerned, they are treated in the chapter 5 on e-government of this report. Thus, for the sake of simplicity, here reference will be made only to B2B online payments.

In the years prior to the Internet revolution, the electronic data interchange (EDI) community was addressing the problem of automating the exchange of trade-related documents between companies. This activity experienced an annual growth rate of around 70 per cent, with the number of EDI users in the United States growing from under 2,000 in 1987 to over 31,000 in late 1992, even though many of the standards to be used for document content and transfer had not garnered widespread support. [26]

When the Internet, in the form of the World Wide Web (www), began to achieve consumer acceptance, the initial wave of e-commerce was driven by the sale of goods to consumers, i.e. the B2C sector. Around 1998, many companies, including some from the EDI community, turned their attention to the huge amount of trade that takes place between companies. Many of the ideas that had been present in the EDI community achieved a new expression with Internet users. New standards for documents have come to the fore — some derived from older EDI standards such as EDIFACT and others that started from scratch using new syntaxes involving XML. The technology and banking communities have also turned their attention to how B2B transactions should culminate in payment.

One of the things that differentiate B2B trading from the consumer market is the fact that the relationship between suppliers and buyers is typically long-lived. Where B2B e-commerce can really make a difference is in bringing together larger groups of traders in an environment that increases choice and stimulates competition (for detailed analysis of various kinds of e-marketplaces, see chapter 4).

(a) B2B e-commerce platforms: from initial participation to payment

A number of specialist companies as well as the more established companies have produced e-commerce platforms that contain all of the ingredients that go to making up Internet sites geared at business-to-business trading. These software suites focus on carrying out a set number of functions, as described below.

(i) Filtering participants

Most B2B commerce sites require a new member to sign up, giving details of their companies. While the initial contact takes place online, there is generally some kind of a vetting procedure before membership is granted. For example, WorldofFruit (www.worldoffruit.com — a site that allows companies in the fruit industry to trade with each other) grants membership only to established companies with annual revenues in excess of $1 million, whereas Ingredientsnet (www.ingredientsnet.com — a site that focuses on the food ingredients industry) requires applicants to have been in business for at least a year with satisfactory credit ratings. These simple checks massively improve the climate of trust that can exist between members of these sites, but fall short of what might be needed to support a financial transaction of a considerable size.

(ii) Networking supply and demand

Easy interfaces are provided to buyers and sellers to specify their requirements or the details of what they are offering or wanting. One of the major advantages of an e-commerce environment is that it can bring an offer to the attention of many more players than would be possible without the use of the Internet. In fact one of the earliest UNCTAD e-commerce initiatives was the so called UNCTAD Global Trade Point Network (GTPNet). The main rationale behind the GTPNet was facilitating SMEs' export potential by giving them an opportunity to offer their products and services through the GTPNet, which became one of the most frequently visited sites on the Net. Similarly CommerceOne links all of its eMarketSites and thereby their buyers/ suppliers together in what they refer to as the Global Trading Web(GTW) to accomplish a similar objective.

(iii) Price negotiation

Online tools are typically provided to facilitate price setting either as a result of a one-to-one negotiation or through the use of an online auction. Payment-related parameters can also be agreed upon at this point. Thus Chematch (www.chematch.com — a petrochemical B2B portal) allows the parties to specify the terms of delivery and also whether letters of credit or other modes of payments will be required. An evolution in purchasing is now occurring whereby buyers are initiating reverse auction, requiring suppliers to bid down in order to secure business contracts. This evolving style of purchasing is proving very successful and is being heavily promoted by the e-marketplaces.

(iv) Payment

Although some of the software suites for e-commerce do have components that help with payments, most of the B2B e-commerce sites do not yet offer this facility online. Since the amounts of each transaction can be quite large (Chemmatch has already had over $425 million transacted with the average transaction exceeding $500,000) companies often resort to appropriate conventional i.e. offline means to effect the payment. However, given the trend, one could presume that this will change. In fact many of the technology providers operating in this market are active participants in the efforts described below to bring these more conventional proprietary electronic high-value payment methods to the Internet.

High-value B2B payments are almost always bank-mediated, and for these systems to move to the Internet, they need to garner the support of the banking industry as a whole. The bankers' communities of both developed and developing countries are usually the leaders in setting the national agenda for the development of Internet trading standards.

(b) Electronic checks: a case for using digital signatures and PKI

It is instructive to look at the initiatives undertaken in developing electronic checks. For some years, many financial service providers grouped in associations or consortia have been working on a specification for electronic check-based payment with a view to developing primarily B2B payments solutions. One of the leading consortia in that respect is the Financial Services Technology Consortium (FSTC) of the United States - an organization made up of the main American banks and banking technology providers. Formed in 1993 to enhance the competitiveness of the United States financial services industry through the use of technology, it made considerable progress in its attempt to make the electronic check a common online payments instrument.

An electronic check is a document containing fields identical to those on a paper check with appropriate digital signatures being added when the check is first issued by the payer and also when it is endorsed by the payee. A pilot run by the United States Treasury and Department of Defense using these checks started in mid-1998, and a new syntax for expressing the check, called the Financial Services Markup Language (FSML), was defined.

Electronic checks expressed in FSML may be exchanged by trading partners in future B2B exchanges. Before these can be processed, though, the banks involved must have the appropriate technological infrastructure to process them and to use the information contained therein in order to effect the inter-account and inter-bank transfers required. The FSTC has laid out an architecture to upgrade a bank's existing technology, to simplify the ACH (and eventually ECP) based interface, and hence to add the capability to handle electronic checks issued and transferred between organizations on the Internet.

Electronic checks are one of the examples which can exist only if secure digital signatures can be applied and thus make them acceptable as an online payment method.

(i) Digital signatures

Digital signatures are produced by electronically digesting the document to be signed and producing a small unique piece of data that represents an electronic fingerprint of the document's contents. This fingerprint is then encrypted using a secret number called the private key. The encrypted fingerprint is the 'digital signature' and the only person that can sign a document is the holder of the private key.

When any other party wants to verify that the signature is correct, they decrypt the document using a non-secret number referred to as the public key. If the result matches the fingerprint of the document they accept the digital signature as a genuine one. In order to use this technique as a substitute for real signatures, the last element needed is a way to associate a person's identity with a particular private key.

When people travel from one country to another, they assert their identity by producing a passport. This document provides a link between their appearance (and their handwritten signature if necessary) and their identity (name and date of birth). It is accepted at border posts because the passport is issued by a national government trusted by those officials.

The electronic counterpart of this is called an X.509 certificate. It is an electronic document that provides a link between a public key and the identity of a person or company and is signed by an entity that is widely trusted and called a Certification Authority (CA). In fact a triangular relationship emerges between the Certification Authority proper, i.e. a public agency defining the rules and criteria for establishing an "electronic passport", the Registry Authority (RA) accepting and verifying persons and entities requesting an electronic signature, and the Certification Company (commonly labeled the Certification Authority), which actually supplies the abovementioned private keys to individual users and makes sure that they are compatible with their own public keys.

Once a single CA or an international network of cooperating CAs that is widely trusted is established, it is possible for people to send signed digital documents such as electronic checks to each other. By including the X.509 certificate with the document, they allow the recipient to verify the signature on the document.

(ii) Public Key Infrastructure (PKI)

A network of cooperating Certification Authorities, Registry Authorities and Certification Companies is often referred to as a public key infrastructure (PKI), and the slow acceptance of this network and the related electronic signature and personal identification technologies has been one of the factors delaying the widespread acceptance of electronic checks and other signed documents that will be essential for B2B e-commerce.

The deployment of PKIs takes a considerable amount of time, and it only becomes useful when very large numbers of users have both the awareness of the contribution it can make to building trust online and also software that supports the verification of online signatures. It is also true that, just like passports or any other identification scheme, systems need to be put in place to cover the full lifetime of the identifying document, including coping with renewal, loss, confiscation or revocation, etc. Clearly, where transactions worth many millions of dollars may be at stake, important issues of liability and negligence might arise for those involved in ensuring the security and reliability of the PKI.

According to one source, the global electronic certification market is highly concentrated and is controlled by three companies, namely VeriSign of the United States, Globalsign of Belgium and Thafte of South Africa.[27] The information on market shares here is based on the estimates of a private source and could be contested, but apparently the market is a heavily concentrated. Certification authorities are also often operated by major postal or telecommunications entities in individual countries. A good example of this is the United Kingdom, where the Royal Mail operates the ViaCode CA and British Telecom competes with them to operate the BT Trustwise service. In Argentina, the Government operates a digital signature infrastructure directly. It is important to note that, for trust to be established across a network, both users of the service must be signed up with the same certification authority. However, in general, these certification authorities do not work together, and the scope of their service is extremely restricted. However it is true that most PKIs that have been built so far have been general-purpose in nature and often limited in their scope to a single country.

An example of a global PKI formed by financial institutions to enable secure online payments of all kinds is the IDENTRUS consortium. Following an initiative that began in November 1997, Identrus™ LLC was launched in April 1999 by its founder members: ABN AMRO, Bank of America, Bankers Trust (since acquired by Deutsche Bank), Barclays, Chase Manhattan, Citigroup, Deutsche Bank and Hypo Vereinsbank. The purpose of this initiative was more precisely to set up a system to allow the circulation of electronic documents in online payments. As chart 16 shows, Identrus LLC operates a common root certification authority on top of local CAs operated by the member banks around the world. Trading partners can exchange signed trade documents with each other using any Internet-related mechanism and these documents can be verified against an identity certified by a trusted banking entity.

In sum the complexity of PKI and various initiatives and systems in this area raises issues of their interoperability, customization, pricing, governance and oversight.

(c) B2B Internet banking

Pending the wide availability of electronic checks, one method of making large business-to-business payments that is becoming increasingly popular is to employ Internet banking. Bank-mediated transfers such as ACH debits or credits, as well as domestic and international wire transfers, which had hitherto required a paper request, can now be initiated directly by companies. This trend pre-dates mass Internet usage and was initially called business banking, where

Chart 16
An e-commerce exchange making use of Identrus certification services

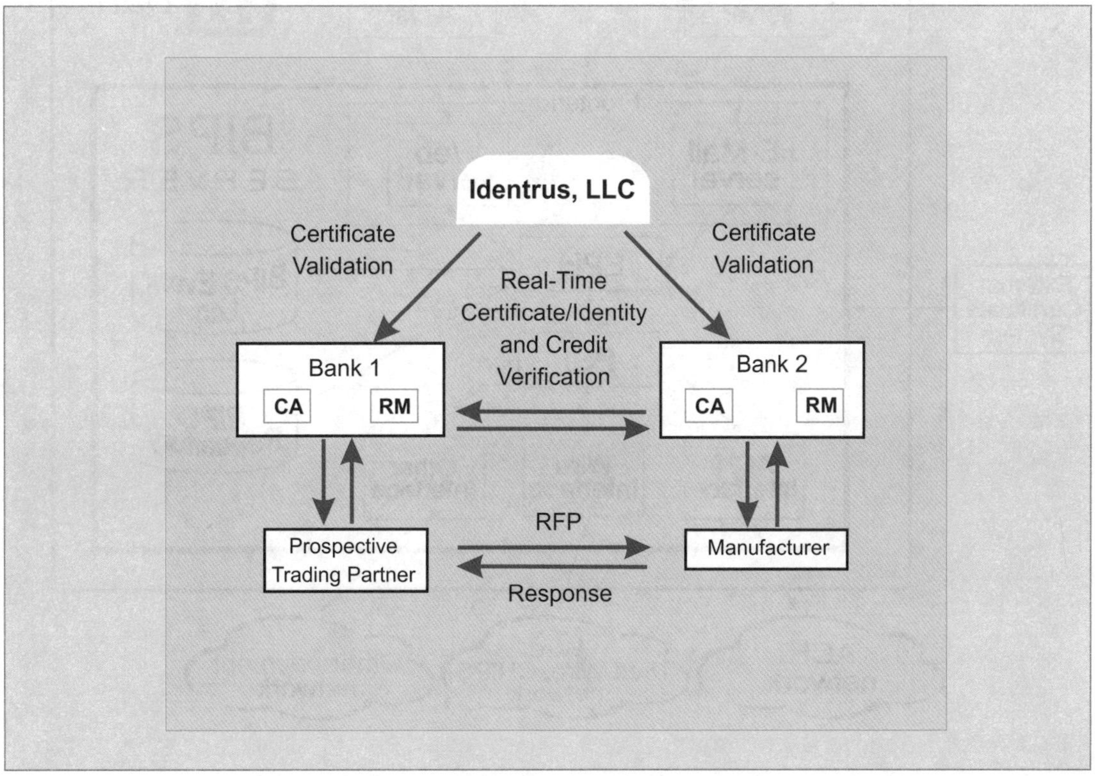

high-value clients were issued with special software which, using a dial-up connection, could monitor the status of their account and also initiate payments. Placing a web base at the front end of this service allows it to be made available to a wider range of banking clients.

Many B2B e-commerce exchanges serve principally to bring together the transacting parties. Once the deal is arranged and the price agreed, the parties can then effect payment using an Internet banking service. This is a system to which all parties are already accustomed and works well even though the payment process is not integrated with other parts of the transaction.

(i) FSTC Bank Internet Payments System (BIPS)

In 1996, the United States Financial Services Technology Consortium (FSTC) initiated a project to come up with a very general way to allow companies easier access to payment services. Their approach involved making as few modifications to the existing United States banking systems as possible. Chart 17 shows how the Bank Internet Payment System (BIPS) acts as an Internet 'frontend' to the existing ACH, wire transfers and other bank networks. Messages such as 'payment requests' can be initiated by either e-mail or web-based software. A Public Key Infrastructure (PKI) is assumed to exist, and this component could be provided either by the Identrus or similar projects described earlier.

BIPS was demonstrated in a number of projects involving Glenview and Mellon banks in the United States in August 1998, but there has been no public progress beyond that. This may change as the Identrus PKI becomes more widespread, enabling many more users to make use of BIPS or BIPS-like services.

Chart 17
The Bank Internet Payment System (BIPS) architecture

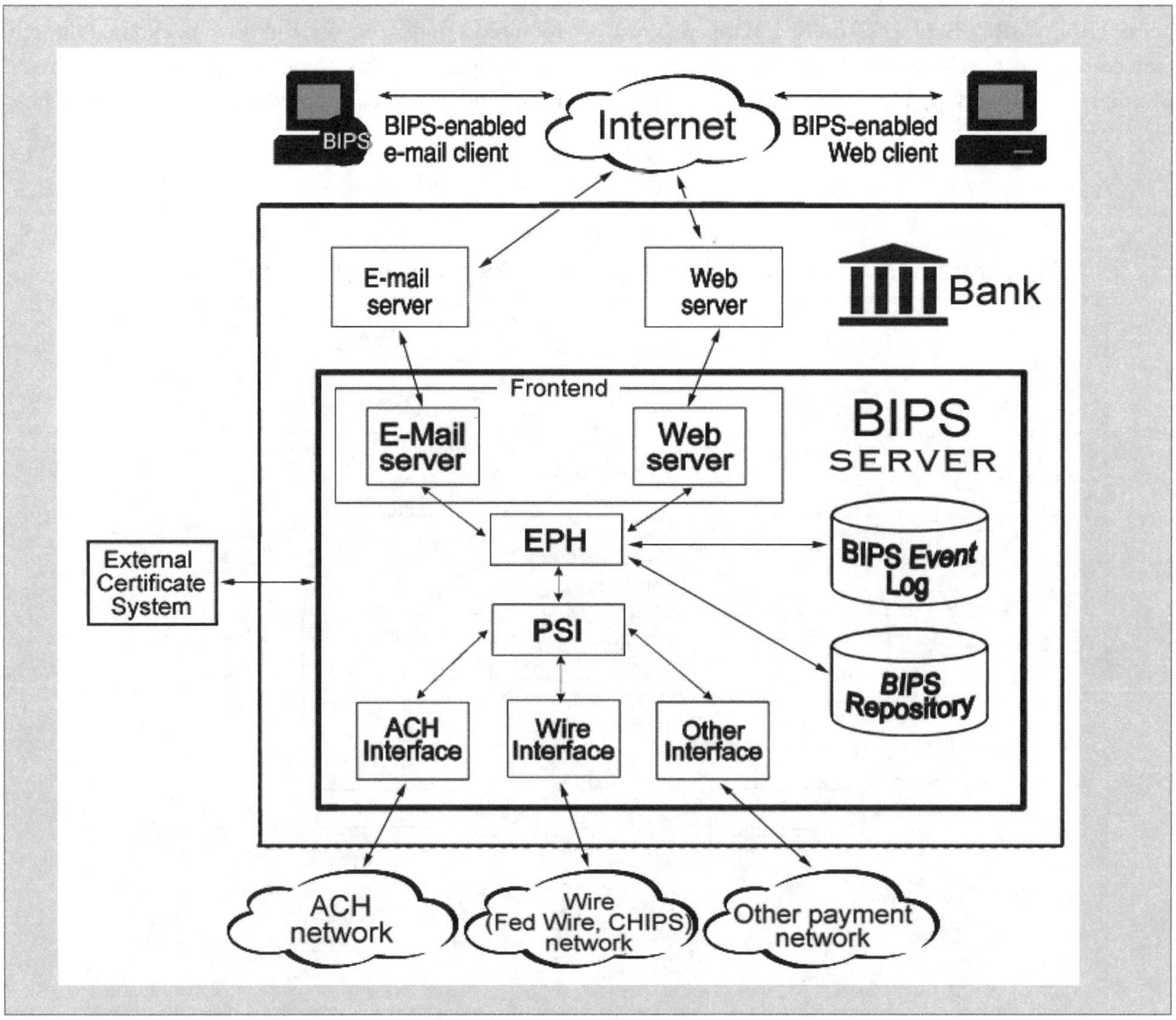

(d) E-Finance for international trade in EDI-like systems

The predecessor of today's B2B e-commerce phenomenon was the Electronic Data Interchange movement of the late 1970s and early 1980s. Prior to the widespread adoption of the Internet and before the World Wide Web was invented, companies that did regular trading with each other were focused on two things. Firstly, great efforts were made to standardize common electronic versions of standard business documents such as invoices, purchase orders, statements of claim (for the insurance business) and a host of others. This had quite a degree of success and led to the adoption of the Electronic Data Interchange for Administration, Commerce and Trade (EDIFACT) syntax and supporting message standards. Secondly, the communities built private or quasi-public networks to allow trade documents to be conveyed. The most highly evolved of these networks supported a derivative of X.400 e-mail referred to as X.435 which had many extra messaging facilities specifically targeted at the EDI user. These networks were referred to as value added networks (VANs).

The emerging model for B2B e-commerce at the beginning of the twenty-first century takes the form of a web portal site concentrating on bringing trading partners together for online negotiation, contracting, delivery and payments. For many industries, this model has a promising future, as the business community may be better served by having a reliable means of exchanging trade documents in the way it was done in the EDI model.

Few Internet-based platforms are trying to face this challenge. One of them is the www.bolero.net — a company created in 1998 from an alliance between S.W.I.F.T. and TT Club (an insurance association for the shipping industry) which tries to provide a neutral platform for simultaneous interchange and certification of all trade-related documents, from sales

Chart 18
The Bolero system

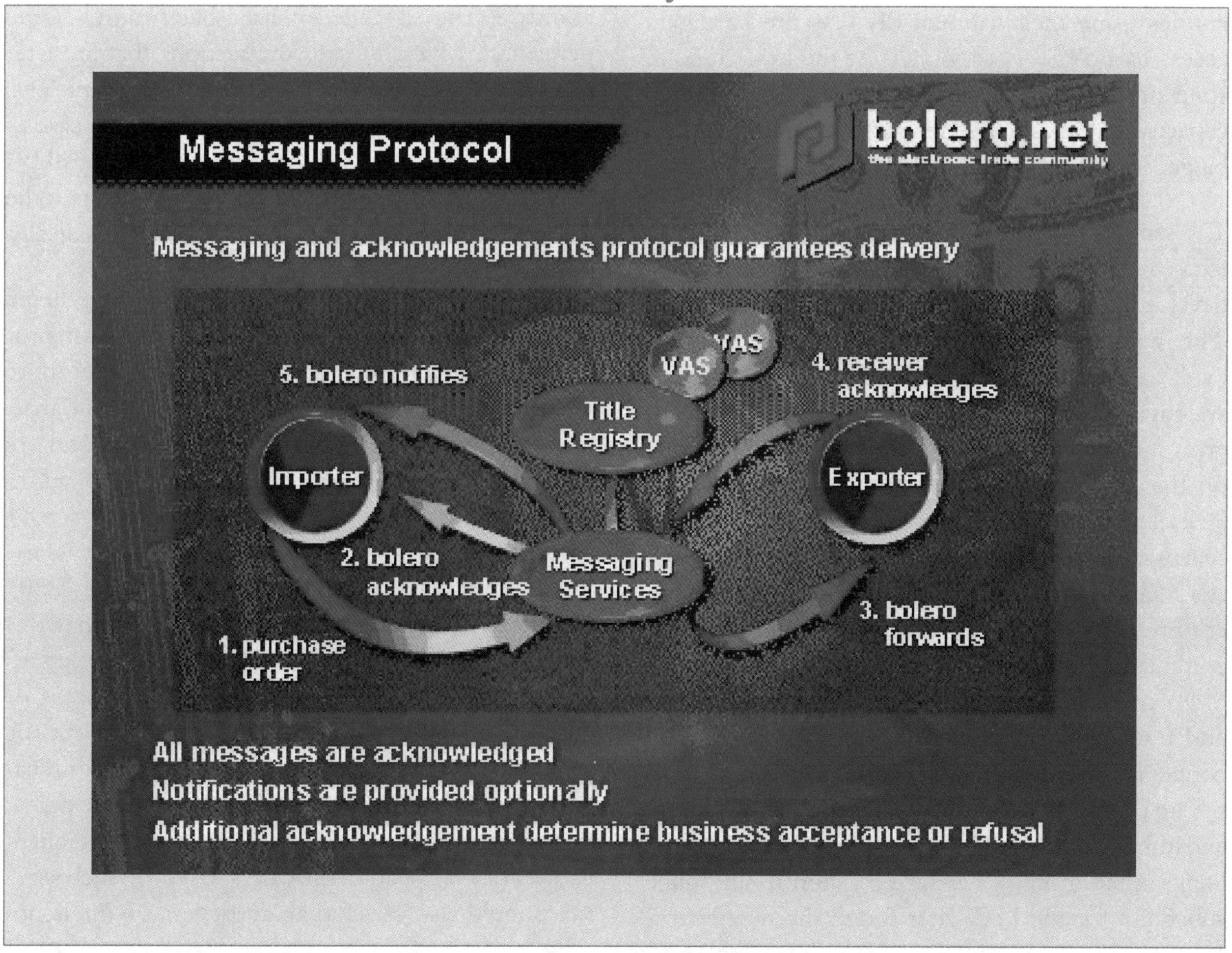

contracts changes of ownership and in some cases payment.

In the case of Bolero, they have built a private network that allows companies to send trade documents to each other. As chart 18 shows, a central function intercepts all messages to provide an audit trail and also to provide explicit acknowledgements of the delivery of documents. The Bolero community has also defined the syntax for a large number of trade-related documents using XML syntax (the messaging service can verify that a document confirms to the syntax before it is accepted into the system). The Bolero system assumes the existence of a PKI and, in addition to certificates issued by itself, it can handle ones issued by other systems. Although payment is not explicitly supported by the Bolero system, one of the message types that is standardized is the "Payment Instruction". This gives a mechanism for a company to instruct a bank to make a payment across the Bolero private network. In fact, to ensure the secure exchange of documents on its platform, Bolero entered into cooperation with Identrus at the end of 2000. The secure keys issued by Identrus participating institutions should be valid in the Bolero online trade system and at the same time permit the Bolero Multiple Certification Authority (MultiCA) to let entities using their national PKA secure keys gain access to Bolero.net services.[28] At the same time in spite of heavy investment in Bolero, the expected capacity utilization has not yet been achieved and bigger turnovers will be required.

The same is true for a finance platform that is more focused on international trade called www.tradecard.com, developed by a US-based company called Tradecard. The intention here was to replace the traditional bank-based letters of credit (L/C) by a similar online system and bring partners together online. Tradecard gives a possibility to buyers and sellers to negotiate on the Internet using all trade-related documents, including the buyer's electronic purchase order, the seller's commercial invoice and packing list, the buyer's payment assurance, the approved logistic provider's proof of delivery documentation, etc. Once the compliance of all these documents is assured, the payment takes place. Tradecard, as far as payments and trade financing solutions are concerned, is in cooperation with such partners as Mastercard (corporate payments solutions), Coface (credit insurance and information) as well as commercial banks.[29] Some banks, after an initial negative reaction to an online substitute for the L/C, later found the new instrument useful and agreed to cooperate. At the same time, although the announced transaction costs of becoming a member and transacting through the system seem to be rather small[30], Tradecard so far proposes only a substitute for a basic L/C and cannot compete with commercial banks by proposing a full range of L/Cs.

In fact online trade finance platforms are continuing to proliferate. They are a result of strategic alliances and co-ownership of banks and technology companies or represent the innovative know-how of some new start-ups. They include the Internet Trade Finance Exchange (ITF), LTPtrade.net, @GlobalTrade and others.[31] At the same time many of those new platforms are for the moment new ventures and need more liquidity injections.

(e) Online payments risk management by third parties

Up to now, most of the fraud that has been perpetrated online has been related to B2C transactions paid for with credit cards. In the United States, just over 3 per cent of the total volume of transactions are fraudulent, but it is suspected that in the Internet world, this percentage is very much higher. In some countries the so called charge-back ratio — the percentage of credit card transactions that are later denied by the cardholder — exceeds 50 per cent. This fraud rate is likely to persist and perhaps increase as long as the predominant security technique is SSL. If SET or some stripped down version of it were to be deployed, this figure could be cut down dramatically.

Normally a B2B transaction takes more time than a B2C one and consequently this allows more time for checking. In the future, as the process becomes more automated, more opportunities for fraud will arise. Since the transactions are fewer in number and are of a typically much higher value, the types of criminals attracted to this area will differ from the credit card fraudsters. Since the primary means for asserting identity in such transactions will be the X.509 Certificate, it will be imperative to ensure that this certification process is not subverted. Many countries in the developed world are in the process of enacting e-commerce legislation which sets out the requirements for entities to operate public certification services. In many cases, there are specific provisions included to deal with negligence and consequent liability of certification providers. Users of such services should also develop an awareness of the issues

Chart 19
The TradeCard Architecture

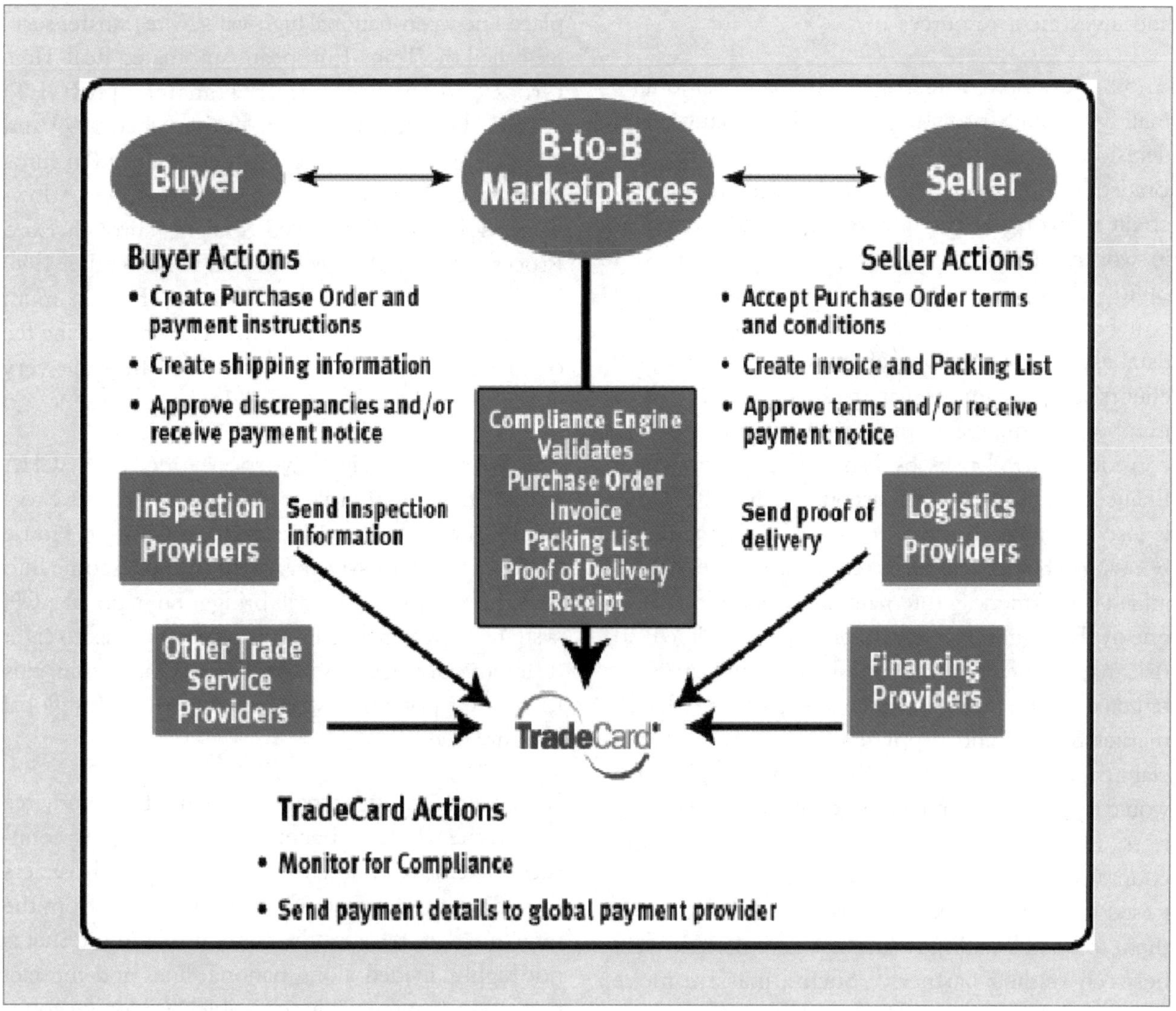

involved and the legal protection afforded to parties contracting with each other using digital certificates.

For a successful B2B transaction to take place, it is not enough for contracting parties to know about each other's existence and credibility. As in the case of the conventional transaction protection by third parties (see section B, subsection 5) the Internet also needs modern tools of risk management. The leaders of industry are moving online to follow their clients and to protect them from political and commercial risks inherent to transactions.

According to one of the biggest global credit insurers — Coface of France — more than 35 million enterprises are going to transact online, and all of them will need to have an image of visibility and credibility on the Internet. To follow them in B2B business, Coface has developed a so called @rating system where enterprises could get various @rating labels depending on the credibility and credit standing of the enterprise and according to the Coface credit information database. The label means that Coface confirms that a given company will honour its debts up to a given sum per transaction. In other words when a company sells to a trading partner which has already got a Coface @label for a given sum, then the former might be insured from the risk of default for that sum. At the same time, the Coface @label could guarantee a trade credit of the same level for the enterprise to finance its exports of goods and services. The labels cover amounts from 20,000 euros to more than 100,000 euros, which corresponds to from 1@ to 3@L respectively.[32] If this system starts to function it might give many third world companies striving to sell abroad but having a problem getting access to pre-export or working capital financing direct access to trade credit on more competitive terms than they might otherwise have received from local banks. That in turn might improve many developing countries' access to international trade finance and investment resources.

Another example of managing company risk online mainly through providing credit information and decision-making tools online concernes Dun and Bradstreet (D&B) of the United States, the biggest credit information provider in the world. Last year its worldwide operations brought the company $1.4 billion in revenues. The company maintains and constantly updates (one million changes a day) databases on 60 million companies. It has 150,000 clients and is famous for its so called D-U-N-S number. Companies which hold this number are considered good risks by banks and can get trade finance and trade on open account.[33] By 2002, D&B is also planning to move to the Web the activities bringing in 80 per cent of its revenues. Last year D&B joined with American International Group Inc. (AIG), one of the biggest insurers, to propose an online B2B risk management product dubbed Avantrust (SM), targeted mainly at online exchanges, Internet-based market makers and supply chain extranets. It was claimed that functions of the Avantrust platform would include confirming the identity of trading partners, inspecting goods, managing and insuring counterparty risks and insuring delivery. It is also supposed to insure eMarketplace web sites, thus helping them to build liquidity, reduce risk and increase trust between trading partners.[34] Such a massive move online of the above and other credit information, credit insurance and other financial services providers will definitely have a major impact on online third party management of primarily B2B credit and performance risks.

(f) New regional and global payment systems and B2B sites: Challenges and opportunities for developing countries

Many of the examples above involve businesses making bank-mediated payments where the most often cited back-end payment method is the Automated Clearing House (ACH). Although most developed countries and many developing ones do have national ACH-like systems, nowhere are these as open and accessible to industry as in the United States. The fact that each of the systems is strictly national, limits their usefulness for international e-commerce. Some new initiatives may be about to change that.

As part of their preparations for monetary union, the Member States of the European Union put in place a new pan-national high-value wire transfer service called the Trans-European Automated Real-Time Gross Settlement Express Transfer (TARGET) system. This has been in operation since 1999 and allows large real-time transfers denominated in euros to be made between participating countries. A low-value variant of this, called Straight Through Euro Processing (STEP), was launched in November 1999 by the Euro Banking Association. The maximum transaction size is □ 50,000, with a low processing fee of □ 0.48. In the future, this could become very important for e-commerce in the euro zone.

At a global level, an initiative spearheaded by NACHA in the United States might give rise in the future to a Worldwide Automated Transaction Clearing House (WATCH).[35] This system, which is due to come into operation in July 2002, will bridge the national ACH systems to provide credit-only transfers in six to eight different currencies as a first step. Once again, this holds great potential as a payment method for global e-commerce.

It is generally thought that the advent of e-commerce will on the whole be beneficial for developing countries. It removes many of the conventional barriers to trade that stem from countries being far from the target market. Because the content of the Internet is not highly divided along national lines and the fact that all content is equally accessible, developing countries can have the same access as their developed counterparts to customers on the Internet.

The economic data so far suggest that the sectors that have benefited most from the introduction of e-commerce are mostly in service areas such as ICT, tourism, finance, publishing and information services, Internet services and other professional services, which were initially of more relevance to developed countries. [36] However the advent of B2B e-commerce could greatly extend the number of services sectors that are and could be of relevance also to developing countries. Computer hardware and software, other types of manufacturing and services, including e-tourism, could be at the forefront of this breakthrough (for more details on e-tourism see chapter 3).

At the same time, the developing countries are still mainly producers of primary goods, semi-manufactures and low-end manufactures, and they should first, capitalize on the many opportunities arising in these sectors. Thus they might take advantage of the fact that many commodity exchanges and large manufacturing systems largely based on subcontracting for procurement are moving online. The competitive terms instantaneously proposed by developing country suppliers to buyers from global e-marketplaces and e-procuring systems should create new business opportunities for them.

Virtually every primary commodity is now served with a B2B e-commerce site. Table 25 shows some representative examples.

Such web sites bring together a community of buyers and sellers based on the products they have to offer or need to purchase rather than the geographic region that they operate in. In that sense, they create a global marketplace to which developing countries should have full access. These sites also may have the effect of causing disintermediation in those markets that could represent both opportunities for developing countries selling to foreign markets and a threat where the flow is in the reverse direction. Developing countries should explore the options available to them to fully participate in and indeed form B2B e-commerce markets in economic sectors that are important to their economies.

As yet, most B2B e-commerce sites support all phases of a transaction but stop short of providing payment services. So, for the present, B2B transactions rely on conventional payment methods. This situation is likely to change in the short term, and one could expect electronic variants of ACH, electronic checks, smart cards, electronic L/Cs and others to be incorporated into the trading dialogues that take place on these marketplaces or integrated foreign trade sites.

Developing countries wishing to be at the forefront of these developments will have to pursue different strategies to support two separate objectives, namely facilitating e-trade with foreign companies and B2B and B2C marketplaces, and starting to develop domestic e-commerce. Where the national payments infrastructure is underdeveloped and has few international linkages, it may be expedient to conclude B2B transactions with the financial transfer taking place between accounts held in countries better connected with trading partners' banking systems. This may involve maintaining business accounts with leading international banks, including for example United States banks giving full access to FedWire, ACH and BIPS-like services, European banks in the euro-zone to access TARGET and STEP services, or banks with a similar level of services in other developed and developing countries.

When it comes to domestic transactions, efforts could be focused on improving the payments infrastructure and conducting initiatives to open up payment services to companies that wish to trade on the Internet. Where it proves to be problematic to institute these changes in national banking systems, consideration should be given to setting up private account-based payment systems that can be used by companies trading on the Internet operating in related areas of business. These private systems would be providing a service akin to private banking and may need regulatory oversight.

In the longer term, developing countries should keep a watching brief on global developments such as WATCH, looking toward the day when a global payments network would be accessible to the majority of developing and transition economies and their companies trading or having prospects of trading on the Internet.

Table 25
Examples of commodity and food related e-marketplaces

B2B e-commerce site	Industry sector
www.forestindustry.com	Forest and wood products
www.chematch.com	Bulk commodity chemicals, polymers and fuel products
www.worldoffruit.com	Global fresh produce industry
www.esteel.com	Global metals supply chain
www.inc2inc.com	Connecting food manufacturers and suppliers of ingredients and packaging
www.rooster.com	Marketplace for farmers, dealers, co-ops and manufacturers to buy and sell the inputs needed for farming

D. Online Payments, Monetary Policy and Financial Stability

Governments regulate conventional commerce to protect both the interests of the parties involved in transactions and the legitimate interests of society at large. Banking organizations and similar financial institutions have their operations overseen by central banks, which have a number of distinct concerns. If a banking organization were to fail or to behave fraudulently this could negatively impact a large section of the population and their savings and could have knock-on effects throughout the entire economy. Clearly, if a non-bank organization is operating either an electronic cash system or one that is based on accounts, it is holding a substantial amount on deposit on behalf of its customers. The European Central Bank (ECB) examined this issue in 1998 and concluded, among other things, that the issuers of electronic money must be subject to prudential supervision and that they should be legally obliged to redeem the electronic money at par value. [37] Historically, the US Federal Reserve has taken a more hands-off approach, opting to let the market for new Internet-based payment methods develop before introducing regulation.[38]

Another concern that regulatory authorities have regarding new methods of payment relates to the effect on a country's money supply of new unregulated organizations issuing cash without recourse to government. The American view on this is that the amounts that are currently stored in electronic purses are so small that they do not constitute any risk. Once again, the European view is stricter and requires e-money issuers to supply the central bank with "whatever information may be required for the purpose of monetary policy". The European Parliament has recently adopted a directive on the regulation of electronic money institutions, which will give legal force to this. [39]

At present, e-finance in developing and transition economies is mainly about the possibilities of the use of online banking and payments for companies participating in B2B e-commerce at the global and regional level. As the residents of those countries are less involved in B2C e-commerce, the questions of e-money, its use and forms are less pressing. However the issues of governance and digital money supply, which are becoming more actual for developed economies, could become equally important for developing ones in the not so distant future. Hence the importance of highlighting the implications of this phenomenon for financial sector governance from the point of view of challenges faced by both central banks and the main payment agents, i.e. commercial banks, themselves.

For central banks, e-money might mean less need for banknotes and hence lower costs related to the issuing and handling of banknotes. The central bank money supply might diminish due to the proliferation of private monies and money substitutes, including client-attracting bonuses such as frequent flyer miles and other purchasing bonuses. The decreasing share of official money might mean less expenditure on its creation and management, but the costs related to the threats of such official money substitution to the stability and credibility of the monetary system could be bigger, as malfunctioning of the various private monies, many of which could be anonymous bearers' instruments, might adversely affect the stature of the national currency and hence its value and exchange rate.

For financial service providers, the risks ahead include business strategy misjudgments, operational issues, legal and regulatory uncertainty and systemic risks. However, even the best private operators have to pass the public's test on the convenience, universality and trustworthiness of their payments instruments. They must also be perceived by digital cash holders as good risks unless the central banks agree to play the role of lenders of last resort and accept from the public the unspent digital cash claims on failed issuers of those monies. In that respect, it will be interesting to know whether lender of last resort arrangements will be provided for the holders of monies issued by the US Digicash venture, which has filed under Chapter 11 of the US Bankruptcy Code.

Other concerns for users include transaction costs, portability and transmitability, and the anonymity of online payment instruments. Thus if various forms of micro and small payments become popular on the Internet, credit card companies will be pressed to adjust their ologopolistic pricing structures downward. While the Internet makes cash easily portable and transmittable, users might have doubts about their anonymity, which might deter them in countries where the informal economy is relatively large and where real cash is still the most trusted and anonymous means of payment.

At the same time, alongside cost and regulatory aspects, one should also stress another important macroeconomic implication: increased use of online payments might increase the income velocity of money circulation and hence decrease the monetary aggregates needed to service a given level of economic activity in a country. An increase in the speed of money circulation, coupled with the sharply decreased transaction costs of online money transfers, might also imply major savings for consumers and financial intermediaries, as well as increasing productivity for the latter. Achieving such a state of development for financial service providers in developing countries implies closer cooperation between local and international financial service providers, as well as concerted technical assistance, including training from specialized international organizations.

Finally, a key parameter of the success of e-finance will be its impact on financial sector stability. Answering the question as to whether online transfer of money increases or decreases systemic risk needs further detailed examination (it is discussed to some extend in the introductory chapter). A preliminary view on this complex issue would be that the impact is positive/neutral. The possibility of transmitting information and payments rapidly through the Internet might greatly contribute to the functioning of early warning arrangements in the international monetary system due to diminishing information asymmetries and possibilities for more precise analysis and fine-tuning. However, unchecked transmission of alarming news could also trigger the herd instinct in a dangerous form of panic, especially from short-term portfolio investors.

The globalized economy raises the issue of how to create built-in buffers and defenses, diminishing the impact of panic waves on the international monetary system. This represents a serious future agenda for regulators and international financial organizations, who will have to think hard about how the world financial sector is going to change its structure. It will pose new challenges for international coordination, given the global character of the Internet. It will be important, by introducing adaptive and flexible regulations and additional prudential buffers, especially for risk-seeking non-bank financial institutions, to ensure the market and operational integrity without impeding the development of e-finance.

Notes

1 For more detail see www.swift.com

2 In this section cards with magnetic strips are reviewed; cards with embedded software chips will be considered under the heading of smart cards in the next online payments section.

3 The first credit card was developed by the Bank of America and was initially known as Americard. Eventually it was transformed into Visa Cards

4 www.visa.com/av/thanksabillion.html

5 "Financial Times" June 13, 2000

6 IMF (2000).

7 BIS (2000a).

8 BIS (2000b).

9 The Banker, 1 February, 2001.

10 Jupiter Communications estimate: $23.1 billion, Activmedia Estimate: $109 billion.

11 The most popular certification authority used for e-commerce applications of this type is Verisign Inc, www.verisign.com

12 In January 2000, a Russian hacker fraudulently obtained a file of of credit card numbers from CD Universe. Initially he attempted to blackmail them for a sum of between $100,000 and $300,000 and when this failed, he published the file on an online site.

13 The Banker, ibid.

14 See www.orbiscom.com, www.americanexpress.com, www.cyota.com

15 BIS (2000b).

16 Mornan-Vaughan and Smith (2001).

17 www.MAOSCO.com

18 MasterCard International (2000).

19 See http://home3.americanexpress.com/corp/latestnews/compaq.asp

20 www.visa.com/av/news/press_release.ghtml?pr_form_edit=365&edit_file=

21 See www.visa.com

22 See www.ubs.com

23 Paydirect.yahoo.com – a division of the Yahoo! Internet portal company

24 www.Paypal.com

25 www.pocketpass.com

26 As reported in Marcella and Chan (1993).

27 Le magazine d'Internet.net, Nu:49, février 2001, p.74

28 See www.bolero.net

29 See www.tradecard.com

30 International Trade Today, November 2000

31 See www.itfex.com, www.ltptrade.net, www.cceweb.com

32 Cazes, Jérôme. "Avec la Solution @rating: L'Afrique sur la route du Commerce B2B". Presentation at the UNCTAD Conference on Building Credit Insurance in Africa and the Mediterranean, Tunis, 23-24 October 2000. See also www.coface.com

33 See www.dnb.com

34 http://investor.dnb.com/ireye/ir_site….dnb&script=460&layout=9&item_id0128344

35 See www.watch.org

36 WIPO (2000).

37 European Central Bank (1998).

38 Gramlich, Edward M. (1999).

39 Directive 2000/46/ELECTRONIC COMMERCE, also known as EMI Directive of the European Parliament and of the Council of Europe, 18 September 2000, on the taking up, pursuit of and prudential supervision of the business of electronic money institutions, http://europa.eu.int/eur-lex/en/lif/dat/2000/en_300L0046.html

References and bibliography

Bank for International Settlements (2000 a). *Clearing and Settlement Arrangements for Retail Payments in Selected Countries*. Basel, Switzerland, September, 45pp.

Bank for International Settlements (2000 b). *Statistics on Payment Systems in the Group of Ten Countries*. Basel, February, www.bis.org/publ, 133pp.

Bank for International Settlements (1999). *Payment Systems in the Southern African Development Community*. Basel, Switzerland, June, 262pp.

Bank for International Settlements (2000 c). *Survey of Electronic Money Developments*. Basel, Switzerland, May, 104pp.

Bank for International Settlements (2000 d). Committee on the Global Financial System. *The Implications of Electronic Trading in Financial Markets*. Basel, Switzerland. November.

Basel Committee on Banking Supervision (2000). *Issues and Principles for Risk*

Management of Electronic Banking. Electronic Banking Group. November.

Bell, Richard (2000). *Internet Banking: The Bank's Perspective*. TowerGroup.

Needham, MA. July.

BIS (2000a). *A Glossary of Terms Used in Payments and Settlements Systems*. Basel, December 2000, p.14 (44pp).

BIS (2000b). *Survey of Electronic Money Developments*. Basel, May 2000.

Bolero, XML Team (2000). *A White Paper on Bolero XML standards*. 21 August. www.bolero.net/downloads/boleroXML_standards.pdf

CEPSCo (2000). *Common Electronic Purse Specifications – Business Requirements*, Version 7.0. March. www.cepsco.com/

Claessens Stijn, Glaessner, Tom and Klingebiel, Daniela (2001). *E-Finance in Emerging Markets: Is Leapfrogging Possible?* World Bank Working Paper, forthcoming.

Crockett, Andrew (2001). *Financial Stability in the Light of increasing Importance of Online Banking and E-Commerce,* BIS Review, May

Europay International S.A., MasterCard International Incorporated, and Visa International Service Association (1996). *EMV '96: Integrated Circuit Card Specification for Payment Systems*. June. www.emvco.com/

European Banking Association (2000). *Straight Through Euro Payment System – Impact Document for STEP1 Banks*, Version 0.3. June. www.abe.org

European Central Bank (1998). *Report on Electronic Money*. August, 1998. www.ecb.int/pub/pdf/emoney.pdf

European Central Bank (2000). *Welcome to the World of TARGET*. August, www.ecb.int

Feghhi, J., Feghhi, J. and Williams, P. (1999). *Digital Certificates : Applied Internet Security*. Addison-Wesley, Reading, Massachusetts, 453 pp.

Financial Services Technology Consortium (1998). *Bank Internet Payment System Specification*, Version 1.0. August. www.fstc.org/projects/bips/index.html

Ford, W. and Baum, M. (2001). *Secure Electronic Commerce : Building the Infrastructure for Digital Signatures and Encryption*, 2nd Edition. Prentice-Hall, New Jersey, 612 pp.

Furst, Karen, Lang, William and Nolle, Daniel (2000). *Internet Banking: Developments and Prospects*. Office of the Comptroller of the Currency. Working Paper. September.

Gramlich, Edward M. (1999). Electronic Money in the United States. Remarks before the Electronic Payments Symposium, University of Michigan, Ann Arbor, Michigan, 17 September 1999.

Group of Ten (2001). *Consolidation in the Financial Sector: Summary Report.* January.

Humphrey, D., Dato, E., Tsurumi, M. and Vesala, J. (1996). *The Evolution of Payments in Europe, Japan and the United States : Lessons for Emerging Market Economies.* World Bank Policy Research Working Paper 1676, October. 44pp.

IMF (2000). *Modern Banking and OIC Derivatives Markets: The Transformation of Global Finance and its Implications for Systemic Risk.* Occasional Paper No: 203. Washington, 2000, p.9 (72pp).

Institute for Prospective Technological Studies (IPTS) (1999). *Study on Electronic Payment Systems for the Committee on Economic and Monetary Affairs and Industrial Policy of the European Parliament.* May, European Commission Joint Research Centre, Seville, Spain, 83pp, www.jrc.es/pages/projects/docs/Final-EPS-Vol.1.pdf

ITU-T Recommendation X.509 (1997): Information Technology - Open Systems Interconnection - The Directory: Authentication Framework, June, 50pp.

Jones, T. (1996). *The Future of Money as it Affects the Payment Systems in the U.S. and Abroad.* Submission to the U.S. House of Representatives, June.

Kravitz, J. (editor) (1999). *FSML – Financial Services Markup Language*, version 1.5. July.

Kountz, Edward (2000). *Wireless Technologies in Asian Financial Services: Business*

Trends and IT Spending. TowerGroup. Needham, MA. August.

Marcella, A.J. and Chan, S. (1993). *EDI Security, Control, and Audit.* Artech House, Norwood, MA., 212pp.

MasterCard International (2000). *Mastercard Delivers the Complete Chip Solution.* www.mastercard.com

Mondex (2001). How does it work? www.mondex.com

Mornan-Vaughan, S. and Smith, P. (2001). Digital money: have banks lost the plot? *"E-mmerce"*, vol. 2, issue 2, February/March 2001, pp 27-29.

NACHA Cross-Border Council Global ACH Working Group (1999). *Concept Paper for a Global Automated Clearing House*, Version 1.4. May. www.globalach.org

National Automated Clearing House Association (2000). *ACH Statistics Sheet – 1989-2000*, www.nacha.org/news/Stats/stats.html

OECD (2001). *Emerging Market Economy Forum on Electronic Commerce.* www.oecd.org/dsti/sti/it/ec/act/dubai_ec/

O'Mahony, D., Peirce, M. and Tewari, H. (1997). *Electronic Payment Systems.* Artech House, Norwood, MA., 254pp.

Schneier, B. (1996). *Applied Cryptography*, 2nd Edition. Wiley, New York, 758 pp.

UNCTAD (2000). *Building Confidence: Electronic Commerce and Development.* United Nations Publication, Sales No. E.00.II.D.16, 175pp.

University of Texas (2000). *The Internet and the Future of Financial Markets.*

Visa International (1999). *Visa, Nokia and MeritaNordbanken Group to Pilot Mobile Payment.* Visa Press Release, May, www-s2.visa.com/pd/eu_shop/presscentre/press_articles

WAP Forum (1998). *The Wireless Application Protocol Architecture Specification.* April, www.wapforum.org

WIPO (2000). Primer on Electronic Commerce and Intellectual Property Issues. May 2000, http://ecommerce.wipo.int

World Bank (2000). *Electronic Finance: Reshaping the Financial Landscape Around the World.* Financial Sector Discussion Paper No. 4. September, 26pp.

Wrona, K., and G., Zavagli (1999). *Adaptation of the SET Protocol to Mobile Networks and to the Wireless Application Protocol.* Proceedings of European Wireless'99. Munich, Germany, Oct. 1999, pp. 193-198.

Chapter 8

E-LOGISTICS: DELIVERING THE GOODS IN E-COMMERCE

A. Introduction

Logistics has been defined as "that part of the supply chain process that plans, implements, and controls the efficient, effective flow and storage of goods, services, and related information from the point of origin to the point of consumption, in order to meet customers' requirements".[1]

It is a broad subject that covers the following functions: production scheduling, order processing, transportation, demand management, warehousing, packaging, information technology, supply chain management, customer services, inventory control, import and export processing, documentation and insurance, payments, customs processing, inspection, returns processing, and implementation of related government regulations such as product and labeling standards, health and environmental protection.

It is clear, therefore, that a comprehensive treatment of the subject would require space beyond the scope of this report. Consequently, this chapter focuses on key issues in logistics that currently affect trading activities, particularly as a result of the Internet and the growth of electronic commerce.[2]

Logistics involves the management of information for the control of interrelated functions in the supply chain. Physical processes are employed to move goods, and information is used by the decisionmaker to control and optimize the physical processes. The central role of logistics in trading activities has been widely recognized. Similarly, the role of trade facilitation as support for logistics functions and trade processing in general has received much attention. In this connection, various initiatives have been taken by a number of organizations, such as UNCTAD, the United Nations Economic Commission for Europe, the World Customs Organization (WCO) and the World Trade Organization (WTO). These are described in section F.

Against this background, this chapter examines the interrelationships between the growth of electronic commerce and the requirements for logistics services, and the role played by technology in enabling service providers to meet the additional demands for logistics services that are imposed by electronic commerce. It outlines the role of order fulfilment in e-commerce (e-fulfilment),[3] the different types of logistics services (e-logistics)[4] and institutions that are emerging to address the critical problems of e-fulfilment and the role of technology and trade facilitation in enhancing logistics functions. It also examines the development of e-logistics in developing countries.[5] The discussion suggests that logistics services could be greatly enhanced through improvements in trade facilitation.

B. The implications of e-commerce for order fulfilment and logistics

The order fulfilment and logistics requirements for handling e-commerce are much greater than those in traditional trade. Traditional trade is associated with fragmented supply chains. Information tends to flow between individual pairs of parties in the supply chain without end-to-end visibility across the chain from producer to consumer. By contrast, e-commerce has given rise to greater integration of information and transactions between participants in the supply chain, leading to the creation of distribution networks in which all the participants can share information.

Apart from differences in information flows, traditional trade is dominated by the movement of large shipments in bulk consignments, often delivered to central distribution points for further distribution to retail stores. The shipments are identified by container or box or pallet or other unit of measurement by which they can be tracked or traced. Also, the demand for shipments tends to be stable and concentrated around a few large buyers and is therefore fairly predictable, and the order cycles tend to be relatively long.

In e-commerce, on the other hand, particularly in B2C trade, the number of buyers placing orders directly with producers or distributors tends to be much larger.[6] Consequently, the total volume of small shipments is much larger, and their origins and destinations are more widely dispersed, while their movements are more frequent and require direct delivery to the final consumer. Order cycles are relatively shorter and the demand for shipments is quite unpredictable and unstable because it arises from orders placed by larger numbers of buyers and a large number of sellers. This gives rise to increased scope for stock-outs and other factors that may cause sellers to fail to fulfil.

Returns tend to be higher in e-commerce than in traditional trade, requiring additional services to deal with them. The high incidence of returns arises from consumers receiving goods that are different from what they expected or ordered and is also due to the failure of the vendor to determine in advance the final landed price of the purchased goods. Online buyers tend to have higher expectations about their purchases. Given that goods can be searched and ordered quickly online, they expect that the information about the status of goods in the supply chain and their transportation and delivery can also be supplied quickly. Customer services thus tend to be responsive, flexible and individualized.

The main characteristics of logistics that are emerging or are expected to emerge as a result of e-commerce are summarized in box 13.

C. How e-fulfilment is handled

Companies that sell merchandise online use a variety of methods and channels to fulfil customers' orders. Three principal channels are used, namely the company handling the fulfilment itself, outsourcing the fulfilment function to third-party logistics service providers and use of drop-shipping.[7] Some companies use various combinations of these methods.

In-house fulfilment services have the advantage of giving the company full control of the fulfilment process and also over costs. They also enable a company to maintain direct relations with its customers and develop collaborative relations with them. However, in-house e-fulfilment involves considerable costs in terms of physical infrastructure and operations. Observers have suggested that where traditional brick-and-mortar companies have used their own distribution systems that had been designed to handle bulk

Box 13
Major characteristics of e-commerce that impose new requirements on logistics services

- Larger number of small parcels or packages due to a larger number of buyers making direct orders and a larger number of sellers than in traditional trade;
- Large numbers of on-line customers, mostly unknown to the sellers;
- Demand for shipments is much more unpredictable and unstable since it originates from more numerous customers;
- Origins and destinations of shipments are more widely dispersed, given that more buyers place direct orders with producers and distributors and more sellers access buyers globally;
- Accountability for shipments extends through the entire supply chain, compared with traditional logistics in which accountability is limited to single links of the supply chain;
- Customers have high expectations about quality of services and demand fast delivery of shipments;
- Higher incidence of cargoes returned to the supplier than in traditional trade;
- Greater demand for and availability of information covering transactions over entire supply chain, thus allowing on-line shipment tracking and other supply chain management functions;
- Greater focus on one-to-one marketing, which creates demand for customized delivery and post-transaction customer services;
- Greater complexity in fulfilling international orders than in traditional trade, thus preventing some retailers and service providers from being involved in international e-commerce;
- The emergence of demand for on-line processing of shipments, including cargo booking, bills of lading/airway bills, freight payment, rate quotation, landed price calculations and tariff management;
- Substantial increase in the volume of small shipments, leading to growth of demand for warehousing, transport and other logistics infrastructure that can handle larger volumes of small shipments;
- Greater scope for customer self-service.

orders, these have proved to be unsuitable for handling small shipments in e-commerce. For example, where a company originally shipped a product only by truckloads to distributors, migration to e-commerce would mean receiving orders from single consumers as well and thus entail the need to create packaging and delivery systems for less-than-truckload shipments. The problem relates not only to a mismatch of physical facilities but also to information transfer. In many cases, orders initiated online have had to be fulfilled using data fed manually into the supply chain and logistics systems, and this has caused considerable inefficiencies and delays.

The second method of e-fulfilment is to outsource the services to third-party logistics service providers. As will be shown later, many companies have established capability to provide logistics services to other companies. Outsourcing is considered to be particularly advantageous for pure-play dot.com companies and start-up companies that do not have experience, capital or the necessary physical infrastructure. It is also a useful method for well-established companies that wish to concentrate on their core businesses.

The third method - drop-shipping - is a fulfilment method whereby the retailer advertises products and, having received orders from customers, places orders for the same products with companies that undertake drop-shipping services. These may be manufacturers or distributors. The retailer tells the drop-shipper where to deliver the goods. He receives payment from the customer and his profit is the difference between what the customer pays for the goods and what the retailer pays to the drop-shipper as his part of the payment. The main advantage of this method for the retailer is that he does not need to make investments in merchandise inventory. Also, it protects the retailer from losses that may arise from goods that cannot be sold. Warehousing, packing and other shipping costs are also met by the drop-shipper. In addition, the method also allows a retailer to deal in a wide variety of goods since no inventory is involved. The retailer may arrange with the drop-shipper to place the retailer's logo on the packing list so that the customer knows where the product was purchased and repeat orders are thus ensured for the retailer.

Drop-shipping may present problems, however, with regard to returned merchandise, especially if a customer orders products that are drop-shipped from several sources, in which case the retailer becomes involved in handling returns and thus in activities in which, according to the method, he should not become involved. Another risk may arise from the fact that not all drop-shippers that fulfil the orders are equipped to deal with retail customer services. Moreover, the system may be unattractive to a customer who orders several products that are eventually shipped to him or her in multiple packages from different drop-shippers at different times. Not only the customer would incur high shipping costs because of the multiplicity of packages, but also the effort to track the shipments would also be greater than if the goods were to be shipped from the same source.

Some retailers employ other strategies, in addition to the three main methods outlined above. For example, some handle some logistics functions themselves but establish partnerships with service providers to deliver other services. For instance, the company could handle warehousing and inventory but make an arrangement with a transportation service provider with which it establishes an alliance to handle transportation, distribution or delivery.

Table 26
Main methods used by e-retailing companies to fulfil orders
(percentages)

Method of fulfillment	Pure-play e-tailers	Multi-channel e-tailers
From company facility	44.5	71.8
Drop-shipped from manufacturers or distributors	30.6	5.1
Outsourced to dedicated fulfillment sources	8.3	17.9
From facility operated by alliance or joint venture partner	8.3	2.6
Electronic fulfillment (e.g. software, information)	5.6	0.0
Other	2.7	2.6

Source: PricewaterhouseCoopers (2001).

Table 27
Methods used by e-retailing companies to handle different kinds of logistics functions
(percentages)

	Inventory warehousing	Picking/ packing	Shipping	Returns	Replenishment
Pure-play e-tailers					
Company handles	47.2	41.6	36.1	63.9	52.8
Outsourced to third party	41.7	44.4	47.2	22.2	25.0
Combination of company and third-party	8.4	11.2	13.9	13.7	16.7
Other methods	2.7	2.8	2.8	0.0	5.5
Multi-channel e-tailers					
Company handles	71.8	69.2	66.7	79.5	76.9
Outsourced to third party	20.5	20.5	23.1	12.8	12.8
Combination of company and third-party	5.1	7.7	7.7	5.2	7.7
Other methods	2.6	2.6	2.5	2.5	2.6

Source: PricewaterhouseCoopers (2001).

Surveys show that there are important differences between various types of online retailers regarding the extent to which they employ the different methods of order fulfilment.[8] They show, for example, that Internet-only or pure-play e-retailers tend to fulfil a large portion of their orders through outsourcing to third-party logistics providers and using drop-shipping. On the other hand, e-tailers that use multiple channels such as physical stores, catalogues and online (multi-channel e-tailers) tend to fulfil a large part of their orders using their own facilities. Table 26 illustrates the main approaches that e-tailers use to fulfil online orders. Table 27 gives a breakdown of logistics services and how different types of e-tailers handle them. These figures show a significant variation in order fulfilment models. In the final analysis, the choice of a model is a strategic decision that an enterprise has to make on the basis of consideration of cost and customer requirements.

D. Capabilities of software applications that support e-logistics

In section B, it was shown that e-commerce gives rise to new features in logistics and transport services that are more demanding than those imposed in traditional trade. These include the need to transact with a large number of disparate customers, the emergence of new business models and practices, an increased demand for higher service levels and a growing demand for collaboration between users and service providers along the supply chain. A major implication of these features is that traditional methods of handling information such as manual methods using e-mails, faxes and the telephone are not sufficient to meet the additional demands. It has therefore become imperative for companies to develop and apply more advanced web-based and other technologies that can automate transactions and also allow the exchange of data and information between different system applications.

Against this background, there has been an upsurge in the development of computer software applications capable of supporting a variety of logistics and transport services over the Internet.[9] These not only reduce the volume of paperwork, but also improve the overall productivity of logistics services and create considerable opportunities for firms to optimize functions over the supply chain. The importance of software applications for e-logistics is demonstrated by the considerable increases in sales of such software. It is estimated that in 2000 worldwide sales of software, hardware and services used in electronic logistics reached $277 billion, and they are expected to reach $1 trillion by 2005. In the United States alone e-logistics software sales are expected to increase from $8 billion in 2001 to $45 in 2004.[10] While these figures appear to be on the high side, they nevertheless provide a useful indication of the importance being attached to the issue of logistics in e-commerce.

This section briefly describes selected applications developed for various types of logistics functions[11].

1. Online order management

Order management applications enable users to perform online order entry, and provide real-time information on all customers and on products ordered in order to enable the seller to set priorities for order fulfilment. Some applications allow customers to specify their needs and requirements in order to allow for the delivery of customized products. The system interactively offers products that match the customer's requirements, and allows him or her to choose on a self-service basis. Some applications automate the allocation to buyers of products that are in short supply according to set criteria. Others make it possible for customers and suppliers to obtain visibility into the status of orders. This enables sellers to commit delivery dates and customers to know when to expect deliveries. Some applications are designed to enable order fulfilment in B2B, many-to-many transactions. They enable order capture from many sources and execute multiple source orders.

2. Shipment tracking

Users can track individual shipments or parcels while they are in transit, and the status of shipments is monitored as it changes at different points along the transport chain. Some applications monitor shipments and can alert the shipper if the shipment is moving behind schedule. Tracking capability requires the seller or shipper to link its website to the carrier's application systems. It enables all parties in the supply chain to share information and to better plan inventory, sales or production. Shipment tracking applications can also be used by a shipper to re-route shipments.

3. Equipment and vessels tracking

The movement and locations of transport equipment such as containers and vessels, trucks and cargo-carrying aircraft can be tracked and fed into shipment tracking. It also enables terminal, port and other facility operators to plan their operations based on real-time information about the location of the vessels, equipment, and so forth.

4. Transportation management and planning

Users can carry out transportation transactions on the Internet, such as freight rate management, freight bill payment and carrier selection. Carriers can optimize route determination and adjust transportation schedules on the basis of incoming orders. Some provide automatic assignment of manifests as shipments are being processed. Manifests are automatically printed on paper and users can transmit them automatically to carriers' billing systems. Others enable shippers to select carriers automatically on the basis of freight cost, transit times and other best-carrier criteria that are specified by the shipper. On the basis of the attributes of a shipment, some applications compute total freight cost, including discounts, additions and surcharges, assign a bill of lading number and remember to assign the same bill of lading number to shipments to be consolidated for delivery to the same consignee.

5. Landed cost calculation applications

These applications are mainly designed for international e-commerce transactions. They permit automatic calculation of the landed cost of a product when received by the consignee. The calculation takes into account information on trade regulations, customs tariffs, government taxes, insurance and transportation costs. To support the calculations, some applications also incorporate large databases on such information as most-favored-nation (MFN) tariffs and tariffs negotiated under bilateral or multilateral trade agreements and preferential agreements such as the Generalized System of Preferences (GSP). Some applications allow shippers to describe their products in plain language, and the software automatically matches the description to Harmonized System Tariff Schedule (HS) codes. Others enable exporters and importers to compare different landed prices automatically for different Incoterms, for example costs, insurance and freight (CIF) and free on board (FOB).

6. Online customer service management

Customer service (or customer relationship management) systems provide capabilities for communication and interaction between sellers, service providers and customers. Customers can access interactively customer service specialists directly and request help online. Responses can be given at virtual help desks. Sellers can contact customers to ask them if they need help. Vendors and service providers can post answers to frequently asked questions (FAQs) and thus provide a form of self-service to customers. Online discussion groups or chat rooms provide useful information to sellers and buyers. Some applications maintain the history of sold items by tracking the serial numbers of the items, contracts and warranty details, and records of after-sales services and agreements.

7. Collaborative logistics management systems

These allow supply chain participants to collaborate in various ways, for example to plan jointly their transport requirements and plans, and to share information on transport capacity availability and thus optimize their vessel scheduling. Participants can also tender for transport or other services. They can also offer customers, producers and suppliers complete visibility into demand data and fulfilment schedules. If exceptions occur that cannot be executed, the trading partners are notified automatically to allow them to quickly resolve the situation.

8. Customs clearance

Customs clearance and compliance applications permit online preparation of import/export documents and provide direct connection to customs services. They also generate automatically customs documents and distribute them to suppliers, buyers, shippers, carriers, freight forwarders and customs brokers. In addition, import data can be filed electronically in advance of the arrival of shipments, thus saving money by reducing the time that goods are held in Customs. Some applications can verify automatically whether imports and exports comply with different countries' trade laws, regulations and procedures, including embargo, boycotts and restricted products.

9. Returns management

A consumer wanting to return a product visits the customer service section of the retailer from whom the purchase was made. The customer selects options for returned products. The program guides the customer through a series of prompts and questions such as the reasons for wanting to return the product. The program may offer some troubleshooting tips if the product is being returned because it is defective. If the customer's decision to return the product is final, he or she is prompted to print a mailing label to effect the return.

10. Integrated all-in-one supply chain management

As opposed to stand-alone solutions designed for single functions, integrated applications attempt to handle multiple supply chain functions starting from the moment an order is placed until delivery to the final customer. A number of logistics companies, in partnership with technology companies, have attempted to develop such applications, although it would appear that integrated systems are not widespread.

11. Summary observations

A large number of software applications are being developed to handle different types of logistics functions. Some of them focus on one or a few functions. Some are designed for B2B transactions, while others are designed for B2C transactions or both. The tendency for software companies to develop differentiated systems, customized for different markets or users, may cause incompatibility between applications.

There is widespread agreement that the integration of software applications systems is essential in order to enable companies to optimize their supply chain functions. For example, automating warehousing and transportation or distribution systems using different systems that cannot exchange data may not bring about much improvement in inventory control. A study by Cap Gemini Ernst & Young found that 80 per cent of users of logistics services indicated that the integration of transportation and distribution systems was important for their overall business strategy[12].

Because of the critical need for the efficient transfer of instructions between different logistics systems, various types of solutions have been sought. The development of XML (Extensible Mark-up Language) is an example of possible solutions to the problem. XML creates formatted messages with metatags that describe the data being transmitted. The receiving system is therefore able to understand how to handle the message. Some logistics service providers have pioneered the creation of XML-based products that can support the integration of supply chain systems[13].

E. E-logistics service providers and outsourcing

There are two broad categories of logistics service providers, namely in-house providers and third-party logistics service providers (3PLs). An in-house logistics provider is a division or department within a company, usually asset-based, that provides such functions as transport, forwarding, warehousing, information technology or other types of logistics functions. A 3PL is an independent, stand-alone entity that is not part of a parent company for which it is supplying logistics functions. Its customers are outside the firm.

A 3PL can be asset-based, in that it owns a fleet of vessels or warehouses, or it can be non-asset-based. Asset-based 3PLs include major integrators such as DHL, FederalExpress and UPS, which play the role of carriers, forwarders and distributors. A distinct category of 3PLs is fulfilment houses and drop-shippers. The latter were described in section B. A fulfilment house stores the e-merchants' merchandise and takes responsibility for getting it to customers. The merchandise and the business are owned by the e-retailer while the fulfilment house provides warehousing, packing, shipping and delivery services. In certain cases its functions may extend to covering credit card processing, packing and order tracking. Fulfilment houses differ from integrators in that in the former case the merchant need not maintain in-house inventory while in the latter case the merchant would require to maintain inventory and carry out online fulfilment processes himself.

In recent years many companies have tended to use the services of more than one 3PL and it has become necessary to nominate a logistics service provider to coordinate the services of the other 3PLs, giving rise to the concept of fourth-party logistics service provider (4PL), also referred to as a lead logistics provider (LLP). A 4PL may also arise where a service provider supplies several services to a company and subcontracts some of them to other 3PLs.

Another group of logistics service providers that can be distinguished from the others are logistics or transport exchanges. These are B2B online market places or trading communities that facilitate trade in freight transportation services between buyers and sellers of such services. Members include shippers (manufacturers, distributors, retailers, 3PLs, freight forwarders and brokers) on the one hand, and carriers or transportation companies on the other. They have evolved from original carrier-shipper matching services into online communities for supply chain collaboration. They also include exchanges established by shippers in partnerships with other companies that function as their logistics service providers. These exchanges undertake such online functions as matching offers of carriers with requirements of shippers through auctions and automatic exchanges, providing price information, freight scheduling and tracking, managing contracts and freight payments, customs compliance and producing user-defined reports.

Another category of 3PLs is providers of logistics management applications. These companies do not provide direct logistics services, but they provide systems that support such functions as described in section D. In certain cases they operate in partnerships with other 3PLs such as integrators or carriers and in other cases they function as application service providers (ASPs). They may do so by hosting web-based logistics/transportation exchanges or providing solutions to buyers and sellers of logistics/ transportation services for their in-house logistics management.

1. Outsourcing of 3PLs

Outsourcing of logistics services was mentioned briefly in section C. It is one of the critical issues in current discussion of e-logistics services. Logistics services are witnessing a considerable expansion of 3PLs, primarily because companies, including e-merchants, prefer to outsource logistics functions. It is predicted that in the United States outsourcing of e-logistics will increase from $12 billion in 2000 to over $71 billion in 2004[14].

The remarkable growth of logistics outsourcing has been attributed to a number of factors[15]. Many companies have installed various types of applications to optimize their in-house logistics functions, and these applications are tending to become increasingly sophisticated and complex. Some companies are unable to cope with the changes and have responded by outsourcing the provision of the applications to specialized technology companies. In other cases, companies have simply not yet installed any logistics applications and outsourcing has been a convenient short cut.

A second factor is companies' desire to concentrate their resources and competencies on their core businesses. A third factor is the avoidance of sunk costs and risks, since outsourcing eliminates the need to incur costs on training logistics staff and acquiring warehouses, equipment and hardware. Fourth, for a start-up company or a company that is expanding quickly, outsourcing allows it to expand the volume of its business quickly with minimum investments, simply by relying on third-party facilities and services. Fifth, by providing services to several firms, 3PLs are in a position to develop large databases and other information that an outsourcing firm can access at lower cost than if it were to collect the same data itself.

Despite the promising benefits of outsourcing, companies still need to carry out a proper assessment of the scope and timing of outsourcing as well as the choice of 3PLs to which outsource. A company must compare the costs and advantages of providing logistics functions in-house with those of outsourcing.

F. E-logistics, e-fulfilment and trade facilitation

Section D outlined the capabilities of software applications in supporting e-logistics functions and e-fulfilment. In addition to the role played by technology, it is widely recognized that trade facilitation has a critical influence on the ability of traders to fulfil orders or deliver goods in e-commerce, especially in international transactions.[16] Furthermore, it could be suggested that even when suitable applications are employed to automate such functions as order management, warehousing, inventory and transport management, most of the benefits could fail to materialize if trade facilitation is inefficient.

Trade facilitation has been defined as the simplification and harmonization of international trade procedures that include activities, practices and formalities related to the collection, presentation, communication and processing of data required for the movement of goods in international trade.[17] It includes such functions as export and import formalities, customs clearance, payments and insurance. There has been widespread concern that in many countries trade facilitation is characterized by a host of inefficiencies that cause delays and high costs. It has been estimated, for example, that the global average of the cost of complying with procedures in international trade amounts to 7 to 10 per cent of the overall value of international trade.[18] Other estimates indicate that potential savings from more efficient information processing in international trade documentation in 1997 would have been of the order of $100 billion, or 30 per cent of the total overhead costs of international trade.[19]

The main problem areas include the following:[20]

1. The existence of a considerable number of documentation requirements, which include government documents, commercial documents and those relating to transportation. A particular international transaction may involve as many as 60 documents,[21] and most of the information they contain is the same. In addition, there is a lack of harmonization of documentation systems between countries and also between the private sector and government. All this contributes to high costs and to delays in processing trade and logistics functions.
2. Variations in the customs valuation of exports and imports, with customs valuation in many countries characterized by such problems as double invoicing and undervaluation, which make of the true value difficult.
3. Although the Harmonized System (HS) has made a considerable contribution in the classification and coding of commodities, some observers are of the opinion that the six-digit codes used in the HS are too broad and that new codes should be introduced gradually in order to provide more trade information. In this regard, the national tariffs of many countries are specified in greater detail beyond the six digits, which means that there is no harmony between the HS classification and the additional levels used in the individual countries.
4. Lack of harmonization of customs procedures and the existence of outdated trade procedures such as exchange controls, long retention of goods in customs custody and regulations that require paper documents.
5. Lack of transparency in many regulations, leading to an inability to predict costs and delivery times.
6. The existence of multiple transport liability regimes, including the Hague Rules, the Hague-Visby Rules, the Hamburg Rules and the United States Carriage of Goods by Sea Act (COGSA), leading to confusion as to which rules to apply in which trade.
7. Customs administrations that are poorly equipped as regards physical infrastructure and human resources, and also lack of cooperation between customs administrations of different countries. Many customs administrations are also prone to

corruption, which leads to delays, high costs and a distortion in trade information.

8. Limited use of automation and information technology in trade facilitation functions, leading to delays, high costs and inefficiencies.

There have been many initiatives and proposals aimed at improving trade facilitation. The following are a few illustrative examples.[22] At the international level, the World Symposium on Trade Efficiency, held in 1994, provided an impetus for efforts to improve trade processing. Linked to the Symposium, the UNCTAD trade efficiency initiative is an example of a programme aimed at addressing problems of logistics in a wider context by promoting the application of information and communication technologies (ICTs) to trade. This is a broad-based initiative focused on simplifying and harmonizing trade procedures worldwide by allowing traders, especially small and medium-sized enterprises (SMEs), access to advanced ICTs.[23] A practical application of this initiative is the ASYCUDA programme, which is widely used by developing countries. This is a computerized customs management system that handles various trade procedures such as manifests, customs declarations and accounting, and utilizes international codes developed by the WCO and the United Nations.[24]

Another development is the revision of the Kyoto Convention, now known as the International Convention on the Simplification and Harmonization of Customs Procedures (as amended), which has been agreed by the WCO. It will come into force when it has been ratified by 40 WCO members.[25] It is expected that the adoption and implementation of the revised Convention by a large number of countries will go a long way to minimizing existing trade facilitation obstacles.

The WTO has included trade facilitation on its agenda. The key issues concerned were articulated at the Trade Facilitation Symposium organized by the WTO in 1998. The symposium covered a wide range of issues, including documentation requirements, official procedures, automation and use of information technology, transparency, predictability and consistency, and modernization of border-crossing administration. A number of areas related to trade facilitation are covered by WTO agreements and the symposium proposed improvements in certain of the rules as well as the incorporation of additional rules on trade facilitation.

As a follow-up to the UNCTAD trade efficiency initiative, the G7 have adopted the G7 Initiative, which is a scheme intended to use export declaration data to process import consignments. It is based on the premise that export declaration data could be used to clear consignments for imports. This would facilitate the movement of goods across borders and would be a step towards the ideal of seamless international trade transactions in which trade participants would supply their information only once and export data and information would equal imports. This ideal could only be realized, however, if all government customs requirements could be simplified and harmonized and the transmission of trade information based on internationally agreed standards.[26] The G7 Initiative is to be applied in international trade transactions between the G7 countries.

A project closely linked to the G7 Initiative is the International Trade Prototype (ITP) project developed jointly by the United Kingdom and the United States customs administrations. The development of the ITP was based on several goals and principles, including the automation and exchange of standardized information that would be agreed by the two countries. Furthermore, it attempted to streamline government reporting requirements in trade transactions and to develop harmonized and simplified messages and procedures that reduce the need for redundant entry or transmission of data. A key element of the ITP is similar to the G7 Initiative, namely developing a process in which data provided for export declaration to the export customs administration are forwarded to the import customs administration and used to process import entry and clearance in the country of destination. The ITP project and the G7 Initiative were merged in 2000.

G. E-logistics in developing countries

The growth of e-logistics is highly correlated with the growth of e-commerce. Consequently, e-logistics and e-fulfilment activities have developed to a much greater degree in developed countries than in developing ones. There is nevertheless scope for the development and growth of these activities in developing countries as well. This section outlines areas in which such countries can exploit available or potential opportunities. These include access to global e-logistics services, participation in Internet-based transportation/logistics exchanges and applying available technologies to B2B transactions in various transportation/logistics services in the developing countries themselves.

1. Access to global e-logistics services

In section II it was pointed out that in e-commerce there is a large volume of small shipments and the deliveries are global. The transportation and distribution of such shipments, both for B2C and B2B transactions, tend to be dominated by global express delivery companies such as DHL, Federal Express and UPS. These companies provide services on a global scale, covering practically all parts of the world, including developing countries. Consequently, shippers are able to use such companies to send shipments to any destination with the frequency and speed that buyers require. A number of service providers offer merchants free online downloads of software from their websites in order to allow them to benefit from tracking, tracing and other logistics functionality and also to integrate their back-end systems with those of the logistics service provider. Also, some developing countries have established firms that provide e-logistics services that shippers can use.

A number of developing country e-commerce sellers are making use of the services of the global logistics service providers to sell in global markets.[27] However, the main constraint relating to these services is the high shipping costs charged. Sellers are able to rely on such service providers if they deal in high-value merchandise.

2. Participation in Internet-based logistics and transportation exchanges

As outlined in section V, logistics/transportation exchanges provide a forum in which service providers and users can conduct transactions.[28] Being Internet-based, in principle any service provider or user should be able to browse the net in order to offer or buy a service and fulfil online the required contractual transactions. The extent to which service providers and users make use of these exchanges, even in the developed countries, has not been well documented. Furthermore, except for the charter of whole vessels, the offers and bids made on the exchanges are in relation to specific trade routes, which may not cover many developing countries. Therefore, overall, the true potential of the exchanges for developing countries has yet to be established.

3. Application of logistics technologies in B2B transactions in the developing countries

Section IV described a variety of technology applications that are being developed or used in providing e-logistics services. Such technologies are made accessible to users in different ways, such as outright purchase from technology developers or vendors, commercial partnerships between technology companies and users, application service providers hosting and servicing the users' websites, or through 3PLs.

Information about the costs of developing or purchasing various types of e-logistics software and applications is not readily available. It suffices to note, however, the growing tendency, even in the developed countries, for logistics companies to rely on 3PLs and partnerships with technology companies as an indication of the high cost and skills requirements involved in the purchase and maintenance of the applications. Outright purchase or in-house ownership would therefore not appear to be a feasible option for logistics companies in developing countries except perhaps for basic applications.

The second option, namely commercial partnerships between logistics service providers and technology companies, is likely to succeed where the user of the application generates sufficient revenues to compensate for the costs incurred by the technology company. A similar condition would apply in the case of an ASP or 3PL arrangement. In principle, any service provider in a developing country that has the requisite volume of services should be in a position to attract partnership with a technology company or be able to engage the services of 3PLs.

Access to technology, however, need not be through direct business affiliation between logistics service providers and technology companies. Instead, a logistics service provider in a developing country could establish a partnership with a service provider in a developed country that already possesses or has access to the required technology. For example, a number of developing country airlines have established alliances with major airlines of developed countries and through such alliances they benefit from a wide range of the latest technologies in the industry.

In addition to accessing technology through commercial partnerships, developing countries may benefit from technical cooperation programmes with multilateral organizations or bilateral donors. Examples of such programmes include the Advance Cargo Information System (ACIS) and the Automated System for Customs Data (ASYCUDA), both of which incorporate elements of e-logistics systems. ACIS is a logistics information system that provides capability to track cargo and equipment of various transportation modes such as rail, road and lake and at interfaces such as ports and inland clearance depots. It is administered by UNCTAD and is being implemented in a number of developing countries.[29] ASYCUDA, on the other hand, is a programme designed to modernize customs, including the automation of customs processes and procedures. It uses information technology to accelerate customs clearance by simplifying documentation. This programme is also administered by UNCTAD and the system has been introduced into a large number of countries.[30] It is an open system that links to traders and carriers, allowing them to perform their customs operations directly.

H. Conclusions and recommendations

Logistics is a broad subject encompassing many activities, and this chapter has dealt with only certain key logistics issues of the day. Electronic commerce is imposing additional requirements on logistics services, but the growth of e-logistics has lagged behind the rapid growth of e-commerce. Logistics service providers have attempted to accommodate the increasing demands by trying to adapt their existing systems and by using 3PLs.

E-logistics services are being provided by in-house departments and 3PLs. There has been a remarkable growth of 3PLs as companies have tried to outsource many of their e-logistics services. While outsourcing is based on a number of sound economic reasons, companies still need to make a proper evaluation of its feasibility for their particular case.

Technology and software applications play a central role in supporting e-logistics services in handling the complex and demanding business models that are emerging. Logistics and transport service providers, supported by technology companies, are making concerted efforts to automate logistics functions in order to cope with the ever-increasing demands of e-commerce.

The development of differing applications to meet the requirements of specific users and functions is a source of incompatibility between applications, even within the same company. There is a critical demand for the integration of systems to ensure that instructions can be efficiently exchanged between different types of logistics applications.

Another impediment to efficient e-logistics is poor trade facilitation. Costly and slow movements of goods in international trade transactions are caused by excessive and unnecessary documentation requirements and official procedures, the lack of adequate automation and of use of information technology, the lack of transparency and predictability in trade processing, and the existence of inefficient and uncoordinated cross-border administration services, especially customs. A large number of international and regional organizations as well as commercial institutions are implementing a variety of measures to improve trade facilitation.

To achieve more efficient e-logistics and e-fulfilment, it is desirable to have a trading environment in which there is perfect information about goods as regards their description, origins and destinations, and costs for different origins and destinations. Sellers and buyers should be able to monitor and track goods at every point along the way from the supplier to the consumer. All stakeholders should be able to check on the Internet the availability and status of orders. All this can be achieved if trade information is simplified, automated and fully harmonized in all countries, and all restrictive government export/import regulations and practices are eliminated. It also requires sophisticated supply chain management systems for compiling and enabling global end-to-end monitoring of trade information.

To achieve these broad objectives and also to take into account the special problems of developing countries, it is recommended that Governments, the international community and the private sector cooperate in promoting the following specific measures:

1. Taking advantage of the great potential provided by Internet technology in order to capture, transfer and monitor trade information over global networks of supply chains in an open fashion;
2. Automating customs declaration systems in order to develop customs-to-customs information exchange and thereby provide a basis for the

elimination of unnecessary export/import requirements, which can instead be replaced by fully integrated international transactions;

3. Harmonizing and improving the classification of commodity tariffs, and facilitating the identification of individual consignments;
4. Providing investment resources especially for customs administrations in order to upgrade their efficiency;
5. Harmonizing and simplifying trade facilitation regulations and procedures, and in particular encouraging greater harmonization of customs procedures through the wide adoption and implementation of the revised Kyoto Convention on the Simplification and Harmonization of Customs Procedures;
6. Promoting cooperation between authorities of exporting and importing countries in order to provide verification and compatibility in trade information. In this context, the International Trade Prototype (ITP) project developed by the United Kingdom and the United States customs administrations could provide a model to be developed at the international level. The international community should give support to further development of the project;
7. Encouraging greater transparency in trade processing activities and taking measures to reduce corruption and other forms of malpractice in customs administration;
8. Promoting partnerships between developing country logistics service providers and developed country logistics service providers that are applying e-logistics systems;
9. Providing technical cooperation programmes to developing countries for the promotion of services that support e-logistics, for example in customs, transportation services, cargo terminals and related services.

Notes

1 Definition adopted by the Council of Logistics Management, http://www.clm.org/mission/logistics.asp.

2 Other dimensions of logistics may be covered in future issues of this report.

3 E-fulfilment can broadly be defined as everything that takes place, in electronic commerce transactions, from the time an order is taken to the time the product is received by the customer.

4 E-logistics is the application of logistics processes to the fulfilment of electronic commerce transactions. It applied to business-to-business (B2B) e-commerce as well as business-to-consumer (B2C) e-commerce. E-logistics differs from conventional or tradtional logistics in that it attempts to satisfy the expectations and requirements of merchants and customers engaged in e-commerce as outlined in table 26. Also, in e-logistics there is more collaboration and sharing of data and information across the supply chain between providers and users of logistics services.

5 Some of the elements discussed in this chapter were reflected in UNCTAD (2000).

6 In B2B e-commerce, while the buyers may be large, some shipments may be small packages. The majority of shipments, however, tend to be larger, palletized, less-than-truckload shipments.

7 For an extended discussion of alternative methods of e-fulfilment, see, for example, PricewaterhouseCoopers (2001).

8 See PricewaterhouseCoopers (2001).

9 It is worth noting that the demand for automated logistics applications existed even in traditional trade. However, e-commerce has undoubtedly spurred the development of new and more powerful applications.

10 See Coleman (2001).

11 For an extended description of the various applications outlined here, see, for example, Bayles (2001), Buxbaum (2001),Tariffc.com, Xporta.com, mycustoms.com, borderfree.com, ClearCross.com, Nextlinc.com, From2.com, Vastera.com, UPS.com, DHL.com, AirborneExpress.com, FederalExpress.com,EmeryWorld.com, Yantra.com and Optum.com.

12 See Cap Gemini Ernst & Young (2000).

13 For a discussion of XML, see UNCTAD (2000) and Bayles (2001).

14 See Buxbaum (2001).

15 For an extended discussion, see Amami and Marelli (1996).

16 While e-commerce relates to both domestic and international transactions, the main issues of trade facilitation concern cross-border trade.

17 See World Trade Organization (2000).

18 See United Kingdom Department of Trade and Industry (2000).

19 Crowhurst (2000)

20 For an extensive discussion of the problems of trade facilitation, see World Trade Organization (1998a, 1998b)

21 See World Trade Organization (1998b).

22 For a description of trade facilitation activities undertaken by various organizations, see World Trade Organization (1997, 1998c) and SITPRO (1998/9).

23 See Columbus Ministerial Declaration on Trade Efficiency (1994).

24 See World Trade Organization (1997, 1998c).

25 See International Convention on the Simplification and Harmonization of Customs Procedures (as amended), http://www.wcoomd.org/ie/Eng/Conventions/Conventions.html.

26 See United States Department of the Treasury (1999).

27 Some of the case studies of e-commerce in LDCs presented in chapter x of this report provide examples of such sellers.

28 The buying and selling of transportation/logistics services is to be distinguished from online buying and selling of goods that are shipped and delivered using the transportation/logistics services.

29 See ACIS, wysiwyg://21/http://www.untad.org/en/techcop/tra0105.htm.

30 See ASYCUDA, http://www.asycuda.org/aboutas.htm.

References and bibliography

Amami, M. and Marelli, M. (1996). *Business Logistics Outsourcing and Inter-organizational Electronic Networks.*

Armstrong and Associates, Inc. (2000). *Who's Who in Logistics: Guide to 3PLs and Global Logistics Services*, ninth edition, Stoughton, WI, U.S.A. Armstrong and Associates, Inc.

Bayles, D. (2001). *E-commerce Logistics and Fulfilment: Delivering the Goods*, Upper Saddle River, NJ, U.S.A.,Prentice Hall PRT.

Buxbaum, P. (2001) *Digital Logistics: Value Creation in the Freight Transport Industry*, First Conferences Ltd., Eyefortransport, www.eyefortransport.com/lasvegas2000/.

Cap Gemini Ernst & Young (2000). *Third Party Logistics Services: Views from the Customers, University of Tennesee, United States.*

Coke, J. (2000). "Who does the best job of e-fulfilment", *Logistics Online, Logistics Management and Distribution Report*, 11 January, www.manufacturing.net/magazine/logistic/archives/2000/1.../1m1100efulfilment.ht.

Coleman, M. (2001). "Software gets its hands dirty", *Investors' Business Daily*, 5 January.

Columbus Ministerial Declaration on Trade Efficiency (1994), http://sunsite.wits.ac.za/untpdc/tei/columbus.html.

Crowhurst, R. (2000). "Trade facilitation: Reducing the economic frictions that get in the way of trading across borders", SITPRONews, July.

Damas, P. (2001). "Building e-logistics networks", *American Shipper*, April, pp. 15-20.

Kapsinow, S. (1999). "Using fulfilment services for e-commerce", *Ecommerce Guide*, 15 April, http://www.internet.com.

McCullough, S. et al. (1999). *Mastering Logistics*, Cambridge, MA. U.S.A. Forrester Research, Inc.

Poirier, C. (1999). *Advanced Supply Chain Management: How to Build a Sustained Competitive Advantage,* San Francisco, Berret-Koehler Publishers, Inc.

PricewaterhouseCoopers (2001). E-fulfilment*: A long last mile*, Columbus, OH, U.S.A., January.

Shelton, B. (1999). "Building customer loyalty on the web", *Ecomworld*, 1 March.

SITPRO (1998/9). *SITPRO Annual Report 1998/9, The Trade Facilitation Year*, http://www.sitpro.org.uk/annual/ar1998-9/pg6a.html.

United Kingdom Department of Trade and Industry (2000*). World Trade and International Trade Rules*, http://www.dti.gov.uk/worldtrade/facilitation.htm.

UNCTAD (2000) Building Confidence: Electronic Commerce and Development. United Nations Publication, Sales No. E.00II.D.16.

United States Department of the Treasury (1999). *U.S. Customs Service, Announcement of a General Test Regarding the International Trade Prototype*, http://www.customs.ustraes.gov/news/fed-reg/notices/fr071999.htm.

World Trade Organization (1997). *WTO Council for Trade in Goods, Trade Facilitation: Background Note by the Secretariat*, C/CW/80, 2 June.

World Trade Organization (1998a). *WTO Trade Facilitation Symposium: Report by the Secretariat*, March.

World Trade Organization (1998b). *Checklist of issues raised during the WTO Trade Facilitation Symposium*, G/C/W/113, 20 April.

World Trade Organization (1998c). *WTO Council for Trade in Goods, Trade Facilitation: Update of Background Note G/C/W/80*, Addendum, 2 December.

World Trade Organization (2000)

Part Four

Experiences and Opportunities

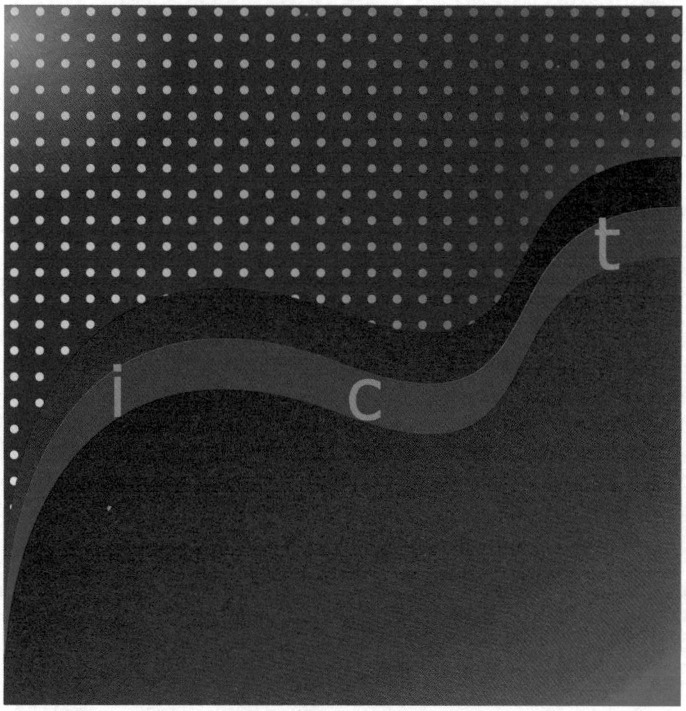

Chapter 9
E-COMMERCE IN THE LEAST DEVELOPED COUNTRIES

A. Introduction

A survey of ten least developed countries (LDCs) was conducted by UNCTAD in preparation for the Third United Nations Conference on the LDCs (Brussels, Belgium, 14-20 May 2001). The purpose of this survey was to identify:

- Enterprises that have successfully applied e-commerce strategies in their business operations;
- Potential business opportunities resulting from the World Wide Web and web-enabled technologies;
- Partners (governmental and non-governmental institutions) that are currently promoting and/or supporting e-commerce initiatives at the enterprise level.

The countries visited were Bangladesh, Cambodia, Ethiopia, Madagascar, Mozambique, Myanmar, Nepal, Togo, Uganda and the United Republic of Tanzania.

The focus of this chapter is on *enterprises* located in LDCs. It recognizes, but does not address important macro issues such as the responsibility of LDC Governments to ensure that civil society is not marginalized by developments in e-commerce, the global information society and the Internet.

A number of enterprises were identified, of which the best 16 cases were selected.[1] Nine enterprises were classified as business-to-business examples (teleservicing[2]) and seven were classified as business-to-consumer examples. The criteria used to identify successful stories included the potential market size, the sustainable competitive advantage, the qualified management and the replicability of the business model.

The biggest challenge facing LDC enterprises is not the technology aspect of e-commerce, but dealing with the business culture and practice changes that will be required within the enterprises in order for them to successfully adopt an e-commerce strategy.

B. Survey findings

Information was gathered via desk research and country visits. Visits lasted on average three days per country. Key people and organizations were identified in each of the countries to assist in identifying e-commerce-active enterprises. Recognized opinion leaders, including business leaders, Internet-service-related business leaders, academics and government officials, were interviewed to obtain an overall picture of the general e-commerce situation in a country.

1. Findings at the country level

The following findings refer only to the LDCs surveyed. The general findings (at the country level) are categorized under the following:

- The physical e-commerce infrastructure which addresses the physical environment needed for an enterprise to carry out an e-commerce strategy. This would include Internet-related services, telecommunications and electronic payment systems;
- The policy and regulatory environment which addresses those policies or regulations which most hinder enterprises from engaging in e-commerce.
- Institutional and human resources which address the national skills base and resource and development capabilities necessary for enterprises engaging in e-commerce strategies.

Information supporting the findings in this section can be found in the Annex, which is a report on selected LDCs.

(a) Physical e-commerce infrastructure

From the enterprise point of view, Internet access is available in all countries surveyed, albeit in a very restricted manner in Myanmar. The quality of Internet access (in terms of number, reliability, capacity, cost and range of services of Internet Service Providers (ISPs)) ranges from very good in cities such as Dhaka, Kampala and Dar-es-Salaam (offering a range of wireless options) to very poor in Addis Ababa and Yangon (prohibitions, long waiting lists, low bandwidth, and high cost).

The availability and the quality of telecommunications have improved dramatically in LDCs. Most enterprises located in urban areas now have access to some form of telecommunication, either a fixed line or a wireless line. The quality and reliability of telecommunications varies between the countries surveyed and between cities and rural areas. Enterprises in Kampala will soon have access to fibre optic telecommunication links, whereas Dhaka still has problems with regular downtimes and low bandwidth.

Most countries surveyed reported relatively high local telecommunications costs (from $10c per minute), with the exception of Ethiopia. This has an impact on use of Internet, as most Internet connections are dial-ups.

There is a correlation, in terms of availability and quality of Internet access, between those countries that have liberalized their Internet access and those that have not. Myanmar and Ethiopia have not issued private ISP licences and as a result have a very poor Internet infrastructure.

All the countries surveyed still rely on Very Small Aperture Terminal (VSAT) gateways. This situation impacts on international bandwidth costs and entails the risk of down time, putting them at a disadvantage in relation to developing and developed countries.

The proliferation of privately owned Internet cafes has surprised many; it provides a viable access option for those enterprises/individuals that do not have their own computers and telecommunications access. Kathmandu (Nepal) has over 1,000 Internet cafes, possibly because of tourism. However, even cities not known as tourist destinations are experiencing growth in this area, for example Lomé (300), Dar-es-Salaam (100), Dhaka (50), Kampala (25) and Maputo (10). The popularity of Internet cafes appears to be unrelated to the cost or quality of ISP services but rather to a greater or lesser awareness on the part of the general public regarding the Internet and its benefits. Most people visiting Internet cafes use the service for e-mail and surfing for news and entertainment.

Most countries surveyed have Global System for Mobile Communications (GSM) cellular networks, and in some cases, more than one operator (i.e. Bangladesh, Uganda, United Republic of Tanzania). Ethiopia and Mozambique have only one State operator. The presence of GSM networks is important for e-commerce because of the number of e-commerce applications now available that can be carried by such networks.

Those countries with more than one mobile operator have benefited from the resulting competitiveness. Mobile operators have built networks covering large parts of the country, reduced call costs, made access easier for the wider population by offering prepaid options, and provided access to subsidized handsets. These product offerings have resulted in unexpected subscriber numbers in excess of 150,000 in countries such us Bangladesh, Uganda and the United Republic of Tanzania.

Joint ventures between ISPs and cellular operators are being set up, enabling ISPs to establish points of presence (POPs) in rural areas. CyberTwiga (ISP) and Mobitel (a cellular operator) in the United Republic of Tanzania have entered into such a relationship.

The banking infrastructure in the LDCs surveyed is not conducive to e-commerce. Most banks are not electronically interlinked, nor even the branches of the same bank. None of the countries surveyed had a national electronic payments clearing system. There are isolated examples of online banking (one bank in Mozambique) and the use of smart cards (one bank in Uganda).

Owing to the lack of a local credit management infrastructure, none of the banks surveyed issue credit cards (not even multinational banks located in LDCs) and very few businesses (usually only hotels and tourist-oriented shops) can accept credit card payments.

(b) Policy and regulation

The LDCs visited, with the exception of Ethiopia and Myanmar, are at various stages in the liberalization of their telecommunications environment, some are in the process of privatizing their State telecommunications company (Mozambique and the United Republic of Tanzania), others have issued second and third private fixed-line licences (i.e. Uganda and Bangladesh), and most have issued private ISP licences.

Some of the countries visited, including Uganda, the United Republic of Tanzania, Bangladesh and Togo, allow private VSAT licences enabling ISPs to purchase their own bandwidth from international satellites. VSAT licences are limited, however, to data traffic.

None of the LDCs visited, with the exception of Togo, allow voice-over IP (Internet telephony). Policing, however, is lax in countries such as Nepal, where IP services are openly offered at Internet cafes.

None of the LDCs visited have an e-commerce policy in place. Bangladesh is at an advanced stage in developing an information technology (IT) policy. Others are at early stages in their e-commerce strategies and IT policy development. None have an e-commerce law as yet (relating to the legalization of digital signatures, cyber crime, protection of databases, copyright issues, etc.)

All LDCs visited have varying degrees of foreign exchange and banking regulations in place which impact on the flexibility of e-commerce strategies aimed at international markets. These include, for example, restricting access to foreign e-commerce-related support services and the holding of foreign bank accounts, and not being able to ship without traditional payment assurances in place, i.e. letters of credit. Other prohibitions, for example on the use of encryption technologies, will impact on the viability of electronic banking and the use of smart cards etc.

(c) Institutional and human resources

Many of the national universities of the countries visited had paid some attention to Internet, IT and e-commerce issues. Initiatives related to IT and e-commerce were found in universities in the United Republic of Tanzania, Uganda, Bangladesh and Ethiopia. Most universities were active in advising government at a policy level.

All the above-mentioned universities have computer science faculties. Bangladesh appears to be by far the most advanced in producing computer science graduates (around 1,300 a year).

The United Republic of Tanzania, Bangladesh and Nepal have a plethora of private colleges offering courses teaching computer skills, web development and programming. Bangladesh produces around 10,000 IT-related graduates per year. This level of skills development is less apparent in the other LDCs, possibly owing to a low local demand for these types of skills and to low levels of awareness of opportunities in this field.

With the exception of Bangladesh and possibly Nepal, the LDCs visited have almost no capacity to develop software. Bangladesh sees software development as a major focus area for future export industries (over 62 software development enterprises are listed in a local association, 10 of which are already servicing international clients).

2. Findings at enterprise level

(a) Business-to-consumer e-commerce examples (international)[3]

Almost all the identified enterprises selling a product or service online were business to ***unique consumer*** e-commerce models. All focused on online selling to a small niche market located in industrialized countries. Examples include Ethiogift.com (Ethiopia) and Munshigi.com (Bangladesh), which market the concept of non-resident Ethiopians or Bangladeshis buying gifts online (sheep, flowers etc.) to be delivered to relatives or friends living at home. Of the 16 enterprises chosen as success stories, seven were classified as business-to-consumer examples. Of those, six were focused on small niche markets such as the diaspora market.

Other examples of unique offerings include enterprises selling traditional textiles, garments, music, food etc. to their respective diasporas living abroad, or to small niche markets. Examples include LifeinAfrica.com (Uganda) selling traditional cloth to African-Americans and promoting African culture, and SimplyAfrican.com (owned by Raha.com, United Republic of Tanzania) selling high-quality African art to art lovers in the United States.

The average annual turnovers of enterprises servicing the diaspora community or small niche markets are between $2,000 and $30,000 a year. Their net profits are low because a large portion of the sales price goes to the original producer and to delivery and payment charges.

Although there is clearly a business model in pursuing unique markets such as the diaspora market, it is limited. Funds transferred from non-residents to their family each year provide an indication of the potential size of the diaspora market. For example, approximately $100 million is transferred home each year by non-resident Ethiopians to support their families. A small percentage of this money is sent to purchase products from home.

Success has come to those LDC enterprises that have been able over a period of time to develop a consumer trust, by creating a loyal subscriber base (i.e. Lifeinafrica.com), offering information about home (i.e. Radio One (United Republic of Tanzania), Simba Radio (Uganda), *The Addis Tribune* (Ethiopia)),[4] or by developing an agent network in the target market (i.e. Ethiogift has a network of Ethiopian restaurants assisting in selling, or facilitating sales and distributing marketing literature).

Enterprises selling products to overseas markets have to charge high delivery costs and provide for longer delivery times. Most rely on local producers who sometimes prove unreliable with regard to delivery and consistency of quality. In order to protect their online reputation, these enterprises have to keep large quantities of stock. Although their international markets are small and niche, they are widely spread, and this makes it difficult to arrange bulk order deliveries; consequently, shipping is a large component of the end price.

The low turnovers of these enterprises limit what they are able to spend on marketing, and consequently they have to rely heavily on word of mouth or advertising and presence on news/information portals. Some news sites (Newafrica.com) claim visitor numbers in the region of 80,000 hits per month. This reflects the hunger of the respective diasporas for information about home; for example, Simba Radio (Uganda) has registered thousands of visitors per week as receiving its audio streaming, mainly from the United States). These portals therefore provide an opportunity to expose appropriate products to a highly targeted online community.

Business-to-consumer e-commerce (international) is an interesting option for medium-sized manufacturing exporters in LDCs, yet only one enterprise was found to be successfully applying an e-commerce strategy, namely Genuine Leather Craft (GLC) of Ethiopia. In the case of GLC, the idea of marketing leather garments directly to the end consumer came as a result of difficulties in getting the support of agents based in the major markets, who preferred suppliers from more established supplier countries (Italy, Turkey and Pakistan). Up to 40 per cent of GLC's sales are now from online orders from consumers around the world, many of which are repeat orders.

Manufacturers wanting to apply business-to-consumer models (i.e. selling directly to the end consumer in a foreign market) have faced a number of hurdles. These include becoming known to their target market, creating consumer trust (these enterprises are not internationally known brands), constantly changing freight charges, trade regulations, and high payment (credit card) commissions. GLC indicated that it did not have the expertise to develop its own online strategy in terms of marketing, website development and back-end processing.

Online businesses selling to international consumers face regulatory problems in countries with exchange controls, particularly those that require proof of payment prior to shipment, or payment before shipment. Export/import regulations may prevent the return and replacement of defective goods. Lengthy customs procedures for exports can also impact on customer service and delivery promises.

All identified business-to-consumer models based in LDCs have their websites hosted in the United States, Canada or another developed country, mainly because credit card payment options can be offered. Other reasons include cheaper and better-quality hosting services, regarding for example website performance and listing.

Obstacles identified by LDC enterprises engaged in online business-to-consumer models include the high costs involved in developing a quality website and acquiring online clients, expensive fulfilment costs, problematic online payment issues, exclusivity of distribution channels and the lack of a domestic market.

(b) Business-to-business e-commerce examples (international)[5]

The business-to-business e-commerce model is the most important form of e-commerce in terms of value. Experts agree that more than 80 per cent of e-commerce transactions will be those between businesses. This percentage will be even higher in LDCs (probably above 90 per cent), particularly if international business is involved, as local business-to-consumer e-commerce is unlikely to reach any significant levels. In that framework, teleservices represent enormous opportunities, mainly because of the huge difference in wages between LDCs (as low as $20 per month but around $500 for highly qualified individuals) and developed countries (from $2,000 to $10,000 per month for similar activities).

A "teleservice" can be defined as a "service which can be executed from a remote location using web enabling technologies". Examples of online and offline teleservices are translation, data scrubbing, copy editing, medical transcriptions, data input, creation of customized marketing databases, creation of (simple) websites, scanning (i.e. digitalization of print documents), call centres, follow-up marketing calls and remote surveillance.

Online teleservices can be divided into interactive and non-interactive. Interactive online services involve real-time involvement by the contracted party. Examples of these types of services include call centres handling airline reservations, telemarketing and after-sales support. Some of these services are being outsourced by large corporations and often to call centres outside the country. The low-cost Internet telephony now allows call centres to be established in a country other than that of the target audience, provided that the call centre, for example situated in an LDC, has reliable low-cost high-bandwidth connections. A report by the Economic Commission for Africa[6] has identified a call centre project in Togo (Café Informatique[7]) which provides call centre services over the Internet for clients based in the United States. The attraction of locations such as Togo is the significant human resource cost advantages. The Café Informatique has secured a pilot contract with a major United States telephone company to update telephone directories. The centre employs over 50 operators. Although an attractive opportunity, online teleservicing has substantial barriers. There are relatively high start-up costs for equipment and high training costs, and the company must have the capacity in place before trying to win a contract. Online contracts often involve 24-hour operations and the skills required are difficult to develop as they involve teaching people not only language but also new cultures and behaviours.

Online non-interactive services include Internet radio stations, or Internet sports sites which provide downloadable but recent news on sports events. Radio Simba[8] could be classified in this category, except that at this stage it is not charging recipients for the service.

Far more attractive options for LDC enterprises are the various forms of offline teleservicing. These include transcription services, data input, software development, remote access server maintenance, web development, creation of databases, digitization of old documents (i.e. architectural drawings), translations and editing. Technosoft Transcription of Bangladesh is contracted to medical practitioners in the United States to transcribe audio patient record files into text. The indications are that this area of teleservicing is a multimillion-dollar industry. Bangladesh believes, on the basis of Indian projections, that if it could capture 5 per cent of the Indian projection, it could generate revenues in excess of $300 million per year.[9] Other types of transcription and data input such as legal transcripting provide similar opportunities.

Offline teleservicing generally involves lower start-up costs. Since operations do not have to be "live", management has the opportunity to intercept poor-quality work prior to delivery. Doticom Services,[10] a four-person company in Uganda, was able to win a contract to input data from scanned invoices into an accounting package for an auditing firm in Canada without a large initial investment.

Offline teleservices offer talented individuals living in LDCs an opportunity to do work for companies based in developed countries. For example, an enterprise in the developed world requires desk-top publishing services for a document. The document is sent by e-mail to the contracted person, who could be situated in any LDC provided that he or she has Internet connectivity. The person works on the document and, once finished, sends it back to the enterprise by e-mail. These services are referred to as offline, as the work is done offline, and only when it has been completed, does the person go online to send it to the customer. Companies in developed economies will increasingly secure these types of services in low-labour-cost countries. The report by the Economic Commission for Africa on electronic commerce in Africa, mentioned earlier, identified a number of examples of offline services: a Moroccan company with a staff of over 70 that digitizes manuscripts for a European publisher; a Moroccan company that offers Internet-based translation services; and a Senegalese company that employs 30 skilled computer-aided design technicians to do architectural detailing for European clients.

Software development and remote access maintenance (RAM) also provide a viable opportunity for low-labour-cost countries that have the required skills base. Unfortunately, most LDCs lack that base for this type of business. Bangladesh, however, has such a capacity in place (it produces 1,300 computer science graduates a year), and Techbangla,[11] a local business initiative, aims to turn Bangladesh into a significant global software exporter with a $1 billion industry. Five companies in Dhaka have already secured international contracts.

However, despite these considerable opportunities, only few larger LDC enterprises provide teleservices to enterprises in developed countries. Obstacles identified by enterprises in LDCs in establishing teleservicing operations include the difficulty selling their services/breaking into established markets, lack of immediate capacity and regulatory hindrances.

3. Technological developments that could benefit LDCs

Promising developments in low-bandwidth cellular applications such as "short message service" (SMS), content push and pull technologies, platforms allowing interface between mobile handsets and computers/databases, and mobile payment solutions will enable the current GSM networks in LDCs to provide the carrier for a local e-commerce infrastructure. Growth in cellular networks has expanded telecommunications and provided thousands of people with handsets. This implies that there are potentially thousands of "points of access" for e-commerce in LDCs.

Wireless solutions are now being deployed which could enable LDCs to leapfrog Internet infrastructure development. Mobitex allows e-mail to go wireless using cellular architecture. In the United States, Mobitex is operational on the 895–910 MHz spectrum. More than 1,500 users can be served through a single base station. Other wireless internet solutions are Ricochet, offering end users rates of 128 kps, and High Data Rate (HDR), which offers high-speed, high-capacity packet data services using GSM infrastructure on an "always connected basis"[12].

The move from highly structured and streamlined electronic data interchange (EDI) standards to XML (eXtensible Markup Language) standards will allow LDC suppliers and buyers easier access to B2B market places and exchanges. This new standard will enable buyers and suppliers to perform full-fledged EDI-type transactions using web-enabling tools (i.e. web browsers). This is a significant development for LDCs in that current EDI systems are the domain of larger companies (of which there are very few in LDCs) since the cost of the customized software and technical coordination is far too high for smaller businesses. This situation is reflected in the OASIS statistics, which show that 95 per cent of Fortune 1,000 companies were using EDI in 2000, whereas only 2 per cent of small and medium-sized businesses are using EDI.[13]

One of the most promising developments for B2B is the Application Service Provider (ASP). ASPs offer business software services on demand over the web without the need to invest in specific products. LDC enterprises will be able to develop their e-commerce strategies without the large investments in software systems previously required. Currently, these services are not widely available in LDCs but could easily be offered from virtually anywhere in the world should the demand justify it.

4. Global developments in B2C/B2C e-commerce important to LDCs

The failing of the "dot.coms" on international stock markets should not affect LDCs in a direct way. The most important e-commerce developments for LDCs are in B2B sector. Although many B2B exchanges and market places have been formed over the past few years, many are not operating as expected. One of the reasons given is that many of these initiatives are being driven by brokers/middlemen who do not have control over the buying or selling and therefore cannot force a change in the buying and selling culture based just on some transaction cost savings. There is, however, a trend whereby traditional market makers are beginning to come together to form B2B markets and exchanges. It is believed that this will most likely be the basis of future e-commerce.

Many of these companies come out of the EDI culture and will develop their business systems further to accommodate open standard buying or selling platforms.

There is no doubt about the cost savings and efficiencies of B2B e-commerce, hence the absolute assurance that it will work one way or another. Cisco Systems claim to have saved over $1 billion thanks to their e-commerce system where they are linked with suppliers.

These developments will no doubt impact on LDCs. Viable B2B portals hold promise for those LDC enterprises that are e-commerce-enabled as the latter will be able to tap into a highly efficient international procurement system, which will save them high marketing and market development costs and provide them with improved market penetration.

There should be no doubt that business is moving in the direction of e-commerce. Jupiter Communications believe that world B2B e-commerce will be worth $6 trillion by 2003,[14] while the Gartner Group has put the figure at around $3.6 trillion.[15] Whatever the prediction, it is clear that business is moving online at a rapid pace. Even small business spending online increased by 138 per cent during the first quarter of 2000 and the number of medium to large businesses engaged in e-commerce is already above 40 per cent.[16] Enterprises in LDCs cannot afford to miss out on these developments.

C. Concluding remarks and recommendations

1. Concluding remarks

E-commerce in LDCs is insignificant when compared with e-commerce in developed and developing countries. However, a number of enterprise case studies were identified of which the best 16 are presented in the annex.

There are several major impediments to the development of e-commerce in LDCs: enterprise managers' lack of initiative and leadership in taking advantage of e-commerce; and the lack of awareness at government level of e-commerce issues, coupled with the need for Governments to assume their role in urgently addressing the lack of an e-commerce culture in their countries. There is an urgent need for enterprises (particularly exporting enterprises) to educate themselves on e-commerce and to become aware of international business-to-business opportunities. Countries in which there have recently been impressive developments in the use of e-commerce (i.e. the United Kingdom and Canada) are countries whose Governments have realized the importance of their role in promoting e-commerce and creating an e-commerce-friendly environment.

The unavailability of electronic banking capabilities in LDCs has a limiting effect on e-commerce, particularly local (domestic) e-commerce. Restrictive regulations such as exchange controls, protection of telecommunication monopolies, restrictive trade practices and prohibitions (i.e. encryption, Internet telephony, own gateway access etc.) are currently more of concern to LDC enterprises wanting to engage in e-commerce strategies than whether or not e-commerce policies and laws are yet in place. The absence of such laws and policies do not therefore prevent e-commerce from taking place but would increase business confidence if they were.

A further problem preventing manufacturers and other medium to large companies from taking e-commerce onboard is the initial costs associated with the change in terms of financial and time investment. Previous bad experiences of IT installations contribute to this concern. Fortunately, the costs are dropping and it is becoming easier to link up with existing market places and exchanges via Internet browsers. The bigger problem faced by many small and medium-sized LDC companies is the lack of internal IT-driven business systems to match the demands that will be placed on a company joining an exchange or market place.

As regards the physical e-commerce infrastructure, most of the countries surveyed had sufficient infrastructure to enable enterprises to implement some form of e-commerce strategy. Certain cities have excellent access to Internet services. Owing to the nature of the Internet, those e-commerce services not available in LDCs can be provided virtually from service providers based in other countries. These include hosting, website maintenance and, payment facilities. Hence, the LDC physical e-commerce infrastructure is limiting but not prohibitive. Even in the current environment, LDC enterprises could engage in e-commerce strategies. Moreover, new technologies (web-enabling cellular applications) offer exciting new opportunities to leapfrog development of a local e-commerce infrastructure.

2. Enterprise-related recommendations

(a) Business-to-consumer e-commerce examples (international)

There are limited opportunities in niche international consumer markets for LDC enterprises that have the appropriate product offering. Enterprises considering such opportunities should ensure that their business model, in terms of overhead structure and expansion plans, takes this limitation into account. It is vital that these companies understand their target market, and structure the offering to meet the need directly. Enterprises with something unique to sell in the international market, whether it is the diaspora market or another market, should work with the appropriate content sites/portals, such as radio stations, newspapers or information portals, that already have a loyal visitor base (e.g. Newafrica.com, Africaonline). Such symbiotic relationships could allow them to:

- Share credit card merchant facilities;
- Share international web-related costs, i.e. web maintenance and hosting;
- Enter joint marketing arrangements;
- Enter joint market research initiatives;
- Enter joint distribution strategies.

(b) Business-to-business e-commerce examples (international)

Business/industry leaders must rapidly become aware of the benefits of using information and communication technology and e-commerce for their enterprises. Current manufacturers/exporters (e.g. the garment industry of Bangladesh, the shrimp/fish industry of Mozambique/United Republic of Tanzania, commodity suppliers) have the most to gain from looking to e-commerce strategies, provided that the opportunity is approached in the correct manner. This includes the realization that an e-commerce strategy is not just a website but provides an opportunity to use information and web-enabling technologies to:

- Improve the efficiency of information sharing and use, such as better access to company and market intelligence;
- Improve internal business practices;
- Improve external business practices, such as the way they deal with suppliers, clients and service providers.

Business/industry leaders must become aware of the implications of adopting an e-commerce strategy. A willingness to address old business cultures, practices and production procedures is vital in adopting an e-commerce strategy. The use of networking, e-mail, intranets and extranets has altered the way companies use and distribute information. This is a fundamental shift in business practice and culture. The only way to achieve cooperation for all parties is for the strategy to be driven and led from the top, and not from the information technology department. In Japan, even companies such as Toshiba, Fujitsu and NEC are in the process of making fundamental changes to business practices and product lines in order to maximize their position on the Internet.

Business/industry leaders must become aware of the penalty for not adopting e-commerce strategies. It is an indisputable fact that business is moving online irrespective of what has happened to many Internet companies, namely dot.com failures. Furthermore, it is important to understand that adopting an e-commerce strategy does not mean turning on traditional and current distribution/sales networks relationships. E-commerce should rather be seen as an enhancer of these relationships.

When considering e-commerce strategies, exporting enterprises in particular must consider joint initiatives with other enterprises in developing their e-commerce strategies. In smaller economies, where human and other resources are scarce, e-commerce strategies/initiatives are best approached at the industry level. Key institutions such as universities could assist in providing guidance, since keeping track of international best practice is very important. Groupings of enterprises could jointly afford the services of top consultants to put strategies in place. Interaction (partnership) with service suppliers such as freight forwarders and banks and with government agencies is critical. The e-commerce strategy could easily be undone by poor services or regulatory interference.

In the case of teleservices, new initiatives should use the cluster approach, all focusing on a particular type of teleservicing with a view to creating a significant capacity for that type of teleservicing in the country. The teleservicing business is very sensitive to reputation, quality assurance and reliability. If enterprises in an LDC focus on one type of teleservicing, i.e. medical transcriptions in Bangladesh, the country will eventually have the critical mass in terms of capacity and reputation to impact on international markets. This will require leadership at the industry/business association level and possible government involvement.

There is sufficient evidence to believe that the potential in offline teleservicing is unlimited, and very viable for LDCs to embark on it with a sense of urgency and commitment. Offline teleservicing (transcription, data input) is more viable than online teleservicing (call centres) for LDCs because of lower start-up costs, manageable quality control and better possibilities to grow from a small capacity with smaller contracts. Also, because of less reliable telecommunications infrastructure and regulatory restrictions for voice-over IP, offline teleservicing is more suited to LDC environments. An offline teleservicing operation in Ghana has just secured a contract to process insurance claims (data input) with a client (an insurance company) in the United States that will eventually create 4,000 jobs.

(c) Local e-commerce

Banks and ISPs should consider installing web-based and other low-cost technologies enabling the roll-out of local e-commerce solutions. The banking community, ISPs and GSM operators must take cognizance of the needs of their clients in order to be able to transact electronically within domestic environments. They must explore the various technologies now available to make e-commerce infrastructure possible and cost-effective.

Local manufacturers and wholesalers must take advantage of any local e-commerce infrastructure initiatives by investigating the possibility of introducing online ordering and payment systems for small retail outlets. Where banks, in particular micro finance banks, are in the process of introducing various forms and levels of electronic banking in certain LDCs, manufacturers and wholesalers should explore the possibilities of providing electronic payment options for their customers using these systems.

3. Recommendations to LDC Governments

Government leaders should become "e-commerce savvy". They should make it an urgent priority to understand what e-commerce is all about, what its benefits could be, and what consequences await LDCs that do not become part of e-commerce developments. They should commission market studies for key industries to determine what should be done, and to where government resources should be directed, to make the biggest impact. This could mean targeting important industry sectors where e-commerce strategies will become most critical.

LDC Governments should create an image of e-commerce awareness and leadership and demonstrate to the business community the importance of e-commerce. They should consider e-commerce issues at the highest level, possibly by creating an e-commerce Cabinet position, as was done in the United Kingdom. E-commerce awareness programmes should be aimed at enterprises and government departments in order to encourage a change in understanding and the approach to e-commerce.

Governments should identify e-commerce as a critical element of international competitiveness, in the same way as many of them have approached export promotion. This would lead them to design policies that would provide an incentive to industry and enterprises to take advantage of e-commerce opportunities. They could adopt e-commerce-type solutions for trade-related services such as port and customs clearance in order to improve trade facilitation. By enabling paperless trading, Governments will play a major role in assisting exporters in becoming e-commerce-ready. Enterprise- and industry-level incentives for applying e-commerce strategies could include special tax incentives, training incentives, investment incentives, establishment of "techno-parks" (similar to an export-processing zone) and provision of special access to finance.

Governments should, in line with their e-commerce strategy, allocate resources to developing their countries human resources and technical capacities. Actions would include a combination of education and training initiatives, including policy-level training for government officials, introduction of incentives to induce non-residents to return home and incentives to encourage inward immigration of talented people in the IT field, and development of international networks of partners and collaborators. For example, LDCs should aim at leveraging IT corridor developments in neighbouring developing and developed countries by entering into joint ventures or partnerships with universities or enterprises in those neighbouring countries.

LDC Governments should address policy and regulatory issues impacting on e-commerce. These would include restrictive telecommunications and trade regulations, laws affecting banking and foreign exchange, establishment of companies abroad, use of foreign hosting services, and encryption limitations. LDCs should develop an e-commerce legal framework in line with international practice. Governments should explore possible cooperation with international organizations active in promoting e-commerce best practice. This must include the development through training of a policy development capacity and a capacity to negotiate at diplomatic level.

E-commerce policy and laws are important, but the lack thereof should not deter enterprises from implementing e-commerce strategies. E-commerce has flourished in the United States for many years without the existence of e-commerce laws. Prohibitive regulations, however, such as foreign exchange laws, telecommunications laws and import/export regulations directly restrict e-commerce development.

Notes

1 The company sheets are presented in the Annex.

2 A teleservicing model is a business model that uses the Internet to service foreign companies on a remote basis. It is explained in section B, paragraphs 2 (b).

3 Business-to-consumer e-commerce (B2C) is the online selling of virtual or physical products to consumers or end users, and is similar to retailing in traditional business models.

4 These examples are discussed in the Annex under their respective countries.

5 Business-to-business (B2B) e-commerce refers to the online buying and selling of virtual or physical products and services between businesses, and is similar to wholesaling in traditional business models.

6 Post-African Development Forum Summit: Electronic commerce in Africa, report by the ECA (http://www.uneca.org/adf99/adf99ecommerce.htm)

7 See Annex in the section on Togo.

8 See Annex in the section on Uganda.

9 See Annex in the section on Bangladesh.

10 See Annex in the section on Uganda.

11 See Annex in the section on Bangladesh.

12 A system known as General Packet Radio Service (GPRS).

13 United States Internet Council, "State of the Internet Report 2000", www.usic.org.

14 United States Internet Council, op. cit.

15 *Businessweek*, European Edition, "Rethinking the Internet", 26 March 2001, p. 51.

16 United States Internet Council, op. cit.

Annex

Report on selected LDCs and companies

Note

A number of enterprise case studies based in LDCs were identified by UNCTAD. The best 16 were chosen for the purposes of this report. Note that information provided in this report about the companies is based on information given by the companies. This information has been accepted at face value and has not been verified.

United Republic of Tanzania

What is striking about Dar-es-Salaam is the extent to which the Internet is becoming part of the daily lives of thousands of Tanzanians (working people, students and school-going children). Internet cafes have sprung up all over the city and outlying areas (there are estimated to be between 70 and 100 privately owned Internet cafes hosting on average between 10 and 20 computers). This is an important development for the United Republic of Tanzania as it points to the possibility of a rapid uptake of local e-commerce solutions. Phone calls are costly, and it is therefore cheaper to spend an hour in an Internet cafe (costing about $1.00) rather than an hour on a dial-up connection from home. In any event, most people do not have the option of accessing the Internet from home.

The United Republic of Tanzania is, relative to other LDCs, advanced in the deregulation of its telecommunications services, particularly Internet-related services. There are a number of private ISPs with a national subscriber population of about 10,000 accounts. Wireless connections are widespread, one ISP reporting that it has installed over 300 antennas in Dar-es-Salaam alone.

A further indicator of the potential uptake of e-commerce in the country is the extent to which and speed at which cellular telephony has taken off (there are now more than 100,000 subscribers, up from 30,000 in 1999). There are three operators, all offering pre-paid services, a fact which indicates that thousands of people in the United Republic of Tanzania are not averse to the concept of a card with a monetary value, which is a good sign for the introduction of digital cash or smart-card-type technology.

The country's lack of business and government leadership in the area of e-commerce is a cause of concern. Very few companies have considered e-commerce strategies and the Government has not yet embarked on any initiatives to create a e-commerce environment.

The financial of the United Republic of Tanzania infrastructure is not e-ready. Credit cards do not exist and even electronic bank transfers are not common-place, many corporate employees still being paid by cheque or in cash. There are interesting plans underway to address the first impediment, which involve certain banks installing intranets and considering the introduction of smart cards. The National Microfinance Bank has plans to link 40 of its 95 branches by intranet, thus enabling rural people to transfer funds to cities. It is considering entering into a joint venture with a multinational bank to introduce smart cards for its 800,000 account holders. These plans are currently on hold as the bank is in the process of being privatized.

Company Sheet No. 1: IPP Ltd (Radio One)

Classification: Business-to-consumer model

Contact, staff and turnover

- IPP Ltd, Mikocheni Light Industry Area, Dar-es-Salaam, United Republic of Tanzania; website: www.ippmedia.com. Telephone: +255 741 786664
- Head: IT IPP Media – Mr. Finehasi Lema; e-mail: lema@raha.com
- Revenues in 2000: Revenues attributed specifically to the Internet project are difficult to determine. The project has, however, enhanced the revenue of Radio One thanks to new international listenership/viewership. This international exposure has led to a 20 per cent increase in spending on the radio.

Main line of business

- IPP is a media conglomerate with a television station, three radio stations and two newspapers. It provides media services to the Tanzanian people.

Line of e-business

- IPPmedia.com is the Internet version of Radio one. The company believes that its Internet strategy is vital to the future of Radio one and of the IPP group and will eventually account for as much as 50 per cent of its revenue within the next 10 years.
- Radio One has a unique visitor rating of approximately 45,000 to 60,000 visitors per week, located mainly in the United States and Europe.
- Online listenership was limited because of the bandwidth (32 people), but now broadcasts are distributed via other servers.
- The company has a fully fledged media division creating web content and maintaining the site. Subcontracting to experts and artists occurs, but most of the work is done in-house. The company is able to leverage the group's resources in news and information gathering and is thus in a position to use mainly its own media content.

Clients

- Current viewership and listenership of the IPP media group;
- Advertisers on radio and TV and in newspapers;
- Clients could include Tanzanian companies wishing to embark on an Internet strategy to promote and sell their products online. These include tour operators and uniquely Tanzanian products, i.e. music, clothing and unique foodstuffs. IPP can provide these companies with exposure to United States and Europe;
- Any company anywhere in the world that needs to expose itself or its product to people who would visit this unique content site.

Modus operandi of the e-business

- Announcements on air about the website;
- Website address in daily newspapers;
- Listing on portals;
- Word of mouth;
- IPP has invested in over 1,800 domain names and intends to create websites based on these models. For example, it has the domain name Serengetti.com and aims to promote Tanzanian products under this brand.

Obstacles

- Local shopping site restricted owing to absence of credit cards; no electronic payment system;
- Problems with local delivery in terms of addresses and cost;
- Bandwidth and other e-commerce infrastructure problems.

Potential business opportunities

- The Tanzanian diaspora may be willing to pay for information about home, i.e. on a subscription basis;
- Product (content) and information are unique, not the focus area for mainline information portals. Opportunity to sell information and products to the larger United States and European portals;
- Able to self-fund new projects as a current revenue stream is in place. Already has resources and capacity to gather news content. Any person anywhere in the world who wants to buy uniquely Tanzanian content, products or services.

Company Sheet No. 2: Newafrica.com

Classification: Teleservicing model

Contact, staff and turnover

- Newafrica.com, Mikocheni Light Industry Area, Dar-es-Salaam, United Republic of Tanzania.
- Contact: telephone: +256 41 2700962; website: www.newafrica.com
- Ms. Roselyne Mariki Nderingo, Managing Director, e-mail: roselyne@newafrica.co.tz
- Revenues in 2000: negligible. Has focused on building a community interested in African information. Began developing revenue models only recently. Financed by a private investor for the past three years. Expects to break even in two years with new revenue models.
- 90 employees.

Main line of business

- Information portal; uniquely African;
- Provides information on a wide range of topics, including business, news, culture and statistics.

Line of e-business

- This is an exclusively online company, and therefore 100 per cent of its business is carried out online;
- Has 70,000–90,000 visitors per month, located mainly in the United States and Europe;
- Many of the staff are young graduates. They regard working for Newafrica as an opportunity to gain experience, despite the low salaries paid. Newafrica employs web designers, software engineers, journalists and researchers;
- Currently Newafrica offers free access to its information sites. It has just received an ISP licence and will be able to generate revenue from subscribers. It plans to start charging for advertising. Up to now, advertising has been free of charge. Plans are afoot to establish a travel booking portal, web hosting services and web design services. It has completed four web design contracts for European companies so far.

Clients

- Current: Companies, institutions and Governments wishing to make public their information and services, and visitors wanting information about Africa;
- Potential: people anywhere in the world wanting to access Newafrica's unique content;
- Commissioned research and creation of customized maps;
- There is a dedicated division that is able to create digital maps of specific regions; limited sales have been achieved in this area;
- Information is unique, not the focus area for mainline information portals; opportunity to sell information to the larger United States and European portals;
- Takes advantage of the LDC diaspora, which wants local information about what is happening at home;
- Currently offers free access to unique information;
- Offers precise information such as statistics and facts about African countries.

Modus operandi of the e-business

- The website is registered on the main search tools/portals, including MSN and Yahoo;
- Publicity due to its uniqueness and through word of mouth.

Obstacles

- Identifying a revenue model. The culture of Internet users is not to pay for information. How to take advantage of 70,000 unique visitors per month;
- Bandwidth and other e-commerce infrastructure problems.

Company Sheet No. 3: Raha.com

Classification: Business-to-consumer model

Contact, staff and turnover

- Raha.com, Raha Towers, Dar-es-Salaam, United Republic of Tanzania; website: www.raha.com; telephone: +255 41 119513; fax: +255 41 138227
- Managing Director: Mr. Hussein Dharsee; email: Hussein@raha.com
- Revenues in 2000: $600,000. 90 per cent Internet service provider accounts, 10 per cent web design, web hosting etc. Self-funded investment of approximately $3 million.

Main line of business

- Internet service provider;
- Also owner of two Internet cafes and a web design studio, and has started a variety of Internet sites such as: www.simplyafrican.com and www.bongoland.com.

Line of e-business

- Raha has 50 per cent of the Tanzanian Internet subscriber market. It offers broadband wireless access to five hubs around the country, providing 6 mbs of raw bandwidth to its server and a 64 K to the international gateway;
- www.Rahanews.com offers 5,000 subscribers news delivered each morning by e-mail;
- www.Simplyafrican.com sells Tanzanian art to the United States.

Clients

- 5,000 subscribers, most corporate and government;
- Advertisers;
- Companies wishing to promote and sell their products online. These include tour operators and uniquely Tanzanian products, i.e. music;
- People in the United States wishing to buy African art. Simplyafrican.com was started six months ago and has achieved $10,000 in sales. Art is bought locally and stored in a warehouse in New York. Deliveries are carried out from New York, and payments are taken by credit card on a website hosted in the United States.

Modus operandi of e-business

- Direct sales, marketing (newspaper advertisements) of ISP services;
- Listings on search engines for sites;
- Free news service to customers;
- Free Internet seminars and training.

Obstacles

- Small cyber population;
- Lack of electronic payment infrastructure;

Potential business opportunities

- There is scope to increase the ISP market, possibly to double the current size;
- There are possibilities for creating websites to sell art, but limited to sales of around $20,000 per year.

ETHIOPIA

Ethiopia still has a highly regulated telecommunications infrastructure. There is only one ISP (state-controlled) and demand for Internet services far outstrips supply (there are approximately 2,000 subscribers with a waiting list of a further 2000). It has been known to take up to a year to secure an Internet account.

More worrying from an e-commerce perspective is that private Internet cafes have been declared illegal except for those in business centres of certain hotels. The Ethiopian Telecommunications Corporation (ETC) is hard at work closing illegal Internet cafes, but demand for these services is so great that the illegal Internet cafes are able to quickly re-establish themselves at another venue. Although the ETC has promised to provide such services, they seem unable to do so, or are slow to meet the demands of the community. Internet access outside Addis Ababa is virtually non-existent. The United Nations Development Programme is currently providing funding to increase bandwidth in Addis Ababa and the roll-out of POPs in rural areas. One positive aspect of telecommunications in Ethiopia is that the cost of local telephone calls seems cheaper relative to other LDCs and will hopefully be maintained at this level in the future.

Ethiopia, probably more so than any other African LDC, has a large and affluent diaspora. Many Ethiopian entrepreneurs are based outside the country, selling various unique Ethiopian-content products online. Foreign-based Ethiopian websites market Ethiopian art, music, designs, Geez Font software etc. Their websites are mostly hosted in Canada and the United States. Some of the newspapers now have online versions attracting large visitor ratings from Ethiopians living abroad wanting to know what is happening at home (for example, www.addisstribune.com). The Ethiopian diaspora therefore provides a market for small Ethiopian business-to-consumer sites.

Despite regulatory and infrastructure problems, there are a few Ethiopian companies identified as e-commerce operations. A poor banking infrastructure, the absence of credit cards and stringent exchange control regulations are significant barriers to development, both restricting the growth of those e-commerce ventures currently operating and turning away possible foreign investment in new initiatives. There is no policy framework or specific regulations in place that deal with e-commerce.

There are a few initiatives by the private sector and donor community to promote e-commerce. The Addis Ababa Chamber of Commerce has taken an interest in e-commerce and has organized a few workshops to highlight the benefits of e-commerce for business and to encourage government to liberalize this sector.

Company Sheet No. 1: Ethiolink PLC

Classification: Business-to-consumer model

Contact, staff and turnover

- Ethiolink PLC was formed about three years ago.
- Addis Ababa, Ethiopia; website: www.ethiolink.com
- Director: Dr. Dawit Bekele (PhD in Computer Science); e-mail: dawit@ethiolink.com
- Revenues in 2000: $50,000. Ethiogift – 20 per cent; network maintenance and lay networks – 25 per cent; web hosting – 20 per cent; design of websites – 15 per cent; training and other – 40 per cent.
- Total self-funded investment of approximately $33,000.
- Ethiolink employs 16 people: two technical departments. The Internet department has four people, all graduates in computer science. There are one computer science and two physics graduates in maintenance, marketing graduate, the other have just finished high school, plus two part-time accountants.

Main line of business

- Ethiolink is an Internet and network maintenance company.
- Ethiogift is one of the online initiatives of Ethiolink. It is an online business-to-consumer site which targets the Ethiopian diaspora and split-markets gifts (on a commission basis) bought by the diaspora for friends and relatives in Ethiopia. These include sheep, cakes and flowers.
- Web hosting. Ethiolink currently hosts around 20 sites.
- Web design services: Ethiolink has designed 10 websites and offers Internet consultancy.
- Networking and maintenance services.

Lines of e-business

- Online selling: Ethiogift sells sheep, cakes, liquor, flowers and chocolates on a commission basis, all of which are typical gifts given on certain holidays and birthdays. For example, during Easter Ethiopians living abroad order sheep to be delivered to their relatives in Ethiopia.
- 50,000 unique visitors to the site so far, mainly from the United States.
- Six staff members dedicated to the e-business side of Ethiolink.

Clients

- Ethiopians living around the world, mainly in the United States.
- Customers: regular month – 50; holiday month – 100 to 300.
- Average spent per customer: $50.
- Average mark-up on products: 15 per cent.
- Not sure of percentage of repeat business.

Modus operandi of e-business

- Radio advertisements in the United States led to an immediate response but owing to a lack of capital, follow-up advertisements were not possible.
- Internet advertisements online Ethiopian newspapers. Advertisements cost around $80 for a banner per week.
- Posters in cities, in Ethiopian restaurants.
- Specially printed Ethiopian calendars which are sent free of charge.
- Ethiopian restaurants become agents, market, sell, receive orders, and take payments, with the main agent e-mailing the order. They set up the agent network by using family connections or meet with Ethiopian restaurateurs on trips to various respective countries. The agent in Johannesburg was signed up by one of the partners who travelled there.
- The server is based in Canada.
- Credit card approvals are done by authorise.net in Canada.
- As soon as payment has been confirmed, the product is delivered to the relative living in Ethiopia.

Company Sheet No.1 (contd.)

Obstacles

- Trying to manage a business that stretches over five continents. Information is slow in coming from partners/agents. Need to communicate and motivate agents to sell and service customers. Ethiogift needs a better management system that can accommodate international requirements.
- Poor local banking infrastructure has obliged Ethiolink to bank in the United States.
- Knowledge of laws in other countries; the company had to be established in the United States in order to open a bank account. The consequence of this is that Ethiogift is subject to United States tax laws. Dawit Bekele is concerned that he does not know enough about the legal consequences of operating in this way.

Potential business opportunities

- There is an Ethiopian diaspora of around one million people living mainly in Europe and the United States (500,000). This diaspora is possibly the most wealthy of the African diasporas. Western Union transfers more than 100 million bir a year to Ethiopia, mainly for family purposes. The potential revenue of Ethiogift could grow 20-fold.
- www.ethiomarkato.com has just been launched. It will sell Ethiopian items to the diaspora and interested people based in other countries, i.e. traditional clothes and spices via direct express delivery. It will not stock products but will have supplier agreements in place. With good marketing it can equal or do better than Ethiogift.
- Becoming an ISP as soon as the ETC permits private licences.
- Intention to create an Ethiopian cyber mall, which would allow incubating companies in Ethiopia to go online. These are companies that have a product but do not have the technical expertise to go online. Ethiolink will design the website, host the site, handle payment and security issues and deal with delivery problems. Ethiolink believes it can succeed as it already has the trust of hundreds of online customers and already has a level of exposure in the international online market place.
- Becoming an online travel agent.
- Local ideas include an online supermarket and the creation of cyber cafes.
- There is one big problem with local opportunities for e-commerce: only 2,500 people in Ethiopia can access the Internet. But for business to business, it may be enough, i.e. small business people from small towns have to come to Addis Ababa to buy their products. If it is possible for them to order and make payment online, the business will send the goods. The banking system is not up to speed yet: there is limited privatization and the Commercial Bank of Ethiopia still controls 90 per cent of the banking market.
- Teleservicing to industrialized companies, offshore software development. There are highly talented students who could perform this service. Dawit Bekele is a lecturer at Addis Ababa University and has direct access to the students.

Company Sheet No. 2: Genuine Leather Craft

Classification: Business-to-consumer model

Contact, staff and turnover

- Genuine Leather Craft started 10 years ago.
- Director: Mr. Teshomo Kebede, telephone: 531894; e-mail: glc@telecom.net.et
- Addis Ababa, Ethiopia; website: www.genuineleathercraft.com
- The company employs 42 people.
- Medium-sized enterprise: turnover about $150,000 a year.
- Leather garments provide 60 per cent of turnover.

Main line of business

- Producer of boutique leather garments.
- Producer of leather bags, leather-upholstered furniture and car seat covers for local market.

Line of e-business

- Sale of leather garments online, business to consumer.
- Outsourcing website maintenance to Ethiolink.
- About four people in production work exclusively on online sales to assure quality and prompt response to orders.
- Started selling online about three years ago, first 8 per cent of garment sales, then 28 per cent, and then 40 per cent in 1999/2000. Sales are now dropping because the company has not been able to make the necessary updates to keep repeat fashion buyers.
- 60 per cent of total business is accounted for by garments.
- The average garment price is $85.

Clients

- United States, Canada, South-East Asia, Japan.
- 25 per cent of sales are to the Ethiopian diaspora.
- 68,000 hits since inception up to September 2000; about 20,000 visitors per year.
- The company has potential in an appropriate regulatory environment, and if its technical problems are solved, it could go 100 per cent online.
- The company does not have applications software to track client behaviour.
- Classic sales are constant, but fashion garments are sensitive to updates. Must keep changing the website to give the right impression.
- When dealing business-to-customer, custom made is a major opportunity. Can charge 20 to 40 per cent more for custom made.

Modus operandi of e-business

- Does not advertise its website.
- Uses the Internet to follow fashion trends visiting competitor websites, international fashion websites, and fashion critic websites.
- It was eight months before the first order was received.
- Client visits website, views garments, prices and options, colour and style selection chart. Under showcase, chooses men's or women's selection. Shows colours, chooses colour, shows image of garment. Bulk order is 500 and above. Free on board (FOB) quoted. Quote delivered worldwide for business-to-consumer.
- Shopping cart collects orders, and then client is required to complete an order form. This will involve supplying credit card details, which are automatically cleared through a United States credit card clearing company. An order coming through to the company means that the card has been approved, and payment is received by the company from the credit card company within three days. The prices online include the fee of the credit card company, which is 8 per cent. The other payment option is payment in advance by wire transfer direct to Ethiopia. The company

Company Sheet No.2 (contd.)

ensures that the client receives the order within 10 days anywhere in world. This is promised on the website. Buyers sometimes do not give all necessary details, and e-mail clarification is required.

Obstacles

- Difficulties in keeping up with the fashions, as most online sales are fashion-sensitive.
- The appearance of the website is fashion-sensitive and must be changed as well; this requires design expertise not available in Ethiopia.
- Difficulties in maintaining the website, which lead to repeat visitors seeing no new changes and therefore no repeat orders.
- Not easy to get service on time from outsourced web maintenance. Urgent changes cannot be made.
- Customs procedures are difficult. With regard to exchange controls, anything over $30 must be approved by the National Bank of Ethiopia, which takes at least half a day.
- Sending five items to five separate buyers needs five separate customs clearances and exchange controls. In-house procedures take an hour or two to respond to an online order received correctly, which then takes two days to leave the country. Also costly in terms of time and actual disbursement.
- Under exchange controls, the National Bank must ensure that payment for anything leaving the country is guaranteed.
- Credit cards are not allowed by enterprises. The company works with a credit card clearing company in the United States; this is not legal but it has no choice.
- Cannot attend to client complaints, it has and will have problems with refunds owing to exchange controls.

Potential business opportunities

- Germany is the biggest consumer of leather garments in the world.
- Develop business-to-consumer market, particularly on the custom-made side.
- To increase rewards and benefits for end buyers.

UGANDA

Uganda, like the United Republic of Tanzania, has taken great strides in deregulating its telecommunications sector. There are two fixed-line operators, three cellular operators and five ISPs. A number of initiatives by cellular operators and ISPs are underway to provide various broadband solutions to the business community. Bandwidth is still expensive, but costs are expected to drop as these solutions are rolled out. Quality Internet access (cost-effective broadband) will be an important comparative advantage for Ugandan enterprises in the context of teleservicing.

Since the introduction of the third cellular licence (MTN) and prepaid phone cards, the cellular subscriber base has grown from less than 30,000 to more than 100,000 subscribers. This, as in the case of the United Republic of Tanzania, is an important indicator as to how rapidly many Ugandans accept useful new technologies. The signs are therefore positive that thousands of Ugandans would quickly see the benefits of e-commerce if they were offered to them.

As is the case in the United Republic of Tanzania, in spite of the favourable telecommunications environment and the advanced technologies now offered by ISPs (i.e. wireless connections), initiatives from the business and government sectors to take advantage of e-commerce opportunities are disappointing.

There is one example of teleservicing in Uganda involving a company (Doticom Services) offering data input services to a Canadian auditing firm. This was the result of an initiative of Infodev, the G77 Chamber of Commerce and private consultants. Another five companies are in the process of being established in a similar fashion.

Simba Radio, a native-language broadcaster, provides an interesting case of how niche radio stations can have success on the Internet. It currently streams its content (African music) over the Internet. Thousands of non-resident Ugandans living in the United States and elsewhere tune in each week. Simba Radio is now considering how to capitalize on this captive audience. Currently, no revenue is derived from its Internet strategy.

There are no credit cards in Uganda, and debit cards are not widely used owing to the poor distribution of points of sale. Banks seem to be content to maintain the status quo, and the Central Bank is in the process of introducing an electronic cheque-clearing facility rather than exploring more modern electronic payment systems. Pride African (headquartered in Kenya) has plans to introduce intranets into its banking operations, which could result in various electronic banking services.

Company Sheet No. 1: Doticom Services

Classification: Teleservicing model

Contact, staff and turnover

- Contact: e-mail: kakooza@hotmail.com; telephone: +256 77 405071; fax: +256 41 256888
- Partners: Mr. Alex Kakooza and Mr. Joseph Sewanyana
- Revenues in 2000: $3,000; 90 per cent in January 2001.
- Target is to sell 2,000 hours per month at $5 per hour.
- Staffing: two people, the aim being to have a total staff of 20.
- Qualifications of staff: at least a diploma in accounting, and computer skills.

Main line of e-business

- Teleservicing: electronic data entry and electronic bookkeeping.

Clients

- One auditing firm, based in Canada. The company could look to the United States for more work.

Modus operandi of e-business

- Client sends scanned images in batches of about 900 images.
- Input data from images into Excel or QuickBooks, charged per hour.
- Hours predetermined in contract according to average productivity in Canada.

Obstacles

- Obtaining trained staff
- Problem with bandwidth: it takes too long to download, and another venue has therefore to be used to download a file.
- Prospective clients insist on tests being done to ensure quality and commitment.They need to know that the work is done, irrespective of holidays, weekends etc. The current perception creates a drawn-out sales cycle which will improve over time with an improved reputation.

Potential business opportunities

- Multimillion dollar industry. A small company of about 20 employees could earn in the region of $15,000 to 20,000 per month.
- Average charge around $5 per hour.

Company Sheet No. 2: LifeInAfrica.com

Classification: Business-to-consumer model

Contact, staff and turnover

- The Life in Africa Foundation; PO Box 28825, Kampala, Uganda; website: www.LifeInAfrica.com
- Telephone: +256/41/236 700 or +256/77/422 303/ E-mail: mzungu@lifeinafrica.com
- Director: Christina Jordan, founding director
- Number of staff: two ful- time staff; 15 volunteers (8 of whom are computer-literate - only two have website design experience, and the rest are learning).
- Revenues in 2000 (turnover) in $: $12,000 ($10,500 in loan donations; $1,500 in revenue).

Main line of business

- Launched at the end of February 2000, www.LifeInAfrica.com raises funds to support micro finance in Africa. Funds raised in 2000 have supported a loan guarantee programme in Kampala, Uganda, which is run by volunteers.

Line of e-business

- The e-business initiative is designed to support both the Life in Africa Foundation and its beneficiaries through selling beneficiary-produced artisan products online. The profit on the sale price is shared between the Life in Africa Foundation and the artisans.

Clients

- Subscribers to Life in Africa publications
- African-American community; educated class with global outlook.

Modus operandi of e-business

- The Life in Africa Foundation marketed the African Crafts Market via regular e-mail newsletters to 1,000+ subscribers. Supplies of goods were purchased (i.e: financed up front) from producers, and then sold via secure credit card transactions on the Internet.
- Secure credit card processing is outsourced to a United States-based company which levies a 6.5 per cent fee on every transaction.
- The company issues a weekly cheque (drawn on a United States bank) representing the transactions made, less the 6.5 per cent fee.
- The Life in Africa Foundation has a United States bank account, in which the cheque is deposited. Every so often a transfer is made to Uganda.
- The producers receive their asking price upfront, and then an additional 10 per cent of the price paid after purchase of an item.

Obstacles

- Shipping is expensive, and international courier service is more expensive than the goods themselves. The Ugandan post can be used for shipping individual orders (registered express mail), but the individual items must be small enough to fit into an envelope (posting boxes is significantly more expensive). Moreover, the shipping charges are not uniform (at one time a certain item would cost $7 to mail, while another time the same item to the same country would cost $10 to mail).
- Pre-financing the stock severely limits the company's ability to offer a range of items. In the future, it will negotiate a different kind of arrangement with producers. For example, it might purchase the inputs, and not pay for the labour until an item has been ordered.

Potential business opportunities

- The African-American market online represents a enormous potential for the kinds of items the company's borrowers can produce, particularly textiles and clothing. The key will be to list the site and/or products in places where the largest potential market will see them. There is much more market research that needs to be done (and is scheduled for the next few months) before this issue can be adequately addressed.

Mozambique

There have been impressive developments in the telecommunications infrastructure in Mozambique, mainly in Maputo, and development is beginning to take place in other parts of the country. Teledata, the State-owned Internet service provider, has installed at least one POP in every province. Access of 64 k is the norm for many businesses in Maputo and an inter-city fibre optic cable will provide high-speed links between Maputo and Beira in the near future. There are ten ISPs, some of which are in the process of installing wireless connections for corporate clients. There are around 8,000 Internet subscribers; this figure may, however, be misleading as the larger corporations and government departments make up the bulk of the subscriptions. There is only one fixed line and one cellular operator in Mozambique (State-owned), but plans are underway to issue a second cellular licence.

Banking in Mozambique is relatively advanced compared with the United Republic of Tanzania, Uganda and Ethiopia, with Banco Standard Totta offering full internet banking services to about 100 clients. Most of the larger banks have automated teller machines (ATMs) and debit card points of payment. Four banks have agreed to enter into a facility-sharing arrangement which will allow their clients access to a better distribution of ATM and to about 500 retail points of sale. Even credit cards appear to be in greater use in Mozambique than in other LDCs visited, with about 2,000 credit card holders and most of the hotels and many restaurants accepting credit card payment.

There are a few Internet cafes in Mozambique but they are not as widespread as in Dar-es-Salaam, and possibly less than in Uganda. The groundswell of popular use of the Internet as seen in the United Republic of Tanzania does not seem to have happened yet in Mozambique. Reasons could include a lack of awareness, cost of access and lack of local or Portuguese content on the Internet. The first information portal has only recently been launched (www.imensis.co.mz).

BANGLADESH

There have been some very promising initiatives over the past year to get e-commerce off the ground in Bangladesh, most notably Techbangla, an initiative of a few businessmen to develop Bangladesh into a billion dollar software exporter. They plan to leverage the non-resident Bangladeshi community based in the United States to create the demand for software development for export. A conference was held in the United States in early 2000 with a follow-up event in Dhaka towards the end of 2000. In association with Harvard University, JOBS-USAID and a number of companies and individuals, Techbangla has conducted an e-commerce readiness assessment for Bangladesh. Information on this assessment can be found on the Techbangla website www.itrc.techbangla.org.

Bangladesh's telecommunications infrastructure is poor, with limited fixed-line access, unreliable connectivity and low bandwidth (9K). Bangladesh use VSAT for international links, and missed out on an opportunity offered a number of years ago to join the undersea cable link. It is now considering joining that link, but will require an investment of about $100 million.

Bangladesh has around 600,000 fixed lines in use and around 257,000 cellular subscribers (as of November 2000). The cellular phone subscribership has grown by 70 per cent (between April 2000 and November 2000. There are four fixed-line operators - one State monopoly (BTTB) and three private sector companies that are licensed to service rural areas. There are four cellular operators: all are private, with Grameen Phone being the largest provider. There are around 50 ISPs: all of them are private and provide a range of ISP services. The Bandwidth offered ranges from 64k to 2mb gateway access. There are limitations as a result of the poor fixed-line connections (9k to 14k). Two ISPs now offer wireless links to overcome this problem. Dhaka and some of the other main centres have privately run Internet cafes available. Grameen Communications and Learn Foundation have projects to introduce Internet cafes into rural areas.

Bangladesh currently produces around 1,300 computer science graduates per year (computer science courses are oversubscribed) and about 12,000 students are trained each year in some category of IT by nine universities and 53 IT education institutions. The quality of some of the education gives cause for concern, and around 80 per cent of graduates and teachers have indicated that they would migrate to other countries if they could. Computer operators and programmers are the most common jobs.

The banking infrastructure in terms of electronic payments and inter-bank connectivity is poor. No local banks issue credit cards and very few companies accept credit card payments.

The Government is using the Internet for information dissemination to a limited extent, for example making official statistics available on the web (www.bbsgov.org). The Stock Exchange was fully automated, two years ago and is now linked to the global system.

Bangladesh is advanced in developing its policies affecting e-commerce. The deregulation of the private use of VSAT has helped ISPs, and the liberalization of the telecommunications sector is well underway. Voice-over IP is, however, still illegal. Also, generous foreign exchange and tax rulings have been made for IT exports, and 100 per cent remittance of capital gains and profits is allowed for foreign investors without approval. A comprehensive ICT policy is to be published shortly.

Many of the Bangladeshi companies that would qualify as e-commerce companies are hosted in United States. Products sold are books, music, flowers and small garments. Many of the sites aim at the Bangladeshi diaspora.

Bangladesh rightly believes that IT offers the most viable future business opportunity. In view of India's success, Bangladesh has reason to believe that it can offer similar services. Such services include coding, remote access server/systems maintenance and web-related work. The two greatest challenges in developing this type of industry are the lack of an international network to secure the work and an insufficient number of trained graduates. However, Bangladesh believes that it could create a billion dollar industry over the next few years. In general, the obstacles to developing this type of industry include the lack of an international marketing network (many of the IT chief executive officers in the United States are Indians and they are channelling work to India), limited capacity (unlike in India), lack of project management skills. Sixty-two Bangladeshi IT companies are listed on a website (www.basisbd.org).

The Government has made an attempt to kick-start the industry by introducing an Entrepreneur Equity Fund of 1 billion taka. This fund has been underutilized so far by the IT sector. As a result, 50 per cent of it has been reallocated to the agro industry. IT managers claim that the administration of the fund was inefficient, that there were no clear guidelines and that many projects were rejected.

Bangladeshis have a particular aptitude for remote web-based services such as transcription and data input. Currently, India is the leading provider of these types of services. Many Bangladeshi companies are securing subcontracts from Indian companies. Those trying to secure contracts directly with United States companies are finding it difficult because of a limited international reputation and marketing infrastructure.

Company Sheet No. 1: Technosoft Transcription Ltd

Classification: Teleservicing model

Contact, staff and turnover

- Contact: telephone: +880 2 9669341; e-mail: techsoft@bdonline.com
- Managing Director: Mr. Sharif N. Ambia: snambia@bdonline.com
- Dhaka, Bangladesh, started in 1999.
- Number of staff and minimum/average qualification: employs 21 people; they are graduates, well versed in American English; they must know medical terminology, the names of drugs, and must have computer and typing skills, and an understanding of American culture and practices. For example, they must know on which side of the road people drive in the United States, and must know that people can get allergies from dogs (many people in developing countries are unaware of such problems).
- Revenues in 2000 (turnover) in $: 40 trained people can produce $200 000 if each transcripts 500 lines a day.

Main line of business

- Remote medical transcription

Line of e-business

- Contracted medical practitioners send audio files containing dictations of patient records, i.e. diagnoses and prescriptions. Operators transcribe the files to text.

Clients

- General practitioners, hospitals, clinics, health service providers, healthcare companies.
- Technosoft currently services 8 to 10 doctors and 200 health care organizations. It is the only company in Bangladesh that is able to contract directly with United States clients.
- Other companies are securing subcontracts from India.

Modus operandi of e-business

- Uses a marketing organization in the United States to secure contracts.
- Has established itself as a “performer” rated company (98.8 per cent accuracy). This rating could improve the turnover of the company tenfold over the next few years.
- Clients send voice files to a server in the United States.
- Technosoft then downloads the voice files from the server.
- Technosoft promises a 24-hour turnaround time.
- Once transcribed, the text files are sent back to the client.

Company Sheet No.1 (contd.)

Obstacles

- The biggest obstacle is marketing. Bangladesh does not have a positive image because of impressions that it is a very poor country.
- Bangladesh does not have a network, unlike India.
- Poor telecommunications, power supply and bandwidth.
- Banks are not very responsive. They are unable to provide finance without physical assets such as collateral. In this business, the intellectual property is the asset, and therefore there is a difficulty with the financing of training.
- Payments from clients are satisfactory, but money transfers to Dhaka are slow.
- It takes four to five months to train staff, although in the case of an emergency it can be done in a month. Internship lasts three months. In order to put 30 stations in place, an investment of $150,000 in training over six months is required, plus about $200,000 for equipment.

Potential business opportunities

- India estimates that it will earn about 300 billion rupees ($6.6 billion) by 2008.
- Bangladesh believes that it could achieve about 5 per cent of this projection ($300 million per year).
- Since this sort of business activity requires a good command of English, the Chinese are not contenders.
- Another reason for optimism for Bangladesh is that there are complaints against Indians by the United States as they have problems with under-capacity.
- The market for offshore transcriptions is growing as it is difficult to make transcriptions. Since transcription is not a pleasant job, people in the United States are moving to other jobs. This has created a worker shortage of 10 per cent.
- The market is also expected to grow because doctors are now being forced to keep records for insurance purposes.
- Technosoft expects to make about $200,000 this year. It aims to grow capacity to 70 stations over the next year.
- Technosoft could consider diversification into legal transcripting since the modus operandi would be similar; however, training would be required in order to become familiar with United States law and the Judicial Code etc.

Company Sheet No. 2: Bangla 2000

Classification: Teleservicing model

Contact, staff and turnover

- Contact: website: www.bangla2000.net; telephone: +88-02-9883642; e-mail: info@bangla2000.net
- Management (name of director): Mr. Mohammad Salimullah Raunak, Chief Technology Officer: e-mail: raunak@bangla2000.com
- Number of staff and minimum/average qualification: Software developers - average qualifications, graduate in computer service; 20 others
- Revenues in 2000 (turnover) in $: $100,000 12 to 15 contracts

Main line of business

- Web-based software development; web-based application development; information portal

Line of e-business

- Coding for software development. 10 per cent of charges of software developers.
- Design of software systems.
- Maintenance – Foreign companies in the United States, ensuring that services are running. Typical contract: $1,000 to $20,000. Its one tenth of charge in USA. Low-end websites Brand name trust is preventing getting high end; it is not an issue of technology, more an issue of capital investment.
- Consulting services for hosting local companies.
- Web marketing – two Swiss-based.
- 30 per cent of staff are dedicated to e-business, and this figure is expected to increase to 80 per cent by 2003.
- 30 per cent of turnover comes from e-business; this figure will increase to 70 per cent.

Clients

- $500,000 to 2 million turnover companies in developed countries, private companies, NGOs, community organizations.
- Potentially larger corporations, once trust is developed.
- Aims to secure as clients two or three Fortune 500 companies by 2005.

Modus operandi of e-business

- Has more than 10 foreign representatives in the United States, Europe and Australia. They make presentations, are trained via online modules, and help to find potential clients.
- The representatives foreign work as a team with a person in Dhaka to find clients.
- Clients complete a brief form on the website to indicate what they want; this helps in formulating proposals. Alternatively, forms can be completed by the representatives.
- Products are developed in Dhaka and are then tested and delivered online.
- Representatives collect payments.

Obstacles

- Trust is the biggest problem: companies still look for a brand name. There is a problem with Bangladesh's reputation.
- The time needed to establish a track record, and the cost involved.
- No venture capital system in Bangladesh.
- No IT policy, no IP law.
- Human resources are manageable.

Potential business opportunities

- In five years, Bangla 2000 will achieve a turnover of about $5 million.
- Bangladesh expects to earn $2 billion in software development by 2008. India is earning about $6 billion now, and is targeting $50 billion by 2008.

MADAGASCAR

Madagascar has a number of ISPs, including DTS (partly owned by France Telecom): which has 5,000 subscribers, Simicron, Network and about nine other small ISPs with a total of 1,000 subscribers. There are estimated to be 10,000 ISP accounts, and 20,000 people have access to the Internet. ISP costs are a fixed cost of about $5 per month and there are variable ISP/telecom costs of about US 9 cents per minute. There are a few Internet cafes in Antananarivo, including Simicron, which has about 6 PCs, and a few others with one PC each. Public access costs: about $8 an hour. Madagascar has access downtime of about 10 per cent (mostly owing to heavy rains).

The local post is said to be unreliable. DHL is reliable in terms of delivery. Internet telephony (i.e. using net2phone.com; delta3.com) is prohibited by law but frequently used by Internet specialists.

Very few people have credit cards and very few companies accept credit cards. Most people pay cash, despite the fact that the largest denomination of banknote is MF 25,000 (about $4). The only way for a Madagascar company to be granted a distance-selling merchant account is to open an affiliate in a country such as France or the United States and then try to get a merchant account through this affiliate. Only a couple of local companies have done that.

Company Sheet No. 1 : Generis Informatique

Classification: Teleservicing model

Contact, staff and turnover

- Contact people: Ms. Clotilde Ranaivoson, Director; Mr. Jaona Ranaivoson, Associate (also director general of ISCAM, a local business college).
- Address : Lotissement Bonnet 31 Ivandry, 101 Antananarivo, Madagascar
- Telephone: +261 20 22 497 00; fax: 261 33 11 022 68; e-mail: igeneris@igeneris.com; www.igeneris.com
- Established in mid-2000
- Number of staff: 7 employees

Main line of business

- Creation of websites for locally-based clients (including affiliates of foreign companies). By January 2001, about 12 websites had been created. Hosting is normally done in United States-based servers through a French company.

Line of e-business

- One intranet site (investment matching) for Fondation EMA (Geneva).
- About 6,000 contacts (name, title, e-mail, faxes) have been gathered from the web and sold to Fondation EMA (0.63 Swiss centimes per contact).
- Other sporadic assignments, initial contacts and projects.
- Most international orders have been obtained through a single personal contact (i.e. Dominique Flaux of Fondation EMA).

Potential business opportunities

- Generis is eager to expand in any promising Internet-related business segment. The most likely exportable services are: creation of relatively simple websites; and creation of customized databases (such as the ones for EMA).

Company Sheet No. 2: Lemurie Tours

Classification: Business-to-consumer model

Contact, staff and turnover

- Contact person : Mr. Haga Rakotoson Director (who is also the Secretary General of the Madagascar Tour Operators Association)
- Address : 119 route Circulaire, Antananarivo 101, Madagascar
- Telephone: +261 20 22 607 07; e-mail: lemurie@dts.mg; www.lemurie.com
- Number of staff: 12 employees

Main line of business

- Local tour operator, i.e. obtains the services of non-exclusive local suppliers (hotels, planes, excursions, rental cars)

Modus operandi of the business

- The company works with a wholesaler in France, who in turn sell its trips to travel agencies.
- It would be too difficult for the company to sell directly to travel agencies in France (lack of trust and financial guarantees).
- It does, however, wholesale directly to two corporate associations (*comités d'entreprise*).
- 30 per cent of its sales are generated by its website. In other words, about 200 tours per year are booked through the Internet.
- The company has about 100 visitors per day on its website
- 60 per cent of its online clients prepay (wire transfer), while the remaining 40 per cent pay upon arrival.
- The website is now in its third generation. The company says that its success is due to its having declared its website in key search tools.
- By selling on the Internet, it circumvents its wholesaler.
- To minimize conflicts, prices online are list prices of its suppliers (hotels etc.) Therefore, a tourist booking online with lemurie.com pays a little more than he would if he booked with a travel agency in France. However, the advantage of booking through lemurie.com is that travelers are free to set up their own agenda.

Clients

- The company's clients are young independent tourists who are somewhat (but not completely) price-sensitive.

NEPAL

Major ISPs include Mercantile and World Link. The estimated total number of Internet subscribers in Nepal is around 25,000 ISP accounts, and approximately 100,000 people have access to the Internet. ISP fixed costs for unlimited access are about $180 per year and variable telecom costs of about US 40 cents per hour.

There are about 2,000 Nepalese websites. None of them take online payments. Internet telephony is illegal in Nepal, but this regulation is not applied.

There are probably close to 1,000 Internet cafes in Kathmandu, many of them being in the tourist area, Thamel. This is a world record in terms of density. Access price is as low as 1 rupee per minute (i.e. about US 90 cents per hour). Access prices started at 30 rupees per minute and gradually dropped to 1 rupee. Many Internet cafes have loaded Asian (mostly Japanese and Korean) fonts. Access speed is typically 19 Kbps using dial-up lines. A few Internet cafes offer Internet telephony. Most have no way of making payment to foreign companies offering this service.

Very few people have (dollar-denominated) credit cards. Distant-selling merchant accounts are non-existent in Nepal; consequently, B2C e-commerce websites ask for prepayment by wire transfer, tourism-related websites take reservations but no online payments. In the case of bank-to-bank wire transfers, the receiving company pay significant banking commissions. Local companies usually need to have accounts in foreign countries to be able to make payments to foreign companies (e.g. web presence providers).

Postal services are generally unreliable, but private courier services are available, including the major international companies. People can move freely between India and Nepal, and work freely in both countries. The language, script and religion are similar. Many Nepalis are trained in India and many Indians work in Nepal.

Company Sheet No. 1: Mercantile Office Systems (MOS)

Classification: Teleservicing model

Contact, staff, and turnover

- Contact people: Mr. Sanjib Raj Bhandari, Chief Executive Officer; Mr. Jai Rajbhandari, Human Resources Manager
- Address: Post Box 876, Durbar Marg, Kathmandu, Nepal
- Telephone: 220 773; e-mail: sanjib@mos.com.np; jai@mos.com.np; www.mos.com.np
- Established in 1994 (but the Mercantile Group has been active as an IT solution provider since 1982)
- Number of staff: About 40 employees

Main line of business

- Since 1982 MOS has been a major local player as an IT solution company, and particularly as a database developer. It is part of the Mercantile Group, one of the pre-eminent industrial groups in Nepal.

Line of e-business

- ISP (since 1994): by the end of 2001, MOS plans to have 35 points of access (POPs), including in some very remote areas where no electricity is available.
- Online development of databases (i.e. clients have online permanent access to the progress made). Without the Internet, it would have been necessary to use a much more sophisticated technology such as a leased satellite line.
- Newly launched: distance learning programme (650 courses) based on the content of and certification from "American Distance Learning". Users pay $200 per year.

Potential business opportunities

- To be launched: Internet-based ASP (accounting, billing, reservations) for small hotels which cannot afford to build their own internal computer department. Goal: to reach 50 hotels within one year.
- In addition, Mercantile owns 50 per cent of Serving Minds (www.servingminds.com), a new multimedia centre (voice, e-mail, chat, co-browsing) which when completed should have about 250 stations and 900 employees.

Modus operandi of e-business

- It is not easy for MOS to sell value-added services (e.g. database development, multimedia centre) abroad owing to a lack of credibility and long-standing contacts.
- So far, international development has occurred slowly.

MYANMAR

There is essentially no web access in Myanmar. Only 15 private leading IT-related companies as well as half of the government agencies have restricted access to the web. Restrictions include the control of incoming content. Free e-mail sites such as Yahoo and Hotmail and free hosting community sites such as Geocities and The Globe are inaccessible. The objective of the Government is twofold: to protect the country from negative external influences and to keep its profitable monopoly in the telecommunication sector (including international phone calls).

Companies can apply to have e-mail access. There is only one e-mail provider namely Myanmar Posts and Telecommunications (MPT), a unit of the Ministry of Communications, Posts and Telegraphs. They have 3,000 to 4,000 clients. Fees are as follows: $150 to set up an account, $150 annual fees and $1 for each set of 1000 characters sent or received. MPT has the right to check the content of e-mails. Previously, an Australian company called Eagle offered email services (xyz@dataserco.com.mm) but has since been expelled from the country.

The Government has announced its intention to open up web access, but it is unclear when this might occur. Currently there are about 1000 Myanmar-related websites. However, only five are hosted by the Myanmar Posts and Telecommunications (TLD = mm). Hosting by MPT is costly (an annual cost of $200 per year for each set of 500 Kb). Many companies have their websites created/uploaded abroad. Some companies use local web designers working offline and then send completed websites by CD-ROM or by FTP to foreign countries from where sites can be uploaded. Most of the Myanmar-related websites are created by Burmese leaving abroad.

Myanmar companies with websites do not have access to the web. They must receive orders, reservations and inquiries through their xyz@mptmail.net.mm e-mail address. Alternatively, they receive information and orders by fax from their foreign-based affiliate.

There is at least one small Internet cafe in Myanmar, located in Ah San Nya University. However, since it does not have access to the web, websites are stored on local hard disks.

The Government is currently preparing a National Intranet, which should be ready in a few months. It should have major commercial, banking and government applications.

Company Sheet No. 1: Design Printing Services

Classification: Teleservicing model

Contact, staff and turnover

- Contact person: Mr. Aye Min Oo-Sonny, Managing Director.
- Address: No. 165/167, Room 4, 1st floor, 35th Street, Kyauk-ta-da Township, Yangon, Myanmar
- Telephone: 051 700 541; e-mail: dps@mptmail.net.mm; website: www.dps.com.mm, www.myanmars.net
- Number of staff: 35 employees

Main line of business

- DPS's main business is to create and distribute high-quality maps of Myanmar. Some maps are very detailed and are sold in small volumes. However, most maps are handed out free of charge to tourists and are financed by advertisements.

Line of e-business

- Most advertisers (i.e. 139) have asked DPS to build websites for them. DPS is therefore one of the leading web agencies in Myanmar.
- DPS also has a website used to promote its clients (i.e. www.myanmars.net).

Potential business opportunities

- DPS plan's to launch a portal site devoted to selling Myanmar local products. However, it is unlikely for many reasons, that it will succeed, the major one being that the Internet is not good for selling an unknown products to new customers.

Modus operandi of e-business

- Since DPS does not have access to the Internet, it loads their completed websites to a ftp site owned by MPT.
- Subsequently, the information is taken from a partner company in Yugoslavia which uploads the websites.

TOGO

About 30,000 people have access to the Internet in Togo. There are about 10,000 Internet accounts, 80 per cent of them being for companies and the remainder for private individuals. In Lomé, there are about 300 Internet cafes. Most of these cafes have one to three PCs while about 20 of them have about 20 PCs each at their disposal. Typical uses are Internet international telephony and web e-mail. Access for one hour costs about CFA 350-800 ($0.6 to 1.3). Major access providers are CAFE Informatique (private) and Togo Télécom (State-owned but likely to be privatised). There are a total of 26 ISPs in Togo.

There are about 1,000 Togolese websites, but few that can be considered to be professionally designed and maintained. Most are amateur sites hosted in free community sites such as Geocities.com and Multimania.com. Websites (excluding those hosted on free community websites) are hosted in Togo (CAFE Informatique), in the United States or France.

No local bank issues credit cards. Togolese owning credit cards obtain them from their foreign banks based abroad. No local bank issues distant-selling credit card merchant accounts. Very few companies (e.g. CAFE Informatique; see http://noel2000.café.tg) have this kind of merchant account needed to accept credit card online payments.

There are no national policies addressing e-commerce and there is a general lack of awareness and understanding of the importance and benefits of e-commerce. There are, however, indications that the Government is beginning to consider these issues. A Danish company has just conducted an IT infrastructure-oriented consultancy for the Ministry of Mines, Energy, Post and Telecommunications.

Company Sheet No. 1: CAFE Informatique

Classification: Teleservicing model

Contact, staff and turnover

- Contact person : Mr. Adiel Akplogan, Directeur du département "Internet et transmission des données"
- Address : Tokoin Casablanca, BP 12596 Lomé, Togo
- Telephone: +228 25 55 55; fax: +228 25 66 66; e-mail: cafenet@café.tg www.cafe.tg
- Established in 1994
- Number of staff: About 60 permanent employees plus at least 50 temporary employees

Main line of business

- ISP: 3,000 clients including 10 with leased lines.
- Website development
- Sales, installation, integration and maintenance of computer hardware and software

Line of e-business

- Telemarketing and data scrubbing using IP telephony (funded by the World Bank).
- The test phase has now been completed (employing 50 temporary employees at night).

Potential business opportunities

- It is hoped to get a major contract from large telecommunications companies.
- Expand to become a major multimedia call centre.

Company Sheet No. 2: Langues et Business

Classification: Teleservicing model

Contact, staff and turnover

- Contact people : Mr. Sylvester Elolo Kumodzi, Member of AIIC (International Association of Conference Interpreters), Rotarian (Club: Lomé Doyen)
- Address : BP 131, Hôtel 2 Février, Lomé, Togo; e-mail: langbus@bibway.com; no website
- Established in 1992

Main line of business

- English/French translation/interpretation (mainly from English to French).
- Texts are regularly transferred by e-mail.
- Four permanent translators and many freelances (about four of them are nearly permanent).
- Sometimes Langues et Business uses Ghanaian freelances for translation from French to English. One freelance can translate from German to French.

Modus operandi of e-business

- Because of its location in a leading hotel, the company can acquire many foreign clients among participants in international conferences.
- Payments are made using bank-to-bank transfers. Only one foreign (Belgian) client has not paid.

Clients

- Foreign clients include WHO (Geneva) and YMCA (Geneva).

CAMBODIA

About 5,000 people have access to the Internet. Most people use it in their office. Dial-up access is typical. There are about 20 Internet cafes in Phnom Penh, most of which have 5 to 15 PCs. Internet cafes tend to serve mostly foreign tourists and the more affluent young Cambodians. Access for one hour costs $2 to 4 (a 30 per cent discount is usually granted to students). Some Internet cafes offer late evening access for $1 per hour.

There are only two ISPs in Cambodia: Telstra's Big Pond (a private Australian-owned company) and Camnet (from the Ministry of Posts and Telecommunications, with the technical support of Canada's International Development Research Center). A third provider - Open Forum of Cambodia (www.forum.org.kh), an NGO - has a licence to provide only e-mail access.

Telstra's Big Pond Internet access fees are as follows: deposit: $100; start-up fee: $30; monthly fees: $50, 13 free hours per month; any hours in excess of the free hours are charged at $2.5 per hour. Camnet charges slightly lower fees.

In 2002, the Government may allow a third ISP. The Government (i.e. the Ministry of Posts and Telecommunications) restricts the number of ISPs as it believes the market is not large enough for more than two or three ISPs.

Voice-over IP is illegal in Cambodia. International calls are expensive (about $3 per minute). None of the four Internet cafes visited provide voice-over IP, which indicates that the Government enforces this law. Power cuts and surges are frequent (at least two power cuts per day). Local telecommunications are poor and relatively expensive.

A major handicap for Cambodians entering the digital economy is language. Very few people speak foreign languages. Most young people, even those active on the Internet, have a very limited knowledge of English.

There are about 100 Cambodian websites. Many of them are very simple and often outdated electronic brochure ware. By law, Cambodian domain name sites (.kh) must be hosted in Cambodia. International domain names (.com, org., net) can be hosted anywhere even though it is difficult for most companies to make payments to foreign registrars and/or to web presence providers.

Credit cards are rarely used in Cambodia. There are no distant-selling merchant accounts, and hence no local Cambodian websites accept online credit card payments. Most travel agencies sites have online booking facilities but payment is done offline, normally through advance wire transfer to a bank account in Cambodia or United States.

Chapter 10
CHINA'S ICT STRATEGY AND E-COMMERCE

A. Information and Communication Technology sector

From 1995 to 2000, China achieved remarkable progress in the ICT sector. The national economy grew at an annual rate of 8.3% while the average growth rate of the information technology industry was 31.4%, three times higher than that of traditional industry. Its contribution to the growth of GDP increased from 5.2% to 12.4% and its share of GDP rose from 2% to 4% in 2000. Exports of electronics and information technology products reached $55.1 billion, accounting for nearly one fourth of total exports. Total investment in the information and communication sector stood at $97 billion. Financing from the overseas stock exchange for telecom enterprises amounted to $20 billion (Xiang, 2001).

The development of e-commerce largely depends on the state of information and communication technology and is related to the growth of the Internet population. Thus, this chapter describes fundamental Internet demographics, the administration of the Internet and the ICT infrastructure in China.

1. China's Internet population[1]

China's Internet population has seen a remarkable increase over the past several years in absolute terms, although its size relative to the total population is still quite low. As of January 2001, China had 22.5 million Internet users and 8.92 million personal computers (PCs) connected to the Internet, representing a threefold increase in comparison with January 2000.[2] Between 1997 and 2000, the number of Internet users has been doubling every six months (see chart 20). There are 122,099 web sites registered under the .cn domain, including 96,221 web sites (78.8% of all registered domain names) that belong to commercial and financial organizations. The sharp increase in the number of web sites in the year 2000 indicates that many companies are becoming Internet conscious and are registering their own web sites with the strong intention of engaging in e-commerce.

The growth of the Internet population is closely related to access capacity. In 1997, China had a capacity of only 24.5Mbps for international Internet access, but this capacity had increased to 2.8Gbps by the end of 2000 (see chart 21). Thanks to the support and investment of the public and private sectors, the bandwidth of the domestic Internet Protocol (IP) phone network expanded from 56Mbps in mid-2000 to 213Mbps by the end of 2000 (CNNIC, 2001). Direct Internet interconnection has been established with the United States, Canada, Australia, the United Kingdom, Germany, Japan and the Republic of Korea.

However, conclusions on the overall impact should take into account the uneven geographical distribution of Internet access. Most Internet users (more than 31% of all Internet users in China) live in big cities, such as Beijing, Guangdong and Shanghai, and in the eastern coastal region. Vast parts of the country's western inland provinces are still not connected to the Internet (see chart 22). There are eleven provinces and territories with less than 2% of Internet users (see chart 23). This imbalance reflects regional disparities in general economic development and level of education.

Due to domestic constraints such as regional economic disparities, low level of disposable personal income and administrative restrictions on the operation of Internet companies, it appears that Internet subscribers are unlikely to sustain as high a growth rate as that experienced in the last several years. From a long-term point of view, a more realistic estimate may be obtained through a simulation model linking Internet user growth rates with average GDP growth rates. The simulation produces a scenario whereby China will have 67.9 million Internet subscribers in 2005, accounting for 5.12% of China's total population and 1.05% of the world total population (see table 28).

Chart 20
China's Internet market

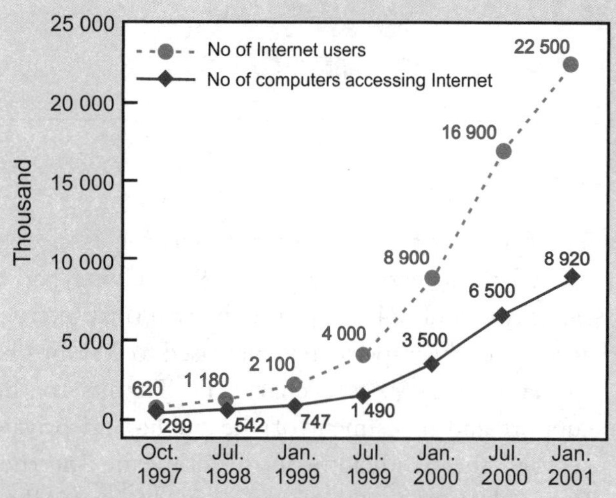

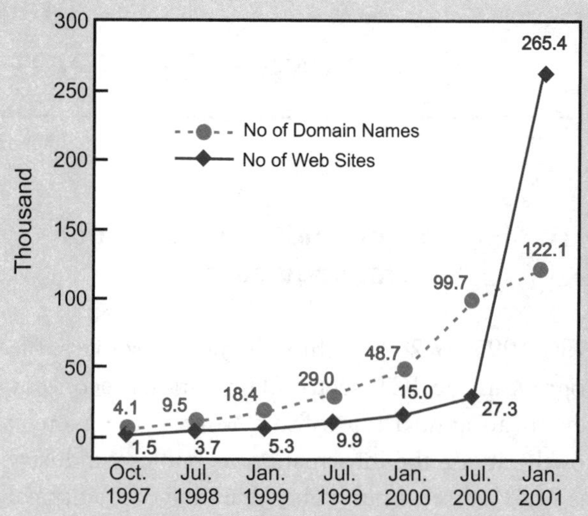

Chart 21
International Internet access capacity

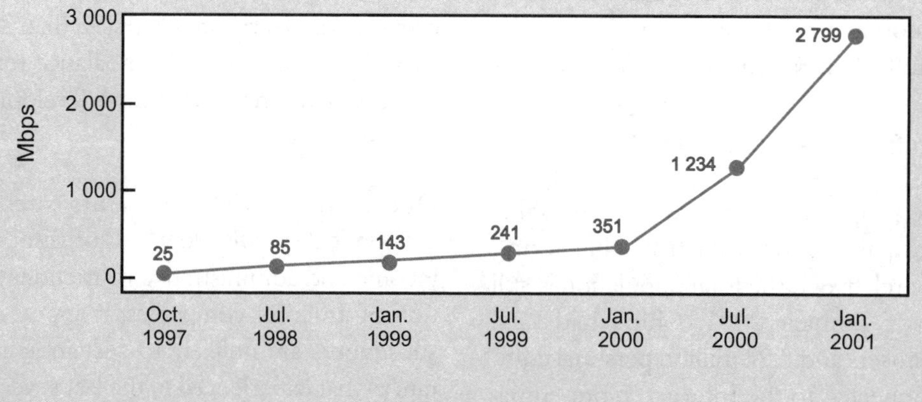

Source: CNNIC survey 1997-2001.

Chart 22
Geographical distribution of Internet users

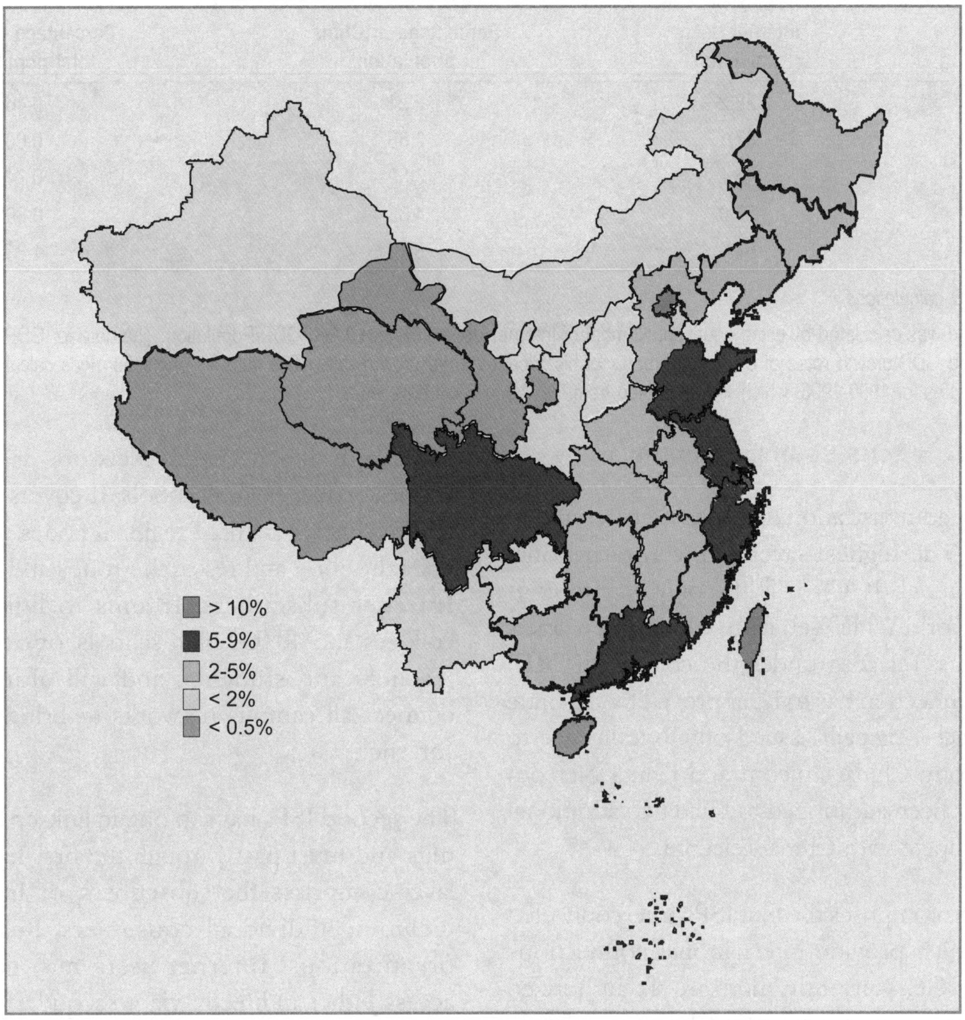

Source: CNNIC survey, January 2001.

Chart 23
Location of users, percentage share of total as of January 2001

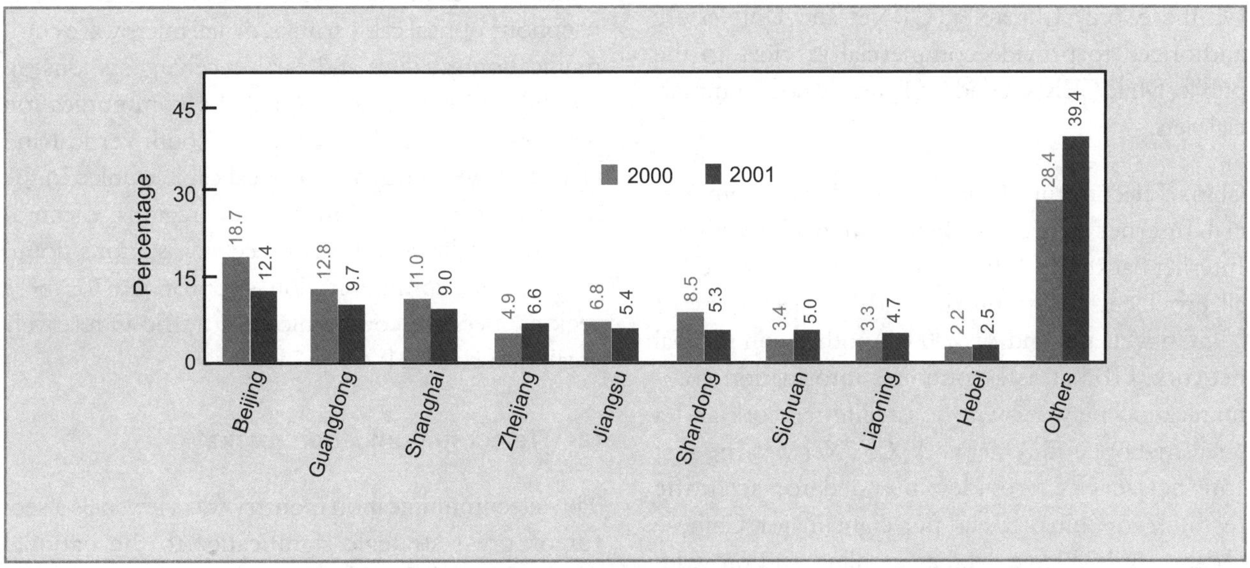

Source: CNNIC survey 2000-2001.

Table 28
Scenario of China's Internet users

Year	Internet users (millions)	Percentage of China population	Percentage of world total population
2001	28.2	2.21	0.46
2002	37.1	2.88	0.60
2003	46.7	3.59	0.74
2004	57.0	4.33	0.89
2005	67.9	5.12	1.05

Source: UNCTAD calculations.

Note: The trend was calculated by using equation: Number of Internet Users=101.23+0.146*GDP/Population. The data for GDP was projected by assuming GDP growth rates of 8% (on the basis of historical average growth rate). The data for population was calculated by using the growth rates for 1990-1998, which was extracted from the World Bank database.

2. Internet administration

The Internet administration in China is structured in four layers. The highest layer is the International Gateway Channel (IGC). It is the only way to connect to the World Wide Web from China and is operated by China Telecom under the control of MII. Each new connection has to be approved by the State Council, which originally issued only one licence to China Telecom. China Unicom and China Netcom have recently been authorized to build two additional IGCs to compete with China Telecom.

The next layer comprises the first ISPs, interconnected networks which provide international connections through the IGC. Currently, there are six authorized interconnected networks, namely ChinaNet (administered by MII), GBNet (owned by Jitong Corporation), CERNet (linking academic institutions), CSTNet (primary network for research institutions and scientists), UniNet (operated by China Unicom) and CNCNet (under construction by China Netcom). Of these, only ChinaNet, GBNet and UniNet are authorized to provide commercial services to the public, while CERNet and CSTNet are non-commercial nets.

China Telecom runs ChinaNet, the largest commercial Internet network, which is now the Chinese Internet backbone. It has 31 regional nodes covering all provinces and territories and had a capacity of 1.95Gpbs at the end of 2000. Another commercial network, GBNet, is a computer information communication network with a satellite network and a terrestrial optic fibre network. CSTNet was the first Internet service provider intended for scientific research in China. It has put eight major Chinese libraries and 23 large databases online, and provides the most extensive search services for scientific research and development. CERNet, the China Education and Research Network, is dedicated to Chinese colleges and schools. It covers 31 provinces and territories, with 24 regional nodes. It is linked to 750 education and research groups and has 4 million Internet subscribers. It aims to link over 1,000 colleges and 40,000 high schools, or over 10 million teachers and students, and will ultimately interconnect all campus networks to bring them to the Internet.

The second ISPs have to obtain link-up business permits and must pass through the first ISPs. The final layer comprises the subscribers, or Internet users, including individual consumers, businesses and organizations. Internet users may gain Internet access either indirectly via a second ISP or directly through one of the six interconnected networks.

3. Internet infrastructure

China's Internet infrastructure is made up of traditional land telephone lines and newly created mobile telephony optical cable trunks, digital microwave communication satellites and earth receiving stations. In coastal and south-east China, the communication network is formed by eight north-south vertical and eight east-west horizontal optical cable trunks. In the north-western and south-western regions, communication satellites and earth receiving stations dominate. Satellite communication is appropriate for these regions, because communication traffic is relatively small (see chart 24).

(a) Telecommunication market

The telecommunication industry was viewed as a sector of great strategic significance to the national economy, and the establishment of MII in 1997 reflected the central Government's desire to stream-

Chart 24
Optical cable trunks network

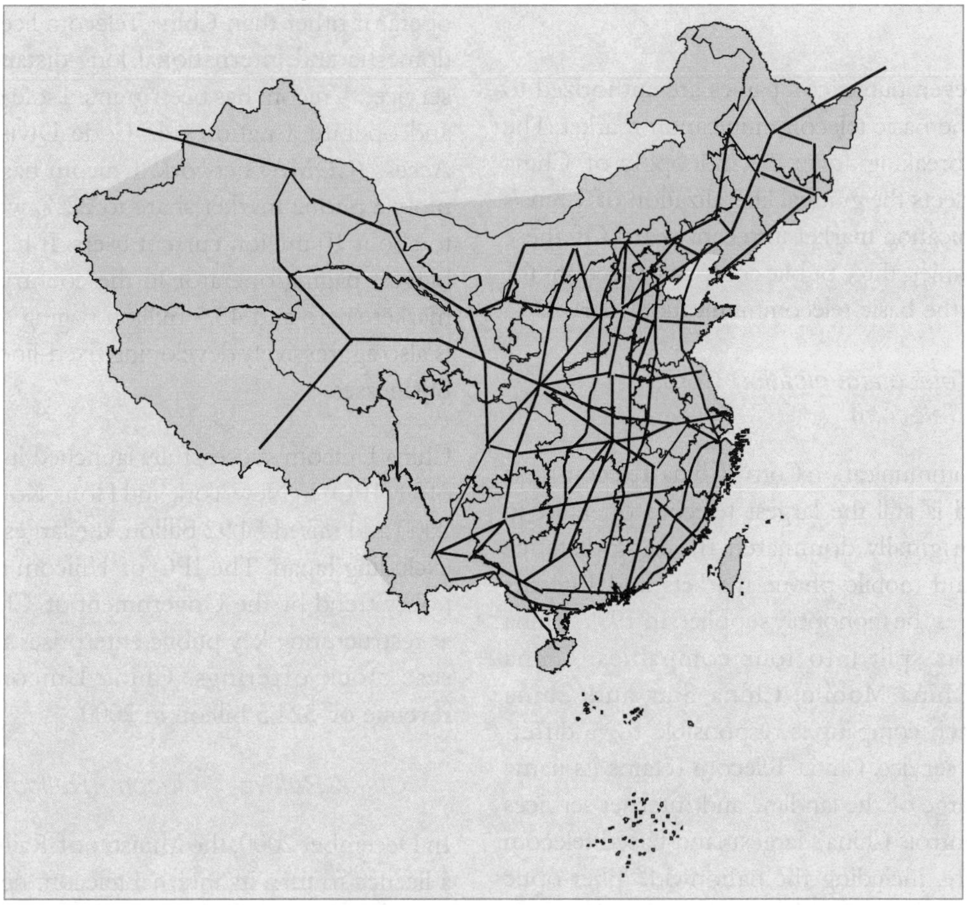

Source: Ministry of Information Industry, 2000.

line the governance of this sector. MII has been given the responsibility for overseeing and regulating national policy concerning China's communications, information technology and software products, initiating research and development programmes, and developing and managing public backbone networks, radio broadcast networks and television cable networks.

Official statistics published by MII demonstrate a significant improvement of the telecommunication infrastructure. China has the world's second largest telephone network capacity in absolute terms, rising from seventeenth place in the 1980s. By the end of 2000, China's teledensity stood at 20.1%, with a daily addition of 170,000 new telephone subscribers, boosting the total to 229 million by 2000. In urban areas, teledencity stood at 39% (Wu, 2001).

Among the new users, 35.6 million signed up for fixed-line service, up 32% from 1999 and increasing the total number of such users to 144 million. Thus, China had 14.1 telephone lines per 100 inhabitants at the end of 2000. In 1999, however, the penetration rate was only 8.6% which was higher than that of India (3.2%) but lower than that of Brazil (14.9%), the United States (67.3%) and the United Kingdom (56.7%) (ITU, 2001). The number of Chinese mobile subscribers grew at an average annual rate of 88% between 1996 and 2000. There were about 41.97 million new mobile phone users in 2000, up 97% from the previous year and increasing the total number to 85.26 million. The nationwide percentage of mobile phone users reached 6.7% of the population (Wu, 2001; China E-commerce Association, 2001), which is much higher than the 0.35% in India but still lower than the 13.6% in Brazil, 40% in the United States and 67% in the United Kingdom (ITU, 2001).

China Telecom is constructing a fiber-optic transmission backbone ring by building 10 trunk lines to connect major cities in the existing grid of eight north-south lines and eight east-west lines. The company worked to extend the international fiber-optic cable network by cooperating with other international carriers to build submarine cables to countries in East and South-East Asia, to Europe and to the United States to handle increased data and Internet traffic. In 2000, 46,000 kilometers of long-distance fiber-optic lines were added, increasing the total length to

286,000 kilometers. Today, the total length of China's fibre-optic cables is 1.25 million kilometers (Wu, 2001).

Currently, seven public companies are authorized to operate in the basic telecommunication market. The process of breaking down the monopoly of China Telecom reflects the gradual liberalization of China's telecommunication market in recent years. Of these seven companies, three public companies account for the bulk of the basic telecommunication market.

China Telecommunication Corp. (China Telecom)

China Telecommunication Corp. (China Telecom) was the first and is still the largest telecom operator in China. It originally dominated the long-distance telephone and mobile phone markets and Internet access and was the monopoly supplier. In 1999, China Telecom was split into four companies: China Telecom, China Mobile, China Star and China Netcom. Each company is responsible for a different telecom service. China Telecom retains its name and is in charge of the landline and Internet services sector. It controls China's largest land-based telecom infrastructure, including the nationwide fiber-optic cable network and ChinaNet, which currently covers 70% of China's Internet market. China Mobile provides mobile communication services and is constructing the world's largest GSM network with a reported capacity of 65 million mobile users. China Star is responsible for developing its satellite communication services, while China Netcom, established in early 2000, concentrates on developing broadband Internet services. In 2000, China Telecom's business revenue was $20.64 billion.

China United Telecommunication Ltd. (Unicom)

As the country's second largest telecom operator established in 1994, China United Telecommunications Ltd. (Unicom) was initially given a license to provide mobile service in 65 cities to break the monopoly of China Telecom. Now, Unicom operates mobile telephony businesses, as well as long-distance, data and Internet businesses. The company is the only operator other than China Telecom licensed to offer domestic and international long-distance telephone services. Unicom has been granted sole rights to build and operate a nationwide Code Division Multiple Access (CDMA) network. Unicom has increased its mobile phone market share to 22%, which amounts to about 10 million current users. It has become the biggest paging operator in the country, with a 59% market share and 43.5 million paging subscribers. It is also aggressively developing fixed-line and Internet businesses.

China Unicom successfully launched its initial public offer (IPO) in New York and Hong Kong in late June 2000 and raised $4.92 billion, the largest IPO in Asia excluding Japan. The IPO of Unicom reflects a new policy trend by the Government of China that aims at restructuring key public enterprises through overseas stock offerings. China Unicom generated revenue of $24.5 billion in 2000.

China Railway Telecom (Railcom)

In December 2000, the Ministry of Railways received a licence to turn its internal telecom network, China Railway Telecom (Railcom), into a commercial system to compete with China Telecom. Railcom was a stand-alone internal telecommunication network (a kind of Intranet) serving the railway sector. It already services 1 million users, mostly railway workers, on a fibre-optic fixed-line network spanning 120,000 kilometers and connecting 500 cities. Railcom provides fixed-line phone, voice-over-Internet protocol (VoIP), paging and Internet access services and will cover 28 of China's 31 provinces.

Future development

China has made initial commitments to progressively liberalize its telecommunication services upon accession to WTO. In value-added and paging services, foreign service suppliers may hold a 30% equity share upon accession, 49% after one year and 50% after two years. Foreign service suppliers can provide e-

Table 29
Multiple service providers

	Fixed line	wireless	IP telephone	Data service	ISP
China Telecom	✓		✓	✓	✓
China Unicom	✓	✓	✓	✓	✓
China Railway Com.			✓	✓	✓

Source: News reports.

mail, voice mail, online information and data base retrieval, EDI, enhanced/value-added facsimile services, code and protocol conversion, online information and data processing, and paging services. The geographic restriction on the above services to the three cities of Beijing, Shanghai and Guangzhou will be lifted two years after accession. In mobile voice and data services, the foreign service supplier will be able to provide all analogue/digital mobile services and personal communication services and hold a 25% share one year after accession, 35% after three years, and 49% after five years. Further, foreign service suppliers can provide services nationwide five years after accession.

In value-added telecommunication services, including the Internet and e-commerce, China's big market is attractive and promising. In the telecommunication hardware market, many foreign telecom companies like Ericsson, Motorola, Nokia and Siemens have decided to further expand their business operations in China in anticipation of China's entry into WTO. In March 1999, AT&T joined two Chinese companies to offer IP services in Shanghai. Until now, it is the first and the only foreign partner allowed to provide telecom services in China. The joint venture is an experimental operation allowing foreign investment in previously restricted network business. In early June 2001, the Chinese computer manufacturer Legend Group and AOL of Time Warner signed a $200 million agreement to establish a joint venture specially for e-commerce.

China's entry into WTO should have a positive effect on e-commerce. It will open the market for foreign investment and create a competitive environment that should bring down the access cost and improve service quality. It will also provide Chinese enterprises with opportunities for cooperation leading to faster adoption of e-commerce practice.

(b) Mobile market

Currently, China has about 85.26 million mobile phone users, much more than the number of PC owners. Accessing the Internet through mobile phones may partly solve China's problem of low levels of PC penetration. Because mobile phone costs are much lower than the price of a personal computer, this approach is more affordable. As mobile phone manufacturers such as Motorola and Ericsson have established production facilities in China, the prices for mobile phones are likely to drop further.

Beginning May 2000, firms throughout China started to offer wireless application protocol (WAP) services to enable more mobile phone users to tap into the Internet using their handsets. China Mobile, China Telecom and China Unicom unveiled their WAP services in the major Chinese cities. But WAP mobile phones have their drawbacks: low speed, lack of a keyboard, small text-only displays, limited security and limited memory are the key problems. The drawback in practical usage is that the WAP services present a graphic display on a small screen and it is especially difficult to enter Chinese characters with the small mobile phone keys.

While WAP has lately been criticized for not meeting the users' needs, General Packet Radio Service (GPRS) should allow for speedier, always-on Internet access. China Unicom is already in the process of rolling out GPRS in major cities throughout China. China Mobil also plans to deliver its GPRS network to four cities (Hangzhou, Chengdu, Tianjin and Beijing) to serve 110,000 subscribers by the middle of 2001.

(c) Computer market

China has a rapidly developing PC market, although there are only about 30 million computers currently in the country. While the growth in demand for PCs in industrialized countries is slowing down, China's demand for PCs has been accelerating. Several factors are at play here. Corporate spending on office automation and individual purchasing was encouraged by retail prices that dropped to a level below the affordability threshold ($1,000). The need for computers in the banking sector for automation and system integration and the modernization of the customs administration and the transport industry also had positive effects. In addition, the decision by the Government to introduce computer courses as a compulsory part of the official school syllabus also had a pulling effect on computer demand. Finally, the surge in enthusiasm in China for the Internet by itself has spurred new demand for PCs. The Chinese market accounted for 36% of the Asia-Pacific market, with 7.17 million PCs sold in 2000, a 45.1% increase over 1999 sales (International Data Corporation, 2001).

The annual production capacity for PCs was 8.6 million units in 2000 (CCID Consulting Co., 2001). Efforts to give online education, training and computer education in schools and initiatives by government and enterprises to go online should stimulate China's PC sales to 17 million units in 2004 (see chart 26).

In spite of the rapid growth in sales, the computer penetration rate is still very low. In the cities, only 5% of Chinese homes have their own PCs, and the figure is less than 3.2% for the whole of China, compared to 105% for TVs, 80% for refrigerators, and 50% for air-conditioners (Merrill Lynch; 2000). Low computer penetration hampers the development of e-commerce in China (see table 30).

Table 30
China's PC penetration rate

Country	%
Per urban household	
China	5
USA	49
Per population	
Mainland China	3.2
Taiwan, Province of China	14
Republic of Korea	15
Hong Kong, China	30
Singapore	36

Source: Merrill Lynch, September 2000 and China E-commerce Association, 2001.

Chart 25
2000 PC shipment growth rate

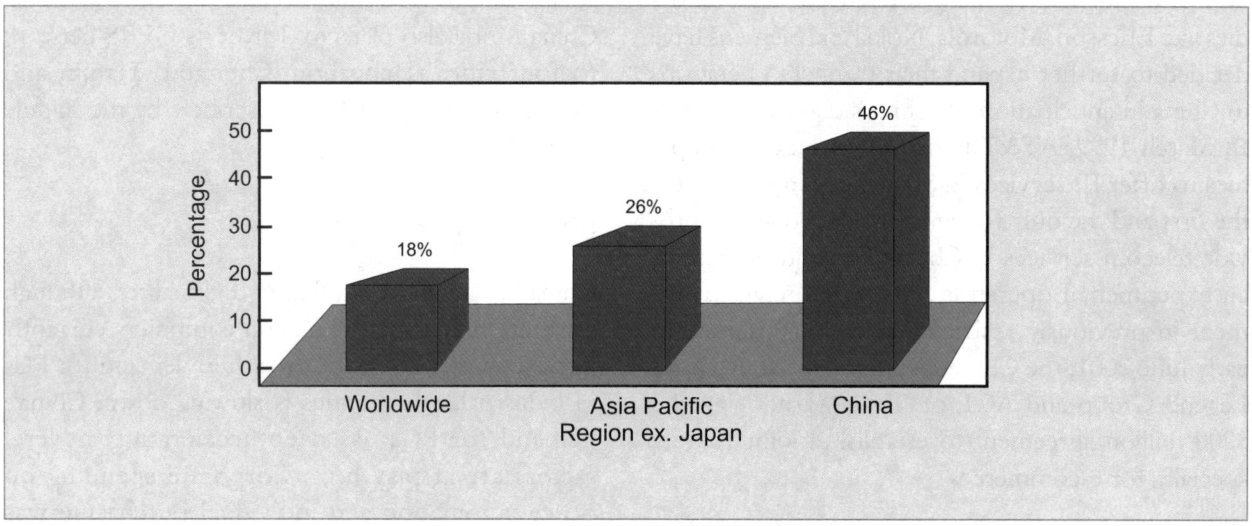

Source: IDC, 2001 and Merrill Lynch, September 2000.

Chart 26
Unit shipment growth of China's PC market

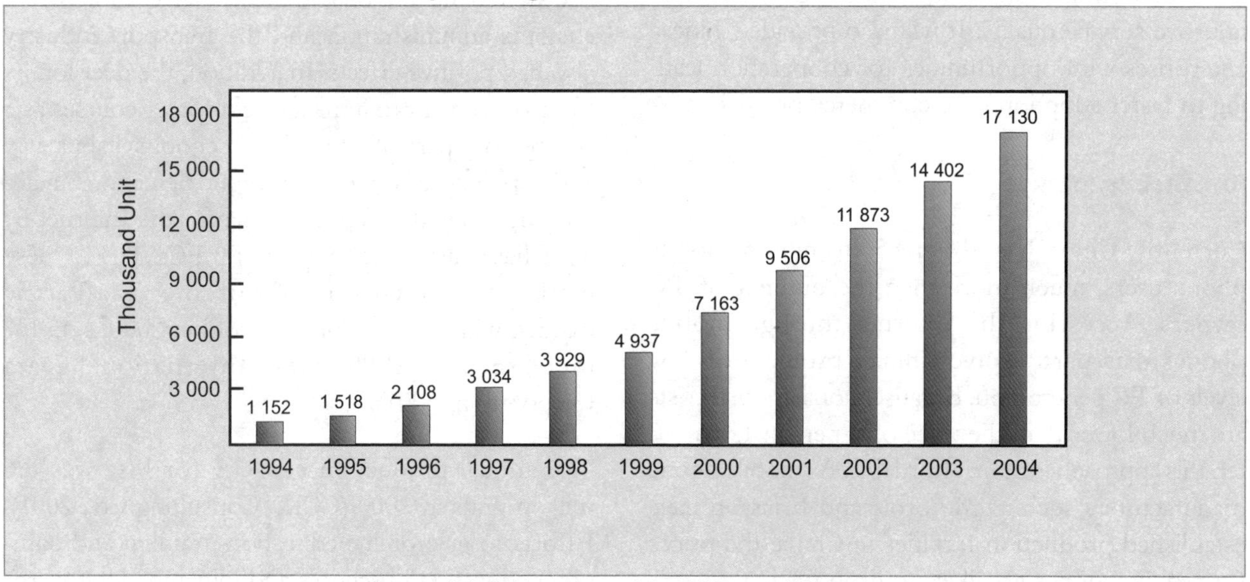

Source: IDC, 2001 and Legend Annual Report, 1998-2000.

B. Government initiatives

In the mid 1980s, the Government launched a comprehensive science and technology development programme that included an information highway development strategy. This early science development programme prepared the way for current initiatives to get electronic commerce off the ground. In 1999, the Chinese Government initiated the "Government Online" and "Enterprises Go Online" projects, and it declared year 2000 the "Year for Chinese Businesses to Go Online". In addition, the Government[3] hosted five sessions of the China International Electronic Commerce Summit in Beijing from 1996 to 2001. Senior government officials and chief executives of prominent multinational enterprises had the opportunity to exchange views in round table discussions. Furthermore, the China E-commerce Association[4] was established in June 2000. These initiatives have undoubtedly contributed to raising awareness among government officials of the implications of e-commerce and provided a forum for discussion on co-operation in e-commerce between Chinese enterprises and foreign enterprises.

1. Golden Projects

China's first move in the direction of building up a national information infrastructure was the initiation of the Golden Projects that aimed at simultaneously developing an information economy and building administrative capacity. The projects, which are supported by a high-level body under the State Council, namely the National Economic Information Council, have the goal of building a national information highway as a path to modernization and economic development by developing information technology in China.

The Golden Projects initially consisted of three elements: the Golden Bridge, the Golden Card and the Golden Gate. Later they expanded their scope to cover other areas (see table 31).

The Golden Bridge project produced the GBNet (described in Section A). Proposed in March 1993, the GBNet is a network composed of satellite and landline networks that tie together 31 provincial and regional nodes with a central hub in Beijing. Designed primarily to serve the finance and business sectors, it plans to cover 180 cities nationwide in 2002 and will link the databases of the national economic management sector, large and medium-size enterprises and major national engineering, scientific and educational bases. By 2000, it had nodes in 60 cities and 15 international lines that connect it to the Internet backbone of China Telecom, AT&T and Global One.

The Golden Card[5] is an electronic money project that was designed to accelerate the development of banking and credit card systems in major cities in China. The project set up a credit card verification scheme and an inter-bank, inter-region clearing system. It plans to issue 200 million credit cards in 400 cities within China by 2003. The total cost for the Golden Card project was estimated to be over $12 billion. By 1999, the progress made was as follows:

- A bankcard information exchange centre and network has been established in each of the 12 trial cities;
- The ATM system had been linked up in 10 of the 12 pilot cities;
- 17 to 20 banks had issued a total of over 140 million bankcards in China. The Industrial and Commercial Bank of China had issued 45.3 million debit cards — the highest issuance rate in China — and covered half of China's debit card market.

First proposed in June 1993, the Golden Gate project is a foreign trade information network. By linking the Ministry of Foreign Trade and Economic Co-operation and the Customs Bureau, it aims at improving import-export trade administration and developing an information network to accelerate China's foreign trade activities. The recent progress will be discussed in Section C.

After the initial three golden projects, a series of other programmes has also been proposed and implemented. The Golden Intelligence project, better known as CERNet (described in Section A), is the vehicle for the Internet's entrance into China by interconnecting campus networks and then connecting them to the global Internet. China's electronic taxation project began in 1996. In the first phase, about 368 tax offices in different cities and regions were connected. At the end of 1996, the second phase of the project was launched, aiming to upgrade and connect tax authorities at the provincial level. In 1998 an e-mail system linking provinces, cities, and local tax bureaus was opened by the State taxation administration, which broadcasts information on tax policies, news and technologies to all tax offices. By 1999, the Golden Tax's network covered 400 cities and 3,800 counties.

The Golden project is an initiative taken by the Government to mobilize all parts of society to prepare to adapt and face the challenge of revolutionary changes that have been foreseen as a result of the application of information technology. It involves almost all economic sectors, i.e. manufacturing, agriculture, services, banking and financing, commerce and international trade, transportation, education and vocational training. It aims to introduce a fundamental reform of the government structure and it touches upon all government institutions. However, many of the activities in the project are still in the process of being implemented, and there is no comprehensive information on which to base an assessment of project performance.

2. National informatization

The Government has an important role to play in building the basic ICT infrastructure and facilitating the development of electronic commerce. At the same time foreign capital is being allowed to participate in the development of e-commerce and to gradually liberalize the information and communication technology industry and create a competitive environment for Chinese and foreign enterprises alike. The Chinese Government has also taken initiatives in term of pushing national informatization. The national informatization programme is given high priority in the 10th Five Year Plan (2001 to 2005). During this period, the information industry is expected to become the pillar industry to spur the national economic growth.

The deployment of city informatization is an important component of national informatization. Several city-based IT projects are under way. Beijing started its "Digital Beijing" project in the experimental zone of Zhong Guan Village, the "Silicon Valley" of China. Shanghai was the first city to embrace the concept of "inforport" and "city informatization". By June 2000, the aspects of Shanghai's city informatization plan that had been completed included:

- Multiple ISPs and broadband Internet access;

Table 31
Summary list of the Golden Projects

Name	Full title	Major ministries, departments
Golden Bridge (JinQiao)	National Public Economic Information Communication Network	Ministry of Electronics, State Information Center, Ji Tong Co.
Golden Card (JinKa)	Electronic Money Project	PBoC, Ministry of Electronics Industry, Ministry of Internal Trade, Great Wall Computer Co.
Golden Sea (JinHai)		State Statistical Bureau, PBoC, State Information Center
Golden Macro (JinHong)	National Economic Macro-Policy Technology System	China ExIm Bank , Ministry of Finance, State Information Center
Golden Tax (JinShui)	Computerised Tax Return and Invoice System Project	Ministry of Finance, Ministry of Electronics Industry, National Taxation Bureau, Great Wall Computer Co.
Golden Intelligence (JinZhi)	China Education and Research Network (CERnet)	State Economic and Trade Commission
Golden Enterprise (JinQi)	Industrial Production and Information Distribution System	State Economic and Trade Commission
Golden Agriculture (JinNong)	Overall Agricultural Administration and Information Service system	Ministry of Agriculture
Golden Health (JinWei)	National Health Information Network	Ministry of Health
Golden Info. (JinFeng)	State Statistical Information Project	State Statistical Bureau
Golden Cellular (GoldenFeng)	Mobile Communications Production and Marketing Project	Ministry of Electronics Industry
Golden Switch (JinKai)	Digital 200 Switch Systems Production Project	Ministry of Electronics Industry, Ministry of Posts and Telecom

Source: Peter Lovelock, 1999.

- Business portals that support electronic certification and online payment;
- Completion of the virtual *Nanjing Road* department store.

C. E-commerce development by sector

1. Internet application and the growth of e-commerce

According to the Ministry of Information Industry (MII), by March 2000 China had 800 online shopping sites, 100 auction sites, 180 remote education sites and 20 remote medical sites. It also had 300 Internet service providers and 1,000 portals. B2C e-commerce was in the start-up phase in 1999, with the total volume of online shopping reaching $3.8 million, accounting for only 0.018% of China's total retail sales. However, recent reports indicate that China's e-commerce transactions in 2000 totaled $9.33 billion, which included $47.17 million in B2C transactions and $9.29 billion in B2B transactions, the latter accounting for more than 90% of total e-commerce in 2000 (Xiang, 2001; CCID Consulting Co., 2001a).

Due to administrative, legal, infrastructure and financial constraints, e-commerce constitutes a small percentage of online activity. Only 31.67% of Internet users actually made online purchases in 2000, although this was double the number of 12 months before (CNNIC, 2001). This shows that China's e-commerce is still in its infancy stage. However, an MII study finds that close to half of all Internet users have expressed interest and enthusiasm for online stores, schools, and brokerage services. In addition, many Internet service enterprises stay in operation without profit with the strategic goal of capturing a market share of the potentially large Chinese market. Anderson Consulting made a forecast that by 2003, China's e-commerce revenue would reach $4.2 billion (see chart 27).

2. Financial services

The People's Bank of China (PBoC) is the country's central bank. The commercial banking system is composed of the main public commercial banks, i.e. the Industrial and Commercial Bank of China (ICBC), the Bank of China (BOC), the Agricultural Bank of China (ABoC) and the Construction Bank of China (CBC), as well as various public and private commercial banks such as the China Merchants Bank (CMB).

PBoC has been cautious in applying Internet-related technologies to financial transactions. PBoC did not begin to make plans for the development of Internet-based technology applications until 1997. In 1998, the PBoC Science and Technology Department and the Beijing Municipal Governments Infoport Office jointly initiated the Beijing Electronic Commerce Project. Since then, PBoC has put the development

Chart 27
China's B2B and B2C market estimates

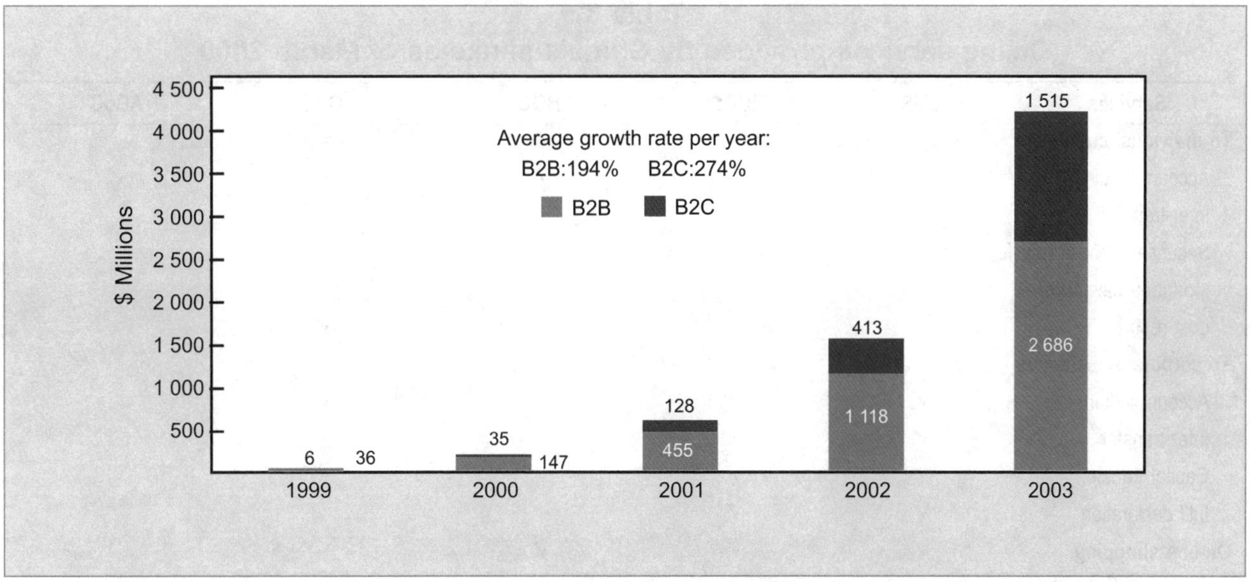

Source: Anderson Consulting, 2000.

of online trading and electronic payment on its agenda.

Meanwhile some commercial banks have also realized the need to develop online services. By March 2000, CMB and four state commercial banks, namely ICBC, BOC, CBC and ABoC were providing online banking services (see table 32).

The five banks provide online services at the basis of two different models. The first is a centralized model. The bank headquarters maintain a centralized web site and all transactions are concluded by the headquarters' Local Area Networks, while the local branches are authorized to accept applications from customers, open accounts for them and distribute software and hardware information. BOC and ICBC follow this model. With the second model, both the headquarters and the local branches have their own web sites, which are interconnected. Local branches complete transactions independently, then transfer the data to headquarters. CBC, ABoC and CMB use this model.

Of all the commercial banks in China, CMB was the first to provide online banking services, Since it launched its B2C online banking service in 1997. Currently, CMB has over 100 million individual customers and 10,000 online institutional customers. Eighty per cent of the e-commerce companies in China prefer CMB's All in One Net card.[6] In the first half of 2000, online institutional customers completed 80,000 transactions.

As the largest commercial bank in China, ICBC has competitive advantages. It runs 8.1 million industrial and commercial business accounts, over half the total for China's financial sector, and has 420 million individual customers. In June 2000, ICBC's online banking service was available in 31 cities, and 500 well-known companies applied for this service. By the end of 2000, online transfers reached $840 million. At present, ICBC has a complete set of e-banking business services, including online corporate banking, personal money management, and B2B and B2C payments.

A number of banks with the intention of entering in the Internet banking business are hesitating for fear of lack of technological capacity to cope with possible hacker attacks and the misuse of customer information and fraud. Some banks have opened special accounts for online banking customers and have set limits on amounts that can be withdrawn to mitigate risks. The establishment of the Certificate Authority (CA) Centre may partly resolve these problems. So far, there are three national CA centres in China, namely the China Financial Certification Center (CFCC), the China international e-commerce CA center, and the China telecommunication CA center.

Initiated by PBoC, along with 12 commercial banks, CFCC was set up in July 2000. The CFCC grants security certificates and digital signature verification to online traders and thus enables secure inter-bank payments and transactions. The security certificate confirms the identity of electronic retailers and online shoppers through a database containing identification information and an encryption system. The CFCC has already completed its first-generation system and is able to issue annually 50,000 corporate

Table 32
Online services provided by China's banks as of March 2000

Services	CMB	ICBC	BOC	CBC	ABoC
To individual customers					
Account inquiry	✓		✓	✓	✓
Inter-transfer	✓		✓	✓	
Securities deposit transfer	✓			✓	
Mortgage calculation	✓				
Lost report	✓			✓	
To corporate customers					
Account inquiry	✓		✓	✓	
Inter-transfer	✓	✓		✓	
Capital transfer	✓	✓		✓	
Int'l declaration	✓	✓	✓		
On-line shopping	✓	✓	✓		

Source: Din (2000).

digital certificates valid for 10 years and 200,000 individual digital certificates.

Two years after China's accession to the WTO, foreign banks will be permitted to conduct Chinese yuan wholesale banking. Finally, five years after China's entry, foreign banks will be entitled to serve individual Chinese customers and also to set up Sino-foreign banks. Foreign banks, with their advanced e-banking systems, capital and experience, are often seen as a future threat to domestic Chinese banks, in particular in the online or e-banking market. This emphasizes the need for good bank supervision and a legal framework that regulates online financial activities, thus supporting fair and competitive market conditions.

3. International trade

Foreign trade is one of the major growth areas in the Chinese economy. In 2000, total international trade was valued at $474.3 billion, an increase of 31.5% over 1999 (MoFTEC, 2001). International trade remains high on the Chinese economic agenda, and there have been persistent attempts to use the Internet as an export market place for Chinese goods and services.

The Ministry of Foreign Trade and Economic Cooperation (MoFTEC) set up its web site in 1998, offering trade information and publicizing China's foreign trade policies. Its web site registers about 700,000 users per day, mostly from overseas. MoFTEC uses the Internet to enhance China's trade transparency and efficiency in trade administration procedures. It established the web site for the China Commodity Trading Market,[7] where business deals can be made online. The China foreign investment databank[8] has also been opened to the public and provides information on China's foreign investment policies, regulations and laws, project invitations, Chinese enterprise profiles, and technology and commodity information. The Chinese Export Commodities Fair, which is China's largest and highest-level trade fair, has also launched its web site[9] covering all sectors of the national economy. Since the initiation of the Golden Gate project in 1993, the computer networks of MoFTEC, the Customs Bureau, the China Foreign Exchange Administration Bureau, the commercial banks, the China Statistical Bureau and some companies have been connected. These provide the tools to substantially simplify trade procedures, cut transaction costs and shorten transaction times.

The China International Electronic Commerce Center (CIECC) was established in 1996. CIECC is administratively managed by MoFTEC, the aim being to assist Chinese enterprises in the use of e-commerce to conduct international trade. Major MoFTEC branches, local offices, and six trade associations are all connected to CIECC (see chart 28). CIECC has the overall responsibility for the construction and operation of electronic trading networks in China and for planning in respect of the role of e-commerce in China's economic development and international trade.

It appears that the main concern of the CIECC is foreign trade administration efficiency and transparency. The following are the main activities of CIECC in promoting trade (Dougan and Fan, 1999):

- Electronically linking with the databases of other countries' customs authorities in charge of textile quota administration;
- Conducting the MoFTEC-Customs trail for online inspection and administration of import-export licences;
- Operating an electronic open bidding system which ensures fairness, openness and transparency, improves efficiency and lowers costs. In October 1998, the introduction of textile export quota electronic bidding saved the bidding enterprises $2 million;
- Harmonizing foreign trade statistics between MoFTEC and the Customs Administration (more than 60 standard trade forms are electronically available) and setting up an import-export statistical database which provides efficient data analysis for China's foreign trade policy makers and for enterprise leaders;
- Launching the electronic certificate of origin nationwide to issue, inspect and manage certificates of origin;
- Setting in operation an electronic inspection and management system for materials processing and manufacturing, a foreign trade practice widely adopted in China;
- Standardizing the coding system for China's export-import enterprises and launching electronic processing, inspection and management systems for a variety of exports and imports from January 1998.

Some commercial web sites concerning foreign trade such as ChinaTradeWorld.com and Chinaproducts.com

Chart 28
CIECC's data communication system

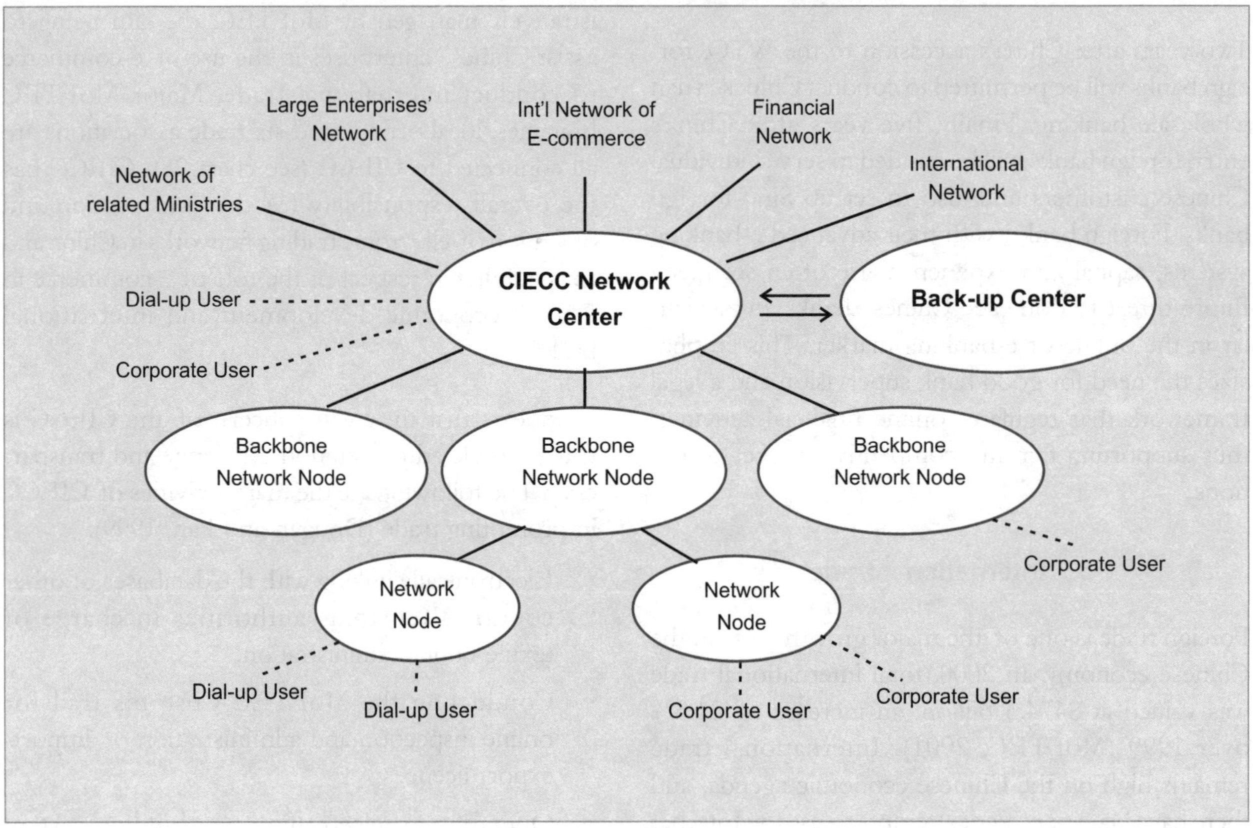

Source: Ministry of Information Industry, 2000.

operate in this sector. Supported by CIECC, ChinaTradeWorld.com aims to become the trade facilitator for China with the rest of the world. Mainly sponsored by the China Council for the Promotion of International Trade (CCPIT), Chinaproducts.com is a B2B trade portal designed to create a marketplace linking China's exporters and manufacturers directly to buyers around the world. These business web sites can normally spread large amounts of trade information covering vast areas and provide a more flexible way of trading than traditional methods.

4. Tourism

Tourism is one of the fastest growing industries in China. In 2000, the number of foreign visitors reached 10.19 million, an increase of 20% over 1999 and China's tourism industry foreign currency revenue amounted to $16.2 billion, up 15% (China National Tourism Administration, 2001).

By the end of 2000, there were over 300 tourism web sites in China. China Travel Network Co. Ltd. (CTN) is one of China's biggest tourism e-commerce web sites. Cost reduction is achieved by attracting more customers by improving the quality of services significantly because, based on real time statistics on customer travelling trends, market analysis reports are provided monthly. CTN differs from other travel agencies in that it provides e-commerce consulting service to more than a thousand travel agencies.

There are three factors that impede the development of etourism. First, e-commerce and tourism cannot be integrated very well at present because some traditional travel agencies are still not aware of e-commerce, while some tourism web sites do not own traditional tourism resources. Secondly, some travel agencies currently limit their services to online air ticket booking and hotel reservation only. Thirdly, since people are still not used to booking online, the ratio of online booking to telephone booking in most travel agencies is 1 to 4 or even less, thus making some online travel agencies actually telephone booking centres.

Table 33
Selected etourism companies

	CTN	Ctrip*	eLong Beijing Ltd.	China Youth Travel Online
Web site	www.ctn.com.cn	www.ctrip.com	www.lohoo.com	www.cytsonline.com
Established	Oct. 1997	May 1999	April 1999	June 2000
Hits/day	300 000	400 000	30 000	N/A
No. of employees	110	323	230	70
Revenue in 2000 ($)	..	12 million	14.5 million	4.8 million
Adv. expenses in 2000	..	0.6 million	0.2 million	0.1 million
No. of hotels included in database	1 100	1 100	3 000	600

Source: Tourism, 2000

* *Ctrip Computer Technology Shanghai Ltd.*

5. Government Online project

In a structural reform launched in 1998, the Chinese Government reduced the number of ministries from 40 to 29 and cut civil servant staffing by half with a view to combating bureaucracy and enhancing efficiency. Achieving this objective should be facilitated by moving much of the administrative work online, which substantially improves transparency and reduces the chance for corruption.

In January 1999, China Telecom and 29 ministries and commissions initiated the project "Government Online". Under the project, more than 80% of the ministries and commissions and all levels of local government will set up web sites on the Internet. The project is to be implemented in three phases. First, both national and local government agencies will put the basic information such as government structures and regulations online. The second step will be to publish rules and regulations, as well as administrative procedures online. The third step will be to operate government administration online. By having different government ministries, offices and information centres nationwide interconnected by an advanced network system, government offices will raise their work efficiency, enhance their policy transparency, improve government procurement and provide better services to the general public.

To date, 4,615 of the 122,099 domain names, i.e. 3.78%, are registered as .gov.cn (CNNIC, 2001). Although the absolute number of registered .gov.cn web sites has increased rapidly after two years of effort, the contents of some web sites are updated slowly and the services offered by most web sites are limited to providing information or reporting news.

6. Enterprises Go Online project

Chinese enterprises are working with poorly developed information technology systems and management. By the end of 1999, there were 15,000 enterprises in China with their own web sites, representing less than 0.1% of Chinese enterprises. Most of them just have a web site with basic contact information and an e-mail address. Few local enterprises are using information technology for enterprise resource management, client-based analysis, or supply-chain management. Furthermore, computers are mostly used for word processing and documentation (96%), followed by e-mail (84%), data processing (79%), and other (less than 50%) (Dougan and Fan, 1999).

In order to help to increase the use of Internet among Chinese enterprises, especially SMEs, the State Economic and Trade Commission, working jointly with MII, launched the "Enterprises Go Online" project at the end of 1999. They intended to get 1 million small enterprises, 10,000 medium-size enterprises and 100 large enterprises online by the end of 2000, and planned to double the number every year in the following three-year period.

7. Online school and distance education

Traditionally, Chinese universities have offered distance learning courses via satellite TV to M.A. and Ph.D. candidates in remote cities, to complement the audio or visual university courses for undergraduates offered by the Central Television. The China Central Radio and Television University (CCRTU) is currently the largest distance education school in China, covering the entire country and targeting adult education and training. The number of graduates totals 2.4 million.

In June 2000, 31 Chinese colleges and universities were permitted to start online classes by the Ministry of Education (MOE). The MOE announced that it would spend $4.8 million on training online teachers and supporting the creation of college-level online teaching materials in 2000. The State Council also allocated $43.5 million to Internet construction for distance education and wants to expand the backbone capacity of CERNet and transform the CCRTU's satellite transmission backbone. In October 2000, the MOE unveiled a satellite-based broadband and multimedia communication platform for distance education. And the distance education programme went into trial operation. The platform will upgrade the satellite TV education system to real-time digital transmission.

Most online high schools and universities are extensions of conventional schools, such as the Beijing High School No. 5 and Beijing No. 101 Middle School, which are known for high rates of university entry. Traditional universities have also allied themselves with some companies to launch online education programmes. In November 2000, CCRTU joined the TCL Group to establish the Modern Distance Learning Cooperation Project in Beijing. The Legend Group has also signed an agreement with the National Higher Education Self-learning Examination Committee to offer e-commerce training courses through its web site FM365.com.

Distance learning is gradually gaining popularity in China for several reasons. First, in the current 10th Five Year Plan, the Government has allocated $1.2 billion for research on crucial technologies and for building an enabling environment for distance education. The target is to equip schools with PCs for education purposes. Administrative regulations require high schools to provide a fixed number of hours of computer instruction per week. Second, only 9.1% of high school students can go on to university, while most parents hope their children will go to university. Parents invest heavily in their children's education, and those who can afford it will not hesitate to buy computers for their children and pay expensive Internet access charges and online tuition. In Beijing at present, 20% of students are attending online high schools. Third, online education for adults is also popular in terms of providing better job opportunities in the rapid transition towards a market economy system.

However, Internet access quality is affecting online education because multimedia applications have to be transmitted over the Internet. Many universities employ several kinds of network combined instead of just a single network. The People's University distance-learning network, for example, has had to send its multimedia course to its twenty-plus instruction locales via satellite and the Internet does the rest. The Tsinghua University uses both a satellite network and a CATV network.

D. Case studies of e-commerce companies[10]

It was not until 2000 that many Chinese traditional companies embraced e-commerce. Several big Chinese companies such as Legend, Haier and Changhong etc. launched their e-commerce operation in that year.

1. Traditional companies

Legend Holdings Limited (Legend)

Incorporated in 1988 and listed on the Hong Kong Stock Exchange in February 1994, Legend Holdings Limited (Legend) is China's largest information technology company and the manufacturer of China's best-selling PCs. For the past few years, Legend has engaged in the design, manufacture and sale of Legend brand PCs, distribution of foreign brand IT products, and the systems integration business. It has already built up a well-known, unique brand name.

Foreign brands such as IBM, Compaq and HP have been competing in China for a long time. However, their aggregate market share declined from over 30% in 1996 to 20% in 1999, while three other local computer manufactures, namely Legend, the Founder and the Great Wall, hold a 30.9% market share (see chart 29). This happened because foreign brands aimed at the corporate sector, while local companies targeted the consumer market, which is the high growth area. Legend built up its market share mainly by selling PCs to Chinese consumers at prices 10-15% lower than comparable foreign brands. In 2000, Legend's PC sales grew by 96% to 2.1 million, which made Legend one of the largest PC manufacturers in the Asia-Pacific region. The operating profits from exports of PCs to North America and Europe represented 5.5% and 5.7% respectively of total operating profits for 2000 (Legend's Annual Report, 2001).

Recently, Legend has been aggressively diversifying its business into the Internet and e-commerce areas. To develop its Internet business, in April 2000 Legend reorganized its existing business into two groups: Legend Computer System Ltd. and Legend Digital China Ltd. On 11 June 2001, Legend and AOL established a joint venture to provide consultancy and technical support for interactive services by using AOL's technology and Legend's mass PC marketing position.

Legend Computer Systems Ltd. is mainly responsible for Internet-related hardware products, wireless devices and Internet services over its web site. Legend has bargaining power with component suppliers because of economies of scale so that it enjoys a pronounced cost advantage over its competitors. In terms of distribution, Legend has been building up a network of its own stores to further cut middleman costs, and it owns over 2,000 distribution points and 70 Legend 1+1 franchise shops. In fiscal year 1999, profits from its Enterprise Resource Planning (ERP) systems were remarkable: online order sheets amounted to over $1 billion. The average period to complete one transaction decreased to 4.5 days from 9 days in 1995, similarly, average inventory days decreased from 30 days in 1998 to 18 days in 1999.

Digital China mainly distributes IT products and provides e-commerce and overall integrated systems planning and servicing. Digital China has so far opened a web site called "E-bridge" and has set up trading platforms in nine major cities in China. Clients can obtain commercial information and complete business transactions through this web site. By the end of 2000, online business had reached $12 million (in three months), representing 22% of total business. Currently, more than 500 different products can be ordered online.

Based on ERP systems, Legend is building its e-commerce model by creating an e-distribution network for IT product vendors, currently focusing on developing a B2B market, and a nationwide logistics system which includes delivery, customs clearance, electronic payment, etc. The full model is expected to be implemented by the end of 2000 (see chart 30).

Like Legend, some local enterprises have also entered the e-commerce market. As one of the most famous consumer electronic manufacturers in China, the Haier Group (Haier) has enjoyed 83% average annual sales increases over the last 15 years. After a pilot e-commerce operation, it set up Haier E-commerce Co. Ltd. in March 2000. Customers could order 456 different products and get their goods within two days through Haier's 10,000 sales points in big cities nationwide. With the biggest CTV market share in China, Changhong Group is integrating its information network, logistics network, service network and settlement network for e-commerce.

Chart 29
China PC market shares in 1998 and 1999

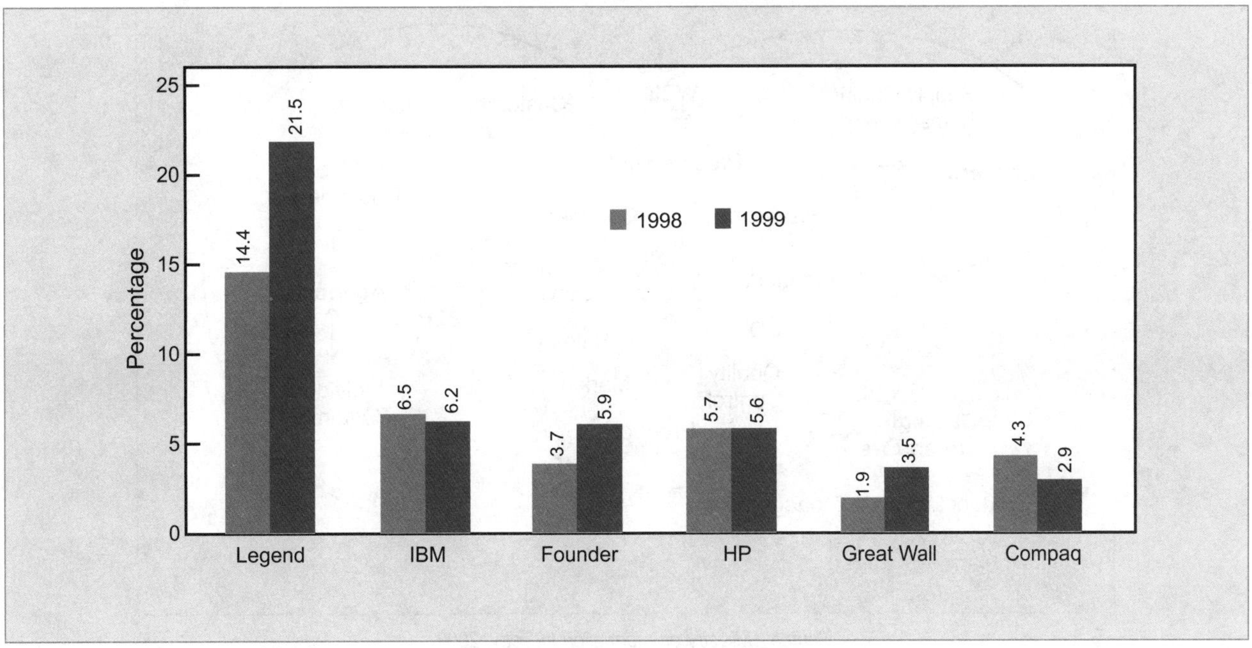

Source: Legend Annual Report 1998-2000.

2. Three portals in China

Sina.com, formed in December 1998, is widely considered the world's largest Chinese-language web site. The company offers Chinese Internet users a range of services from news and information to online community services. E-commerce facilities consist of an online shopping mall, online ticketing and a co-brand debit card with China Merchant Bank.

Sohu.com's initial web site was launched in February 1997. Soon after, the company developed the first Chinese language online directory and search engine. The company's new focus is on the e-commerce platform for B2C and B2B auctions. In September 1999, Sohu.com announced the construction of its e-business commercial network.

Founded in 1997, Netease.com is largely known for its e-mail and community services. In July 2000, Netease.com launched the first online auction in China on its own software platform.

All three portals generate revenues from software licensing and related integration projects, advertising services, and e-commerce related services in China. Although none of these three portals is profitable yet, they are optimistic that they may break even by 2002 or 2003. The portals chose to stay in operation without profit with a long-term objective of capturing a big share of the potential market growth.

Table 34 shows that the three portal companies, and particularly Sohu.com relied heavily on advertising as the major source of revenue.

The three portals are all B2C focused. Sina.com and Netease.com focus on online shopping malls and online auctions respectively, while Sohu.com concentrates on both. In the short term, e-commerce is unlikely to be the main source of revenue for the three portals. The percentage of e-commerce revenue in total revenue in the first half of 2000 for Sina.com, Sohu.com and Netease.com was 1.2%, 6% and 13% respectively. All three talk about new initiatives and will probably reveal new e-commerce revenue models during 2001. They have all shown their interest in potential e-commerce growth rather than immediate profit. They apparently hope that their active promotion of e-commerce will eventually be rewarded by their capturing a major share of the new market as a result of being among the early entities in this field.

Meanwhile, all three portals have already developed WAP pages for mobile operators (wap.sohu.com; wap.sina.com.cn; wap.163.com). An alliance has been

Chart 30
Legend's e-commerce model

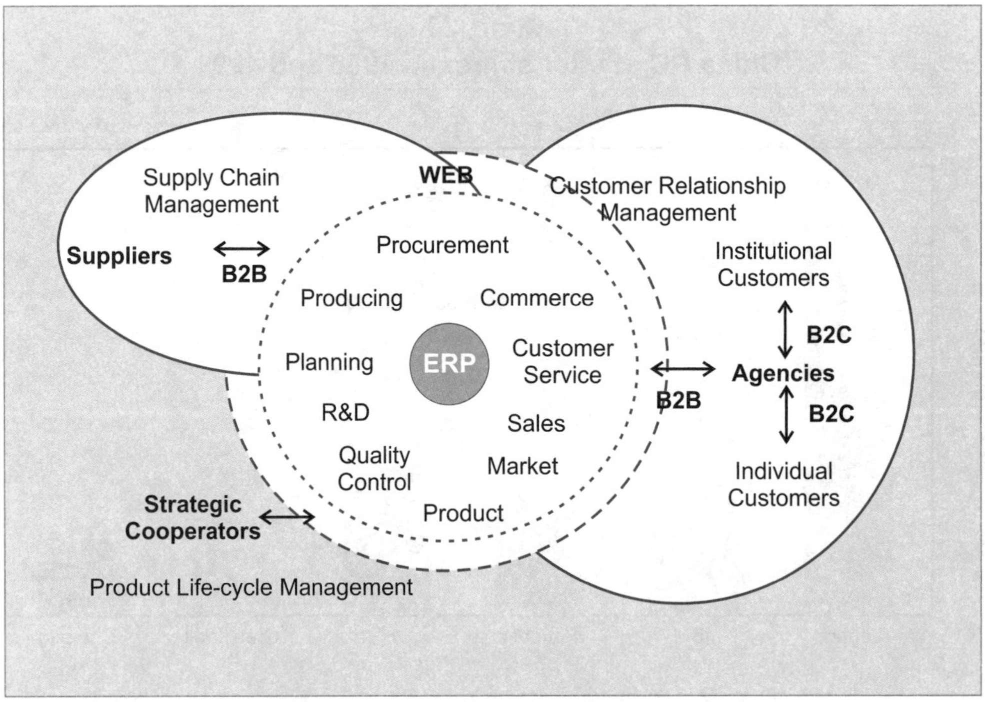

Source: Ministry of Information Industry, 2000.

formed between equipment producers and mobile operators. In July 2000, for example, Sohu.com was able to offer WAP Internet access in nine provinces by working with Nokia, Siemens and regional telecom companies.

Sina.com, Netease.com and Sohu.com were listed on the NASDAQ in 2000. The IPOs raised $68 million for Sina.com, $69.75 million for Netease.com and a total of $59.8 million for Sohu.com. Before the IPOs, they chose to move offshore and spin off China-based assets in order to avoid conflict with Chinese Government restrictions on foreign investment in Internet content providers (ICPs), which fall within the category of value-added services. ICPs in China need approval both from the securities regulators and from MII in order to list overseas. The capital raised by the three portals fell far short of expectations. In the fact of the share-price collapse of Internet companies listed in the NASDQ exchange, investors are questioning the sustainability of Internet ventures. Asian Internet start-ups are subject to even greater scrutiny because of concerns about government regulation, consumer buying power, and the physical and financial infrastructure of developing countries.

3. Chinese dot companies

E-commerce in China began with B2C. The major products sold over the Internet are books, gifts and flowers, CDs, computer hardware and software, communication and office devices, toys, ticket reservations, stocks and travel services. E-commerce companies generate revenue through different business models and bypass current obstacles in e-commerce by employing a number of creative solutions discussed below.

8848.com

8848.com began operation in May 1999 and soon became the largest online store in China. It now offers approximately 300,000 different items. To solve the online payment problem, beginning from June 2000, 8848.com supports 19 methods of payment such as CMB's All in One Net Card, credit cards, debit cards, deposit books of ICBC, VISA and Master Card, etc. It offers cash on delivery service in 470 cities. 8848.com also promises to deliver goods to customers in 78 cities in China within 48 hours by establishing strong alliances and partnerships with professional express forwarding companies such as China Post, National and Overseas EMS, and also manufacturers.

8848.com generates revenue from B2C and B2B business and advertising. In November 2000, 8848.com's B2C business volume increased 12 times over the previous year. In April 2000, it stepped into B2B e-commerce to provide e-commerce services and solutions to Chinese traditional enterprises, especially for small and medium-size enterprises (SMEs). By 2000, its B2B business represented 80% of total earnings.

Yabuy.com and Eachnet.com

Established in June 1999, Yabuy.com owns the largest Chinese auction platform, with 15 categories and 5,000 subcategories of auction products. It provides both online and offline auction. Yabuy.com does not get involved in the financial transaction process, but provides the auction services, thus getting commissions. Yabuy.com hopes to break even in 2001.

Eachnet.com began its B2C and C2C second-hand goods online auction business in September 1999, and six months later it increased its market share to 50% of China's auction business. To solve logistical and credibility problems, Eachnet.com encourages customers to do business within the same city so they can meet before exchanging goods and cash. 40% to 50% of the average monthly turnover of $2.5 million involves transactions where the buyer and seller actually meet physically.

Table 34
Revenue breakdown for fiscal year 1999

Year ending	Sina		Sohu		Netease	
31 Dec. 1999	*($ 000)*	*% of total*	*($ 000)*	*% of total*	*($ 000)*	*% of total*
Advertising	3 544	47	1 504	93	1 303	64
Software sales	3 936	52			424	21
Others	92	1	113	7	297	15
Total	6 574	100	1 617	100	2 204	100

Source: Company Annual Report; financial year-end is June 30 for Sina.com.

Yestock.com

Yestock.com is a pioneer in technology involved in remote security trading via short message services (SMS) of mobile phone operators. Mobile phone operators in China normally charge $0.012 per SMS message or $3 per month for unlimited use. Yestock.com has different revenue sharing schemes with different mobile operators in different provinces. Started in 1999, Yestock.com's network covers 14 provinces and 110 brokerages in China. Yestock.com makes money by charging stock brokerages installation, connection and maintenance fees and by sharing mobile phone operators' short message revenue generated through its trading platform.

Alibaba.com's Global Trade Information Network

E-commerce platforms create many opportunities for SMEs to access international markets directly without the mediation of trading companies and offer SMEs easy access to information about international trade.

Alibaba.com is an online B2B marketplace for global trade and plays host to China's trade communities. Its web sites allow users to browse company information and to trade in 27 industrial categories and 700 product subcategories. The membership of Alibaba.com comprises 500,000 enterprises in 202 countries and regions, and more than half of the exchange's participants are based in China. Based on an online survey in December 2000, Alibaba.com claims that 31.6% of its members have successfully made deals since January 2000, while 97% of the offers posted have received feedback.

Alibaba.com's revenue comes from four sources:

- Revenue sharing from third party services: Alibaba.com shares revenues with shipping, insurance, hotel and travel services. Recently, Alibaba.com contracted with four international logistics companies and planned to provide international transportation services to all members in 2001.
- Online business promotion and advertising: this includes web hosting services, priority placement on Alibaba.com searches, banner link advertising and other related services.
- Premium membership services: while basic services on Alibaba.com will remain free, members will be charged for certain premium services in the future, such as the ability to post additional trade leads and product samples.
- Transactional revenues: when the e-commerce market matures, Alibaba.com will derive revenue from service charges for facilitating transactions among members.

MeetChina.com

Founded in 1998, MeetChina.com is a B2B e-commerce platform and consultancy that offers international retailers access to an expanding database of over 76,000 Chinese suppliers, especially SMEs, and their products. MeetChina.com allows online negotiations and hosts virtual "storefronts" for manufacturers.

However, the low penetration of personal computers in China hinders the company's business expansion. While half of MeetChina.com's first group of manufacturers had e-mail accounts, few checked them regularly, so MeetChina.com had to call or fax its clients, which was costly and inefficient. Motorola and MeetChina.com devised a relatively primitive paging service for Chinese companies with few computers, allowing messaging directly to factories without having to use the Internet. In addition, the company worked with Motorola and China Wireless Information Network to broadcast purchase inquiries and trade leads via mobile phones. This would allow MeetChina.com to reach some 2 million manufacturers that do not have PCs.

Although its operations in mainland China broke even in 2000, it has not been able to make many online transactions. MeetChina.com's revenue still comes mostly from membership fees and from site hosting and advertising. The company hopes to move to a transaction-based business model, whereby firms pay a referral fee of 2–6 % for using the site to make deals.

It is worth mentioning that China's government procurement sector began to cooperate with some e-commerce companies in order to save cost, enhance work efficiency and transparency, and accelerate government informatization. Founded in December 1999, sunbuyer.com reported that it can shorten the government procurement purchasing cycle by 50–80% and cut procurement costs by 5–50% via its new government procurement model. At the moment, government procurement business accounts for 20–

30% of sunbuyer.com's total business volume. The application of e-procurement could save substantial transaction costs and make a major contribution to combating bureaucracy and corruption.

E. Internal regulatory environment

China's international trade law has incorporated the basic principles and rules prescribed by the WTO and WIPO, as well as other relevant laws and regulations from developed countries. As the Internet and e-commerce are relatively new, there has not been a comprehensive law addressing all aspects of e-commerce to date. The rapid growth of Internet applications has found many government institutions without a mandate to address many of the legal issues arising from the emergence of e-commerce. All government institutions that come across such issues have to take the initiative and propose to the State Council (cabinet) rules and regulations on issues within their responsibility. As a result, enforcement of regulations relating to the Internet and e-commerce is shared by different institutions. The major government agencies involved are shown in table 35.

1. Internet-related regulations

In general, the *Interim Provisions on the Administration of Computer Information Networks and the Internet*, published by the State Council in 1996, provide the basic organizational and administrative structure for China's information networks. To address issues relating to the establishment of interfacing networks and their connection to the international computer network, the *Implementation Procedures* for the above provisions were revised in 1997 and issued in 1998; they set out the four-layer system of international linkups of China's computer network (described Section A).

In September 1998, the State Council issued the *Notice on Relevant Issues Concerning Implementing A Business Permit System for Operating International Connections to Computer Information Networks*, which requires approval for business permits from relevant government agencies for engaging in Internet-related services. MII and its local branches are directly responsible for examining and approving business permits for operators engaged in networking at all levels.

The State Council issued the *Telecommunications Administration Regulations* and the *Internet Information Service Management Regulation* on 25 September and 1 October 2000 respectively. The new regulations do not change the existing rules but clarify them further and eliminate ambiguity. The regulations empower the MII to regulate both ISPs and portals.

Content restriction

To ensure Internet security, the Ministry of Public Security issued the *Circular Concerning the Record of Computer Information Systems Linked to Foreign Networks* in December 1997, which requires all Internet users to register with the local public security bureau within 30 days of the establishment of a subscription with an ISP. It also empowers the public security authorities to shut down computer network operators that engage in any acts which jeopardize the safety of any other computer network.

The Provisions on the Administration of the Maintenance of Secrets in the International Networking of Computer Information Systems, which was published by the State

Table 35
Government agencies involved in Internet regulations

Name	Areas of responsibility
Ministry of Information Industry (MII)	Examination and approval of licenses for ISPs and portals, and overseeing the listing of Chinese firms.
Ministry of Public Security (MPS)	Network security State.
Administration of Industry and Commerce	Registration of ISPs and portals.
Ministry of Culture	Supervision of media and Internet content.
State Press and Publications Administration	Overseeing Net publishing and book selling.
State Administration of Radio, Film and Television	Monitoring online video and sound.
State Encryption Administration Commission	Registration of encryption technology.
China Securities Regulatory Commission (CSRC)	Overseeing IPOs of dotcoms and regulating online security brokerage services.
Internet News Administrative Bureau of the State Council's Information Office	Formulating regulations and overseeing content of web site news.

Secrets Bureau and came into effect in January 2000, regulates information flows through the Internet related to state secrets. Anyone who places information on the Internet must take responsibility for that information, including e-mail and chat room discussions, to ensure that there is no violation of the law.

In November 2000, MII issued new rules to control content in Internet public forums. *Rules on Net Bulletin Board Systems* provided that anyone posting information on Internet bulletin board systems (BBS) will be held responsible for the content. The regulations require that BBS providers keep records of content, posting time and referred Internet protocol addresses or domain names cited in the posts. Backups of this information must be kept for 60 days and surrendered to the authorities on demand.

Contract law and dispute resolution

The new *Contract Law*, which came into effect on 1 October 1999, incorporates a new provision recognizing electronic contracts. It expressly provides for electronic messages, including telegrams, telexes, faxes, electronic data interchange (EDI), and e-mail, to be considered as instruments that parties may use to enter into contracts. The law also includes provisions tailored to e-commerce on the formation and validity of contracts. However, there are no provisions governing electronic signatures and dispute resolution online.

To meet existing needs until a more complete regulatory environment for e-commerce is established, the central bank has set up the Finance Certification Policy and Management Direction to help settle e-commerce disputes.

In March and April 2000, the China Securities Regulatory Commission (CSRC) issued the *Provisional Administrative Measures on Securities Brokerage Commission Over the Internet and the Verification* and *Approval Procedures for Securities Brokerage Commission*. These two standards set the guidelines that must be met by securities companies planning to offer online security brokerage services. At the beginning of 2001, the CSRC had certified 23 security brokers to trade online, which marked the first time that brokerage houses had been allowed to trade online since the regulations were issued. The companies are required to inform the CSRC of any major changes, including technical upgrades, to online trading systems, as well as operational or management changes.

In addition to national authorities, local government authorities have also issued rules and regulations. In March 2000, the Beijing Municipal Administration for Industry and Commerce issued the *Circular of the Beijing Municipal Administration for Industry and Commerce Concerning E-commerce Activities Registration* which requires e-commerce dealers to apply for e-commerce operations registration. The *Provisional Measures of Shanghai Municipality on the Price Administration of E-commerce* strengthened the management of the pricing of e-commerce digital certificate authentication and standardized service charges in relation to the authentication of digital certificates.

In April 2000, *Draft Guidelines for China's E-commerce Development* formulated by MII were submitted to the State Council for approval. The guidelines will cover a wide range of issues such as permission for foreign businesses to enter China's Internet market, e-commerce operations logistics, transaction security, IPR protection, consumer privacy, tariffs and taxes. This reflects a strong attempt by the Government to develop a comprehensive regulatory framework. There is need for a uniform state law to ensure certainty and transparency and avoid undue administrative interference in the development of e-commerce.

2. Foreign investment

The progressive liberalization of China's telecommunication services culminated in the promulgation of *The Telecommunications Administration Regulations* in September 2000. The regulations clearly define basic service and value-added services. Private investors involved in basic telecom services in China can hold up to 49% of shares and must get official approval before investing. The regulation provides greater possibilities than the previous situation, where foreign investments in telecommunication services were prohibited. Opening China's Internet market to the outside world will benefit e-commerce companies in terms of gaining access to foreign venture capital, and will thus foster economic growth.

3. E-commerce taxation

China has not yet developed full tax regulations for e-commerce. The present tax regulations do not explicitly state how to tax economic activity on the Internet. China's State Administration of Taxation (SAT) was considering taxing e-commerce in the same way as traditional business. In its view, the electronic form of e-commerce does not change the nature of trade. A research group created by the SAT to examine the issue is expected to work out new measures.

F. Obstacles to e-commerce development

1. High Internet access costs

The high cost of Internet access and of telephony has long been a point of contention for Internet users and operators in China. The Internet access fee is composed of a connection service fee and a telephone communication fee. The communication fee is currently $0.14 per hour, while the connection service fee is $0.48 per hour. Given the low level of personal disposable income, the access charge is extremely high. Communication services users argue that the high connection fee charged by ISPs is caused by China Telecom's monopoly of the basic telecom services.

Hosting charges for web sites with sufficient bandwidth are so high that most e-commerce service providers can only afford to rent narrow bandwidth, leading to long waiting times to download. 46.4% of users are not satisfied with the slow access speed, and 20.8% complain about high Internet access fees (CNNIC; 2001). Even if the hardware and connection are available, consumers will most likely choose not to engage in e-commerce if transmission is slow. Often it is more efficient and enjoyable simply to walk to a store and purchase the desired goods or services.

In 1999, connection service charges were considerably reduced by administrative decision, and there were substantial improvements in service. But costs still remained far too high to allow for a rapid expansion of e-commerce. Responding to domestic consumer complaints, the MII lowered Internet connection fees again in March and October 2000. By launching a new half-price Internet Access Card (IAC) in August 2000, China Telecom has been trying to expand its Internet business. The IAC charged customers on the basis of the actual time they use the Internet and their phone charges for access to the Internet, which are half those for the regular local phone calls. Furthermore, beginning January 2001, long-distance charges were also reduced. Domestic long-distance calls were reduced to $0.08 per minute, with an average 25% decrease. International calls are $0.96 per minute, down 45.8% from 1999.

In fact, some problems of China's e-commerce development stem from China's Internet population itself. For people using the Internet on a regular basis, their purpose in getting online has a direct impact on the prospects of e-commerce growth. The main purpose of 68.8% Internet users is to get the latest information from the Internet, while 13.3% go online for education (CNNIC, 2001). In addition, the monthly personal incomes of Internet users are still pretty low. They do not have enough purchasing power to have an impact on e-commerce. About 51% of Internet user have a monthly family income of only between $61 and $241 (see chart 31).

2. Lack of credit cards and a nationwide credit card system

A major obstacle to the development of e-commerce in China is the limited availability of credit cards and a nationwide credit card system. As described in section 2, most Chinese bankcards issued by commercial banks are actually debit cards, drawing money against previously deposited funds. The cards charge a high fee for an overdraft, and some cards simply refuse an overdraft. At present, people with a foreign currency deposit with BOC, ICBC and Guangdong Development Bank are eligible to apply for an international credit card, but only a few such cards are actually issued.

In addition, a nationwide financial network is still in the preparatory stage, as the financial industry has not yet become fully electronic. Commercial banks issue their own bankcards and most bankcards are only linked to their own issuing banks, thus requiring a retailer to connect to each of these facilities one by one. If a merchant does not set up a mechanism to clear transactions with the specific bank which issued the card, then purchase is impossible. Although MasterCard and Visa operate in China, the absence of a central clearing house prevents them from becoming a popular financial instrument.

Although many commercial banks have ambitious plans to develop online banking services and invested have heavily, the currently available services are still limited and most online banking services are only operated in a few cities where the Internet is much more popular than in other areas. Only CMB has begun to service customers in some inland cities such

Chart 31
Average monthly income of user's family

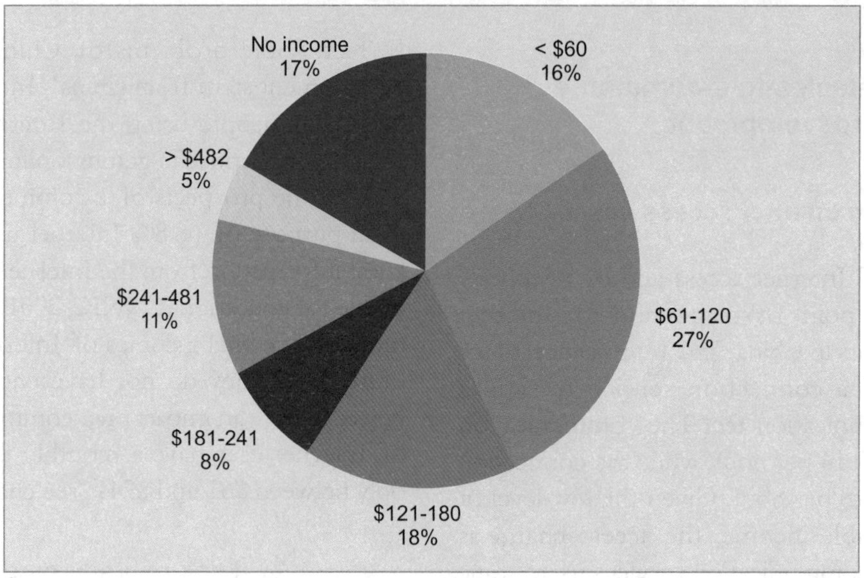

Source: CNNIC survey, January 2001.

as Xi'an and Shengyang. Most companies continue to employ offline payment methods such as cash on delivery (COD), account transfers through banks, or remissions through banks or post offices for online purchasing. As chart 32 shows, COD accounts for the most important part of the payments for online transactions. Account transfers and remittances from banks and post offices make up the remaining small fraction of payments.

3. Transportation infrastructure: slow and uncertain delivery

Although most Chinese online shoppers prefer fast delivery, some of China's web sites do not provide 24-hour delivery services, and most of the time a product can only be delivered in three days, sometimes even taking more than a month to reach the customers. Though partly due to delays in the interbank transfer of payments, late delivery is mainly caused by an inefficient national postal system. E-commerce companies have developed a number of alternatives to the postal system to meet distribution needs. Like most e-commerce companies elsewhere, companies in China usually sign contracts with a number of delivery firms. National couriers such as China Postal or EMS are regularly used. Companies also rely on their own door-to-door delivery teams or on the services of smaller, specialized, local delivery systems. They thus currently rely on hybrids of online shopping and traditional labour-intensive delivery systems. Several Chinese companies, for example Legend, Haier and Changhong, have already built up their nationwide distribution network, so that they can distribute their products to customers by their own sales teams in most big cities in China. Most newly established pure-play e-commerce companies, like 8848.com and Yabuy.com, rely heavily on specialized local delivery companies.

A local delivery company, Eguo.com, has set up a delivery station and over 50 substations around Beijing and guarantees delivery in one hour within central Beijing. With a 400-person delivery team, Eguo.com provides service 24 hours a day. It delivers larger or more distant orders by truck and smaller local orders by bicycle. Another approach is to use a taxi company to deliver goods purchased online. The San Francisco-based MyWeb Inc. entered into an alliance agreement with Beijing YinJian Taxi to deliver goods ordered online.

Having developed its Physical Delivery Postal Network, the Green Card financial network and the Postal Integrated Computer Network[11], China Post also has an important role in the development of e-commerce; using these networks for e-commerce activities may partly solve the above-mentioned financial and logistics problems.

4. Network security

Although government departments attach great importance to the security of information systems, in practice network operators suffer from insufficient budgets. Moreover, considerable security problems

Chart 32
Payment methods

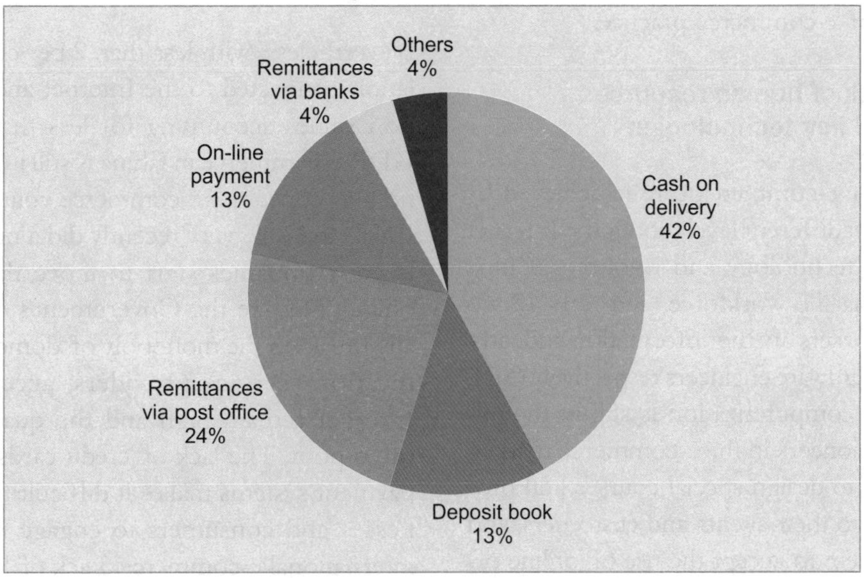

Source: CCID Consulting Co., 2001a.

remain in certain industries. For example, some computer networks use open operating systems with low security, making them vulnerable to hackers. The information systems of some industries were developed entirely without security safeguards. Because security has lagged behind systems development, some national communications network equipment has not been tested. In financial services, some units' security systems are primitive and unprotected.

Government agencies have already taken a number of steps to address the network security problem, including:

- In August 1997 the National Committee of Information Technology and Standardization established an Information Technology Security Subcommittee;
- The State Council Automation Leadership Team Office announced the establishment of the China Internet Security Products Authentication Center. Tests on the first batch of products have been completed;
- The State Technology Supervisory Bureau and the Ministry of Public Security (MPS) established the MPS Computer Information Systems Security Product Quality Supervision and Testing Center. Over 60 products have been tested to date, providing a reliable technological basis for the MPS to issue sales permits for information security products.

5. Trust

What hinders the development of full-fledged B2B in China is the large amount of accounts receivable and the non-performing loans between companies. The uneasy relations between industry and commerce make this the only way for commercial corporations to pay back manufacturers after they actually sell products. This circumstance makes the advantages of online purchase and payment systems irrelevant.

In China, an abundance of counterfeit and low-quality products are already on the market. In addition, some of China's e-commerce vendors cannot provide the services that customers are expecting: reduced prices, usually lower than those found in conventional stores; 24-hour, 7 days per week service; reliable delivery systems; a better selection of products; and a no-risk return policy. Consequently, many Chinese enterprises and consumers are skeptical of the price and quality of online products, as well as of the promises regarding post-sales service and the reputations of online retailers. Most consumers want to see and touch to ensure product quality prior to purchase. Lack of mutual confidence is why most Chinese consumers do not favour online payment but prefer the COD method so that they can check the quality of the goods before paying. Most enterprises are used to becoming trust-based partners and do business only after engaging in face-to-face discussions, visiting the factory and inspecting product samples.

To establish conditions of trust, it is necessary to create a legal and regulatory environment that defines standard norms of e-commerce practice.

6. Lack of human resources and key technologies

The promotion of e-commerce can be achieved by educating people at different levels about the Internet and e-commerce technology and resources. China lacks a professional IT workforce, and only 12.5% and 6.25% of workers in the information industry are software and hardware engineers respectively (MII, 2000). Enterprise computerization is still in the initial phase. Many pioneers in the e-commerce market, like Legend, have to design special courses and provide free training to their agents and customers, and try to convince them to accept the use of online ordering systems.

Other factors such as lack of self-developed core technologies and lack of sufficient investment and human resources to promote e-commerce are also problems. Although Chinese enterprises such as Datang Telecom Co., Huawei Technology Co., Great Dragon Co., Jinpeng Co. and ZTE Corp. have entered the mobile switch and base stations market, some key technologies and equipment are still imported. In 1999, the market share of China-made base stations, mobile phones and switching systems stood at 2%, 3% and 4% respectively.

7. Content restriction

Content restriction on national security grounds may affect business in the field of information services, such as the media and the entertainment sector. Since the Internet grows especially fast in this sector, Chinese business may not be able to take fully advantage of these new opportunities, even though the same restrictions apply to offline services. These regulations will also add to the administrative burden of ISPs or portals and increase their operating costs.

G. Conclusion

Over the past few years, the Chinese Government has made a considerable effort to promote the development and use of information technologies across the country and hence laid an important foundation for the growth of e-commerce in China. In particular, heavy investments in the country's telecommunications infrastructure have resulted in steep growth rates in the number of telephone, mobile phone and — particularly — Internet subscribers.

Nevertheless, with less than 2 per cent of the population connected to the Internet and online transaction values accounting for less than 1 per cent of GDP, e-commerce in China is still in its infancy. Business-to-consumer e-commerce volumes remain very small, and only very recently did a number of mainly larger companies start to move their transactions online. Despite the Government's efforts to gradually break up the monopoly of domestic telecommunications service providers, access costs to the Internet remain high and the quality uneven and often poor. The lack of credit cards or other online payment systems makes it difficult for Chinese businesses and consumers to engage in domestic and international e-commerce. Lack of knowledge about the Internet and its potential business opportunities, combined with limited foreign language skills and a business environment that favours trust-building through interpersonal rather than online contacts, further contributes to the low level of e-commerce.

A number of developments and initiatives currently under way indicate, however, that significant changes may be expected in the short to medium-term. For example, the exponential growth rates in the numbers of Internet subscribers during the past year and predictions for the following years suggest that a large number of Chinese (in absolute terms) will be connected in the near future. China's accession to the WTO, to be expected by the end of this year, will progressively liberalize the domestic telecommunications sector and thus create a more competitive environment. This is expected to result in cheaper and higher-quality Internet services - although some of the commitments will come into operation only after five years. Continuity in the Government's current policy of gradually breaking up the monopoly and encouraging competition in the telecommunications sector would therefore be important in order to achieve faster results in this area. This, combined with efforts to improve access to the Internet throughout the country and to move the financial sector towards incorporating online payment systems, will greatly facilitate the growth of e-commerce in China. Further improvements are needed to lower the administrative burden for ISPs, to put in place a harmonized legal framework for conducting business online, and to provide the Chinese with the skills needed to use the Internet and new information technologies in their businesses.

Notes

1 The figures in this chapter do not include the data on Hong Kong, Taiwan Province of China and Macao.

2 China Internet Network Information Center (CNNIC) seventh semi-annual survey on January 2001. According to CNNIC, the statistics of its semi-annual survey are collected by software-driver online searching and posting online.

3 MII, the State Economic and Trade Commission, and the China Council for the Promotion of International Trade.

4 China Electronic Commerce Association (CECA) is a non-profit association, which aims to be the bridge for e-commerce cooperation between China and other countries.

5 A related project is Green Card Engineering which began in 50 cities in 1996 and was administered by the State Postal Bureau. The planned target of Green Card Engineering in the 9th Five Year Plan was that a nationwide network be installed in 500 large and medium-sized cities of 31 provinces, municipalities and autonomous regions by 2000. More than 10,000 post-depositing network offices distributed in 500 cities, counties and some rural and township will be online to permit depositing and withdrawing money.

6 The main functions of All in One Net card are: foreign currency deposits, telephone banking, account inquiries, inter-transfers, online payments, money withdrawals, securities transactions, and long-distance telephone calls.

7 http://www.chinamarket.com.cn/E/

8 http://www.chinainvest.gov.cn/

9 http://www.cecf.com.cn/e_cecfol/e_index.asp

10 Companies' information and statistics are derived from their web sites and/or interviews with these companies in China from Dec. 2000 to Jan. 2001.

11 The Physical Delivery Network covers almost every city and county in China. There are 236 postal centres forming a physical distribution network linking up urban and rural areas. There are 67,000 post offices and bureaus, and 2,200 cities with EMS services, which make up the largest delivery network in China. By the end of 1999, as the result of the Green Card Engineering project, 800 counties in 31 provinces were connected to the Green Card financial network and the Computer Network of Postal Savings and Remittances which has 7,200 points allowing cross-region savings deposits and withdrawals. The Postal Integrated Computer Network is a backbone network system supporting informatization of exchange technology in China Post. Applications of ATM technology in the platforms of LANs enables online transmission of data, voice and video. The network covers 31 capital cities and 205 regional cities (State Post Bureau; 2000).

References

Anderson Consulting (2000). *The development strategies for Chinese companies.* Presentation by Anderson Consulting. Beijing, China 2000.

Bath, Vivienne (2000). *E-commerce in China.*

http://www.coudert.com/practice/ecommerce_china.htm

CCID Consulting Co. (2001a). *The current situation and prospects of China's E-commerce market.* http://www.ccidnet.com/market/report//2001/02/02/19_1710.html

CCID Consulting Co. (2001b). *The research report on China's IT market.* http://www.ccidnet.com/market/report//2001/03/02/72_1777.html

China Council for the Promotion of International Trade (2000). *Boosting the export of Chinese businesses in E-commerce Era-opportunities & Challenges facing China's Export Promotion Mechanism.* http://www.intracen.org/execforum/docs/ef2000.htm

China E-commerce Association (2001). *The Research Report on China's E-commerce.* March, 2001.

China Internet Network Information Center (CNNIC, various years). *Semi-annual survey* (1997-2001). http://www.cnnic.com.cn/develst/e-index.shtml

China National Tourism Administration (2001). *Have plan, will travel: China unveils tourism strategy.* http://www.chinaonline.com/topstories/010117/1/C01011102.asp

Din, Ming (2000). *The current situation and prospects of China's Internet Banks* (People's Bank of China survey report). http://www.drcnet.com.cn

Dougan, Diana Lady and Fan, Xing (1999). *Scaling the Great Wall of E-commerce: Strategic Issues and recommended actions* (China Electronic Project Report 1999, 2nd edition). Cyber Century Forum, Washington D.C..

HSBC (2000). *China's Portals.*

International Data Corporation (2001). *China's PC sales up 45%, tops most other Asia-Pacific countries.* http://www.chinaonline.com/topstories/010207/1/C01020502.asp

International Telecommunication Union (ITU, 2001). *Basic Indicators, Cellular subscribers.* http://www.itu.int/ITU-D/ict/publications/

Legend Group. *Annual Report* (1998-2000). http://www.legend-holdings.com/

Lovelock, Peter (1999) *E-China: Putting Business on the Internet.* http://www.virtualchina.com/archive/infotech/analysis/e-business-print.html

Merrill Lynch (2000). *China PC Industry.*

Ministry of Foreign Trade and Economic Cooperation (MoFTEC, 2001). *Statistics report on international trade.* http://www.moftec.gov.cn

Ministry of Information Industry (MII, 2000). *Promoting City Information for Social and Economic Development.* Speech at High-Level Forum on City Informatizatin in the Asia-Pacific Region. Shanghai, China; June 2000.

Ministry of Information Industry (MII, 2000). *China E-commerce 2000*, 24 issues.

State Post Bureau (2000). *China Post and E-commerce.* Speech at the 4th China International Electronic Commerce Summit.

The Economist Intelligence United Ltd. (2000). *Country Commerce, China.*

UBS Warburg (2000). *Global Equity Research: Legend.*

US Department of Commerce (1999). *Market Assessment: the development of e-commerce in China.* http://strategis.ic.gc.ca/engdoc/main.html

Wu, Jichuan(2001). *Achieving the leap-frog development embracing the new century challenges.* Speech at Symposium on Network Economy and Economic Governance. Beijing, China; April 2001.

Xiang, Huaicheng (2001). *Fiscal policies of China and network economy.* Speech at Symposium on Network Economy and Economic Governance. Beijing, China; April 2001.

Zeng, Peiyan (2001). *Develop network economy and speed up informatization progress.* Speech at Symposium on Network Economy and Economic Governance. Beijing, China; April 2001.

كيفية الحصول على منشورات الأمم المتحدة

يمكن الحصول على منشورات الأمم المتحدة من المكتبات ودور التوزيع في جميع أنحاء العالم. استعلم عنها من المكتبة التي تتعامل معها أو اكتب إلى: الأمم المتحدة، قسم البيع في نيويورك أو في جنيف.

如何购取联合国出版物

联合国出版物在全世界各地的书店和经售处均有发售．请向书店询问或写信到纽约或日内瓦的联合国销售组．

HOW TO OBTAIN UNITED NATIONS PUBLICATIONS

United Nations publications may be obtained from bookstores and distributors throughout the world. Consult your bookstore or write to: United Nations, Sales Section, New York or Geneva.

COMMENT SE PROCURER LES PUBLICATIONS DES NATIONS UNIES

Les publications des Nations Unies sont en vente dans les librairies et les agences dépositaires du monde entier. Informez-vous auprès de votre libraire ou adressez-vous à : Nations Unies, Section des ventes, New York ou Genève.

КАК ПОЛУЧИТЬ ИЗДАНИЯ ОРГАНИЗАЦИИ ОБЪЕДИНЕННЫХ НАЦИЙ

Издания Организации Объединенных Наций можно купить в книжных магазинах и агентствах во всех районах мира. Наводите справки об изданиях в вашем книжном магазине или пишите по адресу: Организация Объединенных Наций, Секция по продаже изданий, Нью-Йорк или Женева.

COMO CONSEGUIR PUBLICACIONES DE LAS NACIONES UNIDAS

Las publicaciones de las Naciones Unidas están en venta en librerías y casas distribuidoras en todas partes del mundo. Consulte a su librero o diríjase a: Naciones Unidas, Sección de Ventas, Nueva York o Ginebra.

Printed in France
GE.01-52924–October 2001–8,000

United Nations publication
Sales No. E.01.II.D.30

UNCTAD/SDTE/ECB/1

ISBN 92-1-112541-3